Martin Luther King, Jr.:

The Making of a Mind

We feel that we are the conscience of America. We are its troubled soul. We will continue to insist that right be done because both God's Will and the heritage of our nation speak through our echoing demands.

—Martin Luther King, Jr., August 5, 1962

Martin Luther King, Jr.:

The Making of a Mind

John J. Ansbro

ORBIS BOOKS
Maryknoll, New York 10545

The Catholic Foreign Mission Society of America (Maryknoll) recruits and trains people for overseas missionary service. Through Orbis Books Maryknoll aims to foster the international dialogue that is essential to mission. The books published, however, reflect the opinions of their authors and are not meant to represent the official position of the society.

Manuscript editor: Robert J. Cunningham

Library of Congress Cataloging in Publication Data

Ansbro, John.
    Martin Luther King, Jr.: The Making of a Mind

    Includes bibliographical references and index.
    1. King, Martin Luther. 2. Nonviolence.
I. Title.
E185.97.K5A79   323.4'092'4   82-6408
ISBN 0-88344-333-3 (pbk.)   AACR2

Martin Luther King, Jr. was the conscience of his generation. A Southerner, a black man, he gazed upon the great wall of segregation and saw that the power of love could bring it down.

From the pain and exhaustion of his fight to free all people from the bondage of separation and injustice, he wrung his eloquent statement of his dream of what America could be.

He helped us overcome our ignorance of one another. He spoke out against a war he felt was unjust as he had spoken out against laws that were unfair.

He made our nation stronger because he made it better. Honored by kings, he continued to his last days to strive for a world where the poorest and humblest among us could enjoy the fulfillment of the promises of our founding fathers.

His life informed us, his dreams sustain us yet.

—Citation of the posthumous award of the
Presidential Medal of Freedom to Dr. King, July 4, 1977.

Volunteers in the Birmingham Movement signed a Commitment Card that read in part:

I HEREBY PLEDGE MYSELF—MY PERSON AND BODY—TO THE NONVIOLENT MOVEMENT. THEREFORE I WILL KEEP THE FOLLOWING TEN COMMANDMENTS:

1. MEDITATE daily on the teachings and life of Jesus.
2. REMEMBER always that the nonviolent movement in Birmingham seeks justice and reconciliation—not victory.
3. WALK and TALK in the manner of love, for God is love.
4. PRAY daily to be used by God in order that all men might be free.
5. SACRIFICE personal wishes in order that all men might be free.
6. OBSERVE with both friend and foe the ordinary rules of courtesy.
7. SEEK to perform regular service for others and for the world.
8. REFRAIN from the violence of fist, tongue, or heart.
9. STRIVE to be in good spiritual and bodily health.
10. FOLLOW the directions of the movement and of the captain on a demonstration.

Acknowledgment is gratefully extended for permission to quote from the following:

Stride Toward Freedom: The Montgomery Story by Martin Luther King, Jr.; Harper & Row, Publishers, Inc., 1958. Copyright © 1958 by Martin Luther King, Jr. Reprinted by permission of Harper & Row, Publishers, Inc. and by permission of Joan Daves.
Strength To Love by Martin Luther King, Jr.; Harper & Row, Publishers, Inc., 1963. Copyright © 1963 by Martin Luther King, Jr. Reprinted by permission of Joan Daves.
Why We Can't Wait by Martin Luther King, Jr.; Harper & Row, Publishers, Inc., 1963. Copyright © 1963, 1964 by Martin Luther King, Jr. Reprinted by permission of Harper & Row, Publishers, Inc. and by permission of Joan Daves.
Where Do We Go From Here: Chaos or Community? by Martin Luther King, Jr.; Harper & Row, Publishers, Inc., 1967. Copyright © 1967 by Martin Luther King, Jr. Reprinted by permission of Harper & Row, Publishers, Inc. and by permission of Joan Daves.
The Trumpet of Conscience by Martin Luther King, Jr.; Harper & Row, Publishers, Inc., 1967. Copyright © 1967 by Martin Luther King, Jr. Reprinted by permission of Harper & Row, Publishers, Inc. and by permission of Joan Daves.
"A Comparison of the Conceptions of God in the Thinking of Paul Tillich and Henry Nelson Wieman" by Martin Luther King, Jr.; Ph. D. dissertation, Boston University, 1955. Copyright 1958 by Martin Luther King, Jr.; Copyright © 1977 by the Estate of Martin Luther King, Jr. Reprinted by permission of Joan Daves,
"A Testament of Hope" by Martin Luther King, Jr. Copyright © 1968 by the Estate of Martin Luther King, Jr. Originally appeared in *Playboy Magazine*. Reprinted by permission of Joan Daves.
All the other material from Martin Luther King, Jr.'s speeches and writings. Copyright © by Martin Luther King, Jr. and the Estate of Martin Luther King, Jr. Reprinted by permission of Joan Daves.
Agape and Eros by Anders Nygren; translated by Philip S. Watson, Published in England by The Society for Promoting Christian Knowledge,

and published in the U.S.A. by The Westminster Press, 1953, and by Harper & Row, Publishers, Inc., 1969. Used by permission of the Westminster Press and The Society for Promoting Christian Knowledge.

Basic Christian Ethics by Paul Ramsey; Charles Scribner's Sons, 1950; University of Chicago Press, 1978. Copyright 1950 by Charles Scribner's Sons; copyright © renewed 1977 by Paul Ramsey. Reprinted by permission of the University of Chicago Press and Paul Ramsey.

The Children of Light and the Children of Darkness by Reinhold Niebuhr, Charles Scribner's Sons, 1944. Copyright 1944 by Charles Scribner's Sons; copyright © renewed 1960 by Reinhold Niebuhr. Reprinted with permission of Charles Scribner's Sons.

Christianity and the Social Crisis by Walter Rauschenbusch; The Macmillan Company, 1907; Harper & Row, Publishers, Inc., Torchbook edition, edited by Robert D. Cross, 1964. Copyright 1907 by The Macmillan Company; copyright renewed 1935 by Pauline E. Rauschenbusch. Reprinted by permission of Carl Raushenbush.

Jesus and the Disinherited by Howard Thurman; Abingdon Press, 1949. Copyright © renewed 1977 by Howard Thurman. Reprinted by permission of Abingdon Press.

Kant's Political Writings, edited by Hans Reiss; translated by H. B. Nisbet; Cambridge University Press, 1970. Copyright © 1970 by Cambridge University Press. Reprinted by permission of the publisher.

Moral Man and Immoral Society by Reinhold Niebuhr; Charles Scribner's Sons, 1932. Copyright 1932 by Charles Scribner's Sons; copyright © renewed 1960 by Reinhold Niebuhr. Reprinted with the permission of Charles Scribner's Sons.

Philosophy and Opinions of Marcus Garvey by Marcus Garvey; edited by Amy Jacques-Garvey; introduction by Hollis R. Lynch; Atheneum, 1969. Copyright 1923, 1925 by Amy Jacques-Garvey; introduction © 1968 by Hollis R. Lynch. Reprinted with the permission of Atheneum Publishers.

Playboy Interviews; Playboy Press, 1967. Copyright © 1967 by HMH Publishing Co., Inc. Reprinted with permission of PEI Books, Inc.

The Power of Nonviolence by Richard B. Gregg; Schocken Books, 1966. Copyright © 1935 by Richard B. Gregg. Second Revised Edition, copyright © 1959 by Richard B. Gregg. Reprinted with permission of Schocken Books.

The Presocratics, edited by Philip Wheelwright; The Odyssey Press Inc., 1966. Copyright © 1966 by The Odyssey Press, Inc. Reprinted by permission of Bobbs-Merrill Educational Publishing.

Racism and the Christian Understanding of Man by George D. Kelsey; Charles Scribner's Sons, 1965. Copyright © 1965 by George D. Kelsey. Reprinted with the permission of Charles Scribner's Sons.

Stokely Speaks: Black Power Back to Pan-Africanism by Stokely Carmichael, edited by Ethel N. Minor; Vintage Books, 1971. Copyright © 1965, 1971 by Stokely Carmichael. Reprinted by permission of Random House, Inc.

A Theology for the Social Gospel by Walter Rauschenbusch; Macmillan Publishing Co., Inc., 1917. Copyright 1917 by Macmillan Publishing Co., Inc.; renewed 1945 by Pauline E. Rauschenbusch. Reprinted by permission of Macmillan Publishing Co., Inc.

A Theology of the Living Church by L. Harold DeWolf; Harper & Row, Publishers, Inc., revised edition, 1960. Copyright © 1953, 1960, 1968 by Harper & Row, Publishers, Inc. Reprinted by permission of Harper & Row, Publishers, Inc.

"God and History" by George W. Davis; *The Crozer Quarterly*, 20, no. 1, January 1943. Copyright © 1942 by Crozer Theological Seminary. Reprinted with the permission of Dr. Kenneth Smith of Colgate Rochester Divinity School-Bexley Hall-Crozer Theological Seminary.

Contents

Preface

Because of the nonviolent methods of his protests and the scope and depth of his active moral concern, the Reverend Dr. Martin Luther King, Jr. occupies a unique position in the history of creative dissent in the United States. Inspired by a vision of the persistent demands of the moral law for human rights, he raised his prophetic voice against the evils of racism, economic exploitation, militarism, violence, and materialism. While he challenged these fundamental evils, he preached and practiced an understanding goodwill toward those who opposed his efforts, and with a majestic altruism he labored and suffered for their transformation. Using methods as diverse as the prayer vigil and mass civil disobedience, he sought to arouse the conscience of the nation to return to the sublime principles proclaimed in the Declaration of Independence and to establish the conditions that would enable every citizen to develop a life consistent with the claims of universal justice and with the sacredness of the human person.

To understand the nature of King's challenge to American society requires a comprehensive and systematic examination of his strategy of nonviolence. In attempting such an examination, this work emphasizes central insights from ancient, medieval, modern, and contemporary thinkers who moved him to construct his own strategy. Studies of his strategy by historians, political scientists, sociologists, and journalists have not explained the doctrines of these thinkers, but have only repeated his usually brief references to them. A few studies by theologians have described the influence of Mahatma Gandhi and theologians such as Walter Rauschenbusch and Reinhold Niebuhr on King, but they have not adequately detailed his extensive dependence on Personalism, which he identified as his own philosophical position and as the source of the metaphysical bases of his idea of a personal God and of his conviction about the dignity and worth of human personality. Nor have these studies by theologians explored his acknowledged debt to a number of philosophers for some of the guiding principles of his nonviolent resistance. In his courses at Morehouse College,

Crozer Theological Seminary, the University of Pennsylvania, Boston University, and Harvard University, he read the works of philosophers such as Plato, Aristotle, Augustine, Aquinas, Kant, Hegel, Marx, and Nietzsche. This work is based on the conviction that there can be no understanding of the foundation, direction, and power of King's strategy of nonviolent resistance without an exploration of these sources of his thought.

This work will also examine King's critiques of the programs for social change by Booker T. Washington, W. E. B. DuBois, Marcus Garvey, Stokely Carmichael, Elijah Muhammad, and Malcolm X. Since King was convinced that oppressed people have a moral obligation to resist nonviolently the evil system that dehumanizes them, he thought it necessary to criticize the inadequacy of these programs either for refusing to resist or for resorting to morally unacceptable means of resistance. Studies on him have not presented any detailed analysis of these critiques, but such an analysis is necessary for a more precise perception of the nature and goals of his resistance to collective evil.

There have been many critics of King's strategy and direct actions for social change. Most of their criticisms have focused on some doctrine or tactic without even attempting to determine how that doctrine or tactic related to the main principles and objectives of his central strategy of nonviolent resistance. This work will seek to examine the validity of these criticisms by viewing them within the context of the central strategy that gave unity and purpose to his crusades. It would seem that King, who identified with Hegel's insight that "Truth is the totality," deserves a comprehensive evaluation.

A few comments about some terms used in this work seem necessary. I have used both of the terms "blacks" and "Negroes" because King and some other thinkers used both of them. King's frequent use of the term "Negroes" derived in part from his opposition to black separatism. I have also retained his references to the Negro male. Then too, almost without exception, the many thinkers who influenced King regularly used the terms "man," "he," "men," and "mankind." In general, King followed this usage. In presenting their positions, I have used the terms "the individual," "the person," "people," "human beings," "humanity," and "human nature," but only where it could be done without interrupting the flow of the arguments and without contradicting their doctrines. Some of these thinkers were not egalitarians. While King tended to adhere to traditional terminology in his references to human nature, he was keenly aware of the many creative contributions of women to the Nonviolent Movement. Moreover, his struggle for the equality of all persons helped contribute to the direction and momentum of the Feminist Movement.

I wish to express my gratitude to Mrs. Coretta Scott King for her warm encouragement and recommendations. In the course of my research I interviewed King's colleagues in the Nonviolent Movement, his professors, and scholars specializing in his life and thought. I am deeply indebted to the Reverend Ralph Abernathy, the Reverend Dr. Wyatt Tee Walker, the Reverend Bernard Lee, and the Reverend Hosea Williams for interviews that proved to be inspirational. I express my gratitude especially to Dr. L. Harold DeWolf, dean emeritus of Wesley Theological Seminary, who was King's mentor at Boston University and who continued to assist and advise him during his crusades. I am also grateful for interviews with Professor Peter Bertocci and Dr. Walter Muelder, dean emeritus of Boston University, Professor Kenneth Smith of Colgate Rochester Divinity School-Bexley Hall-Crozer Theological Seminary, and Professor Morton Enslin, both of whom taught King at Crozer, Clinton Powers, former administrative vice-president of Crozer, Dr. Benjamin Mays, Dr. Brailsford Brazeal, dean emeritus of Morehouse College, Professor George Kelsey, who taught King at Morehouse, Dean Willis Hubert and Dr. Melvin Watson of Morehouse, Dr. Robert Green, dean of the College of Urban Development at Michigan State University and former educational director of the Southern Christian Leadership Conference, Dr. Kenneth Clark, Julian Bond, Ramsey Clark, Harry Wachtel, a former vice-president and attorney for the Martin Luther King, Jr. Center for Nonviolent Social Change, the Reverend Calvin Morris, the former executive director of the Center, Dr. Richard Long, director of Afro-American Studies at Atlanta University, and the Reverend George Thomas of the Interdenominational Theological Center for the Religious Heritage of the Black World.

I am indebted also to Mrs. Minnie Clayton, former librarian of the Martin Luther King, Jr. Center for Nonviolent Social Change, for her invaluable assistance in locating source material, Dr. Howard Gottlieb, chief of the Special Collections Division of the Mugar Memorial Library of Boston University, and Charles Niles, his assistant, for their kindness during my research on the King Collection, the staff of the library of the Boston University School of Theology for their assistance with the Faculty Papers, the staff of the Zion Research Li-

brary of Boston, the staff of the Atlanta Public Library for their help
with the Samuel Williams Collection, the staff of the Trevor Arnet
Library that services Morehouse College, Morris Brown College,
Clark College, Spelman College, and Atlanta University, and the staff
of the library of the Interdenominational Theological Center.

I am especially indebted to the officers of the Ford Foundation for
providing me with the "travel and study grant" that made this work
possible.

Chapter 1

The Redemptive Power of *Agape*

Two months before his assassination, Dr. Martin Luther King, Jr. gave a sermon on death to his congregation in Atlanta. Sensing that the end of his own life was imminent, he alluded to his death and funeral. He told the congregation that whoever was to give his eulogy was not to refer to his Nobel Peace Prize, to his four hundred other awards, or to the schools he had attended. No, whoever was to give the eulogy was to say that Martin Luther King, Jr. tried to feed the hungry, clothe the naked, visit those in prison, and love and serve humanity as a drum major for justice, peace, and righteousness.[1] Such a eulogy could not have been more appropriate. In the Montgomery Boycott and in all his other crusades for social justice he had instructed his followers in the necessity of a love for all men *(agape)*. He had taught them that only in this way could they elevate their own souls and also creatively transform society.

The Early Struggle with Nietzsche's Revaluation

Although King became convinced that a love for all men must permeate every successful crusade of nonviolent resistance, he had to experience an intellectual and emotional crisis before he could reach the point where this belief proved to be the dominant force in his life. The crisis occurred when he was a student at Crozer Theological Seminary in Chester, Pennsylvania. There he read Friedrich Nietzsche's *The Genealogy of Morals* and *The Will to Power,* which contain vehement attacks on Christian ethics. In commenting later on this period of his development in *Stride Toward Freedom,* King explained that perhaps as a result of his study of Nietzsche's attack on the Hebraic-Christian ethic as a glorification of weakness, he had almost despaired of the power of love for solving social problems.[2] Nietzsche argued that we may define goodness as everything that heightens the feeling of power in man, the will to power, power itself, and that we may define as bad whatever is born of weakness. Nietzsche considered happiness to be the feeling that power is growing and that resistance is being overcome. He contended that Christianity with its active pity for all the failures and all the weak was more harmful than any vice since it had made an ideal of anything that contradicts the instinct of the strong for self-preservation. Pity deprives us of the strength that is the essence of life. Pity defends those who have been disinherited and condemned by life, and it gives life itself a gloomy aspect by the abundance of the failures of all kinds that it preserves.[3]

In *The Genealogy of Morals* Nietzsche charged that Jews and Christians, driven by hatred and resentment against the noble and the powerful, had developed a "slave ethic," which extolled love and compassion for the poor, the powerless, the suffering, the sick, and the ugly as a substitute for the "noble morality" of the ancients, which had promoted the robust ideals of power, self-affirmation, health, and beauty.[4] In *The Will to Power* he attacked the Christian duty to love all humanity as a glorification of weakness. He saw this love as favoring all the suffering, botched, and degenerate, and as fostering the instincts of decadence by denying values such as pride, pathos of distance, great responsibility, exuberant spirits, splendid animality, the instincts that rejoice in war and conquest, the deification of passion, anger, revenge, cunning, adventure, and knowledge.[5] In place of these values Christianity extolled the virtues of modesty, reverence, resignation, moderation, piety, pity, leniency, simplicity, and obedience. Nietzsche protested that while the human species demands the suppression of the weak, Christianity through its emphasis on love favors only the solidarity of the weak and reveals its hostility to all that is natural, including the drives of the body. He distinguished three elements in Christianity: the oppressed of all kinds who struggle against the political nobility and its ideal, the mediocre of all kinds who fight against those who are spiritually and physically privileged, and the discontented and diseased of all kinds who oppose the natural instinct of the happy and the sound.[6] Confronted with this critique of the value of love for social good, King, while still a student at the seminary, had about concluded that Jesus' ethical message of "Turn the other cheek" and "Love your enemies" is effective only in conflicts among individuals, but is not useful in resolving conflicts among racial groups and nations.[7]

The Restoration of Faith in Love through Satyagraha

In the midst of this crisis King heard a sermon on Mahatma Gandhi's life and philosophy by Mordecai Johnson, president of Howard University. The sermon was so inspirational that he read several books on Gandhi. This reading soon restored his original faith in the power of love. He came to recognize that when love pervades nonviolent methods, far from being a symptom of weakness, it is a potent force for social transformation. Years later, in describing the Montgomery Boycott, he explained that Christ had furnished the spirit and the motivation while Gandhi had provided the method:

> Gandhi was probably the first person in history to lift the love ethic of Jesus above mere interaction between individuals to a powerful and effective social force on a large scale.[8]

In a sermon at The Riverside Church, in New York City in 1967, King reaffirmed this commitment. "We will return good for evil. We will love our enemies. Christ showed us the way and Gandhi showed us it could work."[9]

In *Stride Toward Freedom* King maintained that he had discovered a profound significance in Gandhi's central concept of satyagraha as a way of life.[10] The term "satyagraha," which Gandhi formed, means "holding on to Truth," and hence "Truth-force." "Satya" is Truth, and "graha" is literally "holding on to" and also means force. Gandhi explained that "satya" is derived from "sat," which means being, and affirmed that nothing exists in reality except Truth. He asserted that Truth is perhaps the most important name of God.[11] His personal view of God was the Hindu view of the all-pervading Brahma. "God is, nothing else is."[12] The true satyagrahi dedicates his life to Truth. "Holding on to Truth" involves a constant pursuit. "But I worship God as Truth only. I have not yet found Him, but I am seeking after Him. I am prepared to sacrifice the things dearest to me in pursuit of this quest."[13] Gandhi affirmed that Jesus and Mohammed were supreme artists because they saw and expressed Truth. They taught that if one first seeks Truth, then he will also begin to achieve Beauty and Goodness.[14] Since Gandhi considered Truth to be Soul or Spirit, he also called satyagraha "Soul-force."[15]

In *Young India* Gandhi indicated the way to God Who is Truth: "For me the only certain means of knowing God is nonviolence—

ahimsa. . . . "[16] *Ahimsa* was a principal tenet of the Jain religion that originated in India in the sixth century B.C. and was widely accepted in Gandhi's home state of Gujarat. His mother had a strong commitment to Jainism. He understood *ahimsa* to mean a renunciation of the will to kill or to damage:

> For we are all tarred with the same brush, and are children of one and the same Creator, and as such the divine powers within us are infinite. To slight a single human being is to slight those divine powers, and thus to harm not only that being but with him the whole world.[17]

But Gandhi understood *ahimsa* also to mean a rejection of the inner violence of the spirit:

> Not to hurt any living thing is no doubt a part of *ahimsa*. But it is its least expression. The principle of *ahimsa* is hurt by every evil thought, by undue haste, by lying, by hatred, by wishing ill to anybody.[18]

He admitted that he had to struggle continuously to follow the law of nonviolence, yet he could claim that as he succeeded on almost all occasions in keeping his feelings under control, his struggle served to endow him with greater strength:

> The more I work at this law, the more I feel the delight in my life, the delight in the scheme of the universe. It gives me a peace and a meaning of the mysteries of nature that I have no power to describe.[19]

Having indicated the basic meanings of *ahimsa,* Gandhi identified *ahimsa* with a positive and active state of love. Because of the role of love in satyagraha, at times he called satyagraha "Love-force."[20] This love is the means to the end of Truth:[21]

> And when you want to find Truth as God, the only inevitable means is love, that is, nonviolence, and since I believe that ultimately the means and the ends are convertible terms, I should not hesitate to say that God is Love.[22]

In the fulfillment of the supreme duty to seek this Truth, the satyagrahi will encounter injustice, cruelty, exploitation, and oppression, but will pursue Truth by doing good even to the evildoer. "Satyagraha means truth even against cunning, nonviolence against violence, forbearance against anger, and love against hatred."[23] Gandhi contended that we do not practice nonviolence if we love only those who love us. He insisted that in the practice of *ahimsa* he had to apply the same rules to the wrongdoer who was his enemy or a stranger to him as he would apply to his father or son when they did wrong.[24]

In 1928 Gandhi could claim that for forty years, due to a long course of prayerful discipline, he had ceased to hate anyone.[25] However, in the same statement he proclaimed that he could and did hate the system of exploitation established by the British in India, and that he hated the evil system of untouchability, which the Hindus supported. While refusing to hate the British and Hindus, he recognized that *ahimsa* could not allow for a toleration of their evil systems. Such a toleration would not have demonstrated a love for those who administered these systems since it would have permitted them to continue in their error. *Ahimsa* required him to attempt to reform evildoers by active opposition to their systems. Nonviolence does not mean meek submission to the will of the oppressor. Rather it means:

> the pitting of one's whole soul against the will of the tyrant. Working under this law of our being, it is possible for a single individual to defy the whole might of an unjust empire, to save his honor, his religion, his soul and lay the foundation for that empire's fall or its regeneration.[26]

When *ahimsa* opposes the evil system by noncooperation, this non-cooperation is not a passive state. Gandhi considered noncooperation an intensely active state, more active than physical resistance or violence. Therefore he came to regard passive resistance as a misnomer for the type of opposition he advocated. In the spirit of *ahimsa,* noncooperation must be neither punitive nor vindictive nor based on malice or hatred.[27] This requires a continual activity. Then too, in the course of his noncooperation with evil, the satyagrahi must be prepared "joyfully" to endure bodily suffering and even death. Gandhi believed that suffering is a necessary condition for progress:

> No country has ever risen without being purified through the fire of suffering. Mother suffers so that her child may live. The condition of wheat growing is that the seed grain should perish. Life

comes out of Death. Will India rise out of her slavery without fulfilling this eternal law of purification through suffering?[28]

Through this suffering without fear or hatred, the satyagrahi can appeal to the conscience and heart of the opponent to abandon his evil ways. Gandhi was convinced that ultimately the moral approach to the conscience of the opponent would be more effective in converting him than the threat of violence. He warned that violence can be effective in suppressing evil only for a time, and then evil will emerge with renewed vigor. He believed that only nonviolence can put a definite end to the evil since it changes the opponent into an ally.

King was particularly impressed by the amazing results of Gandhi's campaign for independence. He could testify that during his trip to India in 1959 he saw no evidence of the hatred that ordinarily follows a violent victory. He saw rather a mutual friendship based on an equality between the British and Indians. This victory for love led him to judge Gandhi to be "by all standards of measurement . . . one of the half-dozen greatest men in world-history."[29] To encourage his followers to persevere in nonviolence, King frequently appealed to the fact that Gandhi had used the weapons of truth, noninjury, courage, and soul-force, and still had been able to challenge the might of the British Empire to win independence for his people.

A preliminary review of the central themes in King's doctrine of nonviolence reveals why he has been called "the American Gandhi." Like Gandhi, he stressed that nonviolence is not passive, but active resistance. Gandhi strengthened King's belief that there is a moral obligation to resist evil. Moreover, King warned that the defeat and humiliation of the opponent do not constitute a victory. In the midst of opposition to the opponent, one must attempt to win his friendship. When the Supreme Court decision integrated the Montgomery buses, one of the "Integrated Bus Suggestions" King gave his followers was, "Be loving enough to absorb evil and understanding enough to turn an enemy into a friend."[30] King was also similar to Gandhi in that he consistently declared that his nonviolent protests were directed against the forces of evil at work in the unjust systems, not against the persons who were involved in administering the systems. He could repeat St. Augustine's plea to hate the sin, but love the sinner. He regarded the Montgomery struggle not as a racial tension, but as a conflict between justice and injustice. Thus he stressed that there would be a victory for justice and a defeat for injustice.[31]

King also shared Gandhi's vision of the value of unearned suffering.

He recognized that the willingness to suffer could arouse the conscience of the opponent, and he drew strength from Gandhi's plea to his followers, "Rivers of blood may have to flow before we gain our freedom, but it must be our blood."[32] During the Montgomery Boycott he warned his followers that their participation might mean jail or even their death, and contended, "But if such physical death is the price that we must pay to free our children from a life of permanent psychological death, then nothing could be more honorable."[33] As will emerge in this study, the redemptive power of unearned suffering was a recurrent theme in King's sermons and writings. He also identified with Gandhi's insistence that nonviolence should include the internal nonviolence of the spirit. In 1959, he felt a special need to reemphasize the necessity for nonviolence of the spirit when he had to repudiate the attempts of some "hate groups" in the black community to preach a doctrine of black supremacy. While expressing his awareness of the patience of most black persons with the brutality of lynch mobs, with the evil of economic exploitation, and with the constant oppression by unjust Southern courts, he still challenged his people to meet hate with love, and to confront physical force with soul-force.[34]

King's description of his debt to Gandhi was revealing since he stated that his study of Gandhi's philosophy caused him to recognize for the first time that "the Christian doctrine of love, operating through the Gandhian method of nonviolence, is one of the most potent weapons available to an oppressed people in their struggle for freedom."[35] This description preserved the central role of Christian love in King's philosophy, and coincided with his claim, cited above, that Christ provided the spirit, and Gandhi the method. Observing this distinction between spirit and method, the remainder of this chapter will examine King's conception of love and determine the ways in which Paul Tillich, Anders Nygren, George Davis, L. Harold DeWolf, Paul Ramsey, and Howard Thurman contributed to the development of this conception, and the fourth chapter will indicate which of Gandhi's tactics King used in his crusades.

Love as Power to Achieve Justice

King's study of the writings of the theologian Paul Tillich served to reinforce his rejection of Nietzsche's critique of Christian love as a glorification of weakness. In *Love, Power, and Justice* Tillich explained that Nietzsche rejected the Christian concept of love because he misinterpreted the nature of this love.[36] Nietzsche restricted this love to its emotional element and thus mistakenly identified love with a resignation of power, and power with a denial of love. Therefore Nietzsche regarded this love as antithetical to the "will to power," the dynamic self-affirmation of life overcoming internal and external resistance. Against Nietzsche, Tillich proclaimed that love should be the foundation of power and that Christian love must be united with power in order to accomplish its twofold goal of negating what is against love and of saving the soul of him who acts against love. In *Where Do We Go From Here: Chaos or Community?,* though he did not refer to Tillich, King presented Tillich's critique of Nietzsche.[37] King objected to the usual contrast that is made between the concepts of love and power as polar opposites. He criticized the identification of love with a resignation of power, and the identification of power with a denial of love. He indicated that Nietzsche, as the philosopher of the "will to power," was guilty of this misinterpretation, which caused him to reject the concept of Christian love. King called for a realization that a power not rooted in love is reckless and abusive while a love devoid of power is sentimental and anemic. Evidently inspired by Tillich's theme of the union of love, power, and justice, he maintained, "Power at its best is love implementing the demands of justice. Justice at its best is love correcting everything that stands against love."[38] In his doctoral dissertation entitled *A Comparison of the Conceptions of God in the Thinking of Paul Tillich and Henry Nelson Wieman,* King referred to Tillich's doctrine that love and justice should not be looked upon as two distinct attributes of God. "Love is the ontological concept. Justice has no independent ontological standing. Justice is dependent on love. It is a part of love's activity."[39]

Eros, Philia, and Agape

To highlight the form of love that should be the regulating ideal of the Nonviolent Movement, King examined the meanings of three Greek words for love: *eros, philia,* and *agape.*[40] He explained that *eros* is a romantic or aesthetic love which Plato presented in his dialogues as the yearning of the soul for the realm of the divine. *Philia* is an intimate affection between friends. In this love we love because we are loved. *Agape* is an understanding, creative, redemptive goodwill toward all men. It enables us to love every man not because we like him or because his ways appeal to us but because God loves him. "It is the love of God operating in the human heart."[41] This love is spontaneous and groundless in the sense that it is not motivated by any attractive quality in the object. In his dissertation King presented Tillich's conception of *agape:*

> All love, except *agape,* is dependent on contingent characteristics which change and are partial, such as repulsion and attraction, passion and sympathy. *Agape* is independent of these states. It affirms the other unconditionally. It is *agape* that suffers and forgives. It seeks the personal fulfillment of the other.[42]

King indicated that *agape* does not require a sentimental or affectionate emotion. He stressed the fact that Jesus said, "Love your enemies," not "Like your enemies." Liking is a sentimental or affectionate emotion. Jesus was advocating *agape,* not *eros* or *philia.* Jesus was not asking us to be affectionate toward a person whose intention is to exploit and even to crush us. King believed that Jesus was not asking him to like those who denied him basic human rights, threatened his life and the lives of his family, and bombed his home. Jesus taught that *agape* is greater than "liking." King was convinced that *agape* could serve as the life force of creative nonviolence because it does not distinguish between worthy and unworthy persons; it does not distinguish between friend and enemy, but attempts to regard every man as a neighbor. "When we love on the *agape* level we love men not because we like them, not because their attitudes and ways appeal to us, but because God loves them."[43] In his "A Christmas Sermon on Peace" King developed Tillich's notion that *agape* is marked by its willingness to suffer as he said to his most bitter opponents:

> We shall match your capacity to inflict suffering by our capacity to endure suffering. We will meet your physical force with soul-force. Do to us what you will and we will still love you. . . . Bomb our homes and threaten our children, and, as difficult as it is, we will still love you. Send your hooded perpetrators of violence into our communities at the midnight hour and drag us out on some wayside road and leave us half-dead as you beat us, and we will still love you.[44]

Nygren's View of Love as Self-Sacrifice

Another source for King's conception of *agape* was Anders Nygren, a Swedish bishop and theologian. This is not to say that King's total conception of *agape* resembled Nygren's conception. As subsequent sections will indicate, King was far more indebted to George Davis and the Boston Personalists, especially L. Harold DeWolf, for the main development of his conception of *agape.* King's commitment to Personalism even caused him to reject some of Nygren's doctrines. But King did identify with certain elements in Nygren's description of *agape* as self-sacrifice that could harmonize with his commitment to Personalism.

As a student at Boston University, King wrote a research paper entitled "Contemporary Continental Theology."[45] One of the works he examined in this paper was Nygren's *Agape and Eros.*[46] King presented Nygren's sharp contrast between *eros* and *agape.*[47] He explained that Nygren maintained that *eros,* as described in Plato's dialogues, loves in proportion to the value of its object. In the process of responding to the value in its objects, the Platonic *eros* moves from an appreciation of the world of sensible beings to a love of immaterial beings such as the nature of beauty itself. In contrast to this Platonic *eros,* Nygren viewed the *agape* mentioned in the gospels and epistles as purely generous and spontaneous, not caused by a value in its objects and not concerned with human merit.[48] *Agape* flows from God into the lives of sinful men, and enables them to realize their sinfulness and to forgive and love their enemies. Though in this research paper King did not further explain Nygren's contrast between *eros* and *agape,* the essence of this contrast remained the basis of all of King's later references to *agape.* An examination of Nygren's development of this contrast will indicate the significance of King's emphasis on the distinction between the two notions as well as reveal to some degree the force of King's belief in *agape* as the foundation of his Movement.

Nygren presented Plato's doctrine of *eros* as unfolded in his dialogues, the *Phaedrus* and the *Symposium.*[49] In these works Plato saw *eros* as a force that causes the soul to turn from a concern with sense objects and drives the soul to seek the ideal world of Truth, Goodness, and Beauty. Stimulated by *eros,* the soul moves from delight in beautiful material objects and ascends to a vision of Beauty itself, the ideal pattern that makes all beautiful things possible. Plato accepted the belief common to the Oriental doctrines of salvation that the human soul has a supernatural divine origin and worth. The soul can experience *eros* and the resultant ascent to the divine because it is divine in origin. Prior to its involvement with the body, the soul had a vision of the divine. It could see the essences of Truth, Goodness, and Beauty without the flaws that accompany their material manifestations. Plato shared the belief of the Pythagorean mystery religion that the soul fell from this state through moral fault, and as a punishment was placed in the "prison" or "tomb" of the body. When the soul enters the body, it partially forgets the absolute truth it knew in its former spiritual existence. However, the soul in its temporal existence, by contact with sensible objects modelled after the eternal patterns, can "recollect" to some degree these patterns. These patterns are the essences that enable human beings to make moral, aesthetical, mathematical, and metaphysical judgments. In the *Symposium* Plato traced the movements of the soul under the influence of *eros*.[50] The soul is at first concerned with beauty in one beautiful body, then with beauty in another, and then with beauty in all bodies. The soul passes from an appreciation of the order, symmetry, and proportion among the parts of these bodies to a love of beautiful actions, and then to a love of souls as the sources of these actions. The soul then proceeds to a love of beautiful forms of knowledge in human laws, institutions, and the sciences until finally the soul attains a knowledge of Absolute Beauty itself. "It is then, if ever, that life is worth living for man, when he beholds Beauty itself."[51]

As part of his effort to contrast *eros* and *agape*, Nygren described the Platonic *eros* as "acquisitive love":

> The most obvious thing about *Eros* is that it is a desire, a longing, a striving. But man only desires and longs for that which he has not got, and of which he feels a need; and he can only strive for that which he feels to be valuable.[52]

Nygren contended that Plato was fundamentally unaware of any form of love other than acquisitive love.[53] He conceded that Plato's *eros* has a religious significance since it raises the imperfect to the perfect, the mortal to immortality, and it is the way by which the soul mounts up to the divine. Nonetheless, he argued that since *eros* is necessarily motivated by the value of the object that can satisfy its need, it is basically a "Will-to-possess."[54] According to Nygren, there was no room in Plato's doctrine for any spontaneous or unmotivated love like *agape*.

Crucial to Nygren's contrast between *eros* and *agape* was his interpretation of the Platonic love as "egocentric love":[55]

> Everything centres on the individual self and its destiny. All that matters from first to last is the soul that is aflame with *Eros*—its Divine nature, its present straits while it is in bondage to the

body, its gradual ascent to the world above, its blessed vision of the Ideas in their unveiled glory.[56]

Nygren argued that the acquisitive nature of the Platonic love implies its egocentric character since all desire (or appetite and longing) is more or less egocentric. He found in the desire of Platonic love for happiness a confirmation of his interpretation that it is egocentric. This love wishes not only to possess the good but also to possess it permanently, and so Plato viewed love also as a desire for immortality, which, for Nygren, further reveals its egocentricity.

Nygren explained that Jesus' notion of *agape* as God's love for sinners is in many ways opposed to the Platonic *eros*, and that the Christian's *agape,* his love for his neighbor, which includes his enemies, should follow the example of the Divine *agape:*[57]

> This Divine love, of which the distinctive feature is freedom in giving, has its direct continuation in Christian neighbourly love, which having received everything freely from God is prepared also to give freely.[58]

He maintained that the most striking feature of *agape* as Divine Love, as Jesus represented it, is its spontaneity. It is "unmotivated" in the sense that you cannot find an explanation of God's love in the character of the person who is the object of His love. It is "groundless" in the sense that there are no extrinsic grounds for it, such as the personal worth of human beings. Jesus sought the company of publicans and sinners. The only ground for it is to be found in God Himself.[59] Motivated love is human. Jesus' unmotivated love refuses to be controlled by the value of its object, but chooses to be determined only by its own intrinsic nature. Jesus has transcended the scheme of legal piety that asserted that God loves only the righteous. With Nietzsche in mind, Nygren claimed that *agape*, with its indifference to the value of its object, achieves something deeper than any "transvaluation," namely, "the principle that *any thought of valuation* whatsoever is out of place in connection with fellowship with God":[60]

> When God's love is directed to the sinner . . . all thought of valuation is excluded in advance. . . . The distinction between the worthy and the unworthy, the righteous and the sinner, sets no bounds to His love.[61]

Since *agape* is Divine Love, it shares in the creativeness that is characteristic of the life of God. It creates values in its object. *Agape* is not directed toward a person because he has worth; rather it endows him with worth.

Nygren was forced by this interpretation to conclude that the notion of the infinite value of the human soul is not a central idea of Christianity. It is *eros*, he maintained, which begins with the assumption that the soul has a divine origin and worth, and that the divine element in the depths of the soul constitutes a basis for contact with God. But *agape* begins with the conviction that the soul is devoid of value:

> When man has fallen away from God, he is wholly lost and has no value at all. But just in this is the "point of contact" for God's *Agape*, since God seeks that which is lost. All thought of "merit" is here excluded.[62]

Nygren rejected the notion that God's love in forgiving sins concentrates on the essence of the personality that sin cannot destroy and that wins His approbation. Such a notion, he argued, negates the fact that God's forgiveness is a gift.

Nygren concluded his discussion of the characteristics that mark the content of the Christian idea of Divine Love by indicating that *agape* is the initiator of fellowship with God. Man does not come to God by his own efforts, as the theory of *eros* maintains.[63] Man cannot claim to arrive at this fellowship by meritorious conduct. *Agape* must "come down" so that God's forgiveness can establish the fellowship for man's salvation. Nygren used the parables of Jesus to attempt to substantiate this interpretation. He asserted that these parables have as their background "the 'unmotivated' Divine love that baffles all rational calculations."[64] The Parable of the Prodigal Son (Luke 15:11–32) reveals the spontaneity of God's love. The Parable of the Laborers in the Vineyard (Matt. 20:1–16) displays God's willingness to enter into fellowship with those not worthy of it. Nygren affirmed that the essential purpose of the latter parable is to exclude completely the principle of justice from the religious relationship. Motivated justice gives way to unmotivated love. The Parable of the Sower (Mark 4:3–29) discloses that *agape* gives and sacrifices even where rational calculation would suggest the futility of any sacrifice. The sower sows even though he knows that the greater part of the seed will be lost. "*Agape* sows its seed in hope, even when there seem to be no grounds at all for hope."[65] The Parable of the Lost Sheep (Luke 15:4–7) illustrates how reason is put aside in the process of unmotivated love. The ninety-nine sheep are left for the one. Finally, the Parable of the Unmerciful Steward (Matt. 18:23–35) teaches the unconditional nature of divine *agape* and requires that the love and forgiveness of those who receive it shall likewise be boundless and unconditional.

God's *agape* serves as a prototype for the *agape* required by the Christian commandment of love of neighbor. The Christian's love for his neighbor must be spontaneous, unmotivated, unconditional, unlimited, and uncalculating.[66] It is not a mere reflection of the attitude of the person who is its object, but has creative power to establish a new fellowship among men.[67] Nygren appealed to Jesus' words, "If you love them that love you, what thanks have you? For even sinners love those that love them" (Luke 6:32).[68] In contrast to natural love, Christian love acts with no extrinsic motive. Nygren rejected as unacceptable even any love for neighbor that is concerned with a supposed divine kernel or essence within the other person, since this would give love an extrinsic motive and would thus disqualify it as *agape*. He asserted that *agape* best reveals its spontaneous and unmotivated nature when it is directed to enemies whose actions would provoke the opposite of love. Just as God loves sinners, so Christians are expected to love their enemies. "When Christian love is directed to enemies . . . It creates fellowship even where fellowship seemed impossible. Thus it shows that Christian love is action, not merely reaction."[69] Unlike *eros*, which seeks the neighbor only insofar as it can utilize him for its own ascent, *agape* is directed to the neighbor himself, including the enemy, "with no further thought in mind and no side-long glances at anything else."[70] *Agape* does not even use love of neighbor to win God's love.

Nygren maintained that *eros* and *agape* have different attitudes toward self-love. While self-love is the basic form of all *eros*, there can be no self-love in *agape*. He claimed that Christianity should not recognize self-love as a legitimate form of love. As Christian love relates to God and neighbor, it must fight and conquer self-love as its chief adversary. He excluded from *agape* not only sinful self-love but all self-love. "*Agape* recognises no kind of self-love as legitimate."[71] His repudiation of all self-love corresponded to his rejection of the intrinsic value of the soul. In referring to St. Paul's principle, "the love of God which is in Christ Jesus," as the direct opposite of acquisitive love, Nygren claimed that St. Paul had condemned all self-love whatsoever.[72] "Christian love must be ready, according to Paul, to sacrifice even its 'spiritual' advantages and privileges, if need be, in the service of its neighbour."[73]

King's description of *agape* was identical in some ways with that of Nygren. King also spoke of *agape* as an "overflowing love which is purely spontaneous, unmotivated, groundless, and creative."[74] He agreed with Nygren that *agape* as "the love of God operating in the human heart" is groundless in the sense that it should not be motivated by the personal qualities or character or actions of the person loved, and that love for one's enemies is the supreme expression of *agape*.[75] He also shared Nygren's vision of the essential role of forgiveness in the life of *agape*. "It [*agape*] is a willingness to forgive, not seven times, but seventy times seven to restore community."[76] Like Nygren, he also rejected the notion that Christian love is a mere reaction. "*Agape* is not a weak, passive love. It is love in action."[77] Moreover, he could approve of Nygren's rejection of the egocentricity of the Platonic *eros*, that would interfere with the acts of forgiveness. Having studied some of the Platonic dialogues with Professor Samuel Williams at Morehouse College and with Professor Raphael Demos at Harvard University, King understood Nygren's references to the self-seeking movements of the Platonic *eros*.[78] He could thus basically endorse Nygren's contrast between *eros* and *agape*, and affirm that *agape* is a disinterested love, that involves a sacrificial will-to-give as it pursues the good of the neighbor. Nygren stressed how St. Paul regarded the sacrifice of Christ on the cross as the sublimest expression of the divine *agape*.[79] King too found in the cross the highest expression of divine *agape*:

> Every time I look at the cross I am reminded of the greatness of God and the redemptive power of Jesus Christ. I am reminded of the beauty of sacrificial love and the majesty of unswerving devotion to truth.[80]

Davis's Conception of the Necessity of *Agape*

King began his study of Personalism at Crozer Theological Seminary under the direction of Professor George Davis. He took nearly one-third of his courses there with Davis, and later asserted that Davis remained a significant influence on his thought. When he was completing his studies at Boston University, he wrote a letter to Davis in which he acknowledged this influence. "I must admit that my theological and philosophical studies with you have been of tremendous help to me in my present studies."[81]

Like Nygren, though not to the same intense degree, Davis stressed the value of altruism as essential to the Christian life. Unlike Nygren, he did not deny the intrinsic value of the human person, and he emphasized the role of altruism in creating community. Thus Davis's articles for *The Crozer Quarterly* contain many references to his conviction that Christianity requires of its followers a passionate concern for the well-being of others. In his evaluation of eighteenth century evangelicalism, Davis regarded the enhanced concern in that movement for the spiritual and material well-being of others as "one of the glorious chapters in Christian faith and life."[82] He praised this movement because it not only sought to spread the gospel but also labored for the educational, social, economic, and political improvement of humanity. He indicated that this altruism of evangelicalism had led to the abolition of the slave trade in the British Empire and to many philanthropic enterprises, including prison reform, establishment of schools and orphanages, care of the poor, protection of children, relief for the mentally ill, and factory reform. But in his analysis of this altruism Davis revealed that his conception of altruism stood in sharp contrast with that of Nygren. After enumerating the material benefits resulting from the altruism of the evangelicals, Davis concluded, "The volume of good coming from evangelicals imbued with such broad regard for personality is indeed beyond computation."[83] He extolled the evangelical altruism because it was rooted in a recognition that persons deserve altruism since they are beings of supreme worth. The evangelicals understood that persons are made in the divine image and are the reason for the sacrifice of Jesus:

One cannot comprehend the truth, the power, and the appeal of evangelicalism apart from its contention that all men are of worth to God and hence should be of worth to one another.[84]

Davis maintained that altruism, to be authentic, must not only be moved by a desire to imitate the love of God, which, according to Nygren, is the sole acceptable motive, but it must also be prompted by the value of the human personality it serves. Moreover, Davis found in the message of Christ the insight that altruism reveals that human personality is itself a value as it cooperates with divine grace:

Made in the divine image, there was resident within men the power of self-determination which, when properly directed, would eventuate in a life of personal quality which God could approve. Because of this inherent capacity men could turn the other cheek, sacrifice coat and cloak, go the second mile, lend to the needy, love their enemies, and pray for their persecutors. Such things they should do not because of any fear that the end of the world is near. Such things they should do because such actions alone express what their authentic nature is. By expressing this, their real nature, they bring forth a life not qualitatively different from the life of God. Thereby, they become sons of their Father who is in heaven.[85]

Guided by this message about the dignity of the self, Davis found no difficulty in identifying with one of Kant's formulations of the moral law:

This essential dignity and worth of the personal constitutes the source of Immanuel Kant's famous conclusion in morals: So act as to treat humanity, whether in thine own person or in that of any other, in every case as an end withal, never as a means only.[86]

In contrast with Nygren, who could discover no value in man, Davis affirmed, "The liberal Christian will refuse to toss lightly aside the dignity, the beauty, and the love discernible in human personality, both non-Christian and Christian."[87]

Furthermore, Davis differed from Nygren by emphasizing that altruism should aim to promote community. "God intends human life to achieve solidarity."[88] Davis affirmed that humanity is under a ceaseless pressure to form larger units of cooperative life or perish.[89] Although Davis did not stress self-sacrifice as intensely and as frequently as Nygren, he did recommend such a sacrifice if it were necessary to promote "the new world of cooperation and brotherhood." There is "not a one of us, probably, who does not feel that need [for this cooperation] and who would not gladly sacrifice his life if through doing so that end could be attained."[90] King's frequent appeals to his followers during his crusades that they be prepared to sacrifice all for the sake of human dignity and for the beloved community revealed his capacity not only to absorb the positive elements in Nygren's conception of *agape* but also to transcend Nygren's negative view of the human personality by affirming with Davis, DeWolf, and other Boston Personalists, as the next section will indicate, that the purpose of altruism is to create a brotherhood in which all individuals may preserve their dignity, realize their rational potential, and fulfill their destiny.

DeWolf's Comprehensive Conception of *Agape*

Although in his references to *agape* King appealed to some of Nygren's reflections and relied on Davis for the outline of a more complete and positive conception, he found in the thought of L. Harold
DeWolf a comprehensive conception of *agape* that provided not only
for the value of the person and for the role of self-sacrifice but also for
the fulfillment of the self in the creation of community. King took six
courses with DeWolf at the Boston University School of Theology and
selected him as the mentor for his doctoral dissertation. In a letter to
George Davis in 1953, King expressed his appreciation of DeWolf's
work *A Theology of the Living Church*, which Davis had highly
praised in a review for *The Journal of Bible and Religion* and had
adopted as the text for his required course in theology. In this letter
King also stated:

> As you probably know, Dr. DeWolf is my major professor and I
> have noticed all along that there is a great deal of similarity be-
> tween your thought and his. Dr. DeWolf refers to himself as an
> evangelical liberal and as I remember, this is about the same posi-
> tion that you would hold. So you can see that it was not difficult
> at all for me to emerge from your classroom to Dr. DeWolf's. I
> found the atmosphere in both classrooms saturated with a warm
> evangelical liberalism. Theologically speaking, I find myself still
> holding to the liberal position.[91]

Years later, when King gave DeWolf a copy of *Why We Can't Wait*, he
wrote on the flyleaf, "To My Dear Friend and Teacher Harold DeWolf
whose friendship I cherish very deeply and whose sound and profound
ideas have greatly influenced my life, Martin." King autographed
similar tributes in two of his other books he gave to DeWolf. In re-
tracing his intellectual formation in *Stride Toward Freedom* King
identified Personalism as his basic philosophical position, and acknowledged his indebtedness to DeWolf and Edgar Brightman for
greatly stimulating his thinking in his studies of Personalism.[92] In her
autobiography, *My Life with Martin Luther King, Jr.*, Coretta Scott
King emphasized the fact that King had chosen Boston University because he wanted to study Personalism with DeWolf and Brightman.[93]
King indicated that Personalism gave him the metaphysical grounding
for the idea of a personal God and for the dignity and worth of all
human personality.

By his doctrine of the sacredness of the human person DeWolf helped King recognize the unacceptability of Nygren's notion that the human soul is devoid of value. DeWolf devoted a chapter of *A Theology of the Living Church* to developing the doctrine that man is made in the image of God—a doctrine that became so crucial to King's defense of the dignity and rights of all men. DeWolf rejected the approach of many Jews and Christians who have condemned their common humanity and, by prostrating themselves before the holy God, have attempted to extol Him by contrasting His righteousness with the wretched depravity of men.[94] In order to develop a balanced description of man instead of such self-abnegation, DeWolf argued that human depravity cannot be total, for then men would be content simply to call evil good. But, though they try to do this, they cannot do it. "At worst they remain restless and discontented, wandering fearfully through the dark passages of their own souls, haunted by the vague but chilling specters of their guilt."[95] Then too, he asked how can we adhere to the doctrine of the total depravity of man in the face of the fact that countless millions of men have openly tried to learn whom they should worship and, despite interminable disappointments and failures, have attempted to obey the call of duty. DeWolf warned against a narrow view of the human scene that, in using Christlikeness for a measure, looks only upon the sins and failures of men and sees a "frightfully dismal picture."[96] He argued that we can view the human scene from another perspective, still retain Christ as our measure, and arrive at quite a different conclusion:

> No less impressive than men's sins are their groping efforts to make amends for them. The sons of Adam are not only hypocrites but also the exposers and despisers of hypocrisy. They are not only cruel but also kind. They are not only licentious but also self-controlled. In moral blindness they yet grope for light. In self-deception they betray their dissatisfaction with what they are.[97]

Because King, as we shall see, accepted such a balanced view of man, he was able to recognize both man's potential for evil as well as his potential for conversion and for membership in the beloved community.

In affirming man's capacity for goodness, DeWolf rejected the theological view that refuses to credit fallen human nature for its finer attributes and traces all goodness to the gracious work of God. He contended that the refusal to regard as a human good the goodness of a Gautama, Jeremiah, Gandhi, or Albert Schweitzer on the ground that God gave them their virtue is comparable to denying that human life exists because it is a gift of God:

> Of course, it is God who gives us life and it is He who empowers us for every good work. But for all that, we do live and we both aspire and in some measure attain to righteousness. We show more gratitude to God by giving Him thanks for these endowments of our common humanity than by gloomy denials.[98]

DeWolf maintained that the Scriptures, while they stress the sinfulness of man, still emphasize his higher nature. Thus Genesis affirms, "God created man in his own image, in the image of God he created him; male and female he created them. . . . God saw everything that he had made, and behold it was very good."[99] He indicated that the Psalmist asserted, "You are gods, sons of the Most High, all of you."[100] St. Paul spoke of man as "the image and glory of God."[101] DeWolf discerned in the pleas by the prophets for justice and mercy an implicit recognition of the inherent dignity of divinely created men. Then too, he cited the appeal of the Letter of St. James in the New Testament for a respectful treatment of human beings when it denounced the misuse of the tongue. "With it we bless the Lord and Father, and with it we curse men, who are made in the likeness of God."[102] DeWolf effectively argued that if it is evidently inconsistent and evil to bless God and curse men "who are made in the likeness of God," it would seem equally inconsistent and evil for some censorious theologies, while praising God, to engage in "unrelieved disparagement of humanity."[103]

DeWolf stressed that man does bear upon his person the stamp of His Maker. He maintained that this fact is evident in four persistent observable qualities of human life.[104] *First*, man has a spiritual nature as indicated by his ability to think, feel, and will. Whatever attributes God may have that are unknown to us and even beyond the possibility of our comprehension, unless He is less and not more than ourselves, He also knows, desires, and wills.[105] *Second*, although there is a vast difference between the righteousness of God and the uncertain, changing, and imperfect moral sense of man, still there is a godlikeness implied in man's power to make moral distinctions and in his abiding concern with the moral dimension of life that is manifest even in his repressed feelings of guilt:

But human beings are like God in being subject also to rightful description in the ethical category of righteousness, however low on that scale man may sometimes fall. This is no small matter. Without this dimension of his being man would not be a real or potential child of God, called to be like Him.[106]

Differences in moral judgments from one individual to another and from one culture to another indicate that our moral sense is not infallible in its contents, but they no more demonstrate that man's sense of duty or his longing for righteousness is illusory than do differences in men's tastes in food demonstrate that hunger is illusory or that we can dispense with the need to make the distinction between healthful and unhealthful foods. While the development of man's moral sense in large part depends on his social experience, that sense remains an inextricable part of his human nature.

Third, man seems perennially religious. Peoples of all the world have discovered or devised objects of reverence and devotion. Even idolatry is evidence of "the unsatisfied and unenlightened but irrepressible longing for the one proper object of absolute reverence."[107] When man's yearning for God does not attain a relationship to Him, it persists by attaching itself to human heroes, living or dead, to animals imaginatively endowed with superhuman status, and to the forces of nature or to monstrous products of mythological art:

So intimate is the proper relation of man's nature to God that without Him no human being can gain the completion of himself. When this completion is not found, all the races of the world persistently keep up the quest.[108]

Fourth, man continuously aspires to good and condemns evil. DeWolf found indications of this tendency in the way that even the most evil world movements must secure support by masquerading as good. The cruelest aggression acts in the name of justice and peace, while slavery is imposed on subjects in the name of freedom and brotherhood. DeWolf explained that when man aspires to goodness, he is responding to the call of God that summons him to a maturation of his humanity. He reaffirmed man's likeness and kinship with the divine when he concluded:

The call of God to the higher life comes to men from the great Other, it is true. Yet it is not a summons to a strange land where

humanity finds itself alien and insecure. It is an invitation home
to our only peace.[109]

In his speeches and writings King frequently referred to this Personalist conviction that man is made in the image of God. Thus in his
1965 speech "Man in a Revolutionary World" he stated:

> Deeply rooted in our religious heritage is the conviction that
> every man is an heir to a legacy of dignity and worth. Our Judeo-
> Christian tradition refers to this inherent dignity of man in the
> biblical term the *image of God*. The innate worth referred to in
> the phrase, the *image of God*, is universally shared in equal por-
> tions by all men. There is no graded scale of essential worth;
> there is no divine right of one race which differs from the divine
> right of another. Every human being has etched in his personality
> the indelible stamp of the creator. Every man must be respected
> because God loves him. The worth of an individual does not lie in
> the measure of his intellect, his racial origin, or his social posi-
> tion. Human worth lies in relatedness to God. An individual has
> value because he has value to God. Whenever this is recognized,
> "Whiteness" and "Blackness" pass away as determinants in a
> relationship, and "Son" and "Brother" are substituted.[110]

It was this conviction about the sacred dignity of the human person
that intensified King's opposition to the evil of segregation. In the
same speech he contended, "Segregation stands diametrically opposed to the principle of the sacredness of human personality. It de-
bases personality."[111]

Because of his commitment to this Personalist view of the human
soul, King could not subscribe to Nygren's contention that *agape* is
absolutely unmotivated by any value in the object. He could agree
with Nygren that *agape* should not be moved by the personal traits of
the person who is loved, but his belief in the sacredness of the human
personality as an image of the divine was for him a principal motive
for the practice of *agape*:

> Man is rather an upstanding human being whose vision has been
> impaired by the cataracts of sin and whose soul has been
> weakened by the virus of pride, but there is sufficient vision left
> for him to lift his eyes unto the hills, and there remains enough of
> God's image for him to turn his weak and sin-battered life toward
> the Great Physician, the curer of the ravages of sin.[112]

King's conviction about man as the image of God and about the basic dignity of all persons also caused him to reject Nygren's denunciation of all self-love as acquisitive love.[113] Unlike Nygren, King could see that not all self-love need be selfish and acquisitive. He recognized that respect for the sacredness of personality involves respect for the sacredness of one's own personality, and that legitimate self-love is necessary for the formation of the Personalist ideal of a community of shared love and justice. However, in extolling the value of self-love, King did not intend that this proper appreciation of the self should interfere with the practice of *agape*, which at times places the other before self.

DeWolf also prepared King to value the necessity of a love that involves self-sacrifice. At the beginning of his treatment of the Kingdom of God in *A Theology of the Living Church*, DeWolf emphasized the importance of the role of this kind of love in the creation of the communal life of the Kingdom:

> The Christian needs to know what is meant by the kingdom of God. For to him the kingdom is the *summum bonum*, "the pearl of great value" for which everything else ought to be willingly sacrificed. . . . Its supreme uniting principle is love. . . .[114]

DeWolf indicated that it is necessary to recall that "Christian love is a reckless, passionate outreach. . . ."[115] His ethical doctrine contained the Law of Social Devotion, which stated, "All persons ought to devote themselves to serving the best interests of the group and to subordinate personal gain to social gain."[116]

Other Boston Personalists who taught King also emphasized the need for sacrificial love. Edgar Brightman asserted that *agape* is a Christian essential regardless of whether Nygren's exact concept of it be accepted or rejected, and affirmed that sacrifice belongs to the essence of Christianity.[117] "*Agape* is Christian love, love sacred, not profane; unselfish, sacrificial redeeming love, greater than faith and greater than hope."[118] Peter Bertocci likewise stressed the value of sacrificial love when he maintained that while martyrdom may not always be the correct choice for an individual, "for many men the supreme self-sacrifice can be 'their finest hour,' the act that symbolizes the very meaning of their own lives."[119] Walter G. Muelder, dean of the Boston University School of Theology, who did not teach King but, according to King's acknowledgement, did influence him, found in the cross of Christianity an expression of the fact that "self-sacrificing and forgiving compassion are the ultimate fulfillment of person-in-community and the ultimate revelation of the character of God."[120]

While stressing the value of sacrificial love, DeWolf was equally emphatic that *agape* in its sacrifice should aim to create community:

> Life under the reign of God is not an individualistic affair. Since love is its dominant principle, it is communal to the very core. This communal life of the kingdom has already begun in some groups and relationships. So far as that love and life are present, the kingdom of God is here.[121]

His fundamental criticism of Nygren's notion of *agape* was that it could not build community. Community depends on sharing values, but Nygren had denied that *agape* can seek to share in values. God calls each Christian to work for the sake of the Kingdom, and each is to perform his tasks "with the dominant purpose of sharing all the endowment and blessing which God has given him with other persons."[122] DeWolf's Law of Cooperation stated, "All persons ought as far as possible to co-operate with other persons in the production and enjoyment of shared values."[123] He affirmed that in a Christian fellowship "the individual self is surrendered, only to be regained and fulfilled in new depth and richness of meaning."[124] DeWolf further helped prepare King for his vision of the beloved community by maintaining, "For the sake of this community [of divine love], we lose ourselves and in it we find ourselves."[125]

> It would be self-contradictory to demand that every person consider himself less than any other person. But it is plain truth that every person is less than the divine-human community and to put that truth into the whole-commitment of faith is to discover *what life can be*. Even God Himself, in all His power and holiness, so far transcending our imaginations, is yet less than the kingdom which includes Him and also all with whom He is permitted to share His glory. Hence, even He stoops in devotion to the kingdom to which He calls us. How much more should we give ourselves to it.[126]

DeWolf asserted that Nygren minimized the "great and first commandment," the commandment to love God, because "it would be quite unthinkable for me, a dependent creature in need of God's mercy, to approach God in the hope of giving Him some good without hope of any spiritual profit to myself."[127] Moreover, how can love consist only in giving, as Nygren claimed, when Christ's second commandment was "You shall love your neighbor as yourself"?

Other Boston Personalists also proclaimed community as the goal of *agape*. A persistent theme in Brightman's writings was the necessity of cooperation for the creation of a community of *shared values*:

> Co-operation differs from other forms of interaction in that it is interaction consciously directed at the production of values (often of shared values) which contribute to the welfare, or at least to the supposed welfare, of the cooperators.[128]

In stating his Law of Altruism, Brightman revealed that altruism can have legitimate rewards for all involved:

> Each person ought to respect all other persons as ends in themselves, and, as far as possible, to co-operate with others in the production and enjoyment of shared values.[129]

Bertocci could not accept Nygren's repudiation of the self since he held that self-respect is the condition for the creation of communal values:

> I respect myself as a moral unit, as having value potential, as an actualizer of values, and I recognize that apart from me and others like me in our mutual realizations of value certain values in particular will not be realized.[130]

Bertocci reaffirmed the right and obligation of the individual to share in the values of the community. He defined love as "the total orientation of a person's thinking, feeling, and willing insofar as his controlling commitment is the ideal growth of personality in himself and in all other persons."[131]

Muelder reiterated this emphasis when he stated that the right kind of altruism "must find its place in the communitarian laws, for its context is the reciprocity of human needs and interests, common needs and common goals."[132] He wrote that a valid altruism does not neglect self but seeks self-identification with the wider claims, needs, and values of other persons.[133] True community emerges from *agape* that is self-giving but not self-repudiating.[134] In opposition to Nygren's emphasis on self-rejection, Muelder indicated that there is a great deal of evidence that shows that if persons have never learned to love or accept themselves, they are ill prepared to try to love others. "If by the repudiation of self-love, a person is led simply to self-contempt, he has missed the point of Christian love and stewardship."[135]

Ramsey's Description of Christian Love

In his explanation of the *agape* that motivated the Montgomery Boycott, King depended in part on Paul Ramsey's description of Christian love, which to some extent resembled that of Nygren. Ramsey developed this description in *Basic Christian Ethics*.[136] King read this work as one of the basic texts for Kenneth Smith's course at Crozer, "Christianity and Society."

In *Stride Toward Freedom* King wrote:

> *Agape* is disinterested love. It is a love in which the individual seeks not his own good, but the good of his neighbor (I Cor. 10:24). *Agape* does not begin by discriminating between worthy and unworthy people, or any qualities people possess. It begins by loving others *for their sakes*. It is an entirely "neighbor-regarding concern for others," which discovers the neighbor in every man it meets. Therefore, *agape* makes no distinction between friend and enemy; it is directed toward both.[137]

At the beginning of the chapter entitled "The Meaning of Christian Love" in *Basic Christian Ethics,* Ramsey had also described this love as a "disinterested love for neighbor," and had referred to 1 Corinthians 10:24.[138] He too had indicated that Christian love is love for the neighbor *for his own sake,* that this love means "an entirely 'neighbor-regarding concern for others' which begins with the first man it sees," and that this love "discovers the neighbor in every man it meets and as such has never yet met a friend or an enemy."[139]

To emphasize the demanding nature of *agape* and to differentiate it from *philia,* King wrote:

> If one loves an individual merely on account of his friendliness, he loves him for the sake of the benefits to be gained from the friendship, rather than for the friend's own sake. Consequently, the best way to assure oneself that love is disinterested is to have love for the enemy-neighbor from whom you can expect no good in return but only hostility and persecution.[140]

Ramsey had written:

> In the case of a friendly neighbor it is possible in loving him to love only his friendliness toward us in return. Then he is not loved *for his own sake*. He is loved for the sake of his friendliness, for the sake of the benefits to be gained from reciprocal friendship. . . . If a person has love for his enemy-neighbor from whom he can expect no good in return but only hostility and persecution, then alone does it become certain that he does not simply love himself in loving his neighbor.[141]

Like Ramsey, King also appealed to the Parable of the Good Samaritan to emphasize that Christian love responds to the need of the neighbor.[142] However, even as King's Personalism caused him to reject Nygren's denial of the value of the self as a motive for Christian love, so it would have led him to negate Ramsey's contention that Christian love "does not rest upon a doctrine of the infinite, inherent value of human personality in general."[143]

King affirmed, "*Agape* is love seeking to preserve and create community."[144] Ramsey had written, "Only an element of concern for the other person *for his own sake* creates community among men."[145] Ramsey drew a distinction between preserving community and creating community.[146] He contended that while appeals to self-love, enlightened self-interest, and mutual love for common values can preserve community, only Christian love performs the "work of reconciliation," and "enters the 'no man's land' where dwell the desperate and the despised outcasts from every human community and brings community with them into existence."[147]

Thurman's Perception of the Range of Christian Love

One of the books that King read during the Montgomery Boycott was Howard Thurman's *Jesus and the Disinherited*.[148] Thurman, a black scholar, was dean of the chapel at Boston University when King was a student there. He devoted a major part of this work to the nature of Christian love and presented several ideas that may be found in King's philosophy of nonviolence. Thurman indicated how Jesus used the Parable of the Good Samaritan to reveal how love of neighbor should respond directly to human need, permitting no barriers of class, race, and condition. "Every man is potentially every other man's neighbor."[149] Thurman stressed that Jesus practiced a love not only for those who acted as personal enemies but also for persons who made it difficult for the Israelites to live without shame and humiliation. He explained that in Jesus' day the tax collectors helped perpetuate the Roman oppression of Israel. They were despised for helping the enemy, and to be seen in their company meant the loss of status and respect in the community. Yet Jesus invited Matthew, a tax collector, to become his disciple:

> When Jesus became a friend to the tax collectors and secured one as his intimate companion, it was a spiritual triumph of such staggering proportions that after nineteen hundred years it defies rational explanation.[150]

Thurman maintained that in every ghetto and dwelling place of the disinherited throughout the ages, there have been those who have tried to prosper by betrayal of their own people:

> To love such people requires the uprooting of the bitterness of betrayal, the heartiest poison that grows in the human spirit. . . . To love them means to recognize some deep respect and reverence for their persons. But to love them does not mean to condone their way of life.[151]

When King was confronted with the deliberate misrepresentations of his position by some in the civil rights movement during the Montgomery Boycott and in later crusades, he had to rely on this Christian Personalism to avoid experiencing the bitterness of betrayal.

Thurman emphasized that the love that Jesus practiced extended also to the Roman, the political enemy. When Jesus spoke with the Roman captain who sought healing for his servant, he claimed that he had not found such faith in all Israel. Thurman explained that in this encounter the Roman, in seeking help from a Jewish teacher, put aside his status as a Roman, and Jesus did not regard him as an enemy but as a person:

> The concept of reverence for personality, then, is applicable between persons from whom, in the initial instance, the heavy weight of status has been sloughed off. Then what? Each person meets the other where he is and there treats him as if he were where he ought to be. Here we emerge into an area where love operates, revealing a universal characteristic unbounded by special or limited circumstances.[152]

King could readily apply these insights to his relationship to the segregationist. While denouncing his acts, King could still revere the personality of the segregationist as an image of God, and regard him as a potential member of the beloved community.

Thurman concluded his treatment of Christian love by referring to the need to forgive our enemy for injury. He contended that in the insistence of Jesus that we should forgive seventy times seven, there seemed to be the assumption that forgiveness is mandatory for three reasons. God forgives us again and again for what we do intentionally or unintentionally; no evil deed represents the full intention of the person; and the evildoer will be punished. "In the wide sweep of the ebb and flow of moral law our deeds track us down, and doer and deed meet."[153] King also appealed to these three reasons for forgiveness of oppressors, although he tended to stress the eventual defeat of injustice rather than the punishment of the persons who perpetuated injustice and were its victims. In this way he was more consistent than Thurman in his presentation of the reasons for forgiveness.

The Three Dimensions of a Complete Life

In a sermon entitled "Three Dimensions of a Complete Life" King stressed the need in every life for concern for the welfare of others.[154] He explained that any complete life has the three dimensions of length, breadth, and height. The length of life is the person's concern for his own welfare and his drive to realize his own purposes. "Love yourself, if that means rational and healthy self-interest. You are commanded to do that."[155] This first dimension does have its role and special value, but nevertheless it is but one dimension. To restrict oneself to this is to doom oneself to a "paralyzing self-centeredness." A meaningful life also includes a second dimension, a breadth by which the person transcends his egocentricity and involves himself in the universal concerns of humanity. "Love your neighbor as you love yourself. You are commanded to do that."[156] "Length without breadth is like a self-contained tributary having no outward flow to the ocean. Stagnant, still, and stale, it lacks both life and freshness."[157] The "I" cannot attain fulfillment without the "thou." For its development the self needs other selves. Tillich had observed that only a "thou" can make man realize he is an "ego."[158]

As meritorious as this second dimension is, life to be complete needs a third dimension, a height in the form of faith and love that reaches to God Who is the Source of all reality. "But never forget that there is a first and even greater commandment: 'Love the Lord thy God with all thy heart and with all thy soul, and with all thy mind.' "[159] Without God, even the most brilliant achievements on the other two dimensions soon prove to be empty and disillusioning.

In challenging every one to live the life of *agape*, King developed the Christian implications of the second and third dimensions of the complete life and in effect maintained that at times the practice of *agape* may require a suspension of the first dimension, immediate self-interest. As part of this challenge, he called for a "creative altruism" that makes concern for others the first law of life. He indicated that Jesus had revealed the meaning of this altruism in his parable about the good Samaritan who was moved by compassion to care for "a certain man" who had been robbed and beaten on the road to Jericho. King asserted that the altruism of the Samaritan was *universal*, *dangerous*, and *excessive*.[160] His altruism was *universal* since he did not seek to inquire into the nationality of the wounded man to determine whether he was a Samaritan or a Jew. He saw that he was "a certain man" in need, and this was sufficient for him to intervene. The Samaritan was a good neighbor because, unlike the priest and the Levite who passed by the wounded man, he was willing to help any person in distress, and he was able to look beyond external accidents to regard the stranger in need as his brother. Jesus gave the command to love one's neighbor, and King explained that through this parable Jesus disclosed his definition of a neighbor:

> He is neither Jew nor Gentile; he is neither Russian nor American; he is neither Negro nor white. He is "a certain man"—any needy man—on one of the numerous Jericho roads of life.[161]

Jesus exhibited this same *universal* altruism in his magnanimous relationships with publicans and sinners. King saw that dehumanization in the form of discrimination, segregation, economic exploitation, and militarism intensified the need for this *universal* altruism.

The altruism of the Samaritan was also *dangerous* since he was willing to risk his own life to help a stranger. King had traveled the Jericho road and could testify to the fact that the many sudden curves on this road provided likely places for ambush. The road was even known as "the Bloody Pass." The Samaritan could not have known whether the robbers were nearby, and yet in his altruism he did not ask what would happen to himself if he helped the man. He was concerned only with what would happen to the man if he did not assist him. In a speech on the night before he died, King referred again to this parable and applied it to the need to improve the working conditions of the sanitation workers in Memphis. He urged his listeners to realize that the question confronting him was not "If I stop to help the sanitation workers, what will happen to all of the hours that I usually spend in my office every day, and every week as a pastor?" or "If I stop to help this man in need, what will happen to me?"[162] He knew the danger and had heard about the threats to his life. Yet despite the risks, he understood that the question confronting him was "If I do not stop to help the sanitation workers, what will happen to them?" and he realized that this question demanded his sacrificial response. He recognized that such altruism was not an impossible ideal that could be found only in a parable. In his sermon "On Being a Good Neighbor," he asked his listeners to dwell on the example of Albert Schweitzer who, oblivious to his own prestige and security, acted as if his sole concern was what would happen to the people of Africa.[163] He referred to Abraham Lincoln who, indifferent to his own safety, manifested this *dangerous* altruism when he issued the Emancipation Proclamation. He pointed to the Negro professional who was willing to risk all in his involvement in the struggle to end segregation. King understood Jesus to be the supreme exemplar of altruism as he deliberately chose the dangerous course of action whenever it was necessary for the completion of his mission.

The altruism of the Samaritan was *excessive* since he was willing to go beyond his ordinary duty to a wounded stranger. He himself not only bound the wounds of the man and brought him to an inn but also, in the spirit of complete love, he went "beyond the second mile" by indicating his willingness to assume all expenses for the care of the stranger. The Samaritan demonstrated a true sympathy through his personal concern and involvement. Jesus taught us the same *excessive* altruism by his suffering and death for others. King indicated that true altruism is more than mere pity. Pity is feeling sorry for someone, and this can be quite impersonal. An expression of mere pity such as financial help can develop into a paternalism which would be unacceptable to persons who wish to preserve their self-respect. King contended that true altruism requires empathy, which is "feeling sorry with someone."[164] Empathy involves sharing the pain, agony, and burdens of the other person. King expressed his doubt that the problems of the ghettos would be solved until the white majority achieved genuine empathy with Negroes and felt the ache and the anguish of their daily lives.

An essential ingredient in the life of altruism which seeks to reach the level of *agape* is the capacity to forgive. Jesus commanded men to love their enemies, to bless those who curse them, and to do good to those who hate them. Mindful of this command, King held that the person who believes in nonviolence must love the person who oppresses him and must demonstrate this love by the act of forgiveness. Such forgiveness no longer allows the evil that has been done to remain a barrier to a loving relationship. Implying a desire for a new atmosphere necessary for reconciliation, it aims to redeem the soul of the other, and to restore community. It seeks to imitate the example of Jesus, who, though crucified by hate, responded with "aggressive love."[165] In response to Peter's question about how many times he should forgive his brother's sin against him, Jesus set no limit on forgiveness, "I say not unto thee, 'Until seven times; but until seventy times seven.' "[166] This forgiveness manifests a belief that some goodness may be found even in the worst enemy. It reveals a conviction that the enemy's evil deeds do not fully constitute him as a person and contains the insight that his evil acts result from fear, ignorance, misunderstanding, and prejudice.

During the Montgomery Boycott King experienced the need to practice this forgiveness in the spirit of aggressive love. He even had occasion during the boycott to demonstrate this love by forgiving one of his most trusted aides who had attacked the Movement. The Reverend U. J. Fields had announced to the press that he was resigning from his position as recording secretary of the Montgomery Improvement Association (MIA). He accused members of the association of misusing donations to the boycott and appropriating them for their own purposes. He also accused many of the leaders of being too interested in perpetuating themselves. Fields' accusations, which echoed the charges by white opponents of the boycott, arose from his indignation at the fact that the executive board of the association had not reelected him to office. His accusations had the immediate effect of alienating the Negro community and of causing his own congregation to reject him. He soon was filled with regret. He met with King and explained that he knew of no misappropriation of funds and that his accusations had been due solely to his desire to retaliate for mistreatment by the board. In the spirit of *agape* King forgave him. The love had to be on the level of *agape*. By his accusations he had not only impugned the integrity of the leaders of the association but could have crippled the boycott by curtailing donations for the car pool. King's forgiveness went "beyond the second mile." He arranged for Fields to speak at a mass meeting. In introducing Fields to the evidently indignant audience, King reminded them of how all individuals are afflicted with human frailty and pleaded with them to recall in the spirit of nonviolence the Parable of the Prodigal Son. "Will we be like the unforgiving elder brother, or will we, in the spirit of Christ, follow the example of the loving and forgiving father?"[167] The audience was so moved by the depth of King's forgiveness that they received Fields' retraction and apology with applause. Fields' congregation felt compelled to reinstate him. King hailed this communal willingness to forgive as a further triumph for nonviolence. He claimed that this situation, which many had predicted would destroy the association, only served to unify it more than ever in the spirit of tolerance.

On another occasion King received word that his home in Montgomery had been bombed. After reassuring himself about the safety of his wife and baby, he had to confront the rage of a crowd of blacks bent on retaliation. As he spoke to them, his own willingness to forgive prompted him to dispel their rage and to renew their commitment to nonviolence:

> We cannot solve this problem through retaliatory violence. We must meet violence with nonviolence. Remember the words of Jesus, "He who lives by the sword will die by the sword." . . . We must love our white brothers no matter what they do to us. We must make them know that we love them. . . . We must meet hate with love.[168]

In *Stride Toward Freedom* he explained that a favorite topic in the mass meetings in the churches during the boycott was the dialogue on forgiveness between Jesus and Peter.[169] Forgiveness remained a dominant theme in the Movement. After the 1963 bombing of a church in Birmingham, where four children were killed, King could still call for forgiveness: "In the spirit of the darkness of this hour, we must not despair, we must not become bitter—we must not lose faith in our *white brothers*."[170] A few days before his death he had to bear the agony of seeing a group of militant black youths called the Invaders convert a peaceful march in Memphis into a nightmare of violence, and yet he could still find the strength to demonstrate aggressive love when the leader of the Invaders came to him to ask for forgiveness.[171]

King regarded Jesus as a "practical realist" since love for one's enemies is an absolute necessity for the survival of humanity. At his Nobel Lecture he indicated that love is the key to the solution of the basic problem of the world, and warned his listeners that humanity can no longer afford to worship the "god of hate" or prostrate itself before the "altar of retaliation." "History is cluttered with the wreckage of nations and individuals that pursued this self-defeating path of hate."[172] Only love can generate a peace that will "transform our imminent cosmic elegy into a psalm of creative fulfillment."[173] King felt that a man can better understand the value of love when he considers the effect of hate on the person who hates. He maintained that hate distorts the personality and scars the soul of the one who hates. Hate destroys a man's sense of values and his ability to make objective judgments. It causes a man to judge the beautiful as ugly and the ugly as beautiful. It robs him of his ability to separate the true from the false. King spoke of the "hard-hearted person" as one who never truly loves, never experiences the beauty of friendship, is not in real connection with humanity, lacks the capacity for genuine compassion, and never sees men as persons, each with his own dignity. Hate further establishes the enemy as an enemy. Only *agape* with its redemptive power can transform enemies into friends and make reconciliation possible. King believed that no matter how low a person sinks into racial bigotry, he can still be redeemed. Thus he could claim that love was the most powerful weapon in the nonviolent army.[174] Moreover, only through love can a person know God and experience the beauty of His holiness. King held that we are potential sons of God, and that only through love can this potentiality become an actuality. Every volunteer in the Birmingham Movement had to sign a Commitment Card. One of the commandments on that card was "Walk and talk in the manner of love, for God is love."[175]

The Vision of Humanity as a Unity

Agape involves recognition of the fact that all human life is interrelated. King asserted that humanity must be seen as a single process. All men are brothers and therefore whatever directly affects one person affects all indirectly.[176] For example, he recognized that not only did the American enslavement of blacks adversely affect the freedom of white labor, which had to bargain from the depressed base imposed by slavery, but also *de facto* discrimination affects poor whites. The weight of discrimination "corrupts their lives, frustrates their opportunities, and withers their education."[177] The existence of injustice anywhere is a threat to justice everywhere. It is then not only appropriate but necessary for each American to be actively concerned about injustices to every other American. Therefore, no American can be judged to be an "outside agitator." If affluent Americans are to respond to the challenge of *agape,* they must confront the question Adolph Eichmann ignored, "How responsible am I for the well-being of my fellows?"[178] To choose to ignore an evil is to become an accomplice to that evil. *Agape* requires that we be our brother's keeper. "He is a part of me and I am a part of him. His agony diminishes me, and his salvation enlarges me."[179] When a police dog is used to attack a child in a Birmingham demonstration, it attacks every American. At the Lincoln Memorial in August 1963, King praised the white persons who had participated in the March on Washington for realizing that their destiny was linked to the destiny of the Negro. "They have come to realize that their freedom is inextricably bound to our freedom."[180]

Nor should concern have national boundaries. Since all persons are interdependent, our destiny as a nation is linked to that of even the underdeveloped countries. Ten weeks after the beginning of the Montgomery Boycott King explained to a Chicago press conference that the boycott was "part of something happening all over the world. The oppressed peoples of the world are rising up. They are revolting against colonialism, imperialism, and other systems of oppression."[181] In a 1960 speech to the Urban League he alluded to the rapid growth of the number of independent nations in Africa, and proclaimed:

> These rapid changes have naturally influenced the thinking of the American Negro. He knows that his struggle for human dignity is not an isolated event. It is a drama being played on the stage of the world with spectators and supporters from every continent.[182]

He described the 1960 student sit-ins as "part of the world-wide movement for freedom and human dignity."[183] In his sermon "Youth and Social Action" in 1967, he urged that if the anger of the peoples of the world at injustice was to be transformed into a revolution of love and creativity, then Americans had to work with all peoples to shape a new world.[184] In a 1968 interview he expressed the hope that American Negroes would contribute to world peace by serving as a bridge between the white civilization and the nonwhite nations of the world because they have roots in both.[185]

King's sermons and activities revealed his consistent commitment to national and international interracial cooperation. In opposition to the proponents of Black Power who had lost faith in the philosophy and methods of nonviolence, he argued that blacks must regard themselves as Americans and that the solution to their problems will not come through the creation of a separate black nation within this nation.[186] Their goal must be full participation in the life of this nation, and this attainment of power and self-fulfillment will come through alliances with dedicated whites. Thus King always insisted that there be whites on his staff in the Southern Christian Leadership Conference. His repudiation of all separation also emerged in his concern for all the poor. He even called for a change of the slogan "Black Power" to "Power for Poor People."[187] Coretta Scott King in her Introduction to *Where Do We Go From Here: Chaos or Community?* could state, "He spoke out sharply for all the poor in all their hues, for he knew if color made them different, misery and oppression made them the same."[188] His conviction that love is the unifying force at the center of the universe caused him to expand his concern to include the poor throughout the world. When he visited India in 1959, he was depressed at the sight of some of the one million poor who had to sleep on the streets of Calcutta.[189] He did not forget these poor in his Nobel Lecture in 1964. In this lecture he not only deplored the evils of racism and militarism but also emphasized that almost two-thirds of the peoples of the world go to bed hungry each night.[190] "The agony of the poor diminishes the rich; the salvation of the poor enlarges the rich."[191] In his "A Christmas Sermon on Peace" he maintained that world peace could be achieved only when individuals and nations would realize the basic fact of the interrelated structure of all reality, and loyalties became "ecumenical rather than sectional."[192] Six weeks before his death, in a speech honoring the achievements of W. E. B. DuBois, he reiterated his abiding concern for the poor throughout the world:

> Let us be dissatisfied until every man can have food and material necessities for his body, culture and education for his mind, freedom and human dignity for his spirit. . . . Let us be dissatisfied until our brother of the Third World—Asia, Africa, and Latin America—will no longer be the victim of imperialist exploitation, but will be lifted from the long night of poverty, illiteracy and disease.[193]

Chapter 2

The Dimensions of Divine Providence

Central to King's conviction that the practice of *agape* would enable humanity to move toward the recognition of human dignity and the universal realization of justice was his belief in an all-powerful and benevolent God Who guides history with His loving purpose. In his sermons and writings he frequently referred to his certainty that the universe is under the spiritual control of a loving purpose and rests on moral foundations.[1] During the Montgomery Boycott he proclaimed, "God is using Montgomery as His proving ground," and assured his followers, "Remember, if I am stopped, this movement will not stop because God is with the movement."[2] At the conclusion of the boycott he could testify, "But amid all of this we have kept going with the faith that as we struggle, God struggles with us, and that the arc of the moral universe, although long, is bending toward justice."[3] He indicated that the Movement was called spiritual because its members had a strong feeling that they had a "cosmic companionship" in their struggle for righteousness.[4] The principal song of the Movement, "We Shall Overcome," revealed this feeling, "Deep in my heart I do believe the Lord will see us through." Because of this belief, the members of the Movement could accept suffering without retaliation.[5] He emphasized that this belief is part of the Christian vision. "There is something at the very center of our faith which reminds us that Good Friday may reign for a day, but ultimately it must give way to the triumphant beat of the Easter drums."[6]

In an interview in 1968 King reaffirmed his belief that God's love governs the direction of history:

People are often surprised to learn that I am an optimist. They know how often I have been jailed, how frequently the days and nights have been filled with frustration and sorrow, how bitter and dangerous are my adversaries. They expect these experiences to harden me into a grim and desperate man. They fail, however, to perceive the sense of affirmation generated by the challenge of embracing struggle and surmounting obstacles. They have no comprehension of the strength that comes from faith in God and man. It is possible for me to falter, but I am profoundly secure in my knowledge that God loves us; He has not worked out a design for our failure. Man has the capacity to do right as well as wrong, and his history is a path upward, not downward.[7]

To understand his conception of God, which was the basis for his confidence that the struggle for social justice would ultimately be victorious, one must turn to the doctrines of L. Harold DeWolf and George Davis.

DeWolf's Conception of the God Who Sustains His Creatures

In *A Theology of the Living Church* DeWolf developed a comprehensive philosophical and theological system that provided King with the reasoned elements of his theism. By presenting DeWolf's examination of some evidences for theism and his doctrine on certain divine attributes, this section will indicate why King maintained that Personalism gave him a philosophical grounding for his idea of a personal God, and will describe how DeWolf, as a leading exponent of Personalism, exerted the dominant influence on his conception of divine Providence.[8] It was this conception that allowed King to transcend not only Brightman's view of the divine nature but also, as the next section will explain, the views of Paul Tillich and of the theologian and philosopher Henry Nelson Wieman.

While acknowledging that human reason cannot attain absolute certainty on such questions as the existence of God, DeWolf presented several evidences to establish the "rational plausibility" of an assent to the existence of a God Who has created man and the world, and Who cares for man—an assent that is a presupposition of the Christian faith.[9] In his examination of the valid evidences for the existence of God, DeWolf first considered the truths of logic and mathematics. He emphasized the fact that when these truths became known, they were not at that time created, but rather were discovered. The thinkers who discovered them recognized that they were always true. Pythagoras, or the Pythagoreans, for example, did not originate the truth of their theorem. DeWolf contrasted sensible objects, which are always subject to change, with the truths of logic and geometry, which as truths are subject to no change whatsoever. "*Men* can be mistaken about such truths but they cannot change them."[10] He discerned an ultimate significance in the facts that these truths are nowhere perfectly represented by material substances and cannot be coherently conceived as having any being apart from their being thought, and that still, evidently, they do have being apart from the thought of man. From these facts he concluded:

> They [the eternal and unchangeable truths of logic and mathematics] must then be timelessly thought in a Mind not human, but a Mind after which human thought at its best is patterned. If there is veritably a God Who has made us, then we can readily understand why our own minds are forever kept in restless searching, progressively satisfied only as we discover what is already in the thought of our Maker.[11]

DeWolf presented Plato's alternative solution to this problem which referred to a realm of intelligible forms or ideals that do not depend for their existence on any mind or on any other object. But DeWolf rejected this realm as unintelligible since it would mean that truth could have existence independent of thought and material existence. "The belief in a Supreme Mind undergirding our own existence seems best to commend itself as the solution of the problem of abstract truths."[12] Appeal to Plato's doctrine on the Demiurge, the intelligent agent who brings order into matter, would not render DeWolf's criticism any less cogent since, according to Plato in his dialogue the *Timaeus*, the Demiurge has to look to the intelligible forms as independent exemplars as he shapes matter in their image.[13]

For another evidence of God's existence DeWolf considered the material world which, as known through common observation and scientific discoveries, is on the whole "a remarkably systematic order."[14] He affirmed that as science progresses, it provides additional evidence of the ordered causal relations among the phenomena of nature. Clearly, he did not accept Hume's theoretical skepticism about man's ability to know with certainty any objective causal relation. DeWolf examined the claim of Auguste Comte, the Positivist, that the discovery of causal law by the sciences was one of the principal influences that were leading to the irretrievable decline of theology. Prompted by his own belief that the formulation of a causal law could adequately explain events described as effects, Comte contended that belief in God would no longer be useful once the sciences through their formulations of causal laws included all natural phenomena. In his response to this contention DeWolf distinguished between formulas, that have been created by the minds of men, and causal laws, that were in operation before men formulated them:

> Where and how did they [the causal laws] have their being before men first discovered them? Did the elaborate formulas which together constitute what we know as the law of gravity originally exist in stones? Do stones know all these intricate mathematical relations? Why does the water of the sea stir when the moon passes overhead many thousands of miles away?[15]

DeWolf explained that a physical law, such as the law of gravity, is a system of meanings, and cannot be understood as capable by itself of causing events in the physical universe. Our own experience tells us that the power of the will is necessary to translate ideas into action. He therefore concluded:

> The relation between the great system of ideas which we know as causal law and the events of the physical universe becomes intelligible only when we conceive of the ideas as occurring, long before men discovered them, in a cosmic Mind in which idea and will are perpetually and intimately conjoined.[16]

In his sermons King appealed to the "magnificent orderliness" of the universe as evidence for belief in the existence of God.[17] He asserted that such an orderliness cannot be the result of a fortuitous interplay of atoms and electrons. He acknowledged that man's technical achievements could tempt man to feel that he, instead of God, is the true master of the cosmic order. To prevent such arrogance, King contrasted the speed of man-made instruments with the speed of Earth, which in its revolution around the sun travels 1.6 million miles a day:

> So when we behold the illimitable expanse of space, in which we are compelled to measure stellar distance in light years and in which heavenly bodies travel at incredible speeds, we are forced to look beyond man and affirm anew that God is able. . . . God is still in His universe. Our new technological and scientific de-

velopments can neither banish Him from the microcosmic compass of the atom nor from the vast, unfathomable ranges of interstellar space.[18]

DeWolf saw as further evidence for God's existence the remarkable adaptation of means to ends in the organic equipment of plants and animals as manifest in the ways in which their parts contribute to the protection and sustenance of the total organism, the complex organization of the organs of higher animals, and the numerous ways in which animals and plants are capable of mutual help. He maintained that all these "suggest" a creation by a Mind that deliberately devises means for the accomplishment of specific purposes. He viewed the process of evolution not as an objection to this argument but as a source of additional evidence of "purposive guidance in the whole process."[19] The principle of the survival of the fittest does not explain the origin and the direction of evolution. "The superior powers of survival in the better equipped organisms are obvious enough. But the acute problem is not of survival but of origin."[20] He praised the philosopher of science Pierre Lecomte du Noüy for employing the principle of statistical probability in his work *Human Destiny* to show what incredible miracles on miracles must have occurred in bewildering succession if no intelligent purpose guided the process. The purpose operative in nature that is distinct from the purposive activities of man and other creatures is explained only by reference to "a purposive cosmic Person."[21]

DeWolf showed that additional evidence for God's existence can be found in five ways in which man is adapted to his environment—ways that cannot be explained without reference to a purpose in the process that produced him and constantly sustains him.[22] *First*, man's body is so well adapted to his environment that he can live in it "with remarkable freedom and versatility."[23] His body requires and is provided with those environmental conditions necessary for his survival, namely, a very limited temperature range, oxygen, water, sources of nutrition, a certain kind of gravitational field, a definite atmospheric pressure, the absence of noxious gases, and other complex circumstances. Here DeWolf again emphasized how the bodily organs are related to each other and how each organ is adapted to the good of the whole organism. All these instances constitute evidence of a purpose which reveals the activity of a Mind responsible for man.

Second, man's mind is so well adapted to his environment that he can predict its events with uncanny accuracy. There is such a parallel between the requirements of man's reason and the realities of nature that human thought has even described things not yet observed on the assumption that what man's reason required could be confidently assumed to exist. Thus, astronomers were able to describe Neptune before they observed it because without it their mathematical formulas could not account for the movements of Uranus. DeWolf indicated that it was significant that the purely theoretical study of mathematics, and not the study of observed data, had generated the most revolutionary recent advances in the scientific understanding of man. To emphasize man's intellectual rapport with his world, he quoted Sir James Jeans, the physicist:

> What remains is in any case very different from the full-blooded matter and the forbidding materialism of the Victorian scientist. His objective and material universe is proved to consist of little more than constructs of our own minds. In this and in other ways, modern physics has moved in the direction of mentalism.[24]

In *Strength To Love* King also quoted Jeans as part of his rejection of a materialistic explanation of human personality. "The universe seems to be nearer to a great thought than to a great machine."[25] DeWolf also emphasized the role of abstract theory in the development of atomic energy. He concluded that only "a belief in the governance of nature by a Mind in whose image our own minds are fashioned" can explain the "real kinship between our minds at their highest reaches of clear consistency and the order of nature."[26]

Third, man is capable of enjoyment of the beauty in natural objects. These objects are not means for man's survival, but they serve to enhance the meaning of life. DeWolf contended that only the theist can explain man's capacity for aesthetic enjoyment:

> It can hardly be denied that human beings have a natural love of beauty nor that nature, from the starry heavens above to the microscopic world of crystals and algae, fulfills and stimulates that love in innumerable ways. To the theist the beauty of nature is a sign of the likeness between man's aspiring soul and the Creator and an evidence of the power, beauty, and love of God Himself.[27]

Fourth, man can use his environment as "a vale of soul-making" insofar as he can use the natural order, especially through the pain and sorrow in his experience, as a place where he can develop courage, self-discipline, loyalty, love, and other virtues. Man's environment thus allows him to adhere to the category of duty and seek the moral good. Without the moral dimension our experience would lack depth. Could a blind process of chance have generated this ethical dimension? DeWolf denied that any coherence of meaning, one of the Personalist norms of truth, could be found between a blind, unknowing process and the meaningfulness of the moral experience:

> Coherence is gained in the account only when it is seen that such an intricate manifold of meaning and value is no accident of blind process but the creation of the God whose purpose governs the course of nature, both in the evolving of man and in the arousing of his moral sense to action.[28]

Fifth, in all ages and throughout the world men have sought help from unseen powers greater than themselves. How can this fact of the appearance and persistence of religious concern be explained? DeWolf replied that if one does not affirm God's existence he must regard such a concern as the result of man's relationships with his fellows and his natural environment. But then, the nontheist must believe—incoherently—that an impersonal, blindly mechanistic world has produced an organism that has "an apparently ineradicable aspiration for winning the favor of powers in a realm beyond the natural world."[29] DeWolf added that sheer chance cannot be used to explain developments in the history of religion toward ethical monotheism. He concluded this argument by quoting St. Paul:

> For what can be known about God is plain to them, because God has shown it to them. Ever since the creation of the world His invisible nature, namely, His eternal power and deity, has been clearly perceived in the things that have been made.[30]

DeWolf considered as another evidence for God's existence the fact that all persons are subject to a system of moral law which they did not create and which they are not able to change. Though there are contrary beliefs about causal law, the true laws of nature are what they are, independent of man's attempts to formulate them. So too, in a similar way, though there is a diversity of moral beliefs, the moral law has a reality that is independent of human opinion regarding it. Moral obligation serves as the foundation for all of man's intellectual life, including natural science. DeWolf claimed that all of modern science may be seen as a result of acceptance by men of a system of ethical law because:

> . . . the superior claim of legitimate science to acceptance in preference to superstition and casual generalization rests upon the assumption that self-discipline is better than unrestrained emotion, that honesty is better than false, or careless report, and that patience is better than impulsive haste.[31]

In order to evaluate the evidence to determine whether human beings are subject to a valid moral law, one must proceed with the presupposition that he should commit his belief under some conditions rather than others. One must acknowledge the obligation to choose the coherent rather than the incoherent, and hence by implication he must acknowledge a whole system of moral law:

> If truth is ever independent of human opinion, then the system of moral law which must be acknowledged by implication in order to discover that truth must itself be a part of the truth which men cannot change.[32]

DeWolf rejected the claim that truth is not independent of human opinion because such a claim would mean that any claim, including this one, may be affirmed or denied with equal validity, which means with no validity. It is impossible not to reject such a self-contradictory skepticism in practice:

> When it [skepticism] is put aside by the barest affirmation of faith in any truth, the believer is implying, whether aware of it or not, that he and all men are subject to a system of moral law which they did not legislate and cannot revoke.[33]

Moral law, as a judgment of what ought to be, involves a mind and will. Yet, man does not create the being and meaning of the moral law; rather he finds himself subject to this law. The source for this law can be found only in an Intelligence Who governs man:

> But if it [the moral law] belongs necessarily to mind and will while having its home outside and above man so that man stands

always under its jurisdiction, it is evident that it is the legislation of a Mind and Will more than human, under whose sovereignty we live.[34]

Whenever man seeks to determine which of two courses of conduct he *ought* to follow, which social system is *truly better*, or which ethical or physical theory he is *truly obliged* to accept, he is in effect paying homage to the perfect and eternal law of God.

DeWolf regarded the experiences of God that men and women in many lands and in all ages have had as further evidence for the existence of God. He stressed the fact that many of these persons have indicated by their lives that their testimony concerning these experiences has been trustworthy. By their "calm courage, self-giving love and spiritual radiance" they have inspired others to believe in their testimony.[35] Ordinary men and women in thousands of communities, who have had experiences of God, by their words and lives have brought God nearer to their friends more effectively than any ideational argument could do. He asserted that a consciousness of the presence of God can best enable a person to appreciate the force of this evidence. The skeptic may persist in dismissing such experiences as forms of self-deception:

> But he who bows in God's presence, experiencing the condemnation of sin by His purity, the perfect beauty of His holiness, the inrush of His power and the comfort of His love, knows this is no delusion. God lives and He is near.[36]

In presenting evidences for the "characteristics of God," DeWolf developed the conception of the "absolute being" of God in the sense that His being is free from dependence upon or limitation by any other being. In contrast to conditioned, dependent, creaturely being, which is not self-explanatory, God is the one being of whom it can truly be said without qualification, "He is."[37] He alone has the ground and explanation of His being within Himself. DeWolf regarded St. Thomas Aquinas' first three ways of demonstrating God's existence as proofs of His unconditioned being since He alone is the unconditioned ground and explanation of the motion, causality, and existence of finite beings.[38] He also is the ground of those absolute ideal norms that endow existence with purposeful direction and meaning. He is the most real being in the sense that He is the source and ground that sustains and gives meaning to all reality. His knowledge embraces all events and His activity is operative everywhere. "No sin can be hidden from His judgment. But neither in this world nor in any other can we pass beyond the bounds of His active concern."[39] In *Stride Toward Freedom* King affirmed his belief in "a creative personal power in this universe who is the ground and essence of all reality—a power that cannot be explained in materialistic terms."[40]

While insisting that God is not perishable, DeWolf affirmed that time is grounded in the very nature of God:[41]

If God is a purposive being, having certain ends in view for the persons whom He has made, as the theistic evidences indicated, then He must be seeking to shape the present to a future which is not yet. The category of purpose is meaningless apart from time. If God were a timeless Platonic perfection or an Aristotelian Pure Form, men might conceivably have purposes related to such a divine ideal, but such a God could have no purpose for men, since for God there would be no future in which purpose might be realized.[42]

DeWolf maintained also that the Scriptures portray God as so intimately concerned with temporal events that He cannot be considered as timeless:

The God of the Scriptures is no Pure Form untouched by men's sin or sorrow, simply being in perfection while men toil and strive. . . . A deity outside of time is a ghostly product of man's abstraction, not the God who is "clearly perceived in the things that have been made" by Him, who enters deeply into the affairs of history and who communes as Father with His children—the only God of whom there is empirical evidence, sensory or spiritual.[43]

DeWolf argued further that God's awareness of changes in the world must involve changes in the content of His own consciousness as events known as future change to events known as present and then as past. DeWolf's position involved a definite departure from the medieval Scholastic doctrine on God with its roots in Aristotle's philosophy, which held that because God is Pure Act without potency for change, His influence on the temporal order must be such that it involves no change in Him. In his *Physics* and *Metaphysics* Aristotle argued that all changes in the world have to be explained in terms of an "Unmoved Mover."[44] This Mover simply by the supremacy of His being would inspire love and activity in certain intelligent beings below Him, but He would not know them. Aristotle denied that this Mover has any knowledge of human events since such knowledge not only would refer to what would be unworthy of his thought, including evil, but also would make Him dependent on these events and render Him changeable like them. But if He too were changeable, then His being could not explain changes in other things, and He would not be God, the Supreme Reality. Aristotle contended that God's entire activity consists only in knowing Himself. "Therefore, it must be of itself that the divine thought thinks (since it is the most excellent of things), and its thinking is a thinking on [its own] thinking."[45]

King accepted DeWolf's critique of the Aristotelian conception of God as unchanging and oblivious to human affairs. In his 1957 Prayer Pilgrimage for Freedom address at the Lincoln Memorial, while affirming that those in the struggle for social justice had a "cosmic companionship," he proclaimed:

> The God that we worship is not some Aristotelian "unmoved mover" who merely contemplates upon Himself; He is not merely a self-knowing God, but an other-loving God Who forever works through history for the establishment of His kingdom.[46]

In *Strength To Love* he wrote of a dynamic Absolute Who immerses Himself in His creation, Who loves and is loved, and suffers with His people as they seek greater freedom and justice. He explained that God must be conceived as both "toughminded," a God of austerity, justice, and wrath, and "tenderhearted," a God of gentleness, love, and grace.[47] He is not merely toughminded since then He would be a cold, passionless despot, contemplating Himself in a remote heaven, like Aristotle's God. He is not merely tenderhearted since then His softness would render Him powerless before the forces of evil. His toughmindedness enables Him to exercise ultimate control over history while His tenderheartedness impels Him to live with us and fill our lives with His grace. "He does not leave us alone in our agonies and struggles. He seeks us in dark places and suffers with us and for us in our tragic prodigality."[48] In "A Theology of Maximun Involvement" DeWolf asserted, "Where Jesus suffered and died on the cross, so profound was the understanding love which united God with him, there God suffered the agony of death for us."[49]

Although DeWolf argued for the presence of the temporal dimension within the divine life, he also presented ways in which God may be said to be above time. Thus of God alone it can be said that there never was nor will there be a time without His existence. He alone is "co-eternal with time."[50] Moreover, God's fundamental nature must be timeless in the sense of unchanging even as are the timeless laws of implication that are grounded in Him. Furthermore, God is above time in the sense of being the author of time:

> By being and creating, God makes time to be real. . . . Therefore, even though in some ways God may be thought of as subject to time, even more meaningfully must time be regarded as subject to God. Not only "our times" but all time is in His hand.[51]

King often appealed to God's power as the basis for his belief that the struggle for freedom would be successful. DeWolf presented a detailed doctrine on God's power.[52] In affirming God's power DeWolf qualified the extent of that power. He denied that God's power is such that He can do anything abstractly conceivable. He cannot make Himself cease to exist, and then, while not existing, make Himself to have twice the unlimited power He had before. It is nonsensical to affirm that He has an unqualified limitlessness of power. DeWolf further qualified God's power by maintaining that if He has chosen to create human beings and to maintain a relationship of Father to them, as Jesus has described, then He has imposed on Himself the restriction of not being indifferent to them. If He has decided to give men some freedom of choice, He has thereby allowed human power to limit His own.[53] DeWolf regarded as "an added glory" to God His creation of the power of human freedom that would share with Him responsibility for the well-being of the individual and the community. He asserted that God's voluntary self-limitations do not constitute a metaphysical finitude of power but rather are manifestations of a moral exercise of power.

After making the above qualifications of God's power, DeWolf still maintained that God can be spoken of as omnipotent since He is the source of all being and all power. His sovereign control extends over all things and no being limits His action except as He wills to permit it.

Furthermore, His omnipotence implies His omniscience. His capacity to do all that can be done implies His knowledge of all that can be known. Such knowledge is necessary for His control over all things. This knowledge must be limited both by His own rational nature and by His purpose. Here again, DeWolf differed from the medieval Scholastic view of God by asserting that when God limited His power by giving men freedom of the will, He thereby limited somewhat His knowledge of the future. "He doubtless knows all things. But what is not yet and indeed is still within the possibility of never coming to be must hardly be knowable to God as future actuality."[54] DeWolf rejected the view that God knows the future free acts of man through an immediate transtemporal perception since this view would have to regard the future as already present, and hence would have to deny the reality of time. He argued that although we have every reason to suppose that God's power of prediction of the free acts of men is far greater than the individual man's power to predict the free acts of his fellows, still "if men have any margin of free will whatever, then God's foreknowledge of some of their choices must be a knowledge of probabilities, not of certainties."[55]

Within his treatment of the holiness of God, DeWolf further developed the intimate relationship that exists between Creator and creature:

> We turn to Him in recognition that without Him we could not even exist, much less find our way to the destiny for which He made us. Since He made us and sustains us, our lives are rightfully His.[56]

He reaffirmed here that God is the powerful and omniscient source of man's existence and that He alone can satisfy man's yearnings for complete security, understanding, and peace:

> Since He knew how to make both ourselves and all else upon which we depend, He must know also how to preserve us and to direct us according to His purpose. . . . Only God knows and can control all things according to His will. Therefore, He alone can be worthy of our absolute submission and trust. In His presence we rightly declare, "Thou only art holy."[57]

When DeWolf proclaimed further that only God possesses absolute moral authority and that only His law is holy and worthy of absolute obedience, he was stating a truth that was later to reinforce King's doctrine of civil disobedience and specifically his opposition to segregation laws conflicting with the law of God. DeWolf declared that laws are frequently unjust and that conscience at times demands the violation of law:

> As far as prudence is concerned, undoubtedly it is infinitely more important to obey God than to obey men. For while human lawgivers can control only some conditions of our earthly life, God controls, so far as He wills, all the conditions of all life here and hereafter.[58]

God's law stands as "the true norm by relation to which all other laws and all of life ought to be judged. . . . It is the law of our being. . . . We can finally be true to ourselves only by being true to Him. His law is not merely power; it is truth both for men and for nations."[59] His perfect law is the ground and meaning of any righteousness. All righteousness ever experienced by men is derived from His perfect righteousness. As the source of the perfect law, He judges all men in terms of this law.

King stated that God placed certain immutable moral principles within the very structure of the universe.[60] One such principle is the law of love. He charged that those who stood against integration were opposing not only the noble precepts of democracy but also these eternal edicts of God.[61] During the Montgomery Boycott he answered the objection that any change in the current conditions would mean going against cherished customs of the community by affirming that if customs are wrong, they should be changed:

> The decision which we must make now is whether we will give our allegiance to outmoded and unjust customs or to the ethical demands of the universe. As Christians we owe our ultimate allegiance to God and His will, rather than to man and his folkways.[62]

In his sermon "Paul's Letter to American Christians" in *Strength To Love*, King reiterated this conviction as he reminded his readers that they have a dual citizenry since they live in both time and eternity:

> Your highest loyalty is to God, and not to the mores or the folkways, the state or the nation, or any man-made institution. If

any earthly institution or custom conflicts with God's will, it is your Christian duty to oppose it. You must never allow the transitory, evanescent demands of man-made institutions to take precedence over the eternal demands of the Almighty God.[63]

DeWolf was concerned to present a balanced view that provided for God's transcendence as well as for His immanence in the world. He affirmed that God transcends all His temporal creation and that His creative power is never exhausted. In His identity He is the "divine other," distinct from His creatures. But he also stressed that God in His love has chosen to share His goodness with His creatures:

God is not an abstract deity nor one who lives out His life in aloof preoccupation with Himself. He is one who gives Himself in creation of other persons to share His bounty and in reconciliation to win their faith for this sharing. All that we know of God we know through His love. It is through His going forth in creation and other revelations of Himself that He is shown to us.[64]

DeWolf regarded God as immanent in man and the world in several ways. God sustains the creatures who continuously depend on Him:

He now makes the lilies to grow and feeds the birds of the air. With yet greater concern He cares for His human children from day to day. It is to Him that we pray, "Give us this day our daily bread," for all food is produced by His sustaining providence. Without the support of His will none of us could exist even for an hour.[65]

God is immanent also as the ultimate source of the truth man attains about logical, moral, and causal law. Man's thoughts are true when they conform to God's own thoughts. Then too, God has an immediate knowledge of man's works and thoughts. Moreover, God is immanent in the sense that His purpose works on men through the physical world that He preserves and they experience. Furthermore, God at times does allow man to experience His presence in a special way. Such mystical experiences do not allow man any significant advance in discursive knowledge about God, but they do allow man a glimpse of Him:

The effulgent love, the all-consuming power, the infinite beauty, the sublime goodness, the absolute holiness, some or all of these, known to identify the One called God, are overwhelmingly felt in the One encountered. His full glory must always pass man by, but even the glimpse of Him occasionally given as He passes can change a life and history.[66]

Equipped with this comprehensive perspective, King in his dissertation contended that the basic weakness in Tillich's system was that he failed to preserve the tension between the transcendence and the immanence of God, which King felt was necessary for a meaningful theistic position. God is not absolutely beyond nor absolutely in the world. Rather, He is both beyond and in the world. "The doctrines of transcendence and immanence are both half-truths in need of the tension of each other to give the more inclusive truth."[67] In *Strength To Love* he again emphasized God's transcendence and immanence:

Genuine faith imbues us with the conviction that beyond time is a divine Spirit and beyond life is Life. However dismal and catastrophic may be the present circumstance, we know that we are not alone, for God dwells with us in life's most confining and oppressive cells. . . . Any man who finds this cosmic sustenance can walk the highways of life without the fatigue of pessimism and the weight of morbid fears.[68]

King explained that through the experiences of everyday life, and particularly of crisis situations, he was able to develop his conviction about the reality of a personal God.[69] He could testify that at times he had a special awareness of the presence of God. In *Stride Toward Freedom* he related that one evening during the Montgomery Boycott he had been so plagued with threats to his life and so drained of courage that in exhaustion he began to think of a way to remove himself from the struggle without appearing to be a coward. Then he prayed:

I am here taking a stand for what I believe is right. But now I am afraid. The people are looking to me for leadership, and if I stand before them without strength and courage, they too will falter. I am at the end of my powers. I have nothing left. I've come to the point where I can't face it alone.[70]

His prayer had an immediate effect:

> At that moment I experienced the presence of the Divine as I had never experienced Him before. It seemed as though I could hear the quiet assurance of an inner voice saying, "Stand up for righteousness, stand up for truth; and God will be at your side forever." Almost at once my fears began to go. My uncertainty disappeared. I was ready to face anything.[71]

DeWolf concluded his treatment of God's Providence by analyzing the problem of evil.[72] How can evil exist in a world created and sustained by a good God? How can a loving God even allow His children to suffer pain, sorrow, and death? DeWolf rejected a number of proposed "solutions" to this problem. He could not accept the solution that claims that such evils are mere illusions or errors in the mind of man and are not real to God. Another solution that views all suffering as a beneficent warning of greater evil does not explain the presence of the greater evil. A third solution that contends that since God is just and rewards all according to their deserts, the sufferer must deserve his suffering, is disproved by experience. As the Psalmist lamented, the wicked man is often the one who is overbearing and towering like a cedar of Lebanon, while the upright are cast down, poor, and needy.[73] A fourth solution claims that suffering is due to the imprudence, ignorance, and lack of psychological skill in self-management, and that God has arranged everything for our health and pleasure so that, to avoid suffering, we need only use the proper scientific techniques. DeWolf argued that if it could be granted, and it cannot, that such techniques could be so effective, two facts would still remain. The beneficiary of these techniques would sooner or later die. Then too, there is no explanation in this solution as to why the world was so designed that countless millions were never given the opportunity to hear of these techniques.

To move in the direction of a real solution to the problem of evil, DeWolf examined the merits of two more serious views. One view, the "finitistic," emphasizes the limitation of God's power:

> It is held that some or all natural evil is contrary to God's will and its existence is due to some uncreated force, being, or aspect of being which opposes, limits, or partially obstructs that will.[74]

The other view, the "absolutistic," emphasizes the transcendent absoluteness of God's power:

> It is stressed that God's power and knowledge far transcend our understanding and that even the worst of the pains we suffer have some good reason in relation to the ultimate purpose of God.[75]

DeWolf indicated the advantages of the finitistic type of solution without giving it his total approbation. *First*, this solution is simple, direct, and intelligible. God did not create a world without its suffering because He was unable to do it. Man can easily identify with the inability to accomplish good or to destroy evil. *Second*, this solution assures the sufferer that God did not will his suffering, and that God is ready to provide sympathy, comfort, and aid. The sufferer is assured that "God, in fact, battles against the same forces which have produced his affliction."[76] *Third*, this solution casts no doubt upon God's perfect goodness. When evil emerges, it is due to His lack of power to accomplish fully His purpose. His goodness is upheld "so long as it is believed He has done as well as He could."[77] *Fourth*, this type of solution, while offering an explanation of suffering, also serves to explain certain features in nature such as the profligate and irrational waste as countless seeds and eggs never develop to maturity, the species that have become extinct in the evolutionary process, and the vast cruelty and destruction as creatures prey upon each other.

DeWolf next explained the advantages of the absolutistic view.[78] *First*, this type of solution avoids the objections that confront the ultimate metaphysical dualism that marks the finitistic view. DeWolf cited the finitistic view of Paul Tillich who spoke of God as *logos* (His rationality) and God as *abyss* (the nonrational aspect). DeWolf contended that Tillich did not make clear why both should be called God and did not explain the relation between them. He also cited the less unsatisfactory view of Brightman, who attributed natural evil to the "nonrational Given" as the content of God's consciousness in contrast to His "rational Given" and His will, but DeWolf found this view to be limited since it still left a self-contradictory relationship within God's consciousness. In contradistinction to this type of solution the absolutistic view attributes all being, directly or indirectly, to the perfection of God's good purpose. While the absolutistic view concedes that man can only partially understand the ways of God and leaves room for mystery, it does not leave any relationship in self-contradiction. In presenting this view, DeWolf indicated that a margin of mystery is to be expected as the human mind attempts to understand the ways of divine wisdom. *Second*, the absolutistic solution of evil allows the sufferer to depend on God and to accept suffering or loss as God's will, whereas the finitistic solution sees God as a sympathetic fellow sufferer Who must endure evils He is not able to prevent or eliminate. Belief in a God Who can only partially control evil cannot generate the unconditioned trust that permeates religious experience at its more profound and creative levels. *Third*, the absolutistic view harmonizes with much of the Scriptures that assumes that all pain, death, and sorrow, whether individual or national, were willed by God for His own purpose. The authors of the Scriptures had to search for the deeper meaning of suffering because they were convinced that God could have prevented it.

DeWolf offered several reflections designed to conserve the truths in both the finitistic and absolutistic solutions. He first observed that the Christian should assign only minor importance to pain and sorrow. The Christian should seek first the reign of God in his heart, mind, and will. Everything else, including pleasure and pain, have their chief importance only insofar as they promote or obstruct the realization of that goal. Pain is of little importance when compared with sin, the chief intrinsic evil, even as pleasure is but a trifle compared with sanctification:

> In the long run of eternity it matters little to me whether my earthly days are long or short, since even a century is but a passing moment. But it matters everything what stewardship I give of the days at my disposal. Whether I am today suffering pain or enjoying pleasurable health will make little difference a thousand years from now. But how my pain or pleasure, weakness or health are related to faith and love will make all the difference.[79]

In "Paul's Letter to American Christians" King repeated this doctrine when he affirmed, "The end of life is not to be happy nor to achieve pleasure and avoid pain, but to do the will of God, come what may."[80]

DeWolf maintained that much of man's pain and trouble is caused by his sin and faithlessness. He drew an interesting parallel between the way man's mind interprets sense data and the way man's attitudes shape his objective world:

Just as Kant showed the deep dependence of our perceptual experience upon the organizing forms which our own minds supply, so recent psychology and medicine have brought forth one evidence after another that much of the character of our experience which we attribute to the objective world is actually due to the operation of our own attitudes.[81]

In the lives of the mentally ill and even of "normal" people, fear and distrust severely aggravate some pains which faith, hope, and love could reduce to insignificance:

How much of earth's pain might be removed if individuals and the whole society in which they live were rid of the fear, hate, guilt feelings and self-pity which sin has engendered![82]

If the goal of life were pleasure, we could readily see that an intelligent creator could have produced a quite different causal order. But pleasure ought not to be the goal. Rather, the purpose of life is to train immortal souls for heroic faith and love. In developing this point DeWolf revealed his keen appreciation of "the powers of the negative":

How would a created person learn courage if there were no peril of real injury? How come to know the deep joy of self-giving love if, with no pain or death, there were no hard sacrifice to make? How learn responsible community if each must bear alone the penalties of his own sin without power to increase or heal real sufferings in others?[83]

He affirmed that if we confront all natural evil with faith, prayer, and courage, we can transform it into a means for good. He pointed to how the anguish of the ancient nation of Israel resulted in the sublime revelations of the exilic prophets, and to how the torture of Jesus became the supreme channel of divine revelation and redemption. DeWolf found in both finitistic and absolutistic theism the belief that in God's sight no human suffering is final. "Because God lives, evil never has the last word."[84] The faith of Christians assures them that in the life hereafter the judgments of God will have the final word over temporal inequities.

At this point DeWolf returned to a consideration of the limitations on God's power. God's omnipotence, although it is power over all, is limited in different ways, namely, by His choice to give power to some of His creatures, by His rational nature, and by the bounds of His own being. DeWolf denied that his emphasis on these limitations constituted his view as finitistic since he was not saying that evil is due to any " 'uncreated force, being or aspect of being which opposes, limits, or partially obstructs' God's will."[85] He differentiated his view from Plato's in which God confronts a Receptacle, from Brightman's, in which God, as *logos*, has to oppose a nonrational Given, and from Tillich's, in which God, as *logos,* must deal with a symbolically indicated potentiality.[86] DeWolf explained that, according to his own view, when God deals with man's free will, He is not confronting anything that He has not created, and when He is limited by His own nature, He fully approves of that nature. While the finitist claims that God could not prevent some natural evil, and that, in spite of this, we should do the best we can with His help, DeWolf contended that we should regard every natural evil as having a positive place in the purpose of God:

> It is, therefore, not to be treated as something *in spite of which* we do the best we can. On the contrary, we are to treat it, as the prophets dealt with the exile and as Jesus and Paul interpreted the cross, that is, as something *by means of which* God's will is being done and hence great new good coming to pass, *good worth much more than all the cost*.[87]

The present world is not the best of all possible worlds, but only the best God can give to His children while they pass from innocence through sin into the early stages of redemption.[88]

King affirmed that his acceptance of this doctrine of suffering as a means of individual and social redemption enabled him to deal creatively with many agonizing situations. His study of Gandhi had prepared him to be receptive to DeWolf's doctrine of the value of suffering, but DeWolf enabled him to assimilate this doctrine within the context of his Christian faith. As King's sufferings during the freedom struggle escalated, he deepened his reliance on this doctrine. Thus, when a second attempt was made to bomb his home after the Montgomery Boycott ended, he tried to prevent an angry crowd from resorting to violence by asserting, "We must somehow believe that unearned suffering is redemptive."[89] In 1960 in an article entitled "Suffering and Faith" he explained:

My personal trials have also taught me the value of unmerited suffering. . . . I have attempted to see my personal ordeals as an opportunity to transform myself and heal the people involved in the tragic situation which now obtains. I have lived these last few years with the conviction that unearned suffering is redemptive. The suffering and agonizing moments through which I have passed over the last few years have also drawn me closer to God. More than ever before I am convinced of the reality of a personal God.[90]

He was careful not to limit the application of this doctrine to only extraordinary events:

Almost anything that happens to us may be woven into the purposes of God. It may lengthen our cords of sympathy. It may break our self-centered pride. The cross, which was willed by wicked men, was woven by God into the tapestry of world redemption.[91]

He was convinced that faith in the power, goodness, and "cosmic companionship" of God could enable believers to deal creatively with suffering, at times voluntarily to seek it, and to apply it to their spiritual advantage. He referred to the example of St. Paul who, though beaten and bloody in a desolate dungeon, "joyously sang the songs of Zion at midnight," to the joy of the early Christians who rejoiced that they had been deemed worthy to suffer for the sake of Christ, and to the Negro slaves who could still sing their spirituals in the midst of the lash and the oppressive heat.[92]

King's position on God's power was quite similar to that of DeWolf and different from that of Brightman. Like DeWolf, he referred to God as "omnipotent."[93] King maintained that central to the Christian faith is the conviction that in the universe there is a God of power "Who is able to do exceedingly abundant things in nature and in history."[94] He emphasized that the Old and New Testaments frequently stress this conviction which, as he indicated, is expressed theologically in the doctrine of the omnipotence of God. He often alluded to the matchless power of God, which is a fit contrast to the sordid weakness of man, and revealed that in the midst of fear and frustration, he had felt the power of God transforming his despair into hope.[95] But he also maintained, as did DeWolf, that there are limitations on God's power. In his dissertation he explained what he meant by God's omnipotence:

It does not mean that God can do the nondoable; neither does it mean that God has the power to act contrary to his own nature. It means, rather, that God has the power to actualize the good and realize his purpose.[96]

In *Strength To Love* King continued to reaffirm DeWolf's doctrine when he stated, "By endowing us with freedom, God relinquished a measure of his own sovereignty and imposed certain limitations upon himself."[97] Unlike Brightman, who argued that God is good but lacks the power to conquer evil, King stressed that God is both good and powerful.[98] King was convinced that God is not only with us in the struggle against the forces of evil, as Brightman held, but also that God has the power to defeat those forces.[99] "But if God is truly God and warrants man's ultimate devotion, he must have not only an infinite concern for the good but an infinite power to actualize the good."[100] In his concern to avoid Brightman's finitism and to affirm God's power to conquer the evils of history, King at times even referred to God's power in an unqualified way, as when he alluded to "the unlimited power of God" and to God as "a Being of boundless power."[101] Because of the crucial role that King assigned to his belief that God's power would bring success to the struggle for freedom, it seems that, if he had not adopted DeWolf's view on the power of God and had instead identified with Brightman's finitistic view, he might not have persevered in this struggle, and its outcome would have been quite different.

DeWolf ended his treatment of the problem of evil by reminding us again that there must always be a vast margin of mystery when we confront the ways of God, and added that if this mystery did not exist, perhaps suffering would fail fully to serve its purpose for us. In a final statement on this problem he revealed his commitment to the ideal of the interrelatedness of all persons and to the community of humanity:

We must not think there is any complete solution for the problem of evil while any neighbor anywhere remains in distress which we could ameliorate. It is probably God's own purpose that we must be perplexed and plagued, intellectually as well as practically, by the very existence of pain and trouble as long as we need them. For their purpose is served only so long as we cannot be at peace with them in our own persons or in any others. Struggle with them we must, at every level, until we enter the heavenly city where sin has no place and all tears are wiped away.[102]

This doctrine served to reinforce King's own conviction that whatever directly affects one person affects all indirectly, and injustice anywhere is a threat to justice everywhere, and that all of us should sacrifice to help to create the just and loving community.[103]

King's Critique of Tillich and Wieman

DeWolf's contribution to King's conception of God assumes an additional significance when it is understood that King in the course of his studies at Crozer Theological Seminary and Boston University was exposed to different and at times conflicting conceptions of God. In his doctoral dissertation on Paul Tillich and Henry Nelson Wieman's conceptions of God, King criticized Tillich for conclusions that tended to regard God as impersonal. He interpreted Tillich's God, "Being-Itself," to be an Absolute devoid of consciousness and life and to be "little more than a sub-personal reservoir of power, somewhat akin to the impersonalism of Oriental Vedantism."[104] Instead of being a supernatural creator, Tillich's God is the "Ground of Being."[105] King admitted that Tillich had warned that God is not less than personal, and that personality is a precious symbol denoting the unconditional and the ground of all being. King still contended, however, that there were elements throughout Tillich's thinking that referred to God as less than personal, and that all of his conclusions tended to point to an impersonal God. "Even those things which Tillich says about God with personalistic implications are finally given impersonal explanations."[106] King cited as an example the way in which Tillich spoke of God as love. King argued that as Tillich developed this doctrine, he regarded love as just "the dialectical principle of the union of opposites."[107] King maintained that this use of the term "love" reminds one of the love and strife principles of Empedocles, the Greek philosopher, who, according to King, meant by love no more than the attraction of the elements for one another.[108] King further charged that when Tillich stressed the "logos" or rational quality of God, he detracted from this emphasis by his insistence that the "abyss" quality of God, which cannot be known by reason, is the primary essence of God. King concluded this criticism by charging that Tillich "chooses the less than personal to explain personality, purpose and meaning."[109] In *Strength To Love* he reaffirmed his defense of the personal nature of God:

> To say that this God is personal is not to make him a finite object beside other objects or attribute to him the limitations of hu-

man personality; it is to take what is finest and noblest in our consciousness and affirm its perfect existence in him. It is certainly true that human personality is limited, but personality as such involves no necessary limitations. It means simply self-consciousness and self-direction. So in the truest sense of the word, God is a living God. In him there is feeling and will, responsive to the deepest yearnings of the human heart: *this* God both evokes and answers prayer.[110]

King also criticized Tillich for doctrines that could be interpreted as monistic. He viewed as monistic Tillich's emphasis on God's participation in every life as its ground. Also, he objected to certain of Tillich's statements that made his view similar to Hegel's philosophy of spirit and Plotinus's philosophy of the One. He felt these statements would incline one to interpret Tillich as "an absolute monist." For example, Tillich asserted:

The finite is posited as finite within the process of divine life, but it is reunited with the infinite within the same process. . . . The divine life is creative, actualizing itself in inexhaustible abundance.[111]

While making this charge, King conceded that there were some passages in Tillich's writings that implied a quantitative pluralism. He mentioned Tillich's affirmation that there would be no history unless man were to some degree free, that is, to some extent independent from God.[112] He admitted that the most persuasive idea in all of Tillich's utterances about man is that man is free.[113] He discerned a clear contradiction in Tillich's thought between this emphasis on human freedom, which implies a "metaphysical otherness," and his basic position of an ultimate ontological monism, both qualitative and quantitative.[114] He claimed that Tillich never resolved this contradiction. After referring to Tillich's assertions about human freedom, he concluded that Tillich held to a monism since he had maintained that God is ultimately the only metaphysical reality and that the life of man is a phase of the actualization of God and not itself a separate metaphysical reality.[115] It was King's Personalist view of God, derived especially from DeWolf, that sensitized him to reject Tillich's attempts to obscure the personal nature of the Absolute and the real distinction between the Absolute and His finite reflections.

In his dissertation King also criticized Henry Nelson Wieman for denying that God is personal. He explained that although Wieman in his earlier works granted the possibility that God is personal, in his later works he emphatically denied that God is personal. King indicated that Wieman, like the philosopher and mathematician Alfred North Whitehead, defined God as "the principle of concretion."[116] Concreteness for Wieman referred to events in their wholeness, their individualized totality, their unique and full particularity.[117] King presented Wieman's other definitions of God as "the growth of living connections of value in the universe," "the growth of meaning and value in the world," and "that interaction between things which generates and magnifies personality and all its highest values."[118] In commenting on the last definition, King emphasized that an interaction is not a thing or a concrete object but a process in which concrete objects affect one another. It is an event rather than a continuing entity.[119] From these definitions he concluded, "Wieman's God is a process, an order of events, a system or pattern of behavior."[120] King viewed this conception of God that rejected His transcendence and denied His personal nature as consistent with Wieman's naturalism but quite antithetical to traditional theism, which has regarded God as an all-powerful personal Being Who is the generator, shaper, and overruler of events.[121] One of the reasons King gave for Wieman's objection to the idea of a personal God was the latter's conviction that personality can be generated only by interaction between individuals. The existence of a trinity of persons in God would serve as a ground for asserting the nature of God to be personal, but Wieman added that there is not the slightest empirical evidence of an ontological trinity.[122]

Wieman explained that the fact that God is not personal does not mean that He is impersonal. He is supra-personal. "God towers in unique majesty infinitely above the little hills which we call minds and personalities."[123] He felt that if he held that God is personal, he would place a limit on God. King understood Wieman and Tillich to be in accord in denying that God is personal even though they affirmed that God is supra-personal.[124] He argued that when they viewed God as "an entity of some sort which is lacking in consciousness or rationality," such a position never revealed whether an unconscious supra-personality is better or worse than personality:[125]

It would be better by far to admit that there are difficulties with an idea we know—such as personality—than to employ a term [supra-personality] which is practically unknown to us in our experience.[126]

He concluded that Tillich and Wieman's conceptions of God were lacking positive religious value. "Both concepts are too impersonal to express adequately the Christian conception of God. They provide neither the conditions for true fellowship with God nor the assurance of his goodness."[127] This critique not only revealed King's acceptance of the Personalist conception of a provident God but also implied his appreciation of the existential implications of such an acceptance for believers who have both the privilege and the obligation to seek fellowship with a God Whose loving purpose directs them.[128]

Davis's Conception of the God in Control of History

One of the principal themes George Davis developed in the several courses King took at Crozer Theological Seminary and in his articles for *The Crozer Quarterly*, which King read, was that God is in control of history and moves it toward the realization of His eternal purpose for humanity. With reference to Jesus' words, "My Father worketh, even until now," Davis described the God of the Bible as a "working, toiling God," Whose purpose permeates the maze of events, causing even the folly and failures of men to praise Him.[129] He affirmed the validity of the Hebraic-Christian linear conception of history as progress toward a predetermined goal, and rejected the ancient Greek conception of history as a process destined to bend back upon itself in endless cyclic repetition.[130] "There is a slow but sure working towards the full realization of the goal which God has in mind."[131] He contended that one of the hard-won gains that we owe to Hegel is the recognition that God is not a Being Who acts arbitrarily but a Being of rational order, whether His activity be discerned in history, nature, or religious experience.[132]

Davis sought an "empirical basis" for determining what God is seeking to accomplish in the historical process. He found this basis in certain "major shifts" in history. His analysis of these shifts to some extent seemed to resemble Hegel's philosophy of history, that traced the progression of the human spirit to higher levels of self-consciousness, freedom, and active participation by the individual in communal activity. The first major shift Davis discovered in the historical process was *the transition from external controls to inner sanctions*.[133] Early man, through fear and threat of human and divine punishment, had to live under outer and physical sanctions, but these gave way, though admittedly not entirely, to inner and spiritual sanctions. Authorities did not make this progression easy for the reformers, nonconformists, separatists, and prophets throughout the ages who followed their consciences and not the mores of the group or the demands of the establishment. Davis found in contemporary democracy evidence of this shift to the inner sanctions, since it arouses the nobler impulses of human nature, and "seeks to establish an inner control, challenging men to be good citizens because of faith in the experiment of common government and because they can help create a community of life beneficial to all. In such an atmosphere absolute power gives way to inner compulsions."[134] Davis also found the shift in the history of religion as it moved significantly from external authority to an inner personal experience of God as the authority over life.[135] He interpreted this dominant direction of the historical process toward the development of man's responsible self-determination in conformity with his understanding of God's intention for his individual life and for mankind as clear evidence of His control of history. He regarded the ultimate failures of attempts to dominate mankind through external controls as further evidence of God's control and the moral purpose of history:

> The "stars in their courses" fight against all who would dominate the human spirit and beat it into humiliating subjection. It matters not whether such a tyrannical spirit is found in a father, an employer of labor, a minister of religion, or an Adolf Hitler. In the long run the tides of history will overtake his kind and destroy him. Such a person fights not alone against his child, his workman, his parishioner, or humanity; he fights as well against God at work in this unquenchable tendency of the ages.[136]

The second major shift that for Davis was evidence of God's control of history was *the transition from the impersonal to the personal*. He conceded that in the course of history there had been a great disregard for the personal, and cited some of the more repugnant examples of the triumph of the impersonal in ancient civilizations such as the slaughter of whole communities by Joshua's armies, the building of the pyramid of Cheops by forced labor at the estimated cost of a hundred thousand lives, the infanticide approved by the Greeks and the Romans, the mistreatment and subjugation of women, the perpetuation of slavery and serfdom, and ostracism because of race, nation, and other conditions. Writing in 1943, he conceded also that there were contemporary attitudes and acts that constituted reversions to the impersonal, such as the persecution of the Jews, concentration camps, the inhuman treatment of Negroes, Japanese, and Germans, the slaughter of the innocent to compensate for the crime of the guilty, the maltreatment of prisoners, the toleration of slums, racial segregation, attempts to reinstitute child labor, and the glorification of war.[137] Nonetheless, despite these evidences of the impersonal, Davis still affirmed his thesis that the dominant trend of history was toward the recognition of the value of the personal:

> Yet sickening as is the story of this ruthless exaltation of the impersonal, we find complementary inspiration in the recognition and refining of the personal. With slow but certain step man enters the appreciation of the values of personality.[138]

Davis emphasized that it was the teaching of Jesus that a loving God is concerned about each of His children and that therefore each individual is "a being of infinite worth" which proved to be the greatest emancipating force for the personal.[139] This view of God and man helped the shift from the impersonal to the personal to make persistent progress throughout the centuries, despite constant and intense opposition. While recognizing that the development was far from complete, Davis presented several examples of this shift, such as changes from the absolute authority of the father in ancient society to the rights of the child in modern society, from the inferiority of women to their equality, from the almost exclusive rights of property to the rights of man, from slavery to freedom, from child labor to the protection of youth, from starvation to a living wage, from the persecution of the mentally and physically ill to their tender care, from the humiliation of old age through charity to its protection through Social Security, and from the glorification to the discrediting of war, even when war is necessary. It is not too difficult to understand how Davis could communicate to King these concerns and could help inspire him to strive to further the development of some of these progressions.

Davis maintained that God intends that each human life express the personal, which includes goodness, truth, beauty, forgiveness, love, and the other qualitative aspects of character. "Part of God's intention in history is to produce free individuals who use their freedom to generate a personal life creative of an inward quality which is harmonious with His own."[140] King also proclaimed that God intends man to progress to an appreciation of the value of personality:

> God has a great plan for this world. His purpose is to achieve a
> world where all men will live together as brothers, and where
> every man recognizes the dignity and worth of all human per-
> sonality.[141]

Davis affirmed that although the realization of God's intention for the
race may be slow of fruition, it nonetheless ripens.[142] "Though the
mills of God grind slowly, yet they grind exceeding small."[143] Charles
Beard, the historian, indicated that this was one of the four major
lessons that he had learned from history. In *Strength To Love* King
also quoted this lesson and the other three as well in order to emphasize his belief that evil contains the seeds of its own destruction and
that right will ultimately triumph. "Whom the gods would destroy
they must first make mad with power. . . . The bee fertilizes the
flower it robs. . . . When it is dark enough, you can see the stars."[144]
King quoted the last also in a sermon the night before his death.[145] His
experiences in the Movement had furnished abundant evidence for
these truths.

While acknowledging the existence of absolutism and autocracy
and their effect on millions of persons, Davis maintained that the third
major shift in history was *the transition from rank individualism to
the solidarity of the social group, which enhances the realization of the
personal*. The rank individualist not only aims to dominate others but
seeks favored treatment because of his birth, native ability, intellectual
achievement, nationality, racial strain, or financial position. He is the
enemy of the personal since he flouts love, "the culminating fruitage
of personal life."[146] Humanity is slowly moving from such individualism to the creation of a form of societal organization that protects the
individual from mob violence, exploitation by privileged groups, and
arbitrary control by any leader or group of leaders:

> One by one the tyrants and dictators fall by the wayside, de-
> stroyed by that which they would themselves destroy. They have
> always flouted the highest personal life which is, of necessity, a
> free life. At long last, that free life asserts itself, carrying within
> its power the nemesis of all dictatorships. History teaches this
> lesson in large, heavy type: *The tide of time pushes resistlessly
> against all crushers of liberty*.[147]

King frequently echoed this theme. Evil in the form of injustice and
tyrannical exploitation cannot survive. "There is something in this

universe that Greek mythology referred to as the goddess of Nemesis":[148]

> History is the story of evil forces that advance with seemingly irresistible power only to be crushed by the battling-rams of the forces of justice. There is a law in the moral world—a silent, invisible imperative, akin to the laws in the physical world—which reminds us that life will work only in a certain way. The Hitlers and the Mussolinis have their day, and for a period they may wield great power, spreading themselves like a green bay tree, but soon they are cut down like the grass and wither as the green herb.[149]

In his analysis of the biblical account of the exodus of the Israelites from Egypt and the destruction of their oppressors in the Red Sea, King found a glaring symbol of the ultimate doom of evil in its struggle with good.[150] God, Who works through history for the salvation of His children and Who struggles against the forces of evil, has placed moral laws within the structure of the universe, and these laws will eventually conquer those who defy them.[151] King asserted that one of the best proofs that reality depends upon moral foundations is the fact that when individuals and governments work devotedly for the good of others, they thereby achieve their own enrichment.[152]

Davis stressed that a shift to the social became apparent as the religious consciousness moved from concern merely with the family to concern for the tribe, for the nation, and for all humanity:

> The spirit of all mature religion is that I am my brother's keeper and my brother is my keeper. For the fully religious man nothing less than the world can be his parish. Such is the case because, having discovered the full beauty and the ultimate significance of personal life, he longs to make it a social possession; that is, he desires precisely that kind of life for every man, woman, and child who enters the world. . . . The pinnacle of personal life is love, and love, by its very nature, is inclusive, shutting no one out of its circle of vision and concern.[153]

The shift to the social was also discernible in the political order in the transition from the patriarchal group or clan, based on blood relationship, to tribes, to nations, and even to attempts to pass beyond the national stage of organization. Davis indicated that when nationalism becomes an absolute devotion, it blocks the way to the larger good God intends for all humanity. "The purpose of God, Jesus taught, is not limited to the nation of Israel, or the race of Abraham, or any family strain. It extends to all human life."[154]

As already indicated, King often reiterated the need for the individual to develop a loving concern for all of humanity. In *Strength To Love* he affirmed, "We are inevitably our brother's keeper because of the interrelated structure of reality."[155] In *The Trumpet of Conscience* he stressed the necessity for Americans to work with all peoples for universal justice so that the world-wide revolutionary spirit might aim to become creative.[156] He emphasized that the conscience of an awakened activist cannot be satisfied with a focus on local problems because he recognizes that they are interconnected with world problems.[157] The awakened activist will be concerned about world hunger and poverty:

> What can we do? The answer is simple: feed the poor, clothe the naked, and heal the sick. Where can we store our goods? Again, the answer is simple: We can store our surplus food free of charge in the shriveled stomachs of the millions of God's children who go to bed hungry at night. We can use our vast resources of wealth to wipe poverty from the earth.[158]

For those who do not comprehend the social implications of Christianity and who need a pragmatic argument King warned, "We cannot long survive spiritually separated in a world that is geographically together."[159]

Davis did not think that the fact that humanity was immersed in World War II was a cogent argument against his thesis that the pressure of the universe is toward an ever-increasing sociality rather than toward racial and social exclusiveness. Rather, he claimed that the war was a convincing argument for his thesis. It was an indication of the working of God in history. The world cataclysm was God's response to the nationalistic man who in his perverseness and ignorance stubbornly resisted the logic of history, which demanded "interdependent living":

> The tragedies of history, which today engulf practically the whole world, are seen to be due to a failure of men and nations to read the directional signs of history and to follow them in attitude and action.[160]

Davis reasoned that if no catastrophe had come to shake the earth to its foundations, then he would be forced to conclude that the logic of history does not favor increasing sociality. But because the storms came, he felt confirmed in his thesis that "history points to the social as the signpost of true progress."[161] Directly or indirectly the moral foundations of the universe reassert themselves. The moral direction of history has been evident in the disintegration of one civilization after another because they ignored the laws of social obligation whose observance alone is productive of unity and strength:

> The ebbing and flowing tides of history disclose that in God's good time judgment and redemption alike come to men and societies.[162]
>
> We know now that we must live together or perish. If we will not have one world, we may have no world.[163]

King repeated these themes when he warned, "Now the judgment of God is upon us, and we must either learn to live together as brothers or we are all going to perish together as fools," and when he stated at the conclusion of *Stride Toward Freedom*, "Today, the choice is no longer between violence and nonviolence. It is either nonviolence or nonexistence."[164]

In explaining God's intention to use history to create the truly inner, personal, and social man, Davis also emphasized the role of man in executing this intention. He repudiated what he regarded as pessimistic tendencies in theologians such as St. Paul, St. Augustine, Luther, Calvin, Kierkegaard, and Barth to minimize and even to deny the freedom of man to contribute to his own salvation and to the introduction of God's kingdom on earth.[165] Man is not a divinely dominated creature, helpless to do good. Religion must be conceived of with the moral optimism of Jesus as a cooperation between God, Who in His love assumes the initiative, and the person who responds to His grace.

King also wished to emphasize that the divine control of history does not negate human freedom. While proclaiming God's power, he warned against portraying God as so absolutely sovereign that man would be considered completely helpless. He rejected any view that regards God as a despot, and man as so absolutely depraved that he can do nothing but wait on God.[166] In contrast to Nygren, he asserted that man can perform meritorious acts to improve his relationship with God:

But man is neither totally depraved, nor is God an almighty dictator. We must surely affirm the majesty and sovereignty of God, but this should not lead us to believe that God is an Almighty Monarch who will impose his will upon us and deprive us of the freedom to choose what is good and what is not good.[167]

King cautioned that while we need prayer to secure God's grace and assistance, we cannot rely on God to the extent that we dispense with intelligence and good works. "Prayer is a marvelous and necessary supplement of our feeble efforts, but it is a dangerous substitute."[168] He contended that the failure of oppressed people to recognize this truth was one of the causes of the continued existence of segregation. While believing in a loving Providence and the movement of history toward the expansion of justice, he maintained that we must still work to "speed up the coming of the inevitable."[169]

Chapter 3

The Sacredness of Human Personality

The first chapter examined how King's acceptance of the Personalist doctrine of man as the image of God, developed especially by DeWolf, enabled him to avoid the negativity in Nygren's view of *agape* and caused him to realize the possibilities for the actualization of the beloved community. This chapter will explore how King's adherence to this Personalist doctrine allowed him to identify with insights on the dignity of the human person from a variety of sources: Immanuel Kant, whose emphasis on rationality, freedom, and responsibility influenced many Personalists; Edgar Brightman, whose moral laws demanded the formation of values in the person and in the community; Reinhold Niebuhr, whose understanding of the potential of individual and collective man for evil challenged any excessive optimism; and the existentialists, both theistic and atheistic, who championed the value of the person while stressing the limitations that beset human freedom. The chapter will also indicate how King understood that racism essentially implies a negation of the value of human personality. Later chapters will explain how his belief in the sacredness of the person helped motivate him to challenge economic exploitation, militarism, and all forms of segregation.

The Appeal to Kant

In order to emphasize the basic immorality of segregation, King in *Where Do We Go From Here: Chaos or Community?* quoted Kant's demand that we should respect the dignity of human personality, "All men must be treated as *ends* and never as mere *means*."[1] According to King, segregation was guilty of this very evil of regarding Negroes as mere means, as "animated tools," rather than as ends-in-themselves,

71

as persons sacred in themselves. Segregation desecrated persons by dealing with them solely in terms of their usefulness to the power structure. With its overt and subtle forms of discrimination and exploitation it reduced persons to things and thereby denied their basic nature. Discrimination hounded Negroes at every level, stultified their initiative, and insulted their being.[2]

In his ethical theory Kant maintained that man's possession of a rational nature qualifies him to be *free* to establish the moral law for himself. However, in the establishment of this moral law the individual must not seek his own goals in an unrestricted and selfish manner. Rather, he should think and function morally as if he were a member of a "kingdom" of ends or rational beings. In the exercise of his freedom he should realize that the moral law dictates unconditionally that he should respect the dignity of every other rational being and that person's capacity to establish the moral law:

> For all rational beings stand under the law that each of them should treat himself and all others never merely as a means but in every case also as an end in himself. Thus, there arises a systematic union of rational beings through common objective laws. This is a realm which may be called a realm of ends.[3]

According to Kant, each man is sovereign in the sense that he is the source of the moral law within himself. As legislator each person is "sublime."[4] "Humanity in his person must be holy to him."[5] Each man is also a subject since he must respect this law and the persons to whom it applies.

King felt that Kant's doctrine of respect for persons was redemptive since it required that we prescind from superficial personal differences, and recognize every man as a man. King contended that segregation based on pride, hatred, falsehood, and irrationality treated the Negro in an inhuman fashion and inculcated in him a sense of inferiority, "a degenerating sense of 'nobodiness.' "[6] Kant's ethics appealed to King as a challenge to segregation since by its reverence for the dignity of man's rational nature, it helped provide a foundation for the belief that all men are created equal. King could never adjust his spirit to separate housing, educational, recreational, travel, and even church facilities because he believed that to be compelled to be separate is to be regarded as unequal. "Numerous people in the North and South still believe that the affirmation, 'All men are created equal,' means 'All white men are created equal.' "[7]

Although King was attracted to Kant's doctrine of reverence for the sacredness of persons, he never commented on Kant's basis for this doctrine, that is, the capacity of the individual to establish the moral law. King's belief that God is the evident source of the moral law would not allow him to endorse the type of autonomy in the form of self-legislation that Kant attributed to the individual. King affirmed that every man ought to be respected not only as a rational being but also as a child of God.[8] He complained that too seldom we see persons in their true humanness since a spiritual myopia limits our vision to external accidents:

We see men as Jews or Gentiles, Catholics or Protestants, Chinese or Americans, Negroes or whites. We fail to think of them as fellow human beings made from the same basic stuff as we, molded in the same divine image.[9]

In his desire to appropriate Kant's insights for his attack on segregation and discrimination, King in effect helped reinforce the interpretation prevalent even in current philosophical circles that Kant was a champion of the freedom and dignity of the individual. This interpretation appears to be valid if we examine the *Critique of Practical Reason* (1788). However, it would seem that this prevalent interpretation must be qualified if we examine also his essay, "On the Common Saying: 'This May Be True in Theory, But It Does Not Apply in Practice' " (1793). In this essay he presented the principles that should constitute the foundation of a "lawful" or rational state. The first of these principles is "the *freedom* of every member of society as a *human being*."[10] Man's freedom as a *human being* consists in his right to pursue happiness in whatever way he sees fit, provided that he does not interfere with the freedom of others to pursue a similar end. No one may compel another to be happy in accordance with his conception of that person's welfare. Kant here denounced any paternalistic government since it would deny that subjects have the capacity to distinguish what is beneficial from what is harmful to themselves. In such a government, which he regarded as "the greatest conceivable despotism," subjects would be obliged to behave passively and to rely upon the judgment of the head of state as to how they ought to be happy. This kind of state would not be rational or just since it would violate the principle of *freedom*.[11]

The second principle of a rational state is "the *equality* of each with all the others as a *subject*."[12] Man's equality as a *subject* consists in the fact that each member of the commonwealth has access to the laws of the state to coerce others to act so that his freedom can coexist with their freedom. "They are all equal as *subjects before the law. . . .*"[13] From this Kant concluded that every member of the commonwealth should be entitled to reach any degree of rank he can earn through his talent, industry, and good fortune. No other subject by the employment of hereditary prerogatives or privileges of rank may prevent him from exercising this right.

If Kant had developed only these two principles of *freedom* and *equality*, his reputation as a champion of the political freedom of the individual would be secure. However, he did develop a third principle, namely, "the *independence* of each member of a commonwealth as a *citizen*."[14] This initial reference to the third principle would not appear to restrict the freedom of the individual, especially since he proceeded to define the citizen as a "co-legislator," that is, one who has a right to vote on laws.[15] Nevertheless, in his explanation of this principle of *independence* he placed a serious limitation on the political rights of certain individuals in his proposed state. He indicated that in the proposed "rational state" not all could be citizens in the sense that not all would have the right to vote and to make laws through their representatives. He maintained that to qualify as a citizen, one had to be an adult male, to be his own master, *and* to have property, which could include a skill, trade, fine art, or science to support himself.[16] If he had to earn his living from others, he had to earn it only by selling that which was his and not by allowing others to make use of him. He stated that domestic servants, shop assistants, and laborers would not be qualified to be citizens since, unlike artists, they would not produce a commodity they could sell as their own property.

In *The Metaphysics of Morals* (1797) Kant reiterated his notion of the *independence* of citizens and distinguished between "active citizens"—those who would be permitted to vote—and "passive citizens"—women, minors, apprentices to merchants or tradesmen, servants not employed by the state, and all those obliged to depend on others for their food and protection.[17] He explained that he was denying the franchise to the passive citizens so as to be certain that those who would be permitted to vote would serve no one but the commonwealth. Evidently, he assumed that if the passive citizens were permitted to vote, then because of their economic situation, they would be incapable of desiring to serve the community. He also arbitrarily assumed here that the possession of land or a skill that would result in a commodity would automatically equip the active citizens with a desire to serve the good of the whole community and to protect the interests of those less fortunate.[18]

Had King known Kant's principle of *independence*, he would have been quick to denounce the contradiction between Kant's ethical emphasis on the freedom and dignity of the individual as a moral lawgiver and this justification of disfranchisement. He would have repudiated this unethical reduction of certain individuals who are poor and unskilled to *mere means* for the economic and political advancement of the already privileged. Guided by Kant's own ethics, King would have rejected the notion that the right to political self-determination should depend on factors extrinsic to one's rational nature such as the possession of property or a skill. King would also have condemned the ways in which this principle of *independence* violated Kant's own principles of *freedom* and *equality.* How can the passive citizen exercise his *freedom* in his own way if he is subject to the vote of the active citizens and to their conception of his happiness? How can the passive citizens be *equal* before the law when only the active citizens select the representatives who shape the law? King regarded the right to vote as a necessary condition for the realization of freedom and equality. He contended that the denial of this "sacred right" to some black citizens had been a tragic betrayal of the highest mandates of our democratic tradition:

> So long as I do not firmly and irrevocably possess the right to vote, I do not possess myself. I cannot make up my mind—it is made up for me. I cannot live as a democratic citizen, observing the laws I have helped to enact—I can only submit to the edict of others.[19]

Since Kant asserted that every member of the commonwealth should be entitled to reach any degree of rank that he could earn through his talent, industry, and good fortune, he did allow individuals the right to earn the economic status that could serve as a condition for obtaining the vote. However, Kant did not consider or did not choose to consider that until the vote would be secured by all, the freedom and equality of the socially and economically less fortunate would be endangered. Without a detailed knowledge of Kant's political theory, King assumed that this theory would be consistent with Kant's ethical pronouncements on the freedom and dignity of the individual.[20] King did not suspect that Kant, in order to make concessions to some of the political judgments of his day, would choose to forego consistency with his ethical theory and would in effect create the second-class citizenship that King was willing to give his life to abolish.[21]

Brightman's Moral Laws

King could be so enthusiastic in expressing his indebtedness to DeWolf and Brightman for providing him with a metaphysical basis for the dignity and worth of all human personality because, long before his contact with Personalism, he had experienced some of the ways in which the evil of segregation systematically does violence to the human personality. He explained that as far back as he could remember he had resented the system of segregation.[22] In his later years he still bore the scars of his boyhood experiences of discrimination. He recalled with pain that even before he entered school, two white playmates had been forced by their parents to terminate their friendship with him.[23] He remembered also the anger of his father when a shoestore clerk refused to serve him if he did not sit in the rear of the store, and his father's words, "I don't care how long I have to live with this system, I will never accept it."[24] As a boy, King could not bring himself to return to a segregated theater where he had to enter a rear door and sit in a filthy gallery. The very idea of separation offended his sense of dignity and self-respect. The first time he was seated behind a curtain in a dining car, he felt as if a curtain had been dropped on his selfhood.[25] In a 1965 interview he recalled how, when he was fourteen, his teacher and he were ordered to surrender their bus seats to whites, and then were cursed by the white driver who felt that they did not move quickly enough. They were compelled to stand for the ninety-mile trip to Atlanta. Ironically, that day King had delivered a speech in an oratorical contest on the topic "The Negro and the Constitution." "That night will never leave my memory. It was the angriest I have ever been in my life."[26] His training at Morehouse College served to reinforce his awareness of the evils of segregation. His major in sociology gave him some understanding of the scope of these evils. Walter Chivers, his sociology professor, had conducted extensive investigations of lynchings in the South.[27] Dean Brailsford Brazeal conducted weekly orientations for the student body in the college chapel, and some of these orientations were lectures on segregation and on techniques for counteracting its effects.[28] Moreover, the civil rights activities of King's father and grandfather reinforced his awareness of the moral need to protest racial discrimination. His father had been in the forefront of campaigns to secure equal salaries for black teachers and to abolish Jim Crow elevators in the Atlanta courthouse.[29] His maternal grandfather, the Reverend Adam Daniel Williams, a charter member of Atlanta's NAACP, had helped lead a successful movement to defeat a city bond issue that had made no provisions for the construction of public high schools for blacks in Atlanta. He had also been one of the organizers of a boycott against *The Georgian*, a local newspaper that denounced the Negro voters who opposed the bond issue—a boycott that ultimately led to the demise of the paper.[30]

In the light of his personal experiences, King did not need Personalism to provide him with the passion to oppose segregation, but Personalism with its emphasis on the value of the person did help formulate the principles for his attack upon this evil. One of the principal sources of Personalism was Edgar Brightman's *Moral Laws*, which contained his ethical system.[31] King's research papers indicate that he studied this work.[32] In *Moral Laws* Brightman developed his conception of the nature of moral law and made a distinction that became central to King's notion of the moral need to protest against segregation codes, especially by means of civil disobedience. Brightman distinguished between a moral law and social codes.[33] While a moral law is a universal principle that the will ought to obey, social codes are sets of principles that society expects or demands that the individual follow in his choices. While granting that it may be, and perhaps usually is, moral to follow social codes, especially if they have been thoughtfully prepared by moral persons, Brightman asserted:

> But no act is moral because it conforms to a code. It is moral because it conforms to moral law. Every code is subject to criticism by the moral law. Convention is sometimes an aid and sometimes a detriment to morality.[34]

Brightman indicated that the term "duty" has a double meaning. It may mean a demand society makes on the individual. In which case it may even be "an act from which my whole moral judgment revolts."[35] Duty may also mean a demand imposed by the enlightened conscience of the individual. "It is what I judge that I ought to do after having consulted my own experience and reason in the light of my highest ideals."[36] Brightman claimed that if the individual always identifies all the duties imposed by society as moral and admits no other duties but those prescribed by society, he surrenders the whole task of morality.

If the individual could discover the moral law by simply looking to the social prescription, then that prescription could never be subjected to intelligent criticism. But then how could good social prescriptions be distinguished from bad ones? Rather, moral duties must be used to judge social duties. Brightman agreed with Kant that the essential characteristic of all moral value in our acts depends on whether the moral law regulates the will:

> If the person chooses determination by moral law, he is moral; but if he is compelled by social authority, military power (or by hypnotism or the will of God or any other form of superior force), his act has no moral quality. It was not determined by moral law. It was social duty or compulsion; it was not moral duty.[37]

In another context Brightman returned to this theme as he quoted the German philosopher and theologian Romano Guardini, "Conscience is the place where the eternal enters time. It is the birthplace of history. . . . History means that through free humanity something eternal comes to pass in time."[38] Then Brightman warned of the necessity of distinguishing between the spontaneous conscience and the critical conscience. When conscience functions spontaneously, it is uncritical and often emotional. With a strong sense of obligation, the conscience reflects the individual's previous moral experience, especially the habits of feeling which have been nurtured by his social environment. The spontaneous conscience usually contains the customs or standards of the person's family, church, schools, and nation. However, to regard as absolutely binding the demands of this uncritical conscience is tantamount to taking either social tradition or individual emotion as the final authority in moral life. How can a spontaneous conscience shaped by the social environment be perfect if that environment is not perfect? Brightman added that many of the strongest demands of the spontaneous conscience are but rationalizations of desire. We say "we ought" when in fact we want. This conscience requires rational criticism in terms of one's highest standards and ideals. How can the individual move from an uncritical conscience to the formation of a critical conscience? Brightman maintained that a complete answer to this question can emerge only after a complete study of all the moral laws of his system. An examination of his formulations of these moral laws will reveal how King could find further support in this philosophy for his protests against segregation.

Brightman's first moral law was the Logical Law: *"All persons ought to will logically*; i.e., *each person ought to will to be free from self-contradiction and to be consistent in his intentions. A moral person does not both will and not will the same ends; this property of a moral person is called his formal rightness."*[39] In calling for consistency, he explained that he meant consistency with reason, which at times may mean criticism of one's own past. Ralph Waldo Emerson stated that a foolish consistency is the hobgoblin of little minds, and Brightman explained that Emerson by this did not intend to condemn the consistency of a rational will, but rather the petty consistency that refuses to learn anything new or to revise any opinion. In an article entitled "Some Definitions for Personalists," Brightman contended that the process of thought is a process of continual redefinition or at least of critical reexamination of definitions.[40] In *Moral Laws* he credited Kant with making fundamental the principle of a consistent will as a result of his emphasis on consistent respect for the moral law.[41] Brightman asserted that one can maintain respect for one's inner life only if one gives sincere allegiance to this Logical Law. In his application of this Logical Law King maintained that a person convinced of the sacred value of human personality should consistently will this value in all his intentions, and thus oppose every act of discrimination and injustice that degrades personality. He recognized that he could not be morally consistent if he demanded that there be respect for human life in the ghettos and did not publicly denounce violence on an international scale.[42]

In the statement of his second moral law, the Law of Autonomy, Brightman reinforced his emphasis on the need to obey the moral law even at times in opposition to the demands of social codes: *"All persons ought to recognize themselves as obligated to choose in accordance with the ideals which they acknowledge. Or: Self-imposed ideals are imperative."*[43] The law is one of autonomy because the person imposes upon himself the ideals, the plans of action, or types of experience he accepts as the best basis of choice. The person must not simply derive them uncritically from his social environment. Again, Brightman acknowledged his dependence on Kant, "who first made the principle of autonomy clear-cut and fundamental."[44] While King could not fully accept Kant's notion of autonomy since it did not derive the moral law from the law of God, King would assert the autonomy of the will to the extent that he would affirm that it is the will as the critical conscience which ought to impose the law of God upon itself. In the light of this self-imposed divine law, all civil laws have to be evaluated to determine whether they contribute to the elevation of the life of each person. Thus King defined as just "any law that uplifts human personality," and as unjust "any law that degrades human personality. . . . An unjust law is a human law that is not rooted in eternal law and natural law."[45]

Although Brightman praised Kant for his emphasis on the necessity of consistency and autonomy in the acts of the will, he did criticize him for failing to recognize that a moral life is not merely conformity to law but rather also involves responses to concrete values.[46] To supplement Kant's purely formalistic ethics, Brightman introduced the Axiological Law: "*All persons ought to choose values which are self-consistent, harmonious, and coherent, not values which are contradictory or incoherent with one another.*"[47] This law does not nullify the Logical Law or the Law of Autonomy, but it does focus on what is chosen. In "Some Definitions for Personalists" Brightman explained that coherence consists of the fulfillment of certain norms:

> Be consistent, be systematic, be inclusive, be analytic, be synoptic, be active, be open to alternatives, be critical, and be decisive. Coherence is a synonym of reason.[48]

This emphasis on coherence reinforced for King the need for consistency in his moral stands. His concern for this Axiological Law was evident in the way in which he stated the argument against his own nonviolent civil disobedience. "This brings in the whole question of how can you be logically consistent when you advocate obeying some laws and disobeying other laws."[49] His concern for logical and moral consistency in response to a moral value led him to reply to this objection by indicating that, even in disobeying the unjust law, the nonviolent disobedient can accept the penalty for his disobedience and thus reveal the "very highest respect for law."[50]

King could find in Brightman's Law of Consequences both moral and pragmatic value for the Nonviolent Movement: "*All persons ought to consider and, on the whole, approve the foreseeable consequences of each of their choices. Stated otherwise: Choose with a view to the long run, not merely to the present act.*"[51] King was most sensitive to the long-range consequences of his decisions. However, at times when he felt the need for compromise on some particular issue, even some of those who identified with his long-range goals thought that he had forgotten those goals.[52] These critics seemed to be unaware of his abiding vision that "Truth is the totality." In 1961, he proclaimed:

Now we must say that this struggle for freedom will not come to an automatic halt, for history reveals to us that once oppressed people rise up against that oppression, there is no stopping point short of full freedom.[53]

In his doctoral dissertation King presented Tillich's view that "man is never satisfied with any stage of his development; nothing finite can hold him."[54] King regarded each conflict as but one campaign in the total struggle against all forms of oppression. Therefore, he could settle temporarily for a partial gain since he did not accept any victory as ultimate. With his sense of the dialectical nature of the historical process, he could view each outcome as but a temporary synthesis that must become a new thesis in the ongoing drive toward complete freedom. Each achievement becomes a new plateau for a further protest, which may have to be quite specific and involve compromise to be effective. In his Nobel Lecture he stated, "We will always be willing to talk and seek fair compromise. . . ."[55] While recognizing that compromise is an "absolute necessity" for achieving total freedom, he warned that it must be "the creative, honest compromise of a policy, not the negative and cowardly compromise of a principle."[56]

Brightman's Law of the Best Possible provided King with additional motivation to wage his struggle for a free society and to be willing to settle temporarily for less than ideal gains: "*All persons ought to will the best possible values in every situation: hence, if possible, to improve every situation.*"[57] This law heightens the effect of the Law of Autonomy since it requires that persons impose the best possible ideals upon themselves. Brightman felt that this law checks the tendency toward abstraction in the previous laws by emphasizing the need to promote the values in every concrete situation. Since the Law of the Best Possible is seeking constant improvement, he called it the Melioristic Law. He also called it the Law of Creativity since the best is achievable in many cases only by a positive control of situations and the production of values which would not exist if they were not willed. King frequently indicated that all of us, whatever our social status, could become creative if we adopted the "creative solution" of nonviolence as our philosophy of life. A commitment to nonviolence would inspire us constantly to devise new ways to produce those human values that belong to the beloved community.

In his desire to make his moral system even more concrete, Brightman added the Law of Specification: "*All persons ought, in any given situation, to develop the value or values specifically relevant to that situation.*"[58] He maintained that although John Dewey probably was extreme in questioning the validity of general principles, he did make a significant contribution by demonstrating that valid generalizations must derive from and apply to concrete and specific experiences. Brightman affirmed that British and American thought had supplied a needed empirical corrective to the abstractness of Kant's formalism. He recognized that every situation is a problem that demands solution, and that the result of one unsolved problem is more unsolved problems. He indicated how different types of individuals will react differently to each situation:

> The passive type will submit to the situation, will accept it, will adjust to it as well as possible. The active type will rebel against the actual situation in the interests of the ideal, and will at once propose some plan of reform or improvement.[59]

While he affirmed that the merit of the active type is his interest in improving social conditions, he asserted that the merit of the passive type who seeks to endure his situation bravely is his respect for fact and for the personalities of others. He claimed that individuals of either type can be morally good, even as one good man may differ from another in temperament and heredity. He apparently believed that acceptance of a situation could itself be a solution to that situation.

Confronted with segregation, King could not accept Brightman's assertion that the passive type of individual respects fact and the personalities of others when this type adjusts his attitude to the situation and refuses to adjust the situation to his attitude. King contended that the passive acceptance of the evil of segregation constitutes even a disservice to the segregator since it allows him to continue in his error. In actively opposing segregation he could attempt to adhere consistently to both the Law of the Best Possible and the Law of Specification. This is not to claim that he was always successful in fully observing the Law of Specification. He acknowledged that he had made a mistake in the Albany Movement by waging a general attack on segregation instead of focusing on "specific, symbolic objectives" such as integrating the buses or the lunch counters. "One victory of this kind would have been symbolic, [and] would have galvanized support and boosted morale."[60] His heightened awareness of the need for specification as a result of this experience later proved to be crucial to the success of the Birmingham Movement.

The Law of the Most Inclusive End goes beyond the previous laws in demanding that the individual form a life plan for his development: *"All persons ought to choose a coherent life in which the widest possible range of value is realized."*[61] Since situations differ and since the endowments and opportunities of each individual differ from those of another, this law implies the uniqueness of each individual life and allows for individual imaginative and aesthetic creation in the construction of a life plan that is structured enough to be reasonably definite, but loose enough to be open to frequent revision and correction. This life plan must make provision for values of bodily enjoyment as well as for the higher ideals of morality. It must be the intelligence of the individual that develops the variety of his possibilities. If the control of one's development is mainly determined by outside forces instead of being autonomous, "it often happens that the most significant possibilities of one's life are choked out by circumstances."[62] "It would be nothing short of cultural and moral calamity if the growth of social standardization should crush out this side of life."[63] King also spoke of the manner in which society can obliterate individual differences. He described our age as one of "jumboism" because people find security in what is extensive—big cities, big buildings, big corporations—and he maintained that the worship of size causes many to conceal their lofty and noble ideals lest they be regarded as different and identified with a minority idea.[64] Reflecting on the Law of the Most Inclusive End, King could also more intensely experience the evil of segregation, which denies some individuals their moral right and duty to form a most inclusive life plan. How can individuals fulfill their obligation to obey the Law of the Most Inclusive End if segregation and discrimination exclude them from those educational, social, political, economic, and even religious opportunities that are the basis of total personal development?

In the Law of Ideal Control Brightman stressed the fact that morality requires self-control: *"All persons ought to control their empirical values by ideal values."*[65] Empirical values are value claims while ideal values are real values. Morality demands that we use our conscious purpose to control our instinctive and impulsive behavior. In extolling the rational control of instinct, Brightman claimed that the international behavior of the modern state had been largely a series of violations of this law. In advocating "ideal control" he warned against the extreme of a too rigid Puritanical repression of natural desires by excessive discipline and against the other extreme of denying the need for control. "Absence of control by ideal purposes is even surer to lead to disaster than is the most fanatical rigorism."[66] This control involves criticism that includes self-criticism. In applying his ideals to life, the individual generates a value experience, but this experience is an empirical value. In conformity with the law, this experience then becomes subject matter for ideal control. Moreover, the individual must be ready to revise his standards if his new moral insights indicate this to be necessary:

> All of the ideals which have hitherto entered into my life should daily be confronted by the standards of the highest insight I have yet been able to attain. This necessarily will mean that I shall have to revise or even reject today some of the standards which seemed final even as recently as four or five years ago. Ideal control is thus a process of never-ending growth.[67]

An absolute concern for mere consistency for its own sake can only stifle the development of ideals. Brightman's previous emphasis on consistency was not meant to endorse a stagnant dogmatism. When King decided to denounce the Vietnam War and when he expanded his conception of the role of civil disobedience in social change, he was not violating the Logical Law requiring consistency; he was exemplifying his conviction that ideal control is a process of endless growth.

King could also find inspiration in Brightman's belief that devotion to ideals not only makes life worth living, but is the most potent force in human history.[68] Did not King often claim that love is the most powerful force in the world? Brightman argued that we can appreciate the power of ideals if we focus on the fear of the possessors of power when they are compelled to confront those who promote these ideals. He pointed to the foes of Jesus and Socrates who in their fear resorted to the death sentence, to Napoleon, who regarded national moral forces as the greatest enemies of his world-empire, and to a government that in wartime conducts fanatical persecution of pacifists. Those in power, beset by fear, use such extreme measures with dissidents because they recognize that a person dedicated to ideal control only develops more energy in the face of ordinary obstacles.

Since King was convinced of the value of a legitimate self-love within the practice of *agape*, he could draw inspiration from Brightman's formulations of the Law of Individualism and the Law of Altruism. The former law states: *"Each person ought to realize in his own experience the maximum value of which he is capable in harmony with moral law."*[69] This law recognizes that society is made up of individuals, and that each person has a moral obligation to himself as a total personality, and therefore must have an interest in the development of value in his own experience. In demonstrating the truth of this law, Brightman argued that if all the actions of the individual were for the sake of the realization of value in others, then no individual would have control over the values realized in his own life, and this would violate the Laws of Autonomy, of Ideal Control, and of the Best Possible and would destroy the motivation for continued social effort. Brightman based the Law of Individualism on the natural tendency in the individual toward self-preservation and on the fact that the realization of value and its actual functioning in experience occur in the consciousness of individuals. While King would recognize the legitimacy of a certain individualism and a proper interest in self, he tended to give less emphasis than Brightman to this Law of Individualism since he was convinced that *agape* may at times demand even the suspension of the law of self-preservation so that through our self-sacrifice we can help create the beloved community. King believed that in such a sacrifice we do not abandon our self-respect and our own interest, but in fact we grow in self-esteem and self-fulfillment by our willingness to risk all to redeem the other.

King could identify more with Brightman's Law of Altruism, *"Each person ought to respect all other persons as ends in themselves, and, as far as possible, to cooperate with others in the production and enjoyment of shared values."*[70] Instead of conflicting with the Law of Individualism, the Law of Altruism requires each person to recognize the right of every other person to fulfill the obligation that the Law of Individualism imposes on him. The Law of Altruism may be seen as a generalization of the Law of Individualism because if each person has an obligation to respect himself as a realizer of value, then he ought to respect other persons as realizers of value and as ends-in-themselves. If an individual does not obey the Law of Altruism, this implies that others need not treat him as a realizer of value. Brightman argued that the Law of Altruism implies that many values are possible only through deliberate cooperation. Without the respect from others that accrues to the individual as a result of the Law of Altruism, the individual is not able to pursue the Axiological Law and the Laws of Individualism, of the Most Inclusive End, or of the Best Possible. Brightman indicated that while Plato, Aristotle, and Epicurus did not emphasize the virtue of benevolence, this virtue was central in Hebrew, Buddhistic, Confucian, and Christian thought. In his Nobel Lecture King also spoke of the perennial religious belief in the power of love:

I am speaking of that force which all of the great religions have seen as the supreme unifying principle of life. Love is somehow the key that unlocks the door which leads to ultimate reality. This Hindu-Moslem-Christian-Jewish-Buddhist belief about ultimate reality is beautifully summed up in the first epistle of Saint John: "Let us love one another; for love is of God: and everyone that loveth is born of God, and knoweth God. He that loveth not knoweth not God; for God is love. If we love one another, God dwelleth in us, and His love is perfected in us."[71]

Brightman regarded Kant as a leading modern proponent of altruism and appealed to his imperative that each person should treat the humanity in himself and in others always as an end and never merely as a means. Brightman found a reemphasis on the theme of altruism in the concern of the philosophers Jeremy Bentham and John Stuart Mill that the aim of the moral man should be "the greatest good of the greatest number."[72] Altruism was also at the heart of the Nonviolent Movement, but as a result of the influence of Nygren, Davis and DeWolf, King's doctrine of altruism was even more open to self-sacrifice than that of Brightman, who stressed that altruism is of value since it is the key to the spiritual and *material* development of all individuals involved.

Brightman concluded his system of moral laws with a statement of the Law of the Ideal of Personality: "*All persons ought to judge and guide all of their acts by their ideal conception (in harmony with the other Laws) of what the whole personality ought to become both individually and socially.*"[73] This law summons individuals to take up the materials of their lives and create the plan of a harmonious whole that they aim to realize:

> The Personalistic Laws and the whole System now find their ultimate unity and consummation in the obligation to form and to apply a conception of a life purpose, which is not only self-imposed and ideal, but also concrete and unified.[74]

King did not have to look to Personalism to discover his moral obligation to form a consistent life plan. Long before his encounter with Personalism, he had chosen to devote his life to the service of others in the ministry, but once he decided that this service involved a total and persistent public assault on segregation, the moral laws of Personalism served to reinforce that commitment.

Toward a Realistic View of Human Nature

While a graduate student at Boston University, King wrote a research paper entitled "How Modern Christians Should Think of Man."[75] The paper was an attempt to synthesize insights in liberal theology about human nature with insights from neo-orthodoxy while avoiding what he regarded as the extreme positions of both schools of thought. The paper revealed his sympathy with the Personalist doctrines on human dignity, reason, freedom, and moral responsibility. At the beginning of the paper he admitted that his thinking about the nature of man was in a state of transition. He explained that at times he leaned toward a "mild neo-orthodox view of man" that stressed the sinfulness of man and the need for perpetual repentance, and at other times he leaned toward liberal theology's view that stressed the essential goodness of man. He indicated that he found some justification for both views in his early experiences in the South:

The former leaning [toward neo-orthodoxy] may root back to certain experiences that I had in the South with a vicious race problem. Some of the experiences that I encountered there made it very difficult for me to believe in the essential goodness of man. On the other hand, part of my liberal leaning has its source in another branch of the same root. In noticing the gradual improvements of this same race problem I came to see some noble possibilities in human nature.[76]

He indicated that he leaned toward liberal theology also because of the "great imprint" many liberal theologians left on him and because of his "ever present desire to be optimistic about human nature."[77] However, in his introduction he also stated that the one-sided generalizations of neo-orthodoxy were not appealing to him, and that liberal theology had too easily cast aside the term "sin" and had failed to realize that many of man's problems result from his sins.

King listed and developed certain truths about the nature of man that modern Christians should believe, namely, man by nature is neither good nor bad, but has potentialities for either, and is a finite child of nature, a rational being, a free and responsible being, a sinner, and a being in need of continuous repentance. In developing the first of these truths, King rejected any one-sided generalization, whether it be a doctrine of original sin or a romantic idealization of man.[78] Neo-orthodox thought, particularly that of Karl Barth, seemed "preposterous" to him, if it intended to claim that through man's misuse of his freedom in the "Fall" he completely lost his goodness and that the image of the divine in him was totally effaced so that he was left totally helpless in his desire for salvation. But extreme liberal and "so-called religious humanistic circles" were also guilty of a one-sided generalization in their sentimental optimism about man's self-perfectibility through the improvement of methods for attaining and applying knowledge. Though he did not indicate it, King was repeating Niebuhr's criticism of liberalism in maintaining that the brutal logic of events discredited this sort of optimism:

> Instead of assured progress in wisdom and decency man faces the ever present possibility of swift relapse not merely to animalism but into such calculated cruelty as no other animal can practice.[79]

In rejecting both of these extreme positions, King stressed the need to return to the life and teachings of Jesus, who emphasized the need for humanity to remain conscious of its humble dependence on God as the source of all being and all goodness. To refute the excessive optimism in some forms of liberalism, King reaffirmed, "There is none good, save one, even God."[80] To refute the pessimism of neo-orthodoxy, he argued that Christ constantly made appeal to a hidden goodness in even the worst of men. The modern Christian must believe that lives are changed when there is a patient belief in the potential good in them and when there is an effort to overcome the potential for evil in them. It was this belief that later became central to the development of his philosophy of nonviolence. *Agape* could confidently and persistently seek reconciliation by appealing to the conscience of the opponent only because of the belief that every man is an image of God and has the capacity with God's grace to turn from evil and to realize his potential for goodness.

In this paper King maintained that every modern Christian should look upon man not only as a being made in the image of God but also as a "finite child of nature."[81] Man is subject to the laws of nature in many of his actions; hence his freedom is limited and is "mixed with natural necessity."[82] Man is not only "a victim of his own sins" but also a "victim of nature" since in many instances the laws of nature interfere with the higher life of man. Moreover, he is a "victim of the blindness and cruelty of his neighbors. . . . This is a liberal emphasis which must not be lost in the modern world, for it takes into account those non-moral sources of evil which often interfere with man and his salvation."[83] Although King did not further develop this point, in effect he did provide an additional reason for opposing segregation. Not only does the cruelty of segregation limit and even deny human freedom and dignity but also it interferes with the salvation of the victims of segregation. Surrounding the victims with hate and injustice spiritually handicaps them daily and makes it all the more difficult for them to be willing to perform the loving and just acts necessary for salvation.

The influences of Kant, Personalism, and liberalism were evident in King's developments of his belief that man is a rational, free, and responsible being. He affirmed that the modern Christian should never lose faith in rationality as one of the supreme resources of man, which enables him to delve into the eternal aspects of reality. While King was mindful of the warnings by many neo-orthodox theologians about the "pride of reason," and although he indicated that this higher power is a peril as well as a supreme gift since it often creates a sense of self-sufficiency in man, still he did emphasize the fact that "reason rightly used remains the prize gift of man."[84] In the exercise of this rationality man is a free and responsible being. "The Kantian 'I ought, therefore I can' should stand out as a prelude in the modern Christian's thinking about man."[85] King here rejected certain attempts in Calvinistic and Barthian thought that claimed that man is a responsible being who is lacking in freedom. Appealing to the Kantian argument, King asked how there could be responsibility without freedom. On this matter he regarded as more logical the tendency of liberal theology to affirm man's freedom and to deny that his conscious purposes are predestined by God. "We must believe that man has the power of choosing his supreme end. He can choose the low road or the high road. He can be true or false to his nature."[86] King's belief in man's psychological freedom became the basis of his confidence that the oppressor, when confronted with *agape* working through nonviolent direct action, could choose to change the direction of his will.

King contended that although some neo-orthodox theologians had overemphasized the sinfulness of man, still the modern Christian should recognize that many evils in the world are due to sin. He characterized as "perilous" the tendency of some liberal theologians to regard sin as a mere " 'lag of nature' which will be progressively eliminated as man climbs the evolutionary ladder. . . ."[87] Even though many of man's shortcomings are due to natural necessities, still ignorance, finiteness, hampering circumstances, and the pressures of animal impulse cannot account for many of his deficiencies, "We must come to see that every human good has its own form of corruption."[88] He here credited Reinhold Niebuhr for highlighting the fact that men sin through intellectual and spiritual pride.[89] The modern Christian must look upon man as a sinner who must ask for forgiveness and be converted. Man is "a being in need of continuous repentance."[90] The turning away from a life of sin because of a change of mind is an event that can occur again and again in a person's experience:

> The habit of perpetual repentance enables us to grow; it helps to keep our conscience awake; it preserves us from the sin of self-righteousness; it helps us to concentrate on our sins rather than the sins of others.[91]

Repentance is an "inestimable privilege." He identified with W. N. Clarke's statement on repentance, "Perpetual repentance is simply perpetual fellowship with Christ. Performed once or a thousand times, it is a most precious act of moral unity with Christ the Saviour."[92] This message of the need for continual repentance proved later to be an essential ingredient of King's doctrine of nonviolence. It served to remind the nonviolent of the need for humility and helped to preserve them from a self-righteousness that would only alienate oppressors and render reconciliation impossible.

The Division within Man

King further examined the complexity of human nature in a sermon entitled "What Is Man?" in *The Measure of a Man*. He explained that the answer to this question about the nature of man mainly determines the political, social, and economic structures of a society, and that the conflict between democracy and totalitarianism is rooted in a division over this question.[93] The manner in which he formulated his position on this question revealed his habitual concern to achieve the more inclusive explanation on any question by synthesizing the partial truths contained in opposing ideologies while avoiding what he regarded as the extreme tenets of these ideologies. As he considered naturalism, he recognized the truth there that man is a biological being and has a kinship with animate nature, but he rejected as pessimistic and false the view of naturalism that man is merely a biological being, that he is a cosmic accident, and that his whole life can be explained in terms of matter in motion.[94] As he reflected on humanism, King accepted the truth there that man possesses noble, spiritual powers, especially the power of reason, but he rejected as excessively optimistic and false the attempt at a glorification of man that borders on deification. The true conception of man does regard man as noble in origin, powers, and destiny. Man is a "marvelous creation" made in the image of God with the unique power to have fellowship with God. In this sense the Psalmist could say of man, "Thou hast made him a little lower than the angels and crowned him with glory and honor."[95] But a true conception of man also regards man as a sinner who has misused his freedom in his individual life and especially in his collective life, and is in need of God's grace.

To emphasize the "strange dualism" and "dichotomy" in man, King quoted Thomas Carlyle:

> There are depths in man that go down to the lowest hell, and heights that reach the highest heaven, for are not both heaven and hell made out of him—everlasting miracle and mystery that he is.[96]

King also alluded to Plato's description of human personality in terms of "a charioteer with two headstrong horses, each wanting to go in different directions."[97] This description, developed in the *Phaedrus*, presupposed Plato's acceptance of the Pythagorean division of the human soul into three "parts," the appetitive, the spirited, and the rational.[98] According to the Pythagorean belief, the appetitive part of the soul is the source of human desires for food, drink, sex, clothing, and shelter. The spirited part causes desires for honor and glory. The rational part enables man to reason and to make choices. In the "myth of the charioteer" Plato stressed the fact that human reason, symbolized by the charioteer who seeks absolute beauty, is confronted with the continuous task of conflicting with the soul's lower desires and of rendering them subordinate to rational ends. In this myth the "good horse," that is "guided by word and admonition only," symbolizes the spirited part since this part is amenable to direction from reason, while the "evil horse," that needs the whip, symbolizes the appetitive part since this part tends to defy reason, be reckless, and disrupt the harmony of the soul.

King asserted that the universal human experience of this perennial struggle causes us to affirm with St. Paul, "The good that I would, I do not; and the evil that I would not, I do," and to cry out with St.

Augustine, "Lord, make me pure, but not yet," as we are aware that "the 'isness' of our present nature is out of harmony with the eternal 'oughtness' that forever confronts us."[99] All of us must decide whether to allow the dichotomy within us to be the source of continual frustration, disillusionment, and bewilderment, or to struggle to transcend this dichotomy and to achieve authentic self-realization and fulfill our destiny by looking to our origin and responding to the love of God.

The Affirmation of the Individual in Existentialism

In explaining his intellectual formation, King indicated that he had read Sören Kierkegaard, Friedrich Nietzsche, Karl Jaspers, Martin Heidegger, and Jean-Paul Sartre. Through a study of the works of Paul Tillich he had become convinced that these existentialists had grasped certain basic truths about the human condition.[100] He thought that they had contributed to our understanding not only of man's "finite freedom" but also of man's estrangement from his own essential nature and of the anxiety that pervades individual and social existence. He deemed it significant that both theistic and atheistic existentialists in their analysis of man's natural condition found it necessary to discuss man's self-estrangement. Although he warned that the existentialists had not provided the "ultimate Christian answer," still he maintained that the Christian theologian might well include insights from them in describing the true state of human existence.

In a research paper at Boston University entitled "What the Mystics Say about God," King referred to Kierkegaard as a mystic and cited passages from his *Purity of Heart Is To Will One Thing*.[101] In this work Kierkegaard raised the ultimate question for his reader "What then must I do?," and gave the answer "Live as an 'Individual.' "[102] He warned his readers that they must work out their existence as individuals and not avoid moral responsibility to God by identifying with "the crowd":

> But the all-knowing One, who in spite of anyone is able to observe it all, does not desire the crowd. He desires the individual.
> . . . But in eternity each shall render account as an individual. That is, eternity will demand of him that he shall have lived as an individual.[103]

The individual is always only one and conscience in its meticulous way concerns itself with the individual. In eternity you will look in vain for the crowd.[104]

He contended that conformity to the crowd destroys the unity of the self and causes self-estrangement.

King could subscribe to Kierkegaard's emphasis on the need for the individual to have a direct relationship with God, a relationship in which one cannot depend on others to make moral decisions for him. When King had to make decisions that would cause him to be denounced by many groups, as was the case when he determined to protest the Vietnam War, he frequently proclaimed that the individual must answer to his own conscience and to God and not conform to the opinions and desires of "the crowd." He called for a "creative maladjusted nonconformity" that would expose the evils entrenched in the status quo and perpetuated by an unthinking majority:

In spite of this prevailing tendency to conform, we as Christians have a mandate to be nonconformists . . . there are some things in our world to which men of goodwill must be maladjusted. I confess that I never intend to become adjusted to the evils of segregation and the crippling effects of discrimination, to the moral degeneracy of religious bigotry and the corroding effects of narrow sectarianism, to economic conditions that deprive men of work and food, and to the insanities of militarism and the self-defeating effects of physical violence. Human salvation lies in the hands of the creatively maladjusted.[105]

King could easily have identified with Kierkegaard's emphasis on the need for each individual to make an absolute commitment to God and to have unquestioning faith in His loving Providence. In "What the Mystics Say about God," King quoted Kierkegaard's assertion, "Yes, to be sure, God knows that man's highest consolation is that God is love and that man is permitted to love Him."[106] Often when King was confronted with seemingly insuperable opposition, he could express his conviction that there would be an ultimate victory for justice because of his belief that "behind the dim unknown standeth God within the shadows."[107]

Another of the main themes in Kierkegaard's works that would have had a special meaning for King was the value of suffering. Kierkegaard claimed that the Christian who lives his faith suffers for several reasons. *First*, he must perform ascetical exercises so that he will not slip into the emptiness of a life devoted to the selfish pursuit of pleasure. *Second*, God does not directly communicate with him, but rather conceals Himself. *Third*, Christ, in whom he believes, defies his intellect since He constitutes a Paradox.[108] How can the eternal and the temporal be combined in one person? Why should Eternal Truth come into the temporal order like any other mortal? Why should He come specifically to suffer?[109] *Fourth*, the authentic Christian must constantly seek to identify with and imitate the suffering Christ.[110] Kierkegaard placed a premium on all these occasions for suffering since suffering can serve to intensify the faith and commitment of the believer. In *Purity of Heart Is To Will One Thing* he stressed the moral necessity of a willingness to suffer all for the Good:

> When the active one suffers, then his suffering has significance for the victory of the Good in the world. When the sufferer . . . willingly takes up his appointed sufferings, he is willing to suffer all for the Good, that is, in order that the Good may be victorious in him.[111]

Although King could share Kierkegaard's concern for the individual and his relationship with God, his commitment to DeWolf's Personalism with its emphasis on evidences for God's existence would cause him to reject Kierkegaard's description of the act of religious faith as a "leap" that contradicts reason.[112] While criticizing Kierkegaard's irrationalism and denying that authentic faith is a "leap in the dark," DeWolf affirmed that faith does involve a leap insofar as the Christian makes an absolute commitment and stakes his all on truths which reason, after having considered all the available evidence, has established as probably true:

> It is the absolute degree of commitment which constitutes a legitimate "leap of faith" beyond rational proof, not the commitment to a belief or cause which one has no reason at all to suppose true or worthy.[113]

Why did King mention Nietzsche among the existentialists who had made such significant contributions to our understanding of man when he clearly rejected his critique of Christian love? It seems evident that no matter how much he rejected his critique of Christianity, Nietzsche did force him to rethink the Christian ethic. No one can read

Nietzsche without being moved by the unique force and imagery in his message. If Nietzsche had not so vehemently condemned Christian love, King might not have defended it so vigorously. His proclamations that Christian love is weakness caused King ultimately to deepen his realization of the power of Christian love, and probably were the reason for his decision to entitle the book containing some of his sermons on love *Strength To Love*. In April 1967, in calling for an unconditional love for all humanity in a sermon entitled "Why I Oppose the War in Vietnam," he explained that the Nietzsches of the world had misinterpreted this love as weak and cowardly and hence had rejected it, whereas in fact, as the supreme unifying principle of life, love is the most powerful force and necessary for the survival of humanity.[114]

It would not have been difficult for King to concur with Brightman's evaluation of Nietzsche. While denouncing Nietzsche's incapacity for pity, his critique of Christianity, and his contempt for the masses, and while granting the existence of errors, ambiguities, contradictions, and exaggerations in Nietzsche's writings, Brightman still attempted to identify insights of permanent value. He found Nietzsche to be a thinker who excelled in sincerity. "Be sincere and courageously pay the full price of sincerity—that is Nietzsche's first truth."[115] He praised Nietzsche for recognizing that personality must challenge convention. Man must free himself from the bondage of custom to give himself to the values that create a great and strong personality. Brightman's own conviction about the duty of the "critical conscience" to scrutinize social mores caused him to be sensitive to the constructive elements in Nietzsche's challenge. He maintained that Nietzsche, by his assault on custom, was following, perhaps unconsciously, Kant's emphasis on autonomy and on a morality structured by values that emerge from personality. Brightman claimed that Nietzsche had the vision to affirm that man, by sheer will power, can become far better than he has dreamed if he struggles against spiritual weakness and exercises his freedom and responsibility. Then too, he saw Nietzsche as proclaiming, "The highest individualism is social."[116] Nietzsche's Zarathustra, like Jesus, spent years in isolation before he came to men, but when he came, he wanted to share his insight with others.[117] Brightman also had praise for Nietzsche as one of the most acute critics of nationalism, and for his opposition to all forms of racializing and especially to anti-Semitism. Brightman charged Hitler with "cultural ignorance" for his distortion and exploitation of Nietzsche's thought. Furthermore, Brightman found in Nietzsche the truth that man needs eternity. He believed that Nietzsche had a profound religious longing in his nature, despite his criticisms of religions. At the conclusion of his evaluation he claimed:

> But it would be difficult to read him with an open mind and not receive an impetus to braver, stronger, more honest living . . . he wrote with beauty and vigor in praise of beautiful and vigorous living.[118]

Although King expressed his indebtedness also to Martin Heidegger, he did not indicate the specific way in which Heidegger had influenced him. But Tillich, the major source of King's interest in the existentialists, in *The Courage To Be* did refer to Heidegger's reflections on the meaning of death.[119] This was a central theme in Heidegger's thought, which he developed in *Being and Time* and which would have appealed to King. King referred to *The Courage To Be* in his doctoral dissertation and used it in writing *Strength To Love*.[120] Even without having a definite belief in an afterlife, Heidegger asserted that every individual ought to respond to the "call of conscience" to form a true attitude toward death as a condition in the process of seeking to overcome self-estrangement and to achieve an authentic existence. In *Being and Time* he stressed the need for the individual to confront the reality of death.[121] He maintained that death is the ultimate possibility for man, a possibility not to be overcome.[122] Death is a prime expression of human finitude. The individual must accept himself as a "Being-towards-Death." When he makes a "resolute decision" to accept himself in all of his negativity, he represents a "freedom toward death." He can then surmount the ordinary fear of death.[123] Heidegger regarded as inauthentic the attitude toward death so prevalent in "everyday existence" whereby one believes that death is a constant occurrence, but speaks of it as if it presents no threat to him.[124] With this inauthentic attitude one obscures and neutralizes the stark reality of death. He reads about death, and may attend funerals, but he tries every possible trick to cultivate an indifference to the potentiality of his own death. He may even consider the abstract and detached proposition, "All men are mortal," without really applying this to himself. The fact that the individual cannot know the time of his death can cause him to blunt his awareness of the inevitable certainty of its occurrence. He then can interpret it as "not yet for the time being." Heidegger described this flight of the individual from death, the innermost absolute potentiality of Being, as a self-alienation.[125] To avoid this alienation from his true self, the individual must in all of his projects "run forward in thought to death," recognize that he lives in the shadow of nonbeing and that death may be imminent at any moment, accept the inevitability of death, and internalize death as the possibility that constitutes the impossibility of existence, which he must face *alone*.

For Heidegger, this acceptance of the reality of death can be beneficial to the individual in several ways. Voluntarily to accept death liberates the individual from the fear that lurks beneath his usual studied indifference toward the possibility of his own death. Then too, since death comes to each individual and thus "individualizes" him, he can achieve a consciousness of the individuality of his own existence only if he isolates himself from the everyday evasive reflections on death that characterize the "one like many," the mass man.[126] His anticipation of his death in his consciousness also permits him a total view of his existence in the world. Moreover, this attitude toward his own death allows him to emerge from some of the restrictions on his freedom in the present, and allows him to live in and for the future.[127] Furthermore, the assimilation of his death in his consciousness can be practically as well as morally beneficial to the individual since it stirs him to attempt to assign only an appropriate significance to his temporal projects and to eliminate concern with the inconsequential. Finally, an authentic attitude toward his death has the effect of vivifying and intensifying the individual's awareness of his most meaningful experiences.[128]

King frequently received threats against his life, and he recognized the need to deal creatively with the imminent possibility of his own death. This was especially true because of his strong belief in an afterlife. He did not permit himself to be crippled by fear. He explained that he did not allow himself to worry about these threats since such a worry would not permit him to function.[129] However, he did recognize the inspirational value of reminding his listeners of the possibility of his assassination as he persistently placed himself in danger. During the Albany Movement he stated, "It may get me crucified. I may die. But I want it said even if I die in the struggle that 'He died to make men free.'"[130] In an interview in 1964 he explained that he felt that his cause was so moral that if he should lose his life, in some way it would aid the cause.[131] Often he told his followers that if a person were cut down in the service of the Movement, no other death could be more redemptive:

Gandhi's death at the hand of an assassin added to the number of distinguished martyrs for a noble cause. But is martyrdom the end? Is it not the beginning of a new life, better and nobler?[132]

The Reverend Andrew Young, who had served as executive vice-president of the Southern Christian Leadership Conference (SCLC), stated that King had known that as the leader of the Movement he would be killed and that he had talked about it "all the time."[133] Young also indicated that in the home of the Reverend Martin Luther King, Sr. death had been a typical topic for a family conversation.[134]

In his notes on the Ante-Nicean Fathers of the Church, King revealed as a graduate student his early fascination with the idea of martyrdom. His only note on St. Ignatius's Epistle to the Romans referred to Ignatius's plea to the Christians of Rome not to save him from martyrdom:

> He asked them to pray rather that he may attain martyrdom. He says that he wants to die willingly for God. He says, "suffer me to become food for the wild beasts, through whose instrumentality it will be granted me to attain to God." Ignatius says in fact that he desires to die, and even if the beasts didn't want to devour him, he would compel them to. He feels that through death he will attain true life.[135]

As a student of church history, King understood the value of the ancient claim that the blood of martyrs is the seed of faith. During the Montgomery Boycott he asked his followers to be willing to die and added, "Once more it might well turn out that the blood of the martyr will be the seed of the tabernacle of freedom."[136] During the Selma Movement he told demonstrators that their willingness to undergo martyrdom in the freedom struggle revealed whether they had discovered a moral significance in their lives:

> I can't promise you that it won't get you beaten. I can't promise you that it won't get your home bombed. I can't promise you won't get scarred up a bit—but we must stand up for what is right. If you haven't discovered something that is worth dying for, you haven't found anything worth living for.[137]

King's colleagues in the Movement shared this "excessive altruism." It was this altruism that inspired SCLC to continue the Mississippi Freedom March in 1966 after James Meredith was shot. This same altruism caused DeWolf, who also participated in this march, to continue to act as mediator between whites and blacks during the crusade in St. Augustine, despite a threat to his life from some whites. It was the recognition of DeWolf's many sacrifices for the Movement and of his crucial role in King's intellectual and moral formation that led the King family to choose him to deliver the eulogy at his funeral. The Reverend Ralph Abernathy also continually demonstrated this spirit of altruism from Montgomery to Memphis. When asked in June 1968 about his reaction to becoming president of SCLC, he explained that he had never expected to succeed King since he had assumed that they would die together.[138]

King stressed that in order for a person who practices nonviolence to be willing to endure suffering and to risk death, he must be able to master fear. He quoted Epictetus, the Stoic philosopher who had been a slave, "For it is not death or hardship that is a fearful thing, but the fear of hardship and death."[139] Epictetus intended to construct a philosophy that would enable man to attain tranquillity. To achieve this state, man must learn to distinguish between events within his power and events not in his power. He must accept the latter as expressions of the divine will. Any discontent with these events is equivalent to rebellion against the divine will. Thus without complaint man must accept sickness, the loss of honors or wealth, prison, and the death of a loved one. His tranquillity depends on his ability to resign himself to them as manifestations of the divine will. Even though man does not have control over these events, he can have control over his judgments about them. The will of man is such that it can determine that no external event can conquer it. "What disturbs men's minds is not events, but their judgments on events."[140] Therefore, not death but rather the fear of death is the cause of a cowardly spirit. Epictetus had praise for Socrates for achieving an indifference to imprisonment, exile, and even death as merely external events.[141] He found special consolation in Socrates' expression of this spirit of indifference at his trial when he instructed his accusers that nothing evil can happen to a virtuous man.[142] Epictetus maintained that to achieve peace of mind, man must order his desires in accordance with right reason, realize what is within his power, and liberate himself from morbid emotions such as the fear of death. God does not give man complete control over external events, but He does give man the power to deal rightly with his reactions to these events.

King often emphasized the Christian and Stoic ideals of the acceptance of the unalterable, resignation to the will of God, and inner peace:

The Christian faith makes it possible for us nobly to accept that which cannot be changed, to meet disappointments and sorrow with an inner poise, and to absorb the most intense pain without abandoning our sense of hope. . . . God is able to give you the power to endure that which cannot be changed.[143]

After his reference to Epictetus on the fear of death King wrote:

A positive religious faith does not offer an illusion that we shall be exempt from pain and suffering, nor does it imbue us with the idea that life is a drama of unalloyed comfort and untroubled ease. Rather, it instills us with the inner equilibrium needed to face strains, burdens, and fears that inevitably come, and assures us that the universe is trustworthy and that God is concerned.[144]

In referring to the peace emphasized by St. Paul, King stated, "True peace, a calm that exceeds all description and all explanation, is peace amid storm and tranquillity amid disaster."[145]

King's conviction about the validity of Personalism could only have been strengthened as he reflected on Karl Jaspers's belief in the unique and irreplaceable value of the human personality and in the principle that whatever I experience as essentially real owes its reality in my experience to the fact that I myself exist as an individual. Jaspers explained that because of this principle, ultimate questions that I might raise about the meaning of the world and about my own identity arise from my personally and historically determined situation.[146]

According to Jaspers, as I look upon my situation, I find everything to be transitory and uncertain, and my lack of certitude about my situation fills me with doubt and anxiety. As a consequence, I look for some kind of "Being" that can give stability and permanence to my self. Neither philosophy nor science can save me from existential uncertainty. Philosophy lacks a factual, objective basis for its assertions, and all scientific theories are but intellectual constructs that are subject to revision and that fall short of absolute truth. In my search for certitude I am thrown back on my self in its concrete situation. Analyzing this self, I recognize that a part of the self can be treated as an object among other objects and can be subjected to scientific examination, but another part of the self, "possible existence," cannot be regarded as a mere object. It is that part of the self that fulfills itself by its free decisions. Existence is real only as freedom. Only in the act of choice do I recognize myself for the first time as my true self.[147] No abstract intellectual operations nor any emotional, sentimental, or instinctive impulses can yield the certitude I achieve through the exercise of my freedom. My acts of free choice allow me to be creative and to transcend *to some degree* the limitations imposed on me by my natural environment. Only through my individual free acts can I attain true personal authenticity. While the self achieves realization through free acts, the self has a history, and so when I choose, the historicity of my self limits the freedom in my choice. My past weighs heavy on my present decisions. My freedom now is limited by my historically molded personality. My present choices are further restricting the freedom of my future choices. Then too, my present decisions cannot take place independently of the world as my natural environment. I must incorporate this environment in my decisions. Thus the world serves not only as the necessary theater for the operation of my will but also as the source of restrictions on my will.

King had found in Personalism a similar emphasis on the limited nature of human freedom. While DeWolf presented arguments for the freedom of the will, he stressed also that man is limited in his physical existence, knowledge, and power, and that his choices are largely subject to forces within him that are out of harmony with his conscious purposes.[148] Brightman maintained:

Man's free choice is always limited by his past, his surroundings and his imaginative powers. Beyond these, no choice is available. All choice is within limits. The field of choice is always limited— by limits some of which are within a given personality and some external to it.[149]

Tillich defined man as essentially "finite freedom," i.e., man "is free within the contingencies of his finitude."[150] In his dissertation King summarized Tillich's appreciation of the role of some of the factors that serve as the context that imposes limitations on the operation of freedom:

Decisions issue from a self which has been formed by nature and history; the self includes bodily structures, psychic strivings, moral and spiritual character, communal relations, past experiences (both remembered and forgotten), and the total impact of the environment. . . . Yet having a destiny does not contradict freedom, as "fate" does, because persons can realize their destinies.[151]

Tillich viewed "destiny" as man himself as he has been formed by nature, history, and himself.[152] In *Strength To Love* King subscribed to this concept of destiny. He asserted that freedom always operates within the context of a "predestined structure." "Freedom is the act of deliberating, deciding, and responding within our destined nature."[153] He also contended that fatalism errs in seeing destiny as the sole determinant of human action. Destiny is but a set of influences on human action that still contains a significant degree of self-determination. "An abiding expression of man's higher spiritual nature is his freedom."[154] He did extol the value of Stoic resignation for responding to evils over which man has no control, but he also claimed that man ignores his own spiritual essence when he resorts to this resignation in the face of the evils of segregation and other forms of oppression which he has the freedom and moral responsibility to resist.

Jaspers affirmed that the individual can attain to "Transcendence," that is, God, through "limit situations," such as extreme suffering, decisive struggle, the consciousness of guilt, and the imminence of death.[155] In these situations man can experience not only the limit of his existence but also at the same time the enveloping presence of the transcendent Absolute. Man's doubt, disquietude, and distress with his situation are the conditions for his successful search for Transcendence. Although, like Jaspers, King had his most profound experiences of God in the midst of deep personal anguish, he would not, like Jaspers, claim that God is experienced only as an "outer limit" of his existence, but was able to relate that he had experienced the reality of the presence of God within himself.[156]

King expressed his indebtedness to the existentialists also for revealing the perilous character of human existence and for recognizing that history is a series of unreconciled conflicts.[157] In his reflections on "the law of the day" and "the passion of the night" Jaspers illustrated the fearful and tragic possibilities and risks that make for such a precarious world.[158] He found contradictions in human existence that cannot be resolved. No good exists without evil, no truth without falsehood, no happiness without sorrow, no freedom without dependence, no communication without solitude, no life without death.[159] History may exhibit signs of progress but it also discloses evidence of progressive destruction. While the law of the day creates order in life, demands coherence and rationality, and seeks to execute meaningful projects, the passion of the night destroys every order and leads man back to chaos. As a result of the opposition by the law of the night, man is destined to suffer "shipwreck."[160] Nonetheless, Jaspers maintained that it is man's privilege to accept the dangers and destructive forces in his existence. He is capable of giving meaning to "shipwreck" and of using it to gain access to Transcendence. When man experiences the nonbeing of all accessible being, he can experience the Being of Transcendence. Strangely enough, Tillich, who spoke of the Transcendent Ground of all existence, reduced Jaspers's appeal for a "philosophical faith" as the means of achieving Transcendence to a recommendation of "a new conformity," despite Jaspers's insistence that such a faith would not be dogmatic.[161]

The freedom of the individual was also the foundation of Jean-Paul Sartre's existentialism. Sartre affirmed that man's existence precedes his essence in the sense that man is only what he wills himself to be.[162] In *The Courage To Be* Tillich claimed that one could consider Sartre's statement "The essence of man is his existence" to be "the most despairing and the most courageous sentence in all Existentialist literature."[163] Sartre asserted that man first exists, encounters himself, surges up in the world, and defines himself afterwards. The objects that surround man constitute "being-in-itself" (*l'en-soi*), which is dense, silent, and self-contained, whereas human consciousness is "being-for-itself" (*le pour-soi*), which expresses its freedom by perpetually attempting to transcend itself. Man feels that he is inferior to the fullness of being and consequently strives to complete himself. In seeking the fullness of being and in wishing to be conscious of this fullness, man is seeking an impossible goal. Consciousness always implies a lack of being and a desire to go beyond the present and therefore cannot coexist with the fullness of being. Since man strives for the impossible, to become a God, Sartre described him as a "futile passion."[164]

Condemned to the exercise of his freedom, the Sartrian man gives meaning to a world he regards as absurd in itself. In his choices man is not subject to a God. God cannot exist. The assertion of His existence would be a denial of the fact of the absolute freedom of man. God cannot exist also because by definition He would have to be the plenitude of being as conscious of itself, but "being-in-itself" and "being-for-itself" are two types of being that exclude each other. Consciousness can never be content to be self-contained. In the absence of a God each man must choose, but in his choices he must be responsible for all humanity.[165] The freedom of others is implied in his own. In his freedom he chooses freedom for all humanity. The happiness and ethical image of humanity depends on him. In requiring the individual to be a self-legislator for humanity, Sartre was in effect revitalizing Kant's demand that we ought to act in such a way that we can universalize our maxims. To illustrate the type of responsibility that he wished every individual to develop, Sartre pointed to the experience of those who had worked for the French Underground in World War II. He explained that every individual in the Resistance Movement was in all circumstances alone. Each was prepared to be arrested alone and tortured alone, and yet, without encouragement, each was protecting all the others. Each could count on himself alone, and yet each fulfilled his responsibility and role in history. In such authentic choice there was no room for "bad faith" or self-deception that marks the coward who evades responsibility by hiding behind norms, necessities, heredity, class, or the state. However, such authentic choices generate anxiety since they must be made with a sense of responsibility for all human beings. Man suffers in these choices because he must make them without any comforting support. He can look to no God for guidance. Nor can traditional values and moral codes help man invent and project himself since these values and codes are only reminders of the decisions of others.

The fact that King mentioned his indebtedness to Sartre indicated the strength of his determination to accept truth from every position, no matter how antithetical to his own. He could see value in Sartre's doctrine of human freedom, even though he would reject the atheism at the basis of that doctrine. In 1956, at the First Annual Institute on Nonviolence and Social Change in Montgomery, King proclaimed, "There is nothing in all the world greater than freedom."[166] He could subscribe to the notion that one must choose for all humanity because of his own conviction about the interrelated structure of humanity, even though he would have to reject Sartre's notion of moral self-legislation, and even though at times he used traditional precedents as moral arguments for his decisions. No doubt King had Sartre in mind when he acknowledged that the existentialists saw that the world is filled with anxiety and threatened with meaninglessness.[167] In *The Courage To Be* Tillich referred to Sartre's play *No Exit* as his attempt at "taking the situation of meaninglessness upon himself."[168] Sartre provided King with a vision of the nothingness that pervades all of man's projects when he claims for himself the self-sufficiency of the Deity as he confronts what he considers to be an absurd world. The anxiety and despair that marred Sartre's conception of the material world and human relations were but negative arguments for King to demonstrate the value of the life of *agape*.

Although in his description of his intellectual formation King did not mention the philosopher Gabriel Marcel as one of the existentialists who influenced his thinking, he did refer to Marcel in *Strength*

To Love as he examined the implications of religious faith in the life of the individual believer. King indicated that the Scriptures speak of two types of faith.[169] In one type "the mind's faith" is directed toward a theory when the intellect assents to a belief that God exists. In the other type "the heart's faith" is centered in a Person when the believer makes a total commitment to God in a trusting act of self-surrender. This latter faith does not rest content with a theory about a Person. King felt that a true relationship to God has to include this faith. He appealed to the claim of Marcel that "faith is *believing in*, not *believing that*."[170] He perceived the value in Marcel's notion that faith may be compared to "opening a credit, which puts me at the disposal of the one in whom I believe."[171]

When Marcel in *The Mystery of Being* introduced this notion of opening a credit as an example of belief, he warned that we should not be hypnotized by the material aspect of this operation in the business world.[172] He quickly moved beyond the restrictions inherent in the notion of credit, and asserted that when my belief places me at the disposal of someone, this means that I pledge not only *what I have* but also *what I am*. Marcel supplemented the notion of credit with the metaphor of "rallying." If I *believe in,* I *rally to;* with that sort of interior gathering of oneself which the act of rallying implies."[173] He thus contended that the strongest or most living belief is one which absorbs most fully all of the powers of our being. He claimed that this act of faith and trust in God rescues the individual from the anxiety, confusion, and even despair that arises from the uncertainty and instability of the human condition. In the act of faith the believer no longer regards God as an objective entity separate from himself, but rather is open to God as "incarnate" in himself, in others, and in the material world. King shared this insight when he affirmed, "We shall be delivered from the accumulated weight of evil only when we permit the energy of God to come into our souls."[174] Marcel compared the believer to a lover who offers his own self and the world to his beloved. In an act of "consecration" the believer offers all to God as his freedom responds to God's freedom. Marcel saw this act of consecration as an act of restitution since God is the creator of the very gift that the believer offers to Him. As King proclaimed the condition for world peace, he revealed that he shared Marcel's vision of the need for men to be open to the gift of God's presence:

Our age-old and noble dream of a world of peace may yet become a reality, but it will come neither by man working alone nor by God destroying the wicked schemes of men, but when men so open their lives to God that He may fill them with love, mutual respect, understanding, and goodwill. Social salvation will come only through man's willing acceptance of God's mighty gift.[175]

Racism — The Denial of Human Personality

In *Where Do We Go From Here: Chaos or Community?* King examined the nature of racism. This work revealed that he had derived his theoretical understanding of the nature of racism mainly from George Kelsey, his professor at Morehouse College, and anthropologist Ruth Benedict. King presented the definition of racism given by Kelsey in *Racism and the Christian Understanding of Man*:

> Racism is a faith. It is a form of idolatry. . . . In its early modern beginnings, racism was a justificatory device. It did not emerge as a faith. It arose as an ideological justification for the constellations of political and economic power which were expressed in colonialism and slavery. But gradually the idea of the superior race was heightened and deepened in meaning and value so that it pointed beyond the historical structures of relation, in which it emerged, to human existence itself.[176]

To explain how racism is a faith Kelsey relied on the definitions of faith of the theologian H. Richard Niebuhr as "trust in that which gives value to the self" and as "loyalty to what the self values."[177] Kelsey contended that racism is a faith because the racist looks upon his race as the source of his personal value. The racist derives the meaning and worth of his life from the fact that it is part of the racial whole. Driven by a sense of insecurity, the racist feels the need to be attached to a power center and seeks an absoluteness and immortality by relying upon what he regards as the wholeness and permanence of his race.[178] He looks upon his race as the value center that illuminates all other values. It is upon the foundation of race that he organizes his private life and public institutions, even his religious institutions. Hence, the racist does not raise questions about the rightness or wrongness of his race. The racist believes that the members of his race, the "in-race," simply because they are members, possess goodness and worth. Thus he even attributes goodness to criminals, degenerates, and enemies if they are members of his race.[179] For him, the primary consideration is whether one belongs to the in-race. Consequently, if a member of the "out-race" gives evidence of possessing a noble character, that individual is nonetheless judged by the in-race to be depraved. As a member of the out-race, he is condemned as a radically defective being, and his nobility is rejected since the in-race has determined that this nobility inheres in his "unalterably corrupt humanity."[180] King further identified with this interpretation when he affirmed:

> Racism is a philosophy based on a contempt for life. It is the arrogant assertion that one race is the center of value and object of devotion before which other races must kneel in submission.[181]

Kelsey claimed that racism as a faith is a form of idolatry since the racist makes his race his god. It attempts to elevate a human factor to the level of the ultimate. Kelsey appealed to Martin Luther's statement that "trust and faith of the heart alone make both God and idol. . . ."[182] That race has become a god to the racist is evident from its power to give substance and direction to all of his cultural institutions. Kelsey argued that if a racist is also a "Christian," he is frequently a polytheist. This "Christian" may think that he is observing God's commandments in most of the areas of his life, but even in some of these areas he allows the idol of race to shape his attitudes, decisions, and actions. Kelsey perceived that this polytheism infects a sizeable group of Christians who will not recognize the religious implications of American racial traditions and practices, but rather maintain that segregationist racial practices indicate merely amoral expressions of private preference. While Christians affirm that all men are created in the image of God and affirm that man's essence lies in his spirit, still when they have to make decisions on race, they make judgments "which clearly indicate their belief that the races are poles apart in the order of humanity and that the ground of the great human differences lies in the genes."[183]

Ruth Benedict defined racism as:

> . . . the dogma that one ethnic group is condemned by Nature to hereditary inferiority and another group is destined to hereditary superiority. It is the dogma that the hope of civilization depends upon eliminating some races and keeping others pure. It is the dogma that one race has carried progress throughout human history and can alone ensure future progress.[184]

Kelsey referred to this definition, and explained that although the elimination of races has not been carried to its logical limit in Western history, racists have employed segregation with its reduction of life through "subordination, suppression, isolation, and deprivation" as a substitute for the elimination of the out-race.[185] Kelsey agreed that the logic of racism is genocide because the racist thinks that the alleged deficiency in the out-race is in the very being of its members, and therefore the racist sees extermination of the out-race as the final solution.

King also quoted Benedict's definition of racism, and affirmed that the ultimate logic of racism is genocide.[186] He contended that Hitler, in his mad and ruthless attempt to exterminate the Jews, carried the logic of racism to its ultimate tragic conclusion. With evident dependence on Kelsey, King asserted that although America had not literally aimed to eliminate the Negro, it had through segregation "substituted a subtle reduction of life by means of deprivation," and that when a man denies that another is worthy of equal employment, housing, or education, "he is by implication affirming that that man does not deserve to exist. He does not deserve to exist because his existence is corrupt and defective."[187]

Kelsey explained that when racist ideology uses stereotypes to describe the hated out-race as a whole, this ideology by means of these stereotypes bypasses precisely what is unique in the individual.[188] It deals with the out-race as an undifferentiated mass. This constitutes a denial of the human existence of members of out-races, since to be truly human is to be a responsible individual.[189] He contended that while stereotypes may contain some truth, this truth is compounded with error, exaggeration, omission, and half-truth. Stereotypes by the in-races in power are not designed to present truth, but rather to justify the existing power structures. Moreover, when the racist with his stereotypes has the power to assign a false definition to a situation, he can provoke a response that makes that originally false definition come true.

The white racist uses his stereotypes to avoid contact with the reality of the Negro. Instead of confronting the Negro and seeing him as having a claim upon his justice, the white racist chooses to deal with his own images of the Negro. To explain this situation, Kelsey utilized categories from Martin Buber. Instead of an "I-Thou" relationship that allows for mutual personal development, the racist "I" never chooses to encounter a "Thou" in the Negro because he has made the "Thou" invisible, hidden by his own stereotypes. The racist has reduced the Negro to "the World of It," the world of objects and things that the racist attempts to manipulate and appropriate.[190] In this process the racist does not achieve authentic self-knowledge since he feels he must always experience the member of the out-race as anti-thetical to himself in the order of humanity, and thereby he excludes the communion that is the condition for this self-knowledge. Only through the "Thou" does anyone become an "I." In this sense King called racism "total estrangement" since "it separates not only bodies, but minds and spirits."[191]

Chapter 4

The Moral Obligation to Resist Collective Evil

Thoreau's Noncooperation with an Evil System

King had his first contact with a theory of nonviolent resistance as a student at Morehouse College. There he read Henry Thoreau's essay "On the Duty of Civil Disobedience." In *Stride Toward Freedom* he explained that he was deeply moved by the essay and fascinated by Thoreau's idea of refusing to cooperate with an evil system.[1] In this essay Thoreau appealed to the citizens of Massachusetts to refuse to cooperate with a system that involved them in the evils of slavery, the mistreatment of Indians, and the injustice of the war with Mexico. He maintained that those who called themselves abolitionists should at once withdraw their support, both in person and property, from the government of Massachusetts. He contended that voting for the right is in effect doing nothing for it. It is only a feeble expression of one's desire that the right should prevail. Wisdom dictates that the individual should not leave the right to the mercy of chance, nor wish it to prevail through the power of the majority. "There is but little virtue in the action of masses of men."[2] He thought it none too soon for all honest men to "rebel and revolutionize" when a sixth of the population of the nation created as a refuge of liberty were slaves, and when the nation unjustly overran a foreign country and subjected it to military law. He emphasized the radical nature of the protest he proposed:

Action from principle—the perception and the performance of right—changes things and relations; it is essentially revolutionary, and does not consist wholly with any thing which was. It not

110

only divides states and churches; it divides families, aye, it divides the *individual*, separating the diabolical in him from the divine.[3]

Thoreau affirmed that in a government that imprisons any unjustly, the proper place for a just man, a free spirit who must resist such a system, is a prison, and it is there that the fugitive slave, the Indian who wishes to plead the wrongs to his race, and the Mexican prisoner on parole should find him.[4] For jail is the only house in a slave state in which a free man can abide with honor. The demands of conscience must come before civil obedience. "I was not born to be forced. I will breathe after my own fashion":[5]

Must the citizen ever for a moment, or in the least degree, resign his conscience to the legislator? Why has every man a conscience, then? I think that we should be men first, and subjects afterward. It is not desirable to cultivate a respect for the law so much as for the right. The only obligation which I have a right to assume is to do at any time what I think right.[6]

Thoreau believed in the effectiveness of a creative minority who serve the state by resisting it with the intention of improving it. A minority is powerless and not even a minority when it conforms to the majority, but "it is irresistible when it clogs by its whole weight."[7] These very few who serve the state with their consciences and for the most part necessarily resist it are the heroes, patriots, martyrs, reformers in the great sense, and *men*. Though the state treats these men of conscience as enemies, they have the capacity to transform the state:

I know this well, that if one thousand, if one hundred, if ten men whom I could name—if ten *honest* men only—aye, if *one* HONEST man, in this State of Massachusetts, *ceasing to hold slaves*, were actually to withdraw from this copartnership, and be locked up in the county jail therefore, it would be the abolition of slavery in America.[8]

These patriots stand in sharp contrast with the mass of men who are commonly esteemed as good citizens and yet serve the state not as men mainly but as machines with their bodies since in most cases they do not exercise moral judgment. Moreover, patriots differ from most legislators, politicians, lawyers, ministers, and officeholders who serve the state chiefly with their heads, but who rarely make any moral distinctions, and who, though they do not intend it, are as likely to serve the devil as God. Thoreau deplored the fact that the majority regards as useless and selfish the patriot who listens to the demands of conscience, rejects the unjust measures of the state, is willing to accept the penalties for his resistance, and gives himself entirely to his fellowmen, while it regards as a benefactor and philanthropist the man who gives himself only partially to his fellowmen. In an address Thoreau delivered at the Anti-Slavery Convention at Framingham, Massachusetts, on July 4, 1854, he proclaimed that individual citizens are the guardians of justice. "The law will never make men free; it is men who have got to make the law free. They are the lovers of law and order who observe the law when the government breaks it."[9]

At the beginning of the Montgomery Boycott, King remembered this essay and became convinced that what he was proposing to do in the boycott was related to Thoreau's principle of noncooperation, and he persuaded his followers to be true to their consciences and their God and not to cooperate with an evil system that refused to recognize their personal dignity.[10] However, despite this acknowledged similarity, there were at least three significant differences between Thoreau and King in their defense of the principle of noncooperation with an evil system. First, Thoreau spoke at times as if he wanted noncooperation to develop into an attempt to destroy the political system. This was evident not only in his pleas that honest men should rebel and revolutionize, that they should withdraw their support from the government of Massachusetts, and that action from principle is essentially revolutionary, but also in his declaration that he could not recognize a slave's government as his government.[11] In contrast, King never intended his own protests to be revolutionary in this sense. His relentless efforts to secure voting rights demonstrated his confidence in the potential of the political system for the promotion of individual freedom. Moreover, when King called for public opposition to unjust segregation laws, he qualified his protest by emphasizing that one's willingness to go to prison for a civil disobedience that seeks to arouse the conscience of the community expresses the highest respect for law. Furthermore, while Thoreau opposed unjust laws because they violated the moral law, King often explained that he wanted to change local segregation ordinances, not only because they violated the moral law but also because they defied the law of the land.[12]

A second difference between the noncooperation of Thoreau and that of King was that Thoreau at times revealed himself to be a philosophical anarchist. Not only was Thoreau opposed to the actions of the existing government, but also his individualism and his belief in the perfectibility of man led him to the conviction that it would be better for man, as he develops himself, to have no government at all.[13] Although in some passages of his essay he reminded men of their moral obligation to improve the government by their protests, still he regarded any government, however improved, as only an intermediate stage and an "impediment" which would become unnecessary when all men as individuals could govern themselves.[14] As a student of Kant's ethics, he valued the principle of moral autonomy and felt the need to secure the independence of the individual in the social sphere. At the very beginning of his essay he disclosed his philosophical anarchism when he asserted:

I heartily accept the motto,—"That government is best which governs least;" and I should like to see it acted up to more rapidly and systematically. Carried out, it finally amounts to this, which also I believe,—"That government is best which governs not at all," and when men are prepared for it, that will be the kind of government which they will have.[15]

King could not subscribe to this negative view of government. His philosophical and theological training especially in Personalism had endowed him with a deep sense of community that caused him to avoid the extreme of Thoreau's individualism. In opposition to this type of individualism, King's vision of the possibilities of the political process inspired him to call for an expanded role for government in the lives of individuals, so that the government as a moral agency could utilize its vast resources to provide the framework necessary for all individuals to develop as persons. While Thoreau urged individuals not to cooperate with the political system, King initiated extensive voter registration drives to assist citizens to become actively involved in the political system.

A third difference between the noncooperation of Thoreau and that of King was that Thoreau approved of violence as a means to achieve social justice. In defending John Brown's raid on Harper's Ferry, Thoreau declared, "I do not wish to kill or to be killed, but I can foresee circumstances in which these things would be by me unavoidable."[16] Thoreau's opposition to the evil of four million black persons in slavery caused him to claim on behalf of Brown, "The Sharps rifles and the revolvers were employed in a righteous cause."[17] Throughout King's protests, despite the countless provocations, as a matter of moral conviction he consistently rejected violence by demonstrators as an instrument of social change.

In his admiration for Thoreau's belief in the supremacy of the moral law, the sacred rights of the individual conscience, and the value of a creative minority in resisting an evil system, King chose not to indicate how Thoreau's philosophy differed from his own. He seemed to accord special treatment to Thoreau in this respect since in his appraisal of other thinkers he usually was quick to point out what he thought were their limitations even when he wished to express his indebtedness to them. His respect for Thoreau only grew as he continued to apply the principle of noncooperation. In 1962, he claimed, "It goes without saying that the teachings of Thoreau are alive today; indeed, they are more alive today than ever before."[18] He maintained that the creative protest expressed in the Montgomery Boycott, the sit-ins, the Freedom Rides, and the Albany Movement was "an outgrowth of Thoreau's insistence that evil must be resisted and no moral man can patiently adjust to injustice."[19]

Socrates' Defense of Civil Disobedience

In defending the moral legitimacy of his civil disobedience, King appealed also to the example of Socrates. In his "Letter from Birmingham Jail" he claimed, "To a degree, academic freedom is a reality today because Socrates practiced civil disobedience."[20] In an attempt to challenge King's right to civil disobedience, an editorial in *National Review* in 1967 asked King to reread the *Crito* in which Socrates rejected the notion that he should disobey the laws.[21]

While it is true that in the *Crito* Socrates expressed his reverence for the laws of Athens and refused to disobey them by escaping from prison, it would not be valid to infer from his obedience to these laws he deemed just that he would endorse obedience to any law anywhere simply because it was a law. His life-long search for a certain knowledge of an authentic objective morality, as well as his conception of himself as a "gadfly" of the state who challenged conventional beliefs and codes of conduct and aroused individuals to care for the moral condition of their souls, would scarcely have allowed him to accept any automatic identification of local legality with universal morality. Then too, as the *Crito* indicated, Socrates was opposed mainly to that type of civil disobedience that would destroy the state.[22] He realized that his own proposed escape might be interpreted by the Athenians as a total disregard for law, and he was concerned lest the example of such an escape might provoke a general spirit of anarchy. King also was concerned that his actions not encourage anarchy, and therefore he willingly accepted the penalty of imprisonment for his civil disobedience to uphold public compliance with the general legal system in which he believed. Moreover, even in the *Crito* Socrates did refer to the fact that the laws offered him the alternatives of obeying them or of persuading them that their commands were unjust.[23] It would be difficult to understand how Socrates could not regard King's civil disobedience as a legitimate means for the persuasion of lawmakers and the moral education of citizens since he petitioned for a redress of grievances before Federal, state, and municipal authorities. Only when necessary did he resort to selective disobedience of unjust laws, while at the same time professing reverence for the notion of law and demonstrating his sincerity by his acceptance of the penalty. Furthermore, in the *Apology*, which contains Socrates' defense at the trial, he explained what his reply would be if the court offered to acquit him on the condition that he would stop his philosophizing. His reply clearly indicated that his first allegiance was religious and moral, and not political:

> I should reply, Gentlemen, I am your very grateful and devoted servant, but I owe a greater obedience to God than to you, and so long as I draw breath and have my faculties, I shall never stop practicing philosophy and exhorting you and elucidating the truth for everyone that I meet.[24]

St. Augustine's Limitations on Civil Disobedience

In developing the defense of his civil disobedience King referred also to St. Augustine's contention in *De libero arbitrio* that an unjust law is no law at all.[25] While St. Augustine did state that there can be laws that do not deserve the name "laws" since they cause injustice, it is evident from his writings that he could scarcely be considered an advocate of civil disobedience. In general, he taught that the authority of the ruler must be obeyed because it comes from God. He quoted Christ's statement to Pilate, "You would have no power over me unless it had been given you from above."[26] Another of his favorite texts was from the thirteenth chapter of St. Paul's Epistle to the Romans:

> Let every person be subject to the governing authorities. For there is no authority except from God, and those that exist have been instituted by God. Therefore, he who resists the authorities resists what God has appointed and those who resist will incur judgment. . . . Therefore, one must be subject, not only to avoid God's wrath, but also for the sake of conscience.[27]

St. Augustine contended that rulers, no matter how wicked or tyrannical they are, should receive from their subjects both obedience and reverence.[28] God uses the evil actions of wicked rulers to punish the actions of the vicious and to test the patience and fidelity of the virtuous. Wicked rulers by their actions serve to instruct the virtuous in humility and in a due dependence on eternal values.

St. Augustine did allow one exception to the general obligation of civil obedience. Civil disobedience would be legitimate and necessary if the laws or the commands of the ruler are contrary to God's ordinances.[29] God as the higher authority must be obeyed. "For as among the authorities of human society the greater authority is obeyed before the lesser, so must God above all."[30] If rulers command us to do what God forbids or omit what God commands, then they must be disobeyed. Christians must disobey when the ruler interferes with the practice of their faith and with the attainment of their eternal salvation, as when the emperor commanded Christians to worship idols.[31]

He further qualified his position when he maintained not only that an individual by appealing to his conscience may decide that certain laws that do not interfere with his faith still do not coincide with God's Will and hence are unjust, but also that the individual must obey them if it is necessary to prevent anarchy. Such an inconsistency would have been repugnant to King, who believed that one should obey a human law only if it conforms to the divine law. In *A Theology of the Living Church* DeWolf had defined the moral obligation to give *absolute* obedience only to God's law, and to disobey any human law which ignores that law:

> God is the one giver of law worthy of absolute obedience. Only the law of the holy God is holy. People in all lands know that prudence requires the paying of some deference to human lawmakers. Legislators have the power to determine what one must do or refrain from doing to avoid the onus and penalties which fall upon the lawbreaker. But conscience may contradict pru-

dence. Legislators are often corrupt or arbitrary and laws are frequently unjust. To do one's duty sometimes requires the violation of law.[32]

St. Augustine advised slaves that they should not be too concerned about being subject to evil masters since all are on earth for but a brief period, and the main concern of all should be eternal salvation. He was strongly influenced by the Stoics, and revealed some of this influence when he reminded slaves that no matter how they were treated by their masters, they still had "inner freedom," the freedom of their minds and souls. "The servitude of the soul is one thing, the servitude of the body quite another."[33] He seemed here to be expressing the very tolerance of injustice that King denounced in contemporary Christians. St. Augustine claimed that slavery, like the state, is a necessary remedial institution for man as a sinner. Slavery is a just punishment for man's sin and "is appointed by that law which enjoins the preservation of the natural order and forbids its disturbance; for if nothing has been done in violation of that law, there would have been nothing to restrain by penal servitude."[34] He did add that a master should love his slave as a fellowman and not treat him as an inanimate possession.[35] Nevertheless, he did not make the further necessary assertion that Christian justice and love demand that the master free the slave. If St. Augustine thought it necessary to support the institution of slavery, there is no reason to doubt that if he were confronted with the system of segregation, he would have taught compliance with the laws perpetuating that system.

St. Thomas's Defense of Civil Disobedience

As part of his justification for the disobedience of unjust laws, King referred to the doctrine of St. Thomas Aquinas that an unjust law is a human law that is not based on the *eternal law* and the *natural law*.[36] King did not explain this reference, but if he had, his own defense of civil disobedience might have received even more acceptance. Aquinas understood the *eternal law* to be God's plan for His creatures which directs their actions to the attainment of their ends. "The *eternal law* is nothing else than the exemplar of divine wisdom, as directing all actions and movements."[37] All creatures below man follow this *eternal law* unconsciously as they follow their natural tendencies. They do not have the freedom to act in opposition to this *eternal law*. However, man is endowed with the freedom to act in ways contrary to this *eternal law*. Therefore, in order that man can observe the *eternal law* in his activities, God endows him with the capacity to reflect on the fundamental tendencies and needs of his nature. Through this use of reason man can come to some knowledge of the *natural moral law*, which is the totality of the universal precepts of right reason concerning the good that is to be pursued and the evil that is to be avoided. This *natural law* is a participation in or a reflection of the *eternal law*, the ultimate rule of all conduct. "The *natural law* is nothing else than the rational creature's participation of the *eternal law*."[38]

Aquinas explained that when man reflects on his basic inclinations, he determines that if he is to develop his potentialities, he ought to live in society. But although it is natural for man to be a social and political being, and it is a part of the *natural law* that he live in a state, this does not mean that any state simply because it is a state automatically enjoys divine approval or that its citizens owe it unquestioning obedience. Aquinas clearly denied that the state has a moral right to pass legislation contrary to the *natural law*:

> Every human law has just so much of the nature of law as it is derived from the *law of nature*. But if in any point it departs from the *law of nature*, it is no longer a law, but a perversion of law.[39]

He concluded that just laws are binding in conscience while unjust laws are not binding in conscience. He was equally clear in his assertion, "He who acts against his conscience sins."[40]

Aquinas's position on the objectives of the state revealed in part his conception of what constitutes a just law. He maintained that the state must promote the common good, the good of the community. The state must therefore preserve internal peace and provide for the defense of the community, must promote the moral well-being of citizens through legislation, and must ensure a sufficient supply of material necessities for the community.[41] He preferred a monarchy that would be most responsive to the needs of the citizens who would have some measure of control through a constitution and through their election of certain magistrates. He argued that legislation must be judged by reason to be just only insofar as it promotes the common good. He stated that a law is unjust if it imposes burdens on citizens merely to satisfy the greed or ambition of the legislator. A law is unjust also if the legislator in its enactment exceeds the powers committed to him, or if the law distributes burdens such as taxes in an unfair and disproportionate manner. "Laws of this kind are acts of violence rather than laws. . . . They do not bind in conscience. . . ."[42]

Aquinas was here denouncing some of the very evils King protested. King saw that violence is systemic when the laws serve only the legislators and those whom they allow to vote, when local legislators to preserve their political and economic power exceed their jurisdiction and through appeals for legal devices, such as interposition and nullification, attempt to block the implementation of Federal laws, and when Federal legislators ignore their obligation to promote the common good by designing that the working poor assume the tax burden of the nation. Then too, when King affirmed that any law that upholds segregation and degrades human personality is unjust and should be disobeyed, he was in effect applying Aquinas's principle that a law that conflicts with the divine law is unjust and ought not be obeyed.[43]

While Aquinas argued that unjust laws, since they are acts of violence, do not bind in conscience, he did add that they would bind in conscience if "the observance of them is required in order to avoid scandal or public disturbance."[44] King also was concerned about the possibility of scandal and the type of public disturbance that would undermine the political structure. He manifested this concern by reminding his followers that they had to be willing to accept the penalty of imprisonment for their public and loving disobedience of unjust laws in order to prove their respect for the very notion of law.[45]

Dialectical Opposition for Total Truth and Freedom

In his 1956 address to the First Annual Institute on Nonviolence and Social Change, King appealed to the thought of Heraclitus and of Hegel to reassure his followers that the rumblings of discontent from Asia, the uprisings in Africa, the nationalistic longings of Egypt, the roaring cannons in Hungary, and the racial tensions in America did not represent retrogression and tragic meaninglessness but rather the necessary pains that accompany the birth of anything new:

Long ago the Greek philosopher Heraclitus argued that justice emerges from the strife of opposites, and Hegel, in modern philosophy, preached a doctrine of growth through struggle. It is both historically and biologically true that there can be no birth and growth without birth and growing pains. Whenever there is the emergence of the new, we confront the recalcitrance of the old. So the tensions which we witness in the world today are indicative of the fact that a new world order is being born and an old order is passing away.[46]

Heraclitus had far-reaching effects on the history of thought as well as on history itself insofar as he strongly influenced not only Plato but also Hegel. Plato depended on Heraclitus for part of his description of changes in the sensible world. Hegel acknowledged his indebtedness to Heraclitus for emphasizing the necessity of opposition for development. "There is no proposition of Heraclitus which I have not adopted in my Logic."[47] In an article, "Hegel's Influence in the Contemporary Social Situation," Brightman maintained, "Hegel's Absolute really resembles the fire of Heraclitus. . . ."[48] Heraclitus chose fire as the primary substance of all things because of the dialectical nature of its existence. In King's seminar on Hegel at Boston University, Professor Peter Bertocci, who had succeeded Brightman, developed the thesis that Heraclitus and Plato were precursors of Hegel's notion of dialectical unity.[49]

Heraclitus affirmed that all things are in a state of constant change. "Everything flows and nothing abides; everything gives way and nothing stays fixed."[50] His predecessors in Greek philosophy had also stressed the role of change in the universe, but he made a significant contribution to the history of thought by his emphasis on the fact that material and spiritual life depends on a tension of opposites. This tension or conflict between opposing forces is essential to reality. Strife is a material and spiritual necessity:

> It should be understood that war is the common condition, that strife is justice, and that all things come to pass through the compulsion of strife. Homer was wrong in saying, "Would that strife might perish from amongst gods and men." For if that were to occur, then all things would cease to exist.[51]

Any life is but a balance of forces struggling with each other for dominance. "Opposition brings concord. Out of discord comes the fairest harmony."[52] He concluded that it is no accident that dynamic balances of opposing forces do exist since a *Logos* (Reason or Law) is present in nature that regulates the struggles between opposites so that they generate desirable vital equilibriums. Man's reason is a participation in this universal reason, and he should strive to recognize the role of conflict in the objective world and in his own spiritual development, the function of reason in directing this conflict, and his obligation to exercise rational control over his individual and political life:

> Men should speak with rational awareness and thereby hold on strongly to that which is shared in common—as a city holds on to its law, and even more strongly. For all human laws are nourished by the one divine law, which prevails as far as it wishes, suffices for all things, and yet is something more than they.[53]

The Personalists frequently appealed to Heraclitus's insights into the nature of reason and change. Thus Ralph Flewelling in "Studies in American Personalism" contended that Personalism "is, in basic principle, as surely expressed in the affirmation of Heraclitus (536–470 B.C.) that the fundamental reality is mind because it alone, of all creation, has the power to differentiate itself from the objective world and even from its own experiences, asserting that this Logos is the permanent principle in a world of change."[54] In presenting his own metaphysics of the person, DeWolf indicated his basic agreement with the message of Heraclitus:

> Everywhere [in the order of nature] there is change and all that can be observed to endure is the orderly pattern or law of change. Like most Personalists, I maintain a dynamic or Heraclitean interpretation of all this, rejecting ideas of unchanging stuff or substance and maintaining instead that various kinds and patterns of process are the very being of reality.[55]

In an examination in DeWolf's course on Personalism, King wrote a summary of Heraclitus's insights into the role of opposition in nature and human development.[56]

Brightman identified with Heraclitus's reverence for the human capacity for rational development. In "A Personalistic View of Human Nature" he explained that Personalism affirms that human nature in some respects is capable of "infinite progress." "It is a denial that any limit can be set, as long as man is conscious, which would render progress impossible."[57] He asserted that reason is the measure of all potentialities and is itself "the seat of inexhaustible further potentialities."[58] Human nature is no definite substantial entity but a process and a "voyage of discovery."[59] Brightman quoted Heraclitus, "The soul's limits thou canst not find as thou goest, even if thou travelest every way—so deep a *Logos* has she. A *Logos* ever-growing is the soul's." He credited him with recognizing that there is an ideal of infinity in the depths of human nature.[60] Such an emphasis by King's professors could only intensify his determination to reject any arbitrary social, political, or economic limitation on the right of individuals to achieve their rational fulfillment.

In an interview with the *Montgomery Advertiser* during the Montgomery Boycott, King stated that Hegel was his favorite philosopher.[61] In *Stride Toward Freedom* he maintained that Hegel's analysis of the dialectical process, despite its defects, helped him see that "Growth comes through struggle."[62] At Boston University he had studied Hegel's *Phenomenology of Mind, Philosophy of History,* and *Philosophy of Right.*[63] These works trace the development of Hegel's Absolute, the Spirit, that includes not only the eternal Trinity, Who must create the world in order to achieve higher levels of self-consciousness through relation to finite spirits, but also the human spirit in its manifestations, especially in its activities in politics, art, religion, and philosophy. The dialectical movements of the Absolute or Spirit in history and in the development of human thought result in the production of greater freedom and truth. The Absolute so guides its dialectical movements that it passes from each position or thesis in history and in thought on to an opposing position or antithesis. This opposing position negates the narrowness and one-sidedness or "abstractness" of the original position, that pretended to represent total truth. At the same time it allows the truth in that position to become explicit. The Absolute thus surrenders its acceptance of the immediate condition of every position so that the truth, however limited, of that position may become part of a more inclusive system. Nor does the Absolute rest content with an opposing position. This opposing position, when seen in isolation, is itself partial and false. The Absolute therefore seeks a synthesis of the limited truths in the opposing positions.

Hegel chose the term *Aufhebung* to designate the stage of synthesis since the term means an annulment, a preservation, and also an elevation. "Because this annulling is an activity of Thought, it is at the same time conservative and elevating in its operation."[64] The synthesis involves an *annulment* of the claim to completeness and universality made by each of the opposing positions. The synthesis involves also a *preservation* of the partial truths of the moments of opposition. Moreover, since the synthesis involves an interrelation of those truths, it thereby constitutes a further *elevation* of the manifestation of the

Absolute in the human community. The dialectical process does not end with any particular synthesis. Each synthesis becomes a new thesis in the search for total truth and freedom. King indicated that Hegel's contention that "Truth is the whole" led him to a philosophical method of rational coherence.[65] As already indicated, rational coherence is one of the Personalist norms of truth.

The Absolute reaches higher levels of self-consciousness by unfolding its inherent contradictions and by attaining the unification of contradictory forces. The Absolute wages a struggle to overcome contradictions in order to bring all that initially stands in opposition to itself into harmony with itself. Under the direction of the Absolute, finite spirits in the world must struggle to overcome their alienation from Spirit by actualizing their spiritual potentialities in self-conscious activities. Thus the Absolute advances as citizens confront their state as an antithesis and pass from their immediate condition of being particular isolated beings by their struggle *both* to identify through obedience and loyalty with the rational content of the laws of the state and to purify the laws of any irrational elements that would obstruct the legitimate exercise of individual freedom. Hegel's assertion that the seriousness, suffering, patience, and labor of the negative constitute the dialectical life of the Absolute in its search for freedom found an echo in King's contention that "Every step toward the goal of justice requires sacrifice, suffering, and struggle, the tireless exertions and passionate concern of dedicated individuals."[66] King further revealed his appreciation of the dialectical process when he explained that blacks should expect that an inevitable counterrevolution will succeed every period of progress, and added:

> A final victory is an accumulation of many short-term encounters. To lightly dismiss a success because it does not usher in a complete order of justice is to fail to comprehend the process of achieving full victory. It underestimates the value of confrontation and dissolves the confidence born of a partial victory by which new efforts are powered.[67]

In the opening paragraph of *Strength To Love* King explained that Hegel held that truth is found neither in the thesis nor in the antithesis, but in the emergent synthesis that reconciles the two.[68] In *Stride Toward Freedom* he used this doctrine to indicate some of the basic aims of nonviolence:

Like the synthesis in Hegelian philosophy, the principle of non-violent resistance seeks to reconcile the truths of two opposites—acquiescence and violence—while avoiding the extremes and immoralities of both.[69]

King recognized that the partial truth in each of these two positions can be included in a meaningful and effective synthesis to achieve social justice, while each of the positions, if considered in isolation from the other, must be rejected as extreme and immoral. He explained that the nonviolent resister can agree with the person who submits to social evils that one should not inflict physical harm on his opponent, and he can also agree with the person who endorses violence that social evils must be resisted. By appealing to the *limited truths in both positions*, the nonviolent resister is able to reject the extremes and pitfalls of *mere* passive acceptance and violent resistance. Hegel's message also enabled King to comprehend the wisdom of Jesus' formula for spiritual success in a hostile world, i.e., for effective nonviolence. After alluding to Hegel in *Strength To Love*, King asserted that Jesus also recognized the need for blending opposites when he asked his disciples to be "wise as serpents and harmless as doves" as he sent them into the world to practice the gospel of love.[70] They would have to possess "incisive thinking, realistic appraisal, decisive judgment . . . firmness of purpose, and solidness of commitment," but they also had to exhibit a capacity for genuine compassion without descending to a weak sentimentality.[71] Inspired by Hegel, King claimed that life at its best is a creative synthesis of opposites in productive harmony.

In developing his own position on human nature, King relied on the same kind of dialectical approach when he maintained, "An adequate understanding of man is found neither in the thesis of liberalism nor in the antithesis of neo-orthodoxy, but in a synthesis which reconciles the truths of both."[72] Then too, in his dissertation he employed this dialectical approach when he warned, "There is always the danger that in revolting against any extreme view one will go to the opposite extreme, failing to see the partial value inherent in the former."[73] He charged that Wieman was guilty of this failure when he so stressed the immanence of God that he completely overlooked the truth in the doctrine of the transcendence of God. In his general evaluation of Wieman and Tillich, King was also quite Hegelian. He contended that both of them were partially correct in what they affirmed and partially wrong in what they denied. Wieman was correct in emphasizing God's goodness but wrong in minimizing His power while Tillich was correct in emphasizing God's power but wrong in minimizing His goodness. King defended the synthesis that affirmed both God's power and His goodness.[74] Furthermore, he was quite dialectical in his attitude toward criticisms leveled at himself and the Movement:

> Whenever we are objects of criticism from white men, even though the criticisms are maliciously directed and mixed with half-truths, we must pick out the elements of truth and make them the basis of creative reconstruction.[75]

King's studies of Heraclitus and Hegel served to heighten his awareness of the dialectic at work in his protests. Thus in "Our Struggle," his analysis of the Montgomery Boycott, he claimed that every attempt to end the protest by intimidation, by the encouragement of Negroes to inform, and by force and violence further unified the Negro community.[76] He cited the following examples to substantiate this claim: (1) The arrest of Rosa Parks served as the catalyst for the inception of the boycott; (2) the Montgomery authorities published a newspaper report about the call for the boycott in the hope of intimidating the Negro population, but by their action they notified thirty thousand Negro readers about the planned protest; (3) the authorities found Rosa Parks guilty and fined her, but this action only increased the number of Negroes who participated in the boycott; (4) the authorities arrested a Negro student on the charge of intimidating passengers on a bus, but since the student was only helping an elderly woman cross the street, this arrest served to solidify the college students' support of the boycott; (5) policemen attempted psychological coercion as they followed each bus on their motorcycles, but this too increased the number of those who joined the boycott; (6) intimidation of Negro taxi drivers caused the creation of a car pool and a resolution to extend the boycott indefinitely; (7) harassment of Negro motorists caused the Negro middle class to join the boycott; (8) the open resistance of the bus company to hiring Negro drivers only intensified the determination of the Negroes not to use the buses; (9) the prediction by the mayor that the Negroes would be back on the buses on the first rainy day only stiffened their opposition; (10) King's arrest for traveling 30 miles per hour in a 25-mile zone just hours before a mass meeting was so provocative that seven mass meetings had to be held to accommodate the numbers willing to attend; (11) the bombing of the homes of King and E. D. Nixon, the former state president of the NAACP, generated moral and financial support from all over the state; (12) the arrest of 89 persons, including 24 ministers, for their participation in the nonviolent protest engendered even further sympathy for the boycott in Montgomery and the nation.[77]

At times King appealed to those insights in Hegel's philosophy of history that could harmonize with the conception of Providence which he had derived from DeWolf and Davis. Hegel had designated as "the Cunning of Reason" the way in which Reason, that is, God, in the pursuit of self-consciousness and freedom uses the passions of individuals to achieve its goals even though these individuals do not have a full consciousness of the implications of their activities.[78] In referring to historically significant individuals, Hegel observed:

> Such individuals had no consciousness of the general Idea they were unfolding, while prosecuting those aims of theirs; on the contrary, they were practical, political men. But at the same time they were thinking men, who had an insight into the requirements of the time—what was ripe for development.[79]

This idea intrigued King. He applied it to Rosa Parks, who was willing to be arrested rather than surrender her bus seat to a white passenger:

> She was anchored to that seat by the accumulated indignities of days gone by and the boundless aspirations of generations yet unborn. She was a victim of both the forces of history and the forces of destiny. She had been tracked down by the *Zeitgeist*—the spirit of the time.[80]

In his 1959 farewell sermon to his congregation at the Dexter Avenue Baptist Church in Montgomery, King returned to this Hegelian insight. "I can't stop now. History has thrust something upon me which I cannot turn away. I should free you now."[81] Though he had not sought leadership, he had come to realize that he himself was in the grip of the *Zeitgeist*. In his Nobel Lecture he reaffirmed his faith in a provident Spirit Who controls the history of the struggle for freedom. He asserted that "something within" had reminded the American Negro of his birthright of freedom, and that "something without" had reminded him that it could be achieved. Then in Hegelian terms he proclaimed:

> Consciously or unconsciously, he had been caught up by the *Zeitgeist*, and with his black brothers of Africa and his brown and yellow brothers in Asia, South America and the Caribbean, the

United States Negro is moving with a sense of great urgency toward the promised land of racial justice.[82]

While King acknowledged his indebtedness to Hegel for certain insights, he did not identify with his general system. Once again, Personalism proved to be the dominant influence on his thinking. In general, the Boston Personalists accepted Kierkegaard's interpretation and criticisms of Hegel.[83] Brightman was the least critical of Hegel. He interpreted all experience in terms of the basic structure of the Hegelian dialectic. In *The Problem of God* Brightman maintained:

Everything which exists stands in contrast with something else . . . every thesis implies some sort of antithesis . . . every opposition leads to a higher level of life, and every struggle points to a higher meaning or synthesis.[84]

He contended that Hegel through his emphasis on the dialectic had made contributions in the philosophy of religion, in the philosophy of history, and in social philosophy, and that Hegel had held that the rights and freedom of the individual reach their true realization in the state. Nonetheless, despite his admiration for Hegel, Brightman added the devastating qualifications, "Hegel sometimes suffered, as A. E. Taylor once remarked, 'from an insufficient sense of the sinfulness of sin, as anyone must who identified the Prussian bureaucracy with the Kingdom of God,' " and "There is in his [Hegel's] doctrine the germ of the regimentation which prevails in the totalitarian state of Hitler."[85]

While King too expressed admiration for Hegel's insights into the dialectical nature of human spiritual development, in *Stride Toward Freedom* he also in effect accepted Kierkegaard's critique of Hegel's pantheism and overemphasis on the World Spirit to the neglect of the individual when he explained, "His [Hegel's] absolute idealism was rationally unsound to me because it tended to swallow up the many in the one."[86] In his dissertation in referring to the systems of Hegel and Spinoza, King contended:

In each of these systems finite individuality is swallowed up in the unity of being. Individual persons become merely transitory modes of the one substance, having no substantial character of their own.[87]

In *Strength To Love* King challenged Hegel's apparent attempt through his system of thought to resolve all of life's conflicts:

> In their revolt against Hegel's essentialism, all existentialists contend that the world is fragmented. History is a series of unreconciled conflicts, and man's existence is filled with anxiety and threatened with meaninglessness.[88]

Thus King attempted to adopt a Hegelian approach even in his interpretation of Hegel. While deeply impressed with those truths he found in Hegel's system, he was not reluctant to reject as false those portions of that system which he thought either ignored or negated the freedom and dignity of the individual.

Gandhi's "Experiments with Truth"

When King chose to pattern his crusades after Gandhi's campaigns, he inherited a doctrine of nonviolence that for thousands of years had been taught in different cultures as the eternal law of life. Gandhi derived his doctrine of nonviolence from the ancient Hindu writings and found confirmation for this doctrine especially in Buddhist, Christian, and Muslim sources. He found in the Hindu *Laws of Manu* the commands, "Let him patiently hear hard words. Let him not insult anybody. Against an angry man let him not in return show anger. Let him bless when he is cursed."[89] The Indian epic *Mahabharata* stressed the necessity of abstaining from injury to all creatures in thought, word, and deed.[90] Gandhi revered the *Bhagavad-Gita*, a part of this epic, because, according to his interpretation, it extolled nonviolence. In this work the warrior Arjuna does proclaim:

> These warriors I do not wish to kill, even though I am killed by them, not even for the dominion over the three worlds, how much less for the sake of this earth. . . . It would be better for me if the sons of Dhritarashtra, weapons in hand, should slay me in the battle, unresisting and unarmed.[91]

Gandhi acknowledged that he had found additional strength for his commitment to nonviolence in the life and teaching of Buddha. "I owe a great deal to the inspiration that I have derived from the life of the Enlightened One."[92] In an attempt to break away from the ritualism of the Vedic religion, Buddha emphasized ethics, and in the process contributed to the development of the doctrine of non-violence. Prior to Buddha, *ahimsa* had consisted mainly in noninjury to living things and in the maintenance of personal purity, but he chose to establish an ethics of compassion that included all creatures.[93] In challenging the value of violence, he taught that hatreds are not quenched by hatred but by love, and defined a "truth-finder" as one who lays aside the sword, "lives a life of innocence and mercy . . . heals divisions and cements friendship . . . for in peace is his delight."[94] Buddha revealed the universal scope of his compassion as he commanded his disciples:

> Go unto all lands and preach this gospel. Tell them that the poor and the lowly, the rich and the high, all are one, and that all castes unite in this religion as do the rivers of the sea.[95]

Gandhi was further moved by the additional appeals for non-violence in the teachings of Confucius, Lao-tse, Moses, and Socrates. He considered Socrates a satyagrahi since he would not refrain from preaching the truth and he bravely suffered the punishment of death.[96] But Gandhi discovered in the New Testament a special confirmation of his faith in nonviolence. He explained that the Sermon on the Mount went straight to his heart, and that he took immeasurable delight in the verses:

> "But I say unto you, that ye resist not evil, but whosoever shall smite thee on thy right cheek, turn to him the other also," and "If any man take away thy coat, let him have thy cloak too."[97]

He called Jesus the "prince of satyagrahis," and claimed that he would readily call himself a Christian if he had to accept only the Sermon on the Mount and his own interpretation of it.[98] Moreover, his appreciation of the life and message of Jesus encouraged him to study the life of Mohammed and the Koran, where he believed he found the same doctrine of nonviolence, pure love, and goodness toward everything that exists.[99] He revered the prophet's bravery and austere living. At the conclusion of the first stage of his studies of Islam, which were encouraged by his Muslim friends in South Africa, he maintained, "The very word Islam means peace which is nonviolence. The sword is no emblem of Islam."[100] Later, in his mass evening prayers he felt the need to include passages from the Koran as well as from the Zend-Avesta, the sacred book of the Zoroastrians.[101]

Leo Tolstoy proved to be a crucial influence in the development of Gandhi's conception of nonviolence. Early in his formation Gandhi experienced a crisis of skepticism about the value of nonviolence for social transformation. In the midst of this crisis he read Tolstoy's *The Kingdom of God Is Within You*. He explained that this work cured him of his skepticism and belief in violence.[102] In *In Search of the Supreme* Gandhi indicated that what appealed to him most in Tolstoy's life was that "he practiced what he preached, and reckoned no cost too great in his pursuit of truth."[103] Tolstoy affirmed that Christ's teaching was distinctive in that it not only acknowledged the law of love as the supreme law of human life but it also provided clear guidance for applying this law, even to enemies. Tolstoy proclaimed that this teaching required "a complete change of the established organization of life, not only in Christendom, but among all the nations of the earth."[104] He affirmed that Christians by nonviolence could attain freedom for themselves and help liberate humanity, and he appealed for a regeneration of society through simplicity of living, the practice of love in all relationships, service to others, and the persuasion of others to follow this way of life. He predicted that the Christian principles of equality and fraternity, community of property, and nonresistance of evil by force would eventually be regarded to be just as natural and simple as the principles of family or social life.[105] At the age of fifty-seven he renounced his life of privilege to live the essence of Christianity by working and suffering with the poor. Inspired by the application of the principle of nonresistance by American Quakers, he petitioned the Russian Government to assist the peasants, to forbid the disregard of Common Law, to eliminate all barriers to education, and to remove all limitations on religious liberty. He devoted much of his energy to feeding the victims of famine, and could only have enhanced Gandhi's conviction that love is an active force when he asserted:

> A good deed does not consist merely of feeding the hungry with bread, but of loving both the hungry and the satisfied. For it is more important to love than to feed, because one may feed and not love, but it is impossible to love and not to feed.[106]

The example of Thoreau further heightened Gandhi's determination to employ nonviolent resistance to achieve social change. It was not difficult for Gandhi to identify with the content of Thoreau's essay "On the Duty of Civil Disobedience." He read the essay while in jail after engaging in civil disobedience against the authorities in South Africa. While he denied that he had gotten the idea of civil disobedience from Thoreau, in a letter to the American people he indicated that Thoreau through this essay provided him with "scientific confirmation" of what he had been doing.[107] He could easily empathize with Thoreau in his public noncooperation with a system that would promote slavery, an unjust war, and injustice to Indians. Thoreau not only refused to pay his taxes to demonstrate his opposition to evils in the system but also used his house as a station for the Underground Railroad, and even escorted a fugitive slave to Canada. Gandhi was impressed by Thoreau's willingness to risk penalties for his convictions, and considered him one of the most moral men America had produced. "He went to gaol for the sake of his principles and suffering humanity. His essay has, therefore, been sanctified by suffering."[108] Gandhi's admiration for the essay led him to change the name of his movement in South Africa from "Passive Non-Resistance" to "Civil Disobedience."[109] He had come to feel that the name "Passive Non-Resistance" conveyed to many, especially Europeans, the impression that his movement and its members were weak and incapable of meeting force with force. Later, he again changed the name to "Civil Resistance" and then to "Nonviolent Resistance" to convey more accurately the philosophy of his movement.

Gandhi understood that the task of a government should be to work for the elevation and liberation of every individual person. Therefore, he felt morally compelled to oppose the British institutions of colonialism that were designed to perpetuate the pauperization and humiliation of the Indians:

> The Government schools have unmanned us, rendered us helpless and Godless. They have filled us with discontent, and providing no remedy for the discontent have made us despondent. They have made us what we were intended to become: clerks and interpreters.[110]

He regarded it as self-evident that since such a government depended for its survival on the cooperation of its people who were its victims, those victims could defeat that government by noncooperation. He declared that noncooperation and even civil disobedience become a sacred duty when a government becomes corrupt and promotes unjust laws:

A citizen who barters with such a state shares its corruption or lawlessness. . . . Rejection is as much an ideal as the acceptance of a thing. It is as necessary to reject untruth as it is to accept truth. . . . Non-cooperation is a protest against an unwitting and unwilling participation in evil. . . . It is not so much British guns that are responsible for our subjection as our voluntary cooperation.[111]

In demanding active resistance to the evils in the system, Gandhi not only repudiated the Indian habits of passivity and submission, which for so long had constituted the major impediments to independence but also challenged the schools of Hindu thought that taught that the individual should never attempt to struggle against evil but rather should seek to transcend evil by cultivating an attitude of indifference toward it.[112]

In the course of his struggles against the apartheid policy in South Africa and against imperialism in India, Gandhi resorted to several forms of direct satyagraha action but often only after first exploring the constitutional means for a redress of grievances.[113] He contended that those about to engage in a satyagraha campaign should first attempt by means of a public inquiry to understand fully not only their own grievances but their opponent's case as well, and then to negotiate with the opponent with the twofold purpose of appealing to his conscience and of arousing a sense of justice in the general public. As part of his negotiations he frequently resorted to petitions to the Government to remedy inequities against Indians because he recognized that the possibility of satyagraha action would compel the Government to give careful consideration to his petitions. If the Government did not respond to the petitions, he would then declare an ultimatum indicating the minimum demands that had to be fulfilled within a specific time. Only when the Government rejected his ultimatum or when it expired did he launch direct satyagraha action.

Gandhi recognized that those who would volunteer to participate in satyagraha had to be trained in the methods and the spiritual implications of nonviolence. He established training camps so that those who intended to be satyagrahis would learn how to abstain from violence in any form as well as how to control crowds and restore order. As part of their training for a campaign, such volunteers were required to take a pledge that they would resist injustice, abstain from violence to the opponent's life, person, and property, and be willing to suffer cheerfully the consequences of their actions. The success of the Salt Satyagraha of 1930, which King so admired, depended on the disciplined efforts of such trained volunteers.

In over fifty years of protest Gandhi utilized a variety of methods in his campaigns: (1) observance of National Days and Weeks to protest refusals by the Government to fulfill its promises and also to encourage renewal of the satyagraha pledge; (2) publication of pamphlets to defy restrictions on the freedom of the press, to invite Government suppression, and to mobilize public opinion; (3) conducting prohibited meetings, demonstrations, and processions both for protest and the education of public opinion; (4) staging ceremonial marches in defiance of Government orders so as to create massive unrest, as in the 1930 Salt Satyagraha; (5) organizing strikes either for better working conditions or for political goals such as the repeal of a tax in South Africa; (6) voluntary closure of shops to protest the arrest of satyagrahis or to demonstrate dissatisfaction with unwarranted laws such as the Asiatic Registration Act in South Africa; (7) application of boycotts of foreign goods, institutions, honors, and official functions to exert economic and political pressure; (8) peaceful picketing to persuade the opponent and to heighten political awareness among participants, as in the movement against the Asiatic Permit offices in South Africa and against liquor shops in India and the sale and use of foreign cloth; (9) peaceful raids against the property of the adversary that is intended for universal consumption, as in raids to occupy salt depots during the Salt Satyagraha; (10) voluntary renunciation of property by selling it or donating it for a public purpose so that the Government cannot seize the property to force individuals to cooperate against their will, as in the Salt Satyagraha and the Second Nonviolent Non-Cooperation Movement (1932); (11) resignation from the Assembly or Council to protest against an official policy; (12) civil disobedience to protest the immorality of laws or to indicate symbolically one's revolt against the state (Gandhi applied it in South Africa by refusing to conform to compulsory reregistration, by boycotting and picketing the permit offices, by refusing to give fingerprints or thumb-impressions, by hawking without licenses, and by entering neighboring provinces without registration certificates. He used it in India by violating laws that banned the publication of certain literature, by distilling salt from sea water, and by cutting palm trees that provided the Government with revenue.); (13) seeking imprisonment by the violation of laws conflicting with one's conscience so that by one's willingness to suffer, one could arouse both the sympathy and respect of public opinion for the justice of one's cause; (14) fasting in response to the call of one's conscience in order to intensify self-purification and to transform the bitterness of the opponent (he resorted to fasting, even "fasts unto death" to challenge Government inequities and against Hindu-Moslem riots and other acts of violence); (15) usurping Government functions; (16) establishment of functions that parallel Government functions; (17) refusal to pay taxes to halt Government functions (two instances in which this method was used as a last resort were the Salt Satyagraha and the Individual Satyagraha of 1940 to protest the involvement of India in the Second World War without its consent).[114]

King could claim that he derived his method of protest from Gandhi since in his crusades he employed most of the above methods. However, he did not encourage the voluntary closure of shops, raids on property, the voluntary renunciation of property, resignations from political groups, fasting, the usurping of Government functions, the establishment of functions that parallel Government functions, or the nonpayment of taxes. Some of these differences in method stemmed from the fact that while Gandhi was seeking independence from an alien system, King's goal was the transformation of the structures of the existing system so that all citizens could experience integration within the system.

Some critics of King's civil disobedience have denounced what they have regarded as his refusals to rely on litigation and petitions to achieve his goals.[115] They have ignored the fact that, in his attempts to transform the political and economic structures, he did make appeals to the courts. These critics have also disregarded his many petitions to Federal, state, and municipal authorities. Petitions were developed for all of his crusades. At times he tried to dramatize the significance of these petitions. In the Selma Movement he arranged for a delegation to attempt to present a petition to Governor George Wallace. In the Chicago Movement, in a manner reminiscent of Martin Luther, he posted on a church door his demands upon the city officials. Apart from his crusades and his books, he presented petitions through a variety of channels, including the Prayer Pilgrimages to Washington, D.C.; the March on Washington; speeches at universities, conventions, and press clubs and before the Platform and Resolutions Committees of the Democratic and Republican National Conventions; sermons; interviews; numerous articles in journals, magazines and newspapers, especially articles in *The Nation*; a detailed petition to President Kennedy, and discussions with him and with Presidents

Eisenhower and Johnson.[116] However, he soon became painfully aware that only when he reinforced the petitions with nonviolent direct actions could he secure some of the necessary legislation, and even its partial implementation.

During the Montgomery Boycott King revealed his conviction that the struggle for civil rights should employ different kinds of methods. Many thought that he was inconsistent because he gave his support to both the NAACP and the Alabama Council on Human Relations.[117] In seeking integration, the NAACP had emphasized mainly legislation and court action while the Council had stressed education. Many felt that these methods were incompatible, but King held that both methods should be used since they were complementary. Legislation and court orders can seek to regulate behavior and control the external effects of the feelings of fear, hate, and prejudice.[118] Thus they can aim to break down the physical barriers to integration. But legislation and court orders alone will not achieve integration. They cannot change the heart and cannot alter the spiritual barriers to integration. Law cannot make us love another.[119] King stressed that we must depend on education and religion to alter the errors of the mind and heart.[120] Through education and religion we can seek to change attitudes, remove feelings of prejudice, and prepare persons for the new order.[121] However, he also emphasized that to rely on education and religion alone for social change is insufficient. "But it is an immoral act to compel a man to accept injustice until another man's heart is straight."[122] Legislation is therefore also necessary. Yet, in 1963 he contended that the failure of the nation to implement the legal decisions in education had caused the Negro to have less faith in litigation as the dominant method to achieve his freedom. "In his eyes, the doctrine of legal change had become the doctrine of slow token change and, as a sole weapon of struggle, now proved its unsuitability."[123] Hence, nonviolent direct action was necessary not only to produce legislation but to secure its implementation:

> Only when the people themselves begin to act are rights on paper given life-blood. A catalyst is needed to breathe life experience into a judicial decision by the persistent exercise of the rights until they become usual and ordinary in human conduct.[124]

However, King cautioned that direct action is not a substitute for work in the courts and the halls of government:

It is necessary to maintain a creative balance between legal action and direct action. . . . Indeed, direct action and legal action complement one another; when skillfully employed, each becomes more effective.[125]

In extolling the value of litigation in the civil rights struggle King was keenly aware of how successful the interracial NAACP had been in the use of this method.[126] In 1958, he stated that the NAACP had done much more than any other organization to achieve the legal and constitutional rights of Negro citizens.[127] He thought that their most notable victory in the courts was the establishment of the right of the Negro to participate in national elections.[128] He frequently praised the role of the NAACP in securing the 1954 *Brown* v. *Board of Education of Topeka* decision.[129] As a member of the NAACP he maintained a close relationship with the organization for several years. In 1962, he indicated that he had addressed NAACP chapters in more than twenty states and had appeared at three of its national conventions. The organization had often assisted him in his crusades. He reported that in response to an appeal from Roy Wilkins, almost every one of its branches gave moral and financial support to the Montgomery Improvement Association (MIA) during the Montgomery Boycott.[130] The members of its legal staff had secured the U.S. Supreme Court decision that desegregated the buses in Montgomery and ended the need for the boycott.[131] He acknowledged that it had provided legal and financial assistance to his Albany and Birmingham Movements.[132] The assistance was especially valuable because of the reliance on mass civil disobedience at Birmingham.

King was constantly concerned that his methods be viewed as consistent with his philosophy of nonviolence. At the beginning of the Montgomery Boycott he was disturbed that his proposed method of protest was being regarded as the same as the one used by the White Citizens Councils to preserve segregation.[133] He began to consider whether the boycott method was an ethical course of action or a basically unchristian and negative approach to the solution of a problem. He reasoned that while the White Citizens Councils had used this method for the unethical purposes of depriving persons of the basic necessities of life and of urging people to defy the law of the land, he and the Negro community would use this method to achieve justice and freedom and to urge people to comply with the law of the land. He concluded that the term "boycott" was really a misnomer for the proposed action since it suggested an economic squeeze and confined one to the negative, while the concern of the Negro community would be positive. "Our concern would not be to put the bus company out of business, but to put justice in business."[134] It was then that he understood that the protesters in withdrawing their economic support from the bus company as an external expression of the system of segregation would be saying, like Thoreau, that they could no longer lend their cooperation to an evil system.

In explaining the main characteristics of the nonviolent resistance in the Montgomery Boycott, King, like Gandhi, emphasized that this resistance was directed against the forces of evil rather than against the persons who happened to be doing the evil.[135] He often proclaimed that nonviolent resistance does not aim to humiliate or defeat opponents but to liberate them from their prejudice and fear. He asserted that segregationists had been taught wrong and were themselves victimized by the evil system they perpetuated.[136] Segregation gave some whites a false sense of superiority, and deprived them of genuine humility, honesty, and love.[137] Years later, when he was beaten by a white youth at a SCLC convention, he refused to press charges and asserted, "This system that we live under creates people such as this youth. I'm not interested in pressing charges. I'm interested in changing the kind of system that produces this kind of man."[138] He stressed that the struggle was not between whites and blacks, but between justice and the injustice of segregation. "While abhorring segregation, we shall love the segregationist. This is the only way to create the beloved community."[139] After the Supreme Court decision on bus desegregation in effect ended the boycott, King told his followers:

> Our experience and growth during this past year of nonviolent protest has been such that we cannot be satisfied with a court "victory" over our white brothers. We must respond to the decision with an understanding of those who have oppressed us and with an appreciation of the new adjustments that the court order poses for them. . . . We must act in such a way as to make possible a coming together of white people and colored people on the basis of a real harmony of interests and understanding. We seek an integration based on mutual respect. . . . We must now move from protest to reconciliation.[140]

Gandhi had called for "an overflowing love for all" and was convinced that this love could convert the opponent and achieve reconciliation. "No human being is so bad as to be beyond redemption."[141] King shared this conviction. "We must continue to believe that the most ardent segregationist can be transformed into the most constructive integrationist."[142] He contended that within human nature there is "an amazing potential for goodness" and that nonviolent behavior can so arouse the conscience of the opponent that it can actualize this potential for goodness. He preserved this conviction throughout his crusades. In her foreword to *The Trumpet of Conscience*, Coretta Scott King could say of him, "Remember him as a man who refused to lose faith in the ultimate redemption of mankind."[143]

King was willing to work for the enlightenment and conversion of opponents through education and moral example as well as nonviolent direct action partly because he believed that much of the wrong people commit is due to their being victims of their own intellectual and spiritual blindness. He cited several examples to illustrate his conviction that people commit evil through ignorance of the good.[144] He referred to the fact that Christ on the cross could say of the men who called for his crucifixion, "They know not what they do."[145] Those who demanded Socrates' death for atheism did so because they were intellectually incapable of accepting an idea of God that had a depth that went beyond their traditional concepts. Saul had integrity in seeking the death of Christians, but not enlightenment. The Christians who conducted infamous persecutions and shameful inquisitions were not evil but "misguided."[146] The clergy who felt that they had a divine edict to oppose the science of a Copernican revolution or a Darwinian theory of natural selection were good men but "misinformed."[147] The Supreme Court justices who rendered the Dred Scott Decision of 1857, affirming that the Negro had no rights that the white man had to respect, were, in King's judgment, decent and sincere men who were also the victims of spiritual and intellectual blindness.[148] Respectable American citizens who opposed disarmament and international negotiation knew not what they did.[149] White Americans who sincerely believed in black inferiority were blinded by myths and by rationalizations, even from the Bible. "Misguided men robbed us of our freedom."[150] He described the officials of Montgomery who resisted desegregation not as bad but as "misguided." "So these men are merely the children of their culture. When they seek to preserve segregation they are seeking to preserve only what their local folkways have taught them was right."[151] After being choked and kicked by Montgomery police in 1958, King expressed his "compassion for them as brothers," and stated that "they were victims of their environment."[152] In "Love, Law and Civil Disobedience" he maintained, "Somehow this is the important thing, to get rid of the evil system and not the individual who happens to be misguided, who happens to be misled, who was taught wrong."[153]

In the above examples King seemed in effect to have endorsed Socrates' understanding of the cause of moral evil. Socrates maintained that if an individual truly knows the moral good, he will do it. Wisdom about the nature of the morally good act and about the capacity of this act to produce harmony in the soul leads automatically to its performance. Socrates concluded that moral evil is due to ignorance of the good act and of its effect on the soul. King studied this doctrine in his Harvard course with Professor Raphael Demos, "The Philosophy of Plato," as indicated by the following underlined entry in his notebook:

> According to Socrates we all want the good, but we don't know any better. Every man is a potential saint. A criminal is a frustrated saint. Evil is misguided idealism. Now we must agree that Socrates is right to a certain extent. We often do evil ignorantly. Jesus realized this when he said, "Forgive them for they know not what they do."[154]

King did not deal with the way that his own conception of the source of moral evil did not harmonize with the contention of the Christian ethic that we can have an intellectual grasp of the virtuous act and still reject it through an act of the will.[155]

In presenting the principles that directed the Montgomery Boycott, King warned that nonviolent resistance is not a method for cowards.[156] He denied that we are truly nonviolent if we act because of fear or because we do not possess violent means. He repeated Gandhi's judgment that if cowardice is the only alternative to violence, it is better to choose violence.[157] To illustrate his total rejection of cowardice, Gandhi related how his eldest son had asked him what action he should have taken if he were present when Gandhi was almost fatally assaulted in 1908 by an Indian extremist. His son asked whether he should have run away and allowed him to be killed or whether he should have used physical force to defend him. Gandhi told him that it was his duty to defend him even by using violence.[158] On another occasion Gandhi stated, "I would rather have India resort to arms in order to defend her honor than that she should, in a cowardly manner, become or remain a helpless witness to her own dishonor."[159]

In a 1965 interview King reiterated his agreement with Gandhi on the rejection of cowardice. "As much as I deplore violence, there is one evil that is worse than violence, and that's cowardice."[160] Courage ranked higher than the rejection of violence on King's scale of values because he regarded courage as essential to freedom. In an appraisal of the Montgomery Boycott he stated:

> Thucydides, that eminent student of the human saga, touched upon lasting truth in his funeral speech for Pericles when he said, "The secret of happiness is freedom, and the secret of freedom, courage."[161]

Tillich's emphasis in *The Courage To Be* on the necessity of courage to affirm oneself "in spite of" the anxiety of nonbeing in all of its forms, including death, could only have enhanced King's appreciation of the value of this virtue.[162] In *Strength To Love* he affirmed, "Our refusal to be stopped, our 'courage to be,' our determination to go on 'in spite of,' reveal the divine image within us."[163] Then too, he witnessed numerous examples in the freedom struggle of the matchless power of the courage of nonviolent resisters. This power, rooted in Christian love, was for him a further refutation of Nietzsche's contention that Christian love is weakness.

Although King agreed with the cardinal tenets of Gandhi's philosophy of nonviolent resistance, he differed from him in at least three ways he did not mention. *First*, Gandhi acknowledged that he had not found the Truth he sought.[164] He had no fixed and final theological or philosophical system apart from his commitment to the principles of nonviolence. This allowed him to choose insights from several creeds and philosophical systems, and caused him in the course of his campaigns to be open to revising not only his tactics but also his strategies so that he could respond to the actions of his opponent. For the sake of harmony he was concerned to demonstrate to the opponent that at times he could be persuaded that the opponent's position was closer to the truth than his own. "We will never all think alike and we shall see Truth in fragment[s] and from different angles of vision."[165] In contrast, King arrived at a system of definite philosophical and theological convictions about the nature of God, human nature, the direction of history, the mission of the Christian Church, and the role of the state in social reform. Unlike Gandhi, after his formal studies King did not pursue answers to the ultimate questions, but rather was seeking the social implementation of the ultimate truths he had already accepted. As a consequence, although, like Gandhi, he could improvise new tactics in the course of a campaign, he was more interested in securing concessions, and was not willing, as was Gandhi, to alter his strategies and basic goals in response to the reactions of the opponent. Although in "Our Struggle" King stated that "man's hostility to man" as the basis of injustice could be attacked only "when we challenge the white community to re-examine its assumptions as we are now prepared to re-examine ours," he revealed his fundamental position when he stated, "We hope we can act in the struggle in such a way that they will see the error of their approach and will come to respect us."[166] Evidently, a reexamination of his assumptions could have caused him to alter his tactics but not to have questioned the justice of his basic demands. In *Stride Toward Freedom* he asserted:

> For while the nonviolent resister is passive in the sense that he is not physically aggressive toward his opponent, his mind and emotions are always active, constantly seeking to persuade his opponent that he is wrong.[167]

However, it seems that King's refusal to be flexible in this regard proved to be a source of much of his effectiveness since the majority of the nation could recognize and appreciate the moral consistency in his crusades in his persistent adherence to his announced goals and to the basic principles of his philosophy of nonviolence.

Second, King differed markedly from Gandhi in the degree of emphasis on the necessity of self-help programs. In 1921, Gandhi proposed to his satyagrahis a program of "self-purification" as a condition for achieving political independence. It included the development of village industries and sanitation, the expansion of basic and adult education with special emphasis on health and hygiene, appeals for the elimination of the use of liquor through peaceful efforts, and the introduction of the spinning wheel in every home so that a greater production of homespun cloth could allow for an effective boycott of foreign cloth.[168] To promote self-sufficiency in the Armedabad Labor Satyagraha in 1918, he required laborers during the strike period to earn a living by working at other tasks, and he employed many in building a weaving school at his *ashram*.[169] During the 1930 Satyagraha he instructed his satyagrahis that if they were not engaged in civil disobedience or in prison, they should be under orders at the spinning wheel or at some other constructive work advancing *swaraj* (self-rule).[170] He criticized philanthropists who gave alms instead of providing work for the poor. Convinced of the necessity of self-help for developing a sense of personal dignity, he contended that if he had the power, he would have stopped the degrading practice of distributing free meals since it only encouraged laziness, hypocrisy, and crime. He recommended that donors establish institutions to dispense meals in a healthy environment to men and women working for them. His guiding principle was "No labor, no meal."[171] "I refuse to insult the naked by giving them clothes they do not need instead of giving them the work they sorely need."[172] "Satyagraha is based on self-help, self-sacrifice, and faith in God. . . ."[173] He maintained that if his people could remove their apathy and inertia, they would attain self-rule. If they continued to attribute all their weaknesses to the Government, they would never eliminate them. He credited John Ruskin's *Unto This Last* with making him realize for the first time that "a life of labour, i.e., the life of the tiller of the soil and the handicraftsman, is the life worth living."[174] At Gandhi's Tolstoy Farm, a kind of "cooperative commonwealth" for civil resisters, members ground their own wheat, labored at constructive work, and avoided any food that was not necessary for health.[175] Chester Bowles, former U.S. Ambassador to India, could claim that Gandhi devoted as much time to providing training in constructive work in the villages as to the effort to achieve national independence.[176]

In contrast to Gandhi, King arrived at the conviction that the Federal Government could and should do more for blacks than they could do for themselves. He believed that only the Government could provide the ultimate solutions in the problem areas of housing, employment, and education. In 1963, he referred to the need for the Government to establish a Bill of Rights for the Disadvantaged, a massive program that would immediately transform the conditions of Negro life.[177] In 1967, he called upon the Government to provide a guaranteed income:

> I am now convinced that the simplest approach will prove to be the most effective—the solution to poverty is to abolish it directly by a now widely discussed measure, the guaranteed income. . . . We must create full employment or we must create incomes.[178]

He felt that it was unrealistic to expect blacks to develop their opportunities without assistance. "When he [the Negro] seeks opportunity, he is told, in effect, to lift himself by his own bootstraps, advice which does not take into account the fact that he is barefoot."[179] He viewed the task of blacks to be one of developing a situation in which the Government would find it prudent to collaborate with them. He was confident that if society placed responsibility on its system rather than on the individual and guaranteed "secure employment or a minimum income," dignity would come within the reach of all.[180]

This is not to say that King did not appeal to blacks to improve their standards. In his *Ebony* column "Advice for Living" in 1958, he urged blacks to practice systematic saving and to pool their economic resources through cooperative enterprises.[181] He maintained that every black community should have credit unions, savings and loan associations, and finance companies. He felt that these could give the increased purchasing power that would make for better housing, health, and educational standards. At the conclusion of *Stride Toward Freedom* he reminded blacks that they not only had to continue to resist the system of segregation but also that they had to work constructively to improve their personal standards.[182] In his 1959 address to the members of the MIA, he could report that the organization had made sizable contributions which made possible the construction of a YMCA in Montgomery and the continuation of Farm and City Enterprise, a cooperative grocery store, that was "a symbol of what the Negro could do by pooling his economic resources."[183] He also indicated that the MIA by encouraging its members to patronize Negro business was largely responsible for the decisive improvement in Negro business since the boycott. In his 1959 *Ebony* description of his trip to India, he spoke with admiration of the support Nehru gave to the movement there that encouraged and expanded handicraft arts, such as spinning and weaving, in home and village, and that allowed "as much economic self-help and autonomy as possible to the local community."[184]

In *Strength To Love* King reminded blacks that "all labor that uplifts humanity has dignity and importance and should be undertaken with painstaking excellence."[185] The MIA had among its aims the improvement of the vocational and professional fitness of individuals and the improvement of living conditions.[186] James Baldwin recounted how during his visit to Montgomery King in a sermon to his congregation spoke of the need for them to work to elevate their own standards of conduct. Echoing the same plea as Gandhi, he told them:

We know that there are many things wrong in the white world. But there are many things wrong in the black world too. We can't

keep on blaming the white man. There are many things we must
do for ourselves.[187]

In 1966, he wrote of the necessity for blacks to organize their unemployed, to unionize businesses within the ghetto, to create collective
bargaining units for tenants, and to establish cooperatives so that they
could build and control their own financial institutions within the
ghetto.[188] SCLC, through Operation Breadbasket, which involved
ministers in negotiations with business executives, was successful in
securing a significant number of jobs for blacks in Atlanta and Chicago.[189]

Nonetheless, despite these references to the necessity for self-
improvement among blacks, King came to believe that the problems
of blacks were so massive that ultimately only the Federal Government had the capacity to solve them. Thus in 1967, while he continued to encourage blacks to use their buying power effectively and
to develop habits of thrift, he contended that "the ultimate answer to
the Negroes' economic dilemma will be found in a massive Federal
program for all the poor along the lines of A. Philip Randolph's
Freedom Budget, a kind of Marshall Plan for the disadvantaged.
. . ."[190] King was convinced that such a program would be of great
assistance to blacks also in the solution of their other problems. While
insisting that blacks should do all in their power to improve their personal standards he maintained:

> The ultimate way to diminish our problems of crime, family dis-
> organization, illegitimacy and so forth will have to be found
> through a government program to help the frustrated Negro
> male find his true masculinity by placing him on his own two
> economic feet. . . .[191]

In February 1968, King was involved in plans for the Poor People's
Campaign. He asserted that he felt that it was time to bring a Birmingham or Selma type of movement to bear on the economic problems confronting the poor people of the nation, and he emphasized
that he was referring not only to black people but also to the poor
people in the Puerto Rican, Mexican American, Indian, and Appala-
chian white communities.[192] The campaign was to involve a series of
massive demonstrations in Washington, D.C., by a nonviolent army
of three thousand cadre members. The demonstrations would be used
to secure from Congress an Economic Bill of Rights for the Disadvan-

taged, that would guarantee a job to all who were able to work and an income for all not able to work, would substantially increase the construction of housing for the poor, and would provide significant aid to ghetto schools.[193] The first week or two, the demonstrators would engage in lawful "First Amendment protests" to attempt to persuade Congress to meet their demands, and if Congress proved to be unresponsive, sit-ins would take place in offices, in Congress, and in the streets. Demonstrators seeking medical care would jam the hospitals.[194] Students would be used for massive protests at the Department of Health, Education, and Welfare, indigent farmers at the Department of Agriculture, and unemployed workers at the Department of Labor. King maintained that as a last resort, he might have to bring the Government machinery to a halt by using human barricades to block bridges and highways.

In a disclosure of his plans King affirmed that it was his intention to lead a protest without destruction of persons or property. "We will never destroy life or property and if the demonstrations become violent, if the people who come to Washington do not abide by nonviolence, we shall call them off."[195] Evidently, he must have regarded the consequences of a temporary interruption of the flow of vital services in the city as relatively insignificant when compared with the evil of massive economic injustice with all of its social implications. His intense awareness of the systemic violence that caused the national "dislocation" of the poor caused him to seek a drastic and massive solution through the "dislocation" of the capital. His Personalism emerged as the driving force behind his motivation in this campaign. "I feel this movement in behalf of the poor is the most moral thing—it is saying that every man is an heir to a legacy of dignity and worth."[196]

Third, King also differed from Gandhi in that he did not share Gandhi's conception of the role of asceticism in the practice of nonviolence. Gandhi chose the ascetical life because he regarded it as necessary for his own self-purification and adherence to nonviolence.[197] He believed that asceticism makes nonviolence possible since it works to eliminate attachment to the flesh and the world that causes the fear which in turn indirectly breeds violence. He believed further that only through self-denial can one feel, think, and aim for the good of others. Regarding renunciation as the highest form of religion, he used the ascetical disciplines (*tapas*) from the yoga tradition of the Hindu sage Patanjali, which cultivated self-control over the mind, spirit, and body, and taught five precepts of discipline, namely, noninjury, truth, nontheft, continency, and noncovetousness.[198] In his pursuit of complete self-discipline he adhered to austere diets, engaged in prolonged fasts, pursued the ideal of nonpossession or voluntary poverty, wore a loin cloth, took a vow of sexual abstinence at the age of thirty-six, chose for his home a very poor village where untouchables predominated, and for more than a total of six years endured the privations of prison life. He felt that these experiences helped him and satyagrahis who followed his example to achieve not only the capacity to avoid the commission of external violence but also the strength to preserve nonviolence of the spirit.

Despite the fact that he agreed with Gandhi on the value of unearned suffering, King, unlike Gandhi, did not emphasize that asceticism is necessary for the practice of nonviolence. In the Montgomery Boycott he achieved a successful display of nonviolence on a massive scale without such an emphasis. However, to say that King did not make asceticism an explicit goal of his philosophy of nonviolence for himself or his followers is not to deny that his life was in effect quite ascetical in many respects. His demanding schedule as pastor and student at Montgomery even before the boycott, his tireless efforts during the boycott, his later willingness to combine his duties as the principal organizer, speechmaker, and fundraiser for SCLC with his duties at his Atlanta church, his insistence that he receive only a minimal salary from SCLC, his eagerness to live with his family in a Chicago slum to develop his empathy with the poor, his acceptance of imprisonment on many occasions, and his readiness to expose himself constantly to the risk of assassination, especially during his crusades, all testified to his capacity to endure sacrifice and suffering for the sake of the cause. Then too, like Gandhi, in the midst of his diverse activities, he often experienced the need for prolonged prayerful self-examination. In a 1965 interview he explained this need:

> I subject myself to self-purification and to endless self-analysis; I question and soul-search constantly into myself to be as certain as I can that I am fulfilling the true meaning of my work, that I am maintaining my sense of purpose, that I am holding fast to my ideals, that I am guiding my people in the right direction.[199]

Gregg's Conception of the Power of Nonviolence

King further developed his understanding of the effectiveness of nonviolence for social change by reading Richard Gregg's *The Power of Nonviolence*. In the course of his research for this work Gregg studied most of Gandhi's writings. From 1925 to 1929 he lived in India, and stayed several months at Gandhi's own *ashram* at Sabarmati. While King was a student at Crozer, he read the 1944 revised edition of this work for a research paper.[200] In 1959, King wrote the foreword to the second revised edition, which contained an account of the Montgomery Boycott.

Central to Gregg's conception of the power of nonviolence was his thesis that nonviolent resistance acts as "a sort of moral jiujitsu."[201] He contended that even as in physical jiujitsu the lack of opposition to the assailant causes him to use his strength to his own disadvantage and lose his balance, so too in moral jiujitsu the nonviolence and goodwill of the victim causes the assailant to misuse his energy and to lose his moral balance. When the assailant encounters no violent resistance from his victim, he loses the moral support that such resistance would give him. If the victim were to attempt to employ violent resistance, the assailant could enjoy the moral reassurance that his attack is morally acceptable since in effect the victim would be assigning the same value to violence as the assailant. But when the victim refuses to employ violence in self-defense, the assailant is compelled to plunge forward into a new world of values. The assailant is startled and loses his moral strength and self-confidence as he confronts a victim who in his self-control rejects the traditional method of violence, readily accepts suffering, and shows no sign of fear or resentment. The assailant becomes uncertain about his own values and method of violence as he begins to realize that the courage of his nonviolent opponent is higher than physical bravery and is a stronger realization of human nature. "The victim not only lets the attacker come, but as it were, pulls him forward by kindness, generosity, and voluntary suffering, so that the attacker loses his moral balance."[202] The victim who employs nonviolence has the distinct advantage in that he knows what he is doing, has the creative purpose of converting his assailant, and therefore can preserve his moral balance. "He [the victim] uses the leverage of a superior wisdom to subdue the rough direct force of his opponent."[203]

The strength of the assailant is further reduced by the anger he feels toward the victim. As Gregg indicated, while anger initially provides muscular and sometimes mental energy, it consumes energy very rapidly, and it may even eventually exhaust the person who indulges in it. Moreover, the assailant loses more energy as the appeals and the moral conduct of his victim begin to arouse his conscience, and the assailant's more decent and kindly motives challenge his own fighting, aggressive instincts, thus introducing a division into his personality. The strength and balance of the assailant is diminished even more if he acts in the presence of spectators:

> Instinctively he [the assailant] dramatizes himself before them and becomes more aware of his position. With the audience as a sort of mirror, he realizes the contrast between his own conduct and that of the victim.[204]

He begins to feel that his violent action is excessive, undignified, and brutal, while he recognizes that the nonviolent victim has remained courageous and generous. He senses that the spectators realize that he has misjudged the nature of the victim. Through his manner, speech, or glance the assailant reveals that he has lost his inner self-respect, and that he has developed a sense of inferiority. The spectators sense this self-condemnation and deny the assailant their support. Gregg affirmed his belief in the basic moral decency of public opinion. "Violence which is not opposed by violence, but by courageous nonviolence, if it is in the open, is sure sooner or later to react against the attacker."[205] Furthermore, the assailant loses even more strength as the surprising nonviolent reaction of the victim creates wonder in the assailant, and forces his imagination and subconscious into a receptive and suggestible state.

In contrast with the assailant, who suffers from the above weaknesses, the nonviolent resister is in a position of poise and power. Though Gregg did not list them separately, in effect he provided at least ten reasons why the position of the nonviolent resister is superior. *First*, the nonviolent resister has the advantage of pursuing a course of action that is unpredictable to his assailant who is accustomed to violence. *Second*, he is in control of the process and is not subject to surprises. *Third*, his self-control and commitment to nonviolence conserve and even enhance his energy. *Fourth*, as a consequence of his sense of direction, he is not in as receptive a state as his assailant. *Fifth*, his voluntary suffering at the hands of the assailant demonstrates his sincerity and creates the image of an integrated self that is "impressive and moving." *Sixth*, his adherence to nonviolence reveals his respect for the personality of his assailant. "Respect for personality is a prerequisite for real freedom and fine human association. It is proof of unselfishness, and of moral poise and understanding."[206] It is this respect for personality by the nonviolent resister that leads the assailant to shame. *Seventh*, the nonviolent resister has the additional advantage that his moral conduct in the struggle encourages the support of the general public:

> When the public sees the gentle person's courage and fortitude, notes his generosity and good will toward the attacker, and hears his repeated offers to settle the matter fairly, peaceably and openly, they are filled with surprise, curiosity and wonder. If they have been hostile to the victim before, they at least pause to think. His good humor, fairness and kindness arouse confidence. Sooner or later his conduct wins public sympathy, admiration and support, and also the respect of the violent opponent himself.[207]

Eighth, when nonviolence wins public support, it makes the assailant realize that the kind of power he uses is disadvantageous, and that he may not be as powerful as he thought. *Ninth*, the nonviolent resister with feelings of security, unity, sympathy, and goodwill can remove the fear and anger of his assailant and thus reduce his cruelty. *Tenth*, the nonviolent resister is in a position to cause the assailant gradually to abandon his other divisive emotions such as pride, contempt, and anxiety.

Gregg emphasized several qualities that endow the nonviolent resister with superior power, namely, a love that is "an interest in people so deep, and determined, and lasting as to be creative," a profound knowledge or faith in the ultimate possibilities of human nature, a courage rooted in a conscious or subconscious recognition of the underlying unity of all life and eternal values, a strong desire and love of truth, and a humility which involves a true sense of proportion in regard to people, things, qualities, and ultimate values.[208] Gregg maintained that love is the most important of all these qualities, and can be seen to be their origin. "It must be patient and full of insight, understanding, and imagination. It must be enduring, kind, and unselfish."[209] It is love, not anger, that can gain the stronger and more lasting support from humanity. Love dominates the purpose of nonviolence. Like Gandhi, Gregg stated that the aim of nonviolent resistance is not to injure, crush, or humiliate the opponent:

> The aim is to convert the opponent, to change his understanding and his sense of values so that he will join wholeheartedly with the resister in seeking a settlement truly amicable and truly satisfying to both sides.[210]

The nonviolent resister seeks to allow the opponent to regain his moral balance on a higher level:

> The function of the nonviolent type of resistance is not to harm the opponent nor impose a solution against his will, but to help both parties into a more secure, creative, happy, and truthful relationship.[211]

Gregg's doctrine helped strengthen King's dependence on Gandhi. King also emphasized that nonviolent resistance involves an active and aggressive struggle with the purpose of surprising the opponent with a new method and of causing him to alter his moral values:

> It [nonviolent resistance] has a way of disarming the opponent. It exposes his moral defenses. It weakens his morale and at the same time it works on his conscience. He just doesn't know how to handle it and I have seen this over and over again in our struggle in the South.[212]

At a commencement address at Lincoln University in 1961 King stated:

> He [the opponent] has no answer for it [nonviolence]. If he puts you in jail, that's all right; if he lets you out, that's all right too. If he beats you, you accept that; if he doesn't beat you—fine. And so you go on, leaving him with no answer. But if you use violence, he does have an answer. He has the state militia; he has police brutality.[213]

Like Gregg and Gandhi, King frequently stressed that it is better to suffer evil than to inflict it. He contended that instead of multiplying violence and bitterness, the nonviolent resister by his willingness to suffer "may develop a sense of shame in the opponent and thereby bring about a transformation and change of heart."[214] King claimed that the oppressor would become ashamed of his methods as he confronted not only this willingness to suffer without retaliation but also the amazing self-respect of the resisters and their dynamic unity.[215] He affirmed that while people often deal with their guilt by engaging more in the act that evoked the guilt in an attempt to drown the sense of guilt, the Nonviolent Movement did not allow the white opponent to feel comfortable with this approach. Rather, the Movement disturbed the conscience of the white opponent and his sense of content-ment.[216] King also stressed the role of public opinion in forcing the opponent who resorts to violence to change his methods. "He [the violent opponent] will be forced to stand before the world and his God, splattered with the blood . . . of his Negro brother."[217] King knew that he had to appeal not only to the conscience of the opponent but to the conscience of the nation as well.

Niebuhr's Demand for Resistance to Collective Evil

In his writings King acknowledged that Reinhold Niebuhr's theology constructively influenced his own thinking on social change. He claimed that Niebuhr's most significant contribution to contemporary theology was his refutation of the extreme optimism about man's natural capacity for good, which characterized a great portion of Protestant liberalism, without falling into antirationalism or semifundamentalism.[218] King confessed that prior to his contact with Niebuhr's thought, he had found such intellectual satisfaction in the insights of liberalism that he had become absolutely convinced of the natural goodness of man and the power of human reason.[219] In his senior year at Crozer he read Niebuhr's works, and later indicated that his study of Niebuhr helped him turn from the sentimentality of liberalism concerning human nature to recognize the complexity of man's social involvement and to become aware of the reality of sin on every level of man's existence, especially the glaring reality of collective evil.[220] He explained that he was thus able to reject the illusions of a superficial optimism about human nature and to avoid the dangers of a false idealism. He still believed in man's potential for good, but Niebuhr caused him to sense the depths of man's potential for evil.[221] He came to realize that any attempt at social transformation could not ignore this potential for evil.

At Boston University King wrote a research paper entitled "Reinhold Niebuhr's Ethical Dualism" for DeWolf's seminar on systematic theology. In his presentation of those elements of Niebuhr's doctrine that most appealed to him, he revealed his conversion from a total acceptance of liberalism. At the beginning of the paper he disclosed his own early passion for social justice by indicating that Niebuhr as a minister "was overwhelmed by the appalling injustices evident in modern industrial civilization, and particularly by the concentration of power and resources in the hands of a relatively small wealthy class."[222] He wrote how Niebuhr in *The Contribution of Religion to*

Social Work declared that economic power had become the greatest source of injustice because "the private ownership of the productive processes and the increased centralization of the resultant power in the hands of a few make inevitably for irresponsibility."[223] This irresponsible use of economic power necessarily leads to injustice, no matter how intelligent the person who wields it. Niebuhr also claimed that no adequate housing for the poor could ever be initiated within the limits of private enterprise. He blamed social work for accepting philanthropy as a substitute for real justice, and criticized it for pretending to be scientific while it was little better than the "most sentimental religious generosity."[224] In this paper King quoted without criticism Niebuhr's appeal for class conflict as the solution to social injustice. "The real problem cannot be solved by increasing social intelligence and humanitarian judgments, but 'only by setting the power of the exploited against the exploiters.' "[225] He referred to Niebuhr's prophecy that the future in an industrial civilization undoubtedly would belong to the modern proletarian.

After this brief presentation of Niebuhr's understanding of the major cause of social injustice and his prediction of the solution, King next examined his contrast between the relatively decent behavior of man as an individual and the behavior of social groups. Niebuhr developed this contrast in *Moral Man and Immoral Society:*

> Individual men may be moral in the sense that they are able to consider interests other than their own in determining problems of conduct, and are capable, on occasion, of preferring the advantages of others to their own. . . . But all these achievements are more difficult, if not impossible, for human societies and social groups. In every human group there is less reason to guide and to check impulse, less capacity for self-transcendence, less ability to comprehend the needs of others and therefore more unrestrained egoism than the individuals, who compose the group, reveal in their personal relationships.[226]

King explained that Niebuhr credited the individual man with being naturally equipped with some unselfish impulses and with a conscience. Niebuhr spoke of individual men as being endowed by nature with a measure of sympathy and consideration for their kind. He felt that educational discipline could refine their sense of justice and purge it of egotistic elements so that they would be able to evaluate a social situation involving their own interests with a fair measure of objectivity.[227] Yet he also felt that the goodness of the individual in his immediate relationships loses its force to a great extent when he acts as a member of a group. One reason why the behavior of groups is so inferior to that of individuals is that it is a revelation of a collective egoism. The egotistic impulses of individuals result in a more vivid expression when they are united than when they express themselves separately.

Niebuhr believed that this conflict between individual morality and societal "morality" generates such a complexity that there can be no hope of finding a *simple* moral program to cover both the individual and collective mind. King explained how Niebuhr turned to "ethical dualism" as a solution. Niebuhr proclaimed that while *agape* or unselfishness remains as a law for the individual who in his inner life in moments of prayerful self-transcendence has been justified in faith and gives his final allegiance to Christ, *agape* suffers in purity as man functions in complex social relations where he must realistically meet power with power:

> Society must strive for justice even if it is forced to use means, such as self-assertion, resistance, coercion, and perhaps resentment, which cannot gain the moral sanction of the most sensitive moral spirit.[228]

King also referred to Niebuhr's *An Interpretation of Christian Ethics*, which asserted that *agape* is, at best, a regulative social norm that tempers whatever realistic means have to be employed to dynamite recalcitrant centers of pride and injustice.[229] Niebuhr maintained that the balanced Christian must be both loving and realistic. He must act as a vicar of Christ in his intentional life and also as a social and political agent in his actual life. The more one attempts to relate the gospel to life, the more he becomes aware that the social unit can accommodate *not agape* but *only justice*.[230]

Because of the human inability to achieve the perfect expression of the regulative norm of *agape* in society, Niebuhr described *agape* as a "possibility-impossibility." He argued that even Christianity has recognized that this ideal possibility is really an impossibility by its doctrine of the Fall that ended the "Age of Perfection." The ideal is an impossibility for society because sin in the human heart and the contingencies of nature prevent men from ever living in that perfect freedom and equality which the whole logic of the moral life demands.[231] The individual must be realistic enough to adjust himself to the fact that the ethic of *agape* which can direct the individual cannot inform the group. Unlike the individual, who can be related to the will of God and His all-inclusive love, the group lacks the organs of self-transcendence to understand *agape*:

> The larger the group the more difficult it is to achieve a common mind and purpose, and the more inevitably will it be unified by momentary impulses and immediate and unreflective purposes.[232]

Therefore, as the individual acts in society he has the moral responsibility to choose a "second-best." He must choose justice, a value for this world, which is morally inferior to *agape,* an eternal value.

King also examined Niebuhr's doctrine that justice does bear some relation to love. Justice emerges here as the negative application of love. Whereas love seeks to fulfill the needs of others, justice imposes limits on freedom to prevent it from infringing upon the rights and privileges of others. Justice can appeal to force if necessary to check the ambitions of individuals seeking to overcome their own insecurity at the expense of others. Justice serves as love's message for the collective mind. In *An Interpretation of Christian Ethics* Niebuhr reaffirmed this theme:

> In a struggle between those who enjoy inordinate privileges and those who lack the basic essentials of the good life it is fairly clear that a religion which holds love to be the final law of life stultifies itself if it does not support equal justice as a political and economic approximation of the ideal of love. . . . The relativity of all moral ideals cannot absolve us of the necessity and duty of choosing between relative values; and . . . the choice is sometimes so clear as to become an imperative one.[233]

King next briefly presented Niebuhr's critique of the inability of orthodox and liberal Christianity to understand the relation between love and justice. Niebuhr praised orthodoxy for properly judging the inevitability of sin in the world and for realizing the consequent defeat of pure love as a moral force, but he denounced its tendency to withdraw from the world in preference to interacting with it. Too frequently, it made individual perfection an end-in-itself. Christian orthodoxy "failed to derive any significant politico-moral principles from the law of love. . . . It therefore destroyed a dynamic relationship between the ideal of love and the principles of justice."[234] While Niebuhr granted that liberalism was enlightened on the law of love, he claimed that it was not sensitive to the inevitability of sin in history. Consequently, it sought in vain to overcome injustice through purely moral and rational suasions:

> The unvarying refrain of the liberal church in its treatment of politics is that love and coöperation are superior to conflict and coercion and that therefore they must be and will be established.[235]

He thought that liberalism confused the ideal with the realistic means which had to be employed to coerce society into an approximation of that ideal. It failed to realize that the simple statement of the moral superiority of brotherhood in the world will not produce perfect justice because men are controlled by power, not by mind alone. He argued that the approach of liberalism to the problem of achieving justice would have been less "inept and fatuous" if it had less moral idealism and more religious realism. The solutions of liberalism never took into consideration the permanent difference between man's collective behavior and the moral ideals of an individual life.

In the second half of this paper King presented Niebuhr's views on the necessity of government to curb man's sinfulness. Niebuhr argued that the very existence of government with its instruments of force would be unnecessary if *agape* were a historical reality in the lives of men. The practice of *agape* would require that preference be given to the needs and security of the neighbor. Government is necessary because men inevitably corrupt their potentialities for love by a lust for self-security that outruns natural needs. Men must be restrained by force lest they destroy their neighbors in a desperate attempt to make themselves secure. It requires the physical might of the social unit to restrain the stubborn force of sinfulness in human nature. King stressed the fact that while Niebuhr saw the need for goverment to restrain the sinful, he warned that government must not be regarded as divine:

> The individual's reverence for government extends only as far as the purpose for which that unit was created. When the government pretends to be divine, the Christian serves God rather than man. The Christian must constantly maintain a "dialectical" attitude toward government while the collective ego remains within

its bounds, while being critical whenever these bounds are over-passed.[236]

Niebuhr chose democracy as the most desirable form of government mainly because "it arms the individual with political and constitutional power to resist the inordinate ambition of rulers and to check the tendency of the community to achieve order at the price of liberty."[237] Democracy includes in its normal operation the right of the individual to criticize the rules. The act of impeachment constitutes the final expression of this right. Niebuhr regarded it as the highest achievement of democratic societies that they embody the principle of resistance to government within the principle of government itself. Equipped with constitutional power, the citizens can resist any unjust measures of government. They can engage in such resistance without necessarily creating anarchy in the community since the democratic government has been so conceived that criticism of the rules need not become a threat to the government but can and should serve as an instrument for the improvement of the government. Niebuhr realized the risk involved in arming people with the power of resistance, but he also realized that the alternative involves a greater risk. He recognized that if society is not empowered with rights to free expression, "it will explode from internal combustion."[238]

Although Niebuhr preferred democracy as the most desirable political system, he did not hesitate to indicate what he considered to be the patent evils of democracy. He believed the most self-evident evil is that democracy is based on an initial deception. While democracy promises the purely moral arrangement that the people, when they wish, may choose to rule through the use of their ballot, the fact is that the issues of government are determined by proud, powerful parties months before the voters have the privilege of selecting what they regard as the lesser evil:

> The factor of consent does not create governments because the general public is never able to conceive political programs or fashion political strategies. It can only say yes or no to various alternatives presented to it. The public as such is without organs of conscious direction.[239]

Neither does the ballot determine which class is to govern the community. It can only determine which faction of the class is to govern, i.e., Democrats or Republicans. For these reasons Niebuhr considered democracy as a perfect shelter for the prides and pretenses of the will-to-power of a bourgeois capitalistic class.

Niebuhr stated that when the selfishness of human communities becomes inordinate, it can be checked only by competing assertions of interest. The pretensions of a collective ego are checked by balancing power against power. "One power is brought to bay through an equally ambitious power over against it."[240] Niebuhr was aware of the danger in this realistic compromise of a balance of power:

> The very essence of politics is the achievement of justice through equilibria of power. A balance of power is not conflict, but a tension between opposing forces underlies it. Where there is tension, there is potential conflict, and where there is conflict, there is potential violence.[241]

King revealed his own dissatisfaction with the morality of this position when he asserted in this paper:

> Niebuhr has no fond illusion either of the moral worth of this solution or of its resulting problems. The best he can proffer is a realistic approach to a wretchedly complex situation, believing only that within the terms of a dialectic balance of righteous and unrighteous insights can the probability of either anarchy or tyranny be lessened.[242]

In his conclusion to this paper King referred to Niebuhr's ethical theory as "stimulating and profound" and as containing "much of permanent value."[243] He came to accept Niebuhr's critique of the naive optimism of liberalism, and to value his vision of the force of evil in the decisions of collectivities and of the need for active resistance to collectivities that use their concentrations of wealth to exploit the masses. However, despite his attraction to Niebuhr's theory on these points, in this paper King again assumed his usual dialectical approach and rejected Niebuhr's restrictions on the potential of *agape* for the transformation of society. He claimed that Niebuhr "fails to see that the availability of the divine *agape* is an essential affirmation of the Christian religion."[244] He rejected Niebuhr's ethical dualism which in the main limited *agape* to the individual life and which spoke of the goal of society in terms of degrees of justice, achieved by physical force, if necessary.

In his rejection of Niebuhr's position on *agape*, King appealed to an article by Walter Muelder entitled "Reinhold Niebuhr's Conception of Man."[245] While Muelder did acknowledge that the strength of Niebuhr's position lay in its critique of "the easy conscience" and the complacency of some forms of perfectionism, he raised several objections to Niebuhr's theory. King endorsed Muelder's objection that Niebuhr's position was weak in that it was not able to deal adequately with the relative perfection that is a fact of the Christian life. King agreed with Muelder that Niebuhr did not deal with the redemptive forces that can be released into history by committed human beings, and with the way that the immanence of *agape* in human nature and in history is to be concretely conceived. King quoted Muelder on Niebuhr's failure to appreciate the historical effectiveness of *agape*:

> There is a Christian perfectionism which may be called a prophetic meliorism, which, while it does not presume to guarantee future willing, does not bog down in pessimistic imperfectionism. Niebuhr's treatment of much historical perfectionism is well-founded criticism from an abstract ethical viewpoint, but it hardly does justice to the constructive historical contributions of the perfectionist sects within the Christian fellowship and even within the secular order. There is a kind of Christian assurance which releases creative energy into the world and which in actual fellowship rises above the conflicts of individual or collective egoism.[246]

King's acceptance of this correction of Niebuhr's view of *agape* by Personalism was crucial to the formation of his philosophy of nonviolent resistance. Inspired by the Personalist vision he derived from DeWolf, Brightman, Bertocci, Muelder and others, King could combine an emphasis on the power of *agape* to create genuine community with a reliance on nonviolent methods of protest for active resistance to the recalcitrant forces of evil in society, industry, and government.

Although King did not mention it in this research paper, Niebuhr in *Moral Man and Immoral Society* maintained that Gandhi's nonviolence had a special strategic value for an oppressed group that is hopelessly in the minority, and claimed, "The emancipation of the Negro race in America probably waits upon the adequate development of this kind of social and political strategy."[247] Niebuhr warned that it would be futile for the Negro merely to trust in the moral sense of the white race to free him completely from the menial social and economic position into which the white race had forced him. He conceded that philanthropic white people had established schools that endowed Negro leaders with the necessary educational advantages, and that the interracial commissions did serve to improve communication and remove some of the misunderstanding. However, he emphasized that these rational and moral efforts were quite limited in their objectives. The Negro schools supported by white philanthropy did not make a frontal attack on the injustices that plagued the Negro. The commissions, in their concern not to antagonize whites, sought only minimum benefits for the Negro, such as improved schools, police protection, and sanitation, but did not attack his political disfranchisement or his economic disinheritance. These commissions had a faith that education and moral suasion would change the heart of the white man, but Niebuhr contended that this faith was filled with many illusions:

> However large the number of individual white men who do and who will identify themselves completely with the Negro cause, the white race in America will not admit the Negro to equal rights if it is not forced to do so. Upon that point one may speak with a dogmatism which all history justifies.[248]

Niebuhr was equally emphatic in rejecting the value of any Negro effort at violent revolution since he was convinced that such an effort would certainly result in a catastrophe for the outnumbered Negro, and agreed with Gandhi that an attempt at violence would only increase the hostility and prejudice of the oppressor. "Ordinary coercive weapons" would evoke the most violent passions that the ignorance of the oppressor could generate. Even if the oppressor did possess some social intelligence, the Negro would still find that the economic interest of the oppressor would offer stubborn resistance to his claims.

Niebuhr did not advocate the technique of nonviolence as a total solution for the social problems that beset the Negro, but he did claim that if the Negro practiced nonviolence with the same patience and discipline displayed by Gandhi and his followers, he could achieve a degree of justice that he could never attain by pure moral persuasion or violence. Niebuhr confidently anticipated the Negro's use of nonviolence because he believed "the peculiar spiritual gifts of the Negro endow him with the capacity to conduct it successfully."[249] He felt that the fusion of the aggressiveness of the young Negro with the patience of the old Negro provided the formula for effective nonviolence. He predicted that the Negro, equipped with this synthesis of aggressiveness without vindictiveness and of patience without lethargy, could expect some measure of success as he waged his "frontal assault" on injustice by such actions as boycotts against banks that discriminate against Negroes in granting credit, against stores that serve Negroes and yet refuse to employ them, and against discriminatory public service corporations. In 1967, in referring to the Birmingham Movement and to Operation Breadbasket, King praised Niebuhr for making this prediction.[250]

The Aggressive Nature of Collective Evil

King's conviction that there had to be a systematic resistance to collective evil intensified as he studied the thought of Henry Nelson Wieman while preparing his dissertation. Wieman partially rejected the medieval Christian conception of evil. Christian doctrine since St. Augustine, in order to preserve belief in the absolute goodness of an omnipotent God Who is the Source of all being, had regarded evil as a privation, that is, as the absence of a good that ought to exist. Thus it regarded moral evil as a privation insofar as the human will fails to realize its proper goal of moral goodness. King presented Wieman's view of the nature of evil, that in effect repudiated this conception. "Evil is not merely a principle of nonbeing or an absence of something. It is both positive and aggressive."[251] In *Strength To Love* he returned to this view. "Evil is stark, grim and collossally real."[252] In his analysis of the biblical account of the Pharaoh's resistance to the struggle of the Israelites for their freedom, he warned:

> This tells us something about evil that we must never forget, namely, that evil is recalcitrant and determined, and never voluntarily relinquishes its hold short of a persistent, almost fanatical resistance.[253]

In his "Letter from Birmingham Jail" King claimed that the Nonviolent Movement had not made a single gain in civil rights without determined legal and nonviolent pressure.[254] At a 1963 prayer pilgrimage in Atlanta he contended, "In the absence of legal, political, economic and moral pressure, not even a city as enlightened as Atlanta is likely to grant the Negro his constitutional rights."[255] In 1967, he warned, "Evil must be attacked by a counteracting persistence, by the day-to-day assault of the battering rams of justice."[256]

King presented a severe indictment of collective evil when he reviewed what he considered to be the three distinct periods in the history of race relations in the United States.[257] The first period from 1619 to 1863 treated the Negro as a depersonalized cog in a vast plantation machine. The Supreme Court gave constitutional validity to the whole system of slavery by the Dred Scott Decision of 1857 that declared the Negro to be merely property and subject to the dictates of his owner. The second period—from the Emancipation Proclamation of 1863 to the 1954 Supreme Court decision on school desegregation—accepted the Negro as a legal fact but failed to accept him as a person. The court established "separate but equal" as the law of the land by the *Plessy* v. *Ferguson* decision of 1896. Though free from physical slavery, the Negro was still plunged in an abyss of oppression in this period of "restricted emancipation" since segregation had been "at bottom a form of slavery covered up with certain niceties of complexity. . . ."[258] The third period, that began in 1954, was the period of "constructive integration."[259] The Supreme Court declared that separate facilities are inherently unequal and that to segregate a child on the basis of his race is to deny him equal protection of the law. Although in 1959 King did call this period one of "constructive integration," he qualified this by indicating that Americans were standing on "the border of the promised land of integration," and by emphasizing that forces of defiance were at work in the South.[260] He referred to the coalition in the Senate of Northern reactionary Republicans with Southerners who through the filibuster attempted to block civil rights bills; to the legislative halls of the South that resorted to interposition and nullification; to the public officials who aroused abnormal fears within the minds of underprivileged and uneducated whites; to the Ku Klux Klan; and to the White Citizens Councils, which used social ostracism and economic reprisals against white moderates.[261] In denouncing the forces that resisted desegregation, he often attacked the covert and more subtle pervasive forms of discrimination in the North.[262] "The racial issue that we confront in America is not a sectional but a national problem."[263]

To accentuate the reluctance of white America to grant freedom to blacks King alluded to the doctrine of Frederick Douglass, the former slave who became the first great national black leader in the United States. He regarded Douglass, his boyhood idol, as "a Negro of towering grandeur, sound judgment and militant initiative."[264] He referred to Douglass's statement that the Emancipation Proclamation placed the North on the side of justice and civilization and would determine whether the national life and character would be "radiantly glorious with all high and noble virtues, or infamously blackened forevermore."[265] He stressed that Douglass soon found that the Emancipation Proclamation gave the Negro only abstract freedom but did not provide him with food, land, and shelter.[266] "Emancipation granted the Negro freedom to hunger, freedom to winter amid the rains of heaven. Emancipation was freedom and famine at the same time."[267] King maintained that this treatment was in sharp contrast to the way the Government in the late nineteenth century gave white immigrants free land and credit to build a useful and independent life.[268] Douglass contended that it was a marvel that Negroes were still alive.[269] Then too, when King wished to stress the fact that the civil rights struggle aimed to emancipate the oppressors as well as the oppressed, he quoted Douglass, "This is a struggle to save black men's bodies and white men's souls."[270]

Even though Douglass was not an advocate of nonviolence, it seems that King could have made further references to his thought to emphasize the basic elements of his own philosophy on the need for resistance to collective evil. For Douglass underscored themes that King found in the doctrines of Hegel, Gandhi, Niebuhr, and DeWolf. Thus in 1857 Douglass proclaimed:

> The whole history of the progress of human liberty shows that all concessions yet made to her august claims have been born of earnest struggle. . . . If there is no struggle, there is no progress; those who profess to favor freedom and yet deprecate agitation are men who want crops without ploughing up the ground; they want rain without thunder and lightning. They want the ocean without the awful roar of its many waters. . . . Power concedes nothing without a demand. It never did and it never will. . . . Men may not get all they pay for in this world, but they must certainly pay for all they get. If we are to get free from the oppression and wrongs heaped upon us, we must pay for their removal. We must do this by labor, by suffering, by sacrifice, and if need be, by our lives and the lives of others.[271]

Chapter 5

The Social Mission of the Christian Church

The Requirements of the Theology of the Social Gospel

One of the principal sources of King's conception of the prophetic role of the Christian Church in challenging and transforming social structures was Walter Rauschenbusch's theology of the social gospel. During his first year at Crozer Theological Seminary he read Rauschenbusch's *Christianity and the Social Crisis* for George Davis's course, "Great Theologians."[1] Davis had studied at Rochester Theological Seminary, where there was a strong emphasis on the doctrine of Rauschenbusch, who had taught there.[2] In *Stride Toward Freedom* King acknowledged that *Christianity and the Social Crisis* left "an indelible imprint" on his thinking by providing him with a theological basis for the social concern he had developed as a result of his early experiences.[3]

Rauschenbusch received most of his theological training at Rochester Theological Seminary. As a consequence of his studies there, he adopted the belief that the primary task of the Church must be to lead individuals to seek their own personal salvation. This almost exclusive emphasis on individual salvation was dominant in the churches of his day. It was only when he became pastor of the Second German Baptist Church of New York that he came to realize that social reform is essential to the mission of the Christian Church. His parish was located near Hell's Kitchen, one of New York City's worst slums. He witnessed the ugliness and desperation of the lives of his parishioners as they struggled with the damning effects of economic exploitation, especially during the depression of the 1890s. He asserted that it was these experiences and not the Church that produced his prophetic passion for social reform. He explained that this passion:

came through personal contact with poverty, and when I saw how men toiled all their life long, hard, toilsome lives, and at the end had almost nothing to show for it; how strong men begged for work and could not get it in hard times; how little children died—oh, the children's funerals! They gripped my heart.[4]

These experiences compelled him to reexamine the Bible and the Christian tradition to determine whether they confronted social evils. As a result of this reexamination he concluded that the prophets, Jesus, and the primitive Church not only concerned themselves with the salvation of individuals but also systematically and consistently condemned the evils rooted in the structures of society.

Rauschenbusch devoted the first section of *Christianity and the Social Crisis* to an examination of the life and thought of the Old Testament prophets since he believed that they had been an integral part of "the thought-life of Christianity."[5] He contended that the prophets were convinced that God demands righteousness and nothing but righteousness, and that it was this fundamental conviction that distinguished them from the ordinary religious life of their day. They regarded sacrificial ritual as a harmful substitute for and a hindrance to ethical religion. Hosea proclaimed, "I desire goodness and not sacrifice."[6] Isaiah affirmed the need for social justice:

> Your hands are full of blood. Wash you! Make you clean! Put away the evil of your doings from before mine eyes! Cease to do evil! Learn to do right! Seek justice! Relieve the oppressed! Secure justice for the orphaned and plead for the widow![7]

Micah also stressed the need for social justice:

> Will Jehovah be pleased with thousands of rams, or with ten thousands of rivers of oil? . . . He hath shewed thee, O man, what is good; and what doth Jehovah require of thee, but to do justly, and to love kindness, and to walk humbly with thy God.[8]

Amos and Jeremiah denied that God had commanded sacrifices at all when He constituted the nation after the exodus from Egypt.[9] They proclaimed that God required only obedience. Rauschenbusch maintained that insofar as the people believed that the traditional ceremonial was what God required of them, they were indifferent to the reformation of social conduct. By rejecting the need for sacrifice, the prophets could affirm that ethical conduct is the supreme and sufficient religious act.

Rauschenbusch emphasized that the prophets were actively involved in the public affairs of their nation, and that some of them were statesmen of the highest type. When they insisted on righteousness, they were concerned about the social morality of the nation rather than about the private morality of detached pious souls. He contrasted their principal concern to combat social injustice and oppression with the major concern of churches in his own day to condemn the private evils of intemperance, unchastity, and sins of the tongue. The prophets began to develop a special concern for the individual life only when foreign invaders crushed the national life of Israel, but, he contended, they insisted on personal holiness then because it was the condition and guarantee of national restoration.[10]

Rauschenbusch also stressed that the sympathy of the prophets was totally and passionately on the side of the poor and the oppressed.[11] They condemned the land hunger of the aristocracy, the ruthlessness that would reduce the poor freeman to a slave to collect a debt, and the venality of the judges who had a double standard of law for the rich and the poor. The prophets' concern for the poor was manifest in their theology when they viewed God as the husband of the widow, the father of the orphan, and the protector of the stranger:

> When the prophets conceived Jehovah as the special vindicator of these voiceless classes, it was another way of saying that it is the chief duty in religious morality to stand for the rights of the helpless.[12]

Jeremiah and the prophetic psalms identified the poor as a class with the meek and godly, and used "rich" and "wicked" as almost synonymous terms. Rauschenbusch maintained that the fact that Israel was in the unique position of having a library of classics in which the spokesmen of the common people had the dominant voice could serve as a strong proof for the divine inspiration of the Old Testament.

King found in the Hebrew prophets a continual source of inspiration for his struggle for social justice. In his "Letter from Birmingham Jail" he explained to the clergymen who criticized him that he had come to Birmingham because he was compelled to carry the gospel of freedom beyond his own home town, "just as the prophets of the eighth century B.C. left their villages and carried their 'thus saith the Lord' far beyond the boundaries of their home towns. . . ."[13] In his youth he had heard frequent references to the prophets in his father's sermons and had studied the prophets in a course on the Bible at Morehouse College, but his study of Rauschenbusch developed his understanding of the social implications of the prophetic mission. His understanding of this mission deepened during his studies at Crozer Theological Seminary and Boston University.

King's writings, sermons, and speeches abounded with references to the prophets. He extolled Amos, Hosea, Isaiah, and Jeremiah for standing up amidst unjust power structures and forces of religious idolatry, and for declaring with prophetic urgency the eternal word of God.[14] In "A Christmas Sermon on Peace" in *The Trumpet of Conscience*, he defined some of the elements of his dream of freedom, equality, justice, and peace by appealing to the words of Amos, Micah, and Isaiah:

> I still have a dream today that one day justice will roll down like water, and righteousness like a mighty stream.[15] I still have a dream today that in all of our state houses and city halls men will be elected to go there who will do justly and love mercy and walk humbly with their God.[16] I still have a dream today that one day war will come to an end, that men will beat their swords into plowshares and their spears into pruning hooks, that nations will no longer rise up against nations, neither will they study war any more.[17] I still have a dream today that one day the lamb and the lion will lie down together and every man will sit under his own vine and fig tree and none shall be afraid.[18] I still have a dream today that one day every valley shall be exalted and every mountain and hill will be made low, the rough places will be made smooth and the crooked places straight, and the glory of the Lord shall be revealed, and all flesh shall see it together.[19]

In his references to the prophets King most frequently quoted Amos's demand, "Let justice roll down like waters, and righteousness like an ever-flowing stream."[20] He contended that even as Amos was "maladjusted" to the injustices of his day, so too he did not intend to adjust to the evils of discrimination, segregation, religious bigotry, militarism, and violence.[21] He stressed that Amos was seeking not consensus but "the cleansing action of revolutionary change," and he called on ministers to imitate Amos by speaking out for righteousness.[22] While admitting that not every Christian minister can be a prophet, he affirmed that some must be prepared for the ordeals of this high calling and be willing to suffer courageously for righteousness.[23] In his special affinity for the message of Amos, King again resembled DeWolf, who in *A Theology of the Living Church* had asked, "Where is such blazing denunciation of hypocritical religion and social unrighteousness as the prophecy of Amos unless, indeed, it be in the words of Jesus?"[24]

Rauschenbusch developed the notion that Jesus by his words and deeds was similar to the prophets in many ways, even though "in the poise and calm of his mind and manner, and in the love of his heart, he was infinitely above them all."[25] Jesus too opposed the ceremonial elements of religion and insisted on the ethical, sided with the poor and oppressed, and was deeply concerned with national and social life. Jesus began his preaching by affirming, "The time is fulfilled; the Kingdom of God is now close at hand; repent and believe in the glad news."[26] Rauschenbusch maintained that Jesus' parables, moral instructions, and prophetic predictions indicate that the Kingdom of God was the center of all his teaching as recorded by the synoptic gospels. "The goodness which he sought to create in men was always the goodness that would enable them to live rightly with their fellowmen and to constitute a true social life."[27] He found in the message of Jesus a definition of goodness that King later found also in Personalism:

All human goodness must be social goodness. Man is fundamentally gregarious and his morality consists in being a good member of his community. A man is moral when he is social; he is immoral when he is antisocial. The highest type of goodness is that which puts freely at the service of the community all that a man is and can [be].[28]

Love was the fundamental virtue in the ethics of Jesus because "Love is the society-making quality."[29] In preparing men for the nobler social order of the Kingdom of God, Jesus aimed to energize the faculty and habits of love and to stimulate the dormant faculty of devotion to the common good. "Love with Jesus was not a flickering and wayward emotion, but the highest and most steadfast energy of a will bent on creating fellowship."[30] This doctrine helped to predispose King to accept the definition of *agape* as an act of the will that for the sake of community transcends expressions of *eros*, which are so dependent on emotion.

Rauschenbusch explained that since Jesus desired to establish a society founded on love, service, and equality, he felt it necessary to warn of the profound spiritual danger involved in the pursuit of wealth insofar as it is difficult to obtain riches with justice, to preserve them with equality, and to spend them with love.[31] In preparing people for the Kingdom of God, Jesus revealed that his basic sympathies were with the poor and oppressed. In his early preaching Jesus appealed to the passage of Isaiah where the prophet proclaimed good tidings to the poor, release to the captives, liberty to the bruised, and the acceptable year of the Lord for all, and Jesus stated that the time of the fulfillment of this proclamation had come.[32] When he wished to offer proof to John in prison that the Messiah had come, he affirmed that the helpless were being assisted and the poor were listening to glad news.[33] His healing power was at the service of any wretched leper but not of the doubting scribes. His parables reveal that he knew how much a strayed sheep or a lost coin meant to the poor. "No man would have laid on the colors in the opening description of Dives at his feasting and Lazarus among the dogs as Jesus did, who had not felt vividly the gulf that separates the social classes."[34]

In concluding his treatment of the social aims of Jesus, Rauschenbusch examined his "revolutionary consciousness."[35] Jesus was aware that he had come to kindle a fire on the earth. While loving peace, he knew that he had come to bring the sword. His revolutionary spirit permeated the beatitudes where we should least expect it. The Kingdom of God would bless those whom the world had not blessed. The poor, hungry, and sad would be satisfied and comforted, and the meek would inherit the earth. His revolutionary spirit was evident also in his attack on the religious leaders and authorities who were the pillars of the Jewish state. He rejected their brand of piety as hypocrisy, and criticized their law as inadequate. Moreover, he showed that he was liberated from spiritual subjection to existing civil powers such as Herod. Furthermore, his revolutionary spirit was apparent in his desire to abolish those titles and badges of rank in which former inequality was incrusted so that the only title to greatness would be distinguished service at cost to self.[36]

King also referred to the revolutionary spirit of Jesus. When asked by a white citizen of Montgomery why he and his associates had come to destroy a long tradition of peaceful race relations, he explained that Montgomery before the boycott had only a negative peace in which the Negro had too often only accepted his state of subordination. He then referred to the words of Jesus "I have not come to bring peace, but a sword," and interpreted them to mean:

I have not come to bring this old negative peace with its deadening passivity. I have come to lash out against such a peace. Whenever I come, a conflict is precipitated between the old and the new. Whenever I come, a division sets in between justice and injustice. I have come to bring a positive peace which is the presence of justice, love, yea, even the Kingdom of God.[37]

Rauschenbusch indicated that although Jesus aimed to establish the Kingdom of God, which involved a thorough regeneration and reconstruction of social life, Christianity in modern times had not undertaken the work of social reconstruction. He argued that the Church as "the incarnation of the Christ-spirit on earth, the organized conscience of Christendom, . . . should be swiftest to awaken to every undeserved suffering, bravest to speak against every wrong, and strongest to rally the moral forces of the community against everything that threatens the better life among men."[38] He rejected the conception of religion that regards as religious only what ministers to souls or what serves the Church:

If now we could have faith enough to believe that all human life can be filled with divine purpose; that God saves not only the soul, but the whole of human life; that anything which serves to make men healthy, intelligent, happy, and good is a service to the Father of men; that the Kingdom of God is not bounded by the Church, but includes all human relations—then all professions would be hallowed and receive religious dignity.[39]

The Church has the moral obligation to condemn all the conditions, especially the economic conditions, that induce a sense of despair and stifle spiritual growth. The Church should belong to the tradition of the Hebrew prophets and reflect the revolutionary spirit of Jesus; therefore, it should use its moral authority to protest all forms of exploitation and oppression: "A Christian preacher should have the prophetic insight which discerns and champions the right before others see it."[40]

King claimed that Rauschenbusch had rendered a great service to the Christian Church by insisting that the gospel deals with the whole man, not only with his soul but also with his body and his material well-being.[41] He indicated that after reading Rauschenbusch, it was his conviction that "any religion which professes to be concerned about the souls of men and is not concerned about the social and economic conditions that scar the soul is a spiritually moribund religion only waiting for the day to be buried."[42] He reaffirmed the judgment, "A religion that ends with the individual ends."[43]

King maintained that Christian belief regards the body as sacred, and that any realistic conception of man must involve a concern about his material well-being.[44] "We have both a privilege and a duty to seek the basic material necessities of life."[45] Religion must seek not only to change the soul of the individual so that he can be one with himself and with God, but also to change the environmental conditions so that the soul can have a chance once it is changed.[46] Christians must think not only about streets in heaven "flowing with milk and honey" but also about millions of persons who go to bed hungry.[47] They must think not only about "mansions in the sky" but also about slums and ghettos. The minister must refer to the new Atlanta and the new Memphis as well as to the new Jerusalem.[48] Religion at its best is aware that the soul is crippled as long as the body is tortured with hunger pangs and harrowed with the need for shelter. The minister who works with the poor knows how poverty influences morality. "It is infinitely harder for the hungry men with hungry children to respect the property of others than it is for the well-fed and the well-housed."[49] While rejecting any religion that would ignore social conditions, King was careful to emphasize that he would also reject any religion that would ignore otherworldly concerns and be completely earthbound. He stated that such a religion is reduced to an ethical system and sells its birthright for a mess of naturalistic pottage.[50]

During his crusades King at times felt compelled to remind Christian ministers of their social mission. He indicated that while prior to the Montgomery Boycott some Negro ministers were aware that the projection of a social gospel is the true witness of a Christian life and therefore were active in NAACP groups, too many Negro ministers remained indifferent to social problems. He asserted that much of this indifference was due to their sincere feeling that ministers were not supposed to be involved in earthly matters, such as social and economic improvement.[51] They believed that their task was to preach the gospel and keep men's minds centered on the heavenly. As the boycott developed, most Negro ministers in Montgomery quickly abandoned this narrow conception of their responsibility. Then too, during the boycott King had to confront the claim of Dr. E. Stanley Frazier, a white segregationist, that the Negro ministers who led the protest were wrong since the task of the minister was to lead souls to God and not to generate confusion by getting involved in transitory social problems. King challenged this claim by stating that if one is truly devoted to the religion of Jesus, he will aim to eliminate social evils since the gospel is social as well as personal.[52] During the Albany Movement he explained, "I feel I am called to preach wherever evil and injustice lie."[53] During the Birmingham Movement he emphasized for Negro ministers the necessity of a social gospel to supplement the gospel of individual salvation. "I suggested that only a 'dry as dust' religion prompts a minister to extol the glories of Heaven while ignoring the social conditions that cause men an earthly hell."[54] He reminded Negro ministers that they were more independent than any other persons in the community and called for their strong leadership in the freedom movement.[55] In 1967, he could still lament the fact that there were still too many Negro churches that were so concerned with a future good "over yonder" that they conditioned their members to adjust to the present evils "over here."[56] During the Memphis Movement in his last sermon he proclaimed that the minister must say with Jesus, "The spirit of the Lord is upon me, because he hath anointed me to deal with the problems of the poor."[57]

Rauschenbusch's conception of the Kingdom of God inspired King to develop further his own notion of the nature of the "beloved community," the ultimate goal of all his endeavors. In *A Theology for the Social Gospel* Rauschenbusch stated, "The Kingdom of God is humanity organized according to the will of God," and affirmed certain convictions about the ethical relations within the Kingdom by interpreting it through the consciousness of Jesus.[58] These convictions reinforced what King had learned in Davis's classes. *First*, "Since Christ revealed the divine worth of life and personality, and since his salvation seeks the restoration and fulfilment of even the least, it follows that the Kingdom of God, at every stage of human development, tends toward a social order which will best guarantee to all personalities their freest and highest development."[59] The Kingdom of God would redeem social life from religious bigotry and from all forms of slavery in which human beings are treated as mere means to serve the ends of others. *Second*, "Since love is the supreme law of Christ, the Kingdom of God implies a progressive reign of love in human affairs."[60] Rauschenbusch maintained that the advance of the Kingdom is evident wherever love rather than force and legal coercion regulates the social order. Such an advance would be manifest in "the redemption of society from political autocracies and economic oligarchies, the substitution of redemptive for vindictive penology, the abolition of constraint through hunger as part of the industrial system, and the abolition of war as the supreme expression of hate and the completest cessation of freedom."[61] *Third*, "The highest expression of love is the free surrender of what is truly our own, life, property, and rights."[62] Rauschenbusch emphasized also that the surrender of any opportunity to exploit individuals, though a lower expression of love, may be the more decisive one. He contended that this involves the elimination of the possession of private property in the natural resources of the earth, and the abolition of any condition in industry that would make monopoly profits possible. *Fourth*, "The reign of love tends toward the progressive unity of mankind, but with the maintenance of individual liberty and the opportunity of nations to work out their own national peculiarities and ideals."[63]

Rauschenbusch affirmed that the Church must exist for the sake of the Kingdom since the Kingdom is the supreme end of God. He maintained that the spiritual authority of the Church depends on the degree to which it fulfills this purpose. "The institutions of the Church, its activities, its worship, and its theology must in the long run be tested by its effectiveness in creating the Kingdom of God."[64] He argued that if the Church were to view itself apart from the Kingdom and to find its aims in itself, it would be guilty of the same sin of selfish detachment as an individual who selfishly separates himself from the common good.

Despite his acknowledgments of Rauschenbusch's role in his own formation, King did not hesitate to indicate what he regarded as defects in his thought. Mindful of Niebuhr's "realism" with its emphasis on the reality of collective evil, King felt that Rauschenbusch had been a victim of the nineteenth-century "cult of inevitable progress," and hence of a superficial optimism concerning human nature, and that he had come dangerously close to identifying the Kingdom of God with a particular social and economic system.[65] It seems that King should have qualified these criticisms since Rauschenbusch emphasized also the power of a "Kingdom of Evil." Thus in *A Theology for the Social Gospel* he asserted, "Depravity of will and corruption of nature are transmitted wherever life itself is transmitted," and in the chapter "The Kingdom of Evil" he maintained, "Yet we ought to get a solidaristic and organic conception of the power and reality of evil in the world."[66] He contended further that humanity in seeking the Kingdom of God on earth will never have a perfect social life. In *Christianity and the Social Crisis* he warned, "At best there is always but an approximation to a perfect social order. The kingdom of God is always but coming."[67]

DeWolf also contributed to King's vision of the social mission of the Christian Church. DeWolf's definition of the purposes of the organized Church in *A Theology of the Living Church* revealed his conviction that the Church should use its spiritual power to resist the many forms of social injustice. While emphasizing that the principal purpose of the Church is the cultivation and expression of the sacred *Koinonia*, a sharing fellowship that participates in the Spirit of God and pursues the more excellent way of love, and that the Church must seek the truth and exhort its members to act upon the truth disclosed as well as provide the means necessary for communal worship and prayer, DeWolf also affirmed that the Church must reach beyond its own borders and work for the extension of love, truth, justice, and peace in the world.[68]

DeWolf maintained that in response to the challenge of Christ, "whoever would be great among you must be your servant, and whoever would be first among you must be the slave of all," the Church must establish schools and hospitals, support the training of doctors and nurses, assist agencies for the relief of poverty, and minister in many other ways to multitudes outside its own membership.[69] Moreover, the organized Church by its words and deeds must strive to share with others the riches of the Kingdom within its own fellowship. A church that is not missionary and evangelistic demonstrates either that it does not possess a life that it values or that it lacks the degree of love that is concerned that others share in that life. Such an organization does not participate in the true spiritual Church and therefore is not a true church.[70]

Furthermore, the organized Church must confront the institutional sources of oppression and injustice:

> . . . the church must incessantly raise its voice in prophetic warning against the social evils in all the institutions of the day. The church must not try to *be* a state or an economic order, but remaining in its own role as conserver and voice of the spiritual life within, it must continually speak to the state and the economic order. In all its judgments it must avoid even the appearance of being one organization competing for power and prestige among other organizations. Its peculiar power lies not in self-seeking but in searching for truth and justice and peace for all, in the spirit of Jesus Christ. For this, too, is part of being "first" by being "slave of all."[71]

The Church must regard social evils as "the denial of God, rebellion against the kingdom and blights upon the priceless, eternal souls of men."[72] DeWolf asserted that while social evils which are tolerated so embitter many persons that they turn against their fellows and become unable to see the light of God, a prophetic act that challenges social injustice and opposes sinful barriers to brotherhood draws many lonely and despairing persons into the kingdom of love and faith.[73]

In *Responsible Freedom* DeWolf indicated that the prophetic function of churches tends to be in conflict with their pastoral function.[74] Thus when the preacher performs the prophetic function by emphasizing the failure of individuals, churches, and society to exemplify Christian ideals, as when he pronounces God's condemnation of racism or calls for policies of aid for the poor, or for a reduction of expenditures on military preparation to allow for more expenditures on housing and training for the unemployed, many people are offended and find it more difficult to accept their preacher's assistance with their personal problems. DeWolf maintained that there is no resolution to this conflict if one conceives of the prophetic function as one of preserving a comfortable peace of mind in individuals and pleasant social compatibility in the congregation. But he contended that such a conception contradicts the message of the New Testament:

> The peace of which the Gospel of John speaks is not the soft peace of conformity with the world. It is the peace of the Christ who has challenged earthly powers, is about to be crucified by them, who gives peace even while promising tribulation, and who says he has "overcome the world."[75]

The obligation of the pastor is not to promote a comfortable self-satisfaction that would interfere with spiritual growth but rather to foster a peace that involves repentance, sacrifice, and risk. DeWolf added that a preacher is not exercising the prophetic function if he resorts to angry denunciations that express his own pride, personal insecurity, or repressed hostility:

> To be truly Christian, a prophetic utterance must arise from love for the victims of injustice or other evil and desire to bring all who are involved into a community of forgiveness, grace, and mutual assistance.[76]

DeWolf asserted that the pastoral and prophetic functions do not really conflict with each other but rather are mutually supporting. At times, only a caring personal ministry can excise the race prejudice, violence, and evil of individuals, and thus can bring them Christ's healing as well as relief to the victims of their vicious conduct. While the Church should publicly condemn the hypocrisy, cruelty, injustice, and folly of society or of people belonging to certain types or classes in terms worthy of an Amos, Isaiah, or Jesus, it should minister to individuals guilty of social injustice in a positive way "which will remove their fears and hostilities, expand their perspectives, and eliminate their prejudiced activities."[77]

Other thinkers contributed indirectly to King's understanding of the social role of the Church. As already indicated, his identification with the social philosophy of the Personalists helped prevent him from accepting any religious approach that would ignore the redemption of the social order while seeking the salvation of the individual. In his dissertation he emphasized Tillich's conviction that the theologian "is involved with the whole of his existence . . . with the healing forces in him and in his social situation. . . ."[78] King's tendency to appropriate the ethical thought of Gandhi would have reinforced his rejection of any religion that concerned itself only with the salvation of the individual. In an address at Howard University he referred to the fact that Gandhi had conceived of man as a social being and had stated that man's individuality comes out best when he works for the social.[79] He then quoted Gandhi's contention, "I do not know of any religion apart from human activity."[80] Gandhi had also asserted, "Religion which takes no account of practical affairs and does not help to solve them is no religion."[81] One of his fundamental teachings was that service of the poor is worship of God.

In his definition of the prophetic role of the contemporary Church King maintained that the churches must make it clear that segregation, whether legal or *de facto*, is morally wrong and sinful, and contradicts the noble precepts of the Judeo-Christian tradition.[82] He contended that the problem of racial prejudice remained America's chief moral dilemma. The churches "must affirm that every human life is a reflection of divinity and that every act of injustice mars and defaces the image of God in man."[83] The churches must denounce the immorality of segregation because it denies the sacredness of human personality and deprives man of freedom, the quality that makes him a man.[84] "Nothing can be more diabolical than a deliberate attempt to destroy in any man his will to be a man and to withhold from him that something that constitutes his true essence."[85] The churches must denounce the immorality of segregation also because it rejects the unity men have in Christ.

King also stressed the obligation of the churches to use their channels of religious education to make the ideal of brotherhood a reality by exposing the irrationality of the fears and suspicions that are the roots of race hate. Churches can teach that anthropological evidence has refuted the myth of a superior or inferior race:

> They [the churches] can show that Negroes are not innately inferior in academic, health, and moral standards, and that they are not inherently criminal. The churches can say to their worshipers that poverty and ignorance breed crime whatever the racial group may be, and that it is a tortuous logic to use the tragic results of segregation as an argument for its continuation.[86]

King maintained that churches can and should aim to reduce racial prejudice by teaching that the true intention of the Negro is not to dominate the nation but to live with all of the rights and responsibilities of a first-class citizen. Churches can assist also by mitigating the prevailing and irrational fears concerning intermarriage. In general, churches can lessen the fears of some whites about integration and the fears of some other whites about social disapproval if they are too liberal on the race question by emphasizing that man owes his ultimate allegiance to God since love for God and devotion to His will casts out fear.[87]

King insisted that churches must take the lead in social reform. They must seek to keep open the channels of communication between the Negro and white communities, especially through interracial ministerial associations. He was careful to stress that if churches are to be effective in their attack on evils in society, they have to remove the yoke of segregation from their own bodies. They also must take an active stand against the injustices and indignities that Negroes and other nonwhite minorities confront in housing, education, police activity, and in city and state courts. They must support strong civil rights legislation and work for economic justice:

> Economic insecurity strangles the physical and cultural growth of its victims. Not only are millions deprived of formal education and proper health facilities, but our most fundamental social unit—The Family—is tortured, corrupted, and weakened by economic injustice. The church cannot look with indifference upon these glaring evils.[88]

Since the Church is the guardian of the morals of the community, it cannot be indifferent to such a "profound moral issue" as discrimination in employment, a deliberate strangulation of the moral, physical, and cultural development of the victims.[89] Therefore the Church is obliged to create the moral climate in which fair employment practices are regarded positively and accepted willingly. The Church should provide the spiritual leadership and guidance to millions of whites who deplore the evils of discrimination in employment but who fear to speak out. The Church should encourage and support the Federal Government when it refuses to give contracts to employers who engage in discrimination or when it determines to make examples of industries by dramatically cancelling contracts where through discrimination the principle of brotherhood is violated.[90]

King's early activities as pastor of the Dexter Avenue Baptist Church in Montgomery revealed some of his vision of the social mission of the Church. When he became pastor, the parish had a Sunday School, a Baptist Training Union that developed Christian leadership, and a Missionary Society that brought the message of the church into the community. He recommended the establishment of several committees that would revitalize religious education, channel and invigorate services to the sick and needy, engage in social and political action, raise and administer scholarship funds for high-school graduates, and encourage promising artists.[91] The congregation enthusiastically approved these recommendations. One of the duties of the Social and Political Action Committee was to emphasize for the congregation the importance of the NAACP and the necessity of being registered voters. This committee created a voting clinic to instruct unregistered members of the congregation in the pitfalls of discriminatory registration procedures, and during state and national elections it sponsored forums and mass meetings to discuss the major issues. It published a biweekly newsletter to inform church members about social and political issues. At that time King joined the local branch of the NAACP and within a year served on its executive committee. He also was vice-president of the Montgomery Chapter of the Alabama Council on Human Relations, an interracial group that aimed through educational methods and action to achieve equal opportunity for all the people of Alabama. As the only truly interracial group in Montgomery, it was able to keep open the channels of communication between the races. Some of the members of this group and of the Social and Political Action Committee later were to become prominent in the bus boycott.

Although King felt the need to criticize some Negro ministers for their lack of active concern about social evils, he was most willing to acknowledge the crucial role of the Negro Church in his crusades. In his "Letter from Birmingham Jail" he stated, "I am grateful to God that, through the influence of the Negro church, the way of nonviolence became an integral part of our struggle."[92] In 1965, he asserted, "I am happy to say that the nonviolent movement in America has come not from secular forces but from the heart of the Negro Church."[93] The Negro Church had perpetuated belief in the Judeo-Christian principles of love and justice that were at the center of the Nonviolent Movement. It had prepared blacks for a practical commitment to nonviolence by its emphasis on the dignity of the self, the value of sacrificial love, the merit of unearned suffering as exemplified in the life of Jesus, and the reality of a personal God Who demands righteousness and seeks justice for His children.[94] King indicated that although it was probably true that most of Montgomery's blacks did not believe in nonviolence as a way of life, they were willing to employ it as a technique because it was presented to them by trusted leaders as a simple expression of Christianity in action.[95] During the Montgomery Boycott he stressed that he was "motivated chiefly by the social gospel," and he and his associates aimed to channel the religious fervor and spiritual energy of the Negro Church into militant nonviolent action.[96] He explained that Christian love allows people to protest with "wise restraint and calm reasonableness."[97] When Gunnar Jahn presented him with the Nobel Peace Prize, Jahn contended that the Montgomery Negroes could not have reached such widespread agreement to spurn the use of violence if they had not been so deeply religious.[98]

In preaching the need for black liberation, King relied on the black religious tradition by referring not only to New Testament themes such as suffering, redemption, and resurrection but also to Old Testament themes such as exodus and deliverance from bondage.[99] Thus he referred to the Southern segregationists as "pharaohs" who had employed legal maneuvers, economic reprisals, and even physical violence to hold the Negro in the "Egypt of segregation."[100] He often assured his followers that they would reach the "Promised Land" of freedom and justice.[101] It would not be difficult for those immersed in the black religious tradition who listened to these references to come to understand his campaigns as religious crusades.

King could say that the Nonviolent Movement came from the heart of the Negro Church also in the sense that the Negro Church was the organizational structure that made the Montgomery Boycott and other crusades possible. The Negro Church had been a center of educational, economic, social, cultural, and political activities as well as a source of leadership for the black community.[102] It had provided its members with that degree of independence from white domination that allowed them to create organized resistance to oppression. During the Montgomery Boycott the Negro Church revealed its effectiveness as an agent for nonviolent protest. It was at the churches that the meetings were held that initiated and sustained the boycott. These meetings served as necessary channels of communication since Montgomery did not have a Negro-owned radio station or a widely read Negro newspaper. The meetings included a statement by King, reports from the strategy, finance, program, and transportation committees, speeches, hymns, scripture readings, hortatory preaching, freedom songs, and discussions of the philosophy of nonviolence. In his statements he emphasized the immorality and impracticality of violence. At each meeting there were prayers for the success of the meeting, for strength of spirit to carry on nonviolently, for strength of body to walk for freedom, for the opponents, and for all men that they might become brothers and live in justice and equality.[103] The meetings rotated from church to church, with speakers from various Protestant denominations and with Catholic participants. In commenting on the willingness of the speakers to transcend denominational lines by their presence, King stressed that the mass meetings accomplished on Monday and Thursday nights what the Christian Church had failed to accomplish on Sunday mornings. Also, the churches made possible the car pool that was essential to the continuation of the boycott. Initially the churches raised most of the funds for the car pool and provided many of the dispatch centers. Furthermore, the churches were a source of special inspiration for the black community when scores of ministers were arrested for their role in the boycott. When the people saw how their ministers were willing to be jailed for the cause, they could readily identify with their references to Jesus and Gandhi.

While King could point to the contributions of the Negro Church to the Nonviolent Movement, he frequently expressed his disappointment with the white Church for not exercising its prophetic function and for not being in the forefront of the struggle for freedom and equality:

So often it [the Church] is an archdefender of the status quo. Far from being disturbed by the presence of the church, the power structure of the average community is consoled by the church's silent—and often even vocal—sanction of things as they are.[104]

Even though he affirmed that he was in the rather unusual position of being the son, the grandson, and the great-grandson of preachers, that he loved the Church, that he was fundamentally a clergyman, "a Baptist preacher," and that the Church was his life, still he felt compelled to reiterate the judgment of Dean Liston Pope of Yale Divinity School in *The Kingdom beyond Caste*, "The church is the most segregated major institution in American society."[105]

King conceded that the National Council of Churches had repeatedly condemned segregation and had requested its constituent denominations to issue similar condemnations, and that most of the major denominations had endorsed the action of the Council.[106] In 1946, the Federal Council of Churches, later succeeded by the National Council of Churches, had issued a statement rejecting segregation:

> The Federal Council of Churches of Christ in America hereby renounces the pattern of segregation in race relations as unnecessary and undesirable and a violation of the gospel of love and human brotherhood. Having taken this action, the Federal Council requests its constituent communions to do likewise. As proof of their sincerity in this renunciation they will work for a nonsegregated church and a nonsegregated society.[107]

In 1963, the National Council of Churches budgeted $300,000 to support civil rights activities, and in 1965, in one of its several projects it built voter education centers in Mississippi to overturn segregation.

King also acknowledged that the Roman Catholic Church had declared that segregation is morally wrong and sinful.[108] After an audience with Pope Paul VI in 1964, he stated, "The Pope made it palpably clear that he is a friend of the Negro people, and asked me to tell the American Negroes that he is committed to the cause of civil rights in the United States."[109] In 1967, the Pope stated, "The Second Vatican Council clearly and repeatedly condemned racism in its various forms as being an offense against human dignity. . . ."[110]

While King approved of the "sublime statements" of Protestant and Catholic Church authorities, he complained that these stands were far too few, and that in actual practice they moved all too slowly down to the local churches.[111] In a 1964 article "The Churches Will Follow" Dr. Benjamin Mays, former president of Morehouse College who had helped inspire King to enter the ministry, lamented the fact that on the local level the majority of churches would practice open membership only when it was considered safe to do so, and that all too many ministers would lead in the desegregation of their churches only when there was widespread acceptance of the idea in their local communities.[112] Mays stated that if the local churches had at once supported the 1954 Supreme Court decision on school desegregation on the basis of religion and morals, the turmoil and bitterness of the previous ten years might have been avoided or at least greatly reduced.

King felt disappointment with the white Church as early as the Montgomery Boycott. At the inception of the boycott he was confident that the white ministers and priests of the South would prove to be among his strongest allies, but his optimism was soon shattered as some of them refused to understand the freedom movement, misrepresented its leaders, and became open adversaries while all too many other clergymen were "more cautious than courageous" and "remained silent behind the anesthetizing security of stained-glass windows."[113] In 1962, he stated:

> As a minister of the gospel I am ashamed to have to affirm that eleven o'clock on Sunday morning, when we stand to sing, "In Christ There Is No East Nor West," is the most segregated hour of America, and the Sunday School is the most segregated school of the week.[114]

When he came to Birmingham, he hoped that the white religious leadership would see the justice of his cause and would assist in transforming the power structure, but once again his hopes were dashed when eight Protestant, Catholic, and Jewish clergymen of Alabama issued a statement criticizing his demonstrations as "unwise and untimely," as "extreme measures" inciting to hatred and violence, and as directed in part by "outsiders."[115] The statement appealed to the black community to withdraw support from the demonstrations and to unite locally and rely on negotiation among local leaders and the courts to achieve "a better Birmingham."[116]

In expressing his disappointment with the white ministers, King did add that criticism should not be directed against those ministers who believed that segregation violated the will of God and the spirit of Christ, were faced with the alternatives of taking a vocal stand and being fired or of keeping silent in order to remain in the situation and do some good for race relations, and chose the latter alternative. He recognized that the replacement of such men by ministers favoring segregation would have only impeded the struggle for freedom.[117]

However, he warned that a minister must never permit the notion that it is better to remain quiet so as to help the cause to become a rationalization for doing nothing. "The most important thing is for every minister to dedicate himself to the Christian ideal of brotherhood, and be sure that he is doing something positive to implement it."[118]

Although King did not mention it in his writings, he must have experienced further disappointment with the white Church when some ministers criticized him for being one of the founders of the Gandhi Society for Human Rights. In 1962, the Reverend John Morris, executive director of the Episcopal Society for Cultural and Racial Unity, described the Gandhi Society as "a symbol of the departure from orthodox Christian tradition of key spokesmen who might otherwise have led in the renewal of the Church in areas connected with race."[119] He accused King and others of seeking a new creedal foundation for nonviolent action and a way of life in Gandhi's thought:

> It is a new crucifixion when Gandhi displaces Christ as the source of power and motivation for those who call themselves Christian. . . . The Way of the Cross is sufficient encouragement to non-violence for Christians.[120]

Morris contended that one may rightly honor Gandhi and his followers, but avoid turning esteem into a new religion. He concluded his critique by denying that King had allowed an authentic role for Christ in his nonviolence:

> The Christ of the overturned tables and crown of thorns calls us to the same commitments and goals. A residual readiness to follow such a Christ might have led to a great awakening had Dr. King felt called in such directions. New prophets must come forward now if Christ is not to be shunted aside in favor of humanistic loyalties which man elevates higher than faith.[121]

The reason King did not allude to this criticism in his writings may have been that four years before he had already rendered it groundless by his explanation in *Stride Toward Freedom* that he combined the love ethic and spirit of Jesus with the nonviolent method of Gandhi.[122] Moreover, his prophetic and pastoral ministry, rooted in his Baptist faith, was a consistent revelation of the role of Christ in his life.

The Challenge and Limitations of Communism

As part of his plea for the Church to be more actively concerned with promoting social justice, King challenged Christians to witness the zeal and commitment of Communists to a cause they believe will create a better world. He marvelled at the Communists' sense of purpose and of destiny, and ardently wished that the fire in Christian hearts burned with the same intensity.[123] In an effort to discover the reasons for the special appeal of Communism for so many, on his own initiative as a student at Crozer Theological Seminary he studied *The Communist Manifesto* and *Das Kapital* as well as some interpretative works on Marx and Lenin.[124] He resumed his study of Marx in a course on the philosophy of history at the University of Pennsylvania and in courses at Crozer on Tillich and Niebuhr, whose early works were influenced by Marx. In *Stride Toward Freedom* he later explained that he had read Marx, as he had read other influential historical thinkers, from a dialectical point of view, combining a partial yes and a partial no with the result that, even though he regarded Communism as "basically evil" and stated that his response to it was "negative," he claimed that he found challenging points in Communism.[125]

King felt a genuine admiration for Marx's "passion for social justice."[126] In *Strength To Love*, in attempting to explain the origin of Marx's concern for the cause of the poor, the exploited and the disinherited, he concluded that Marx was the champion of the poor because he had been nourished by both the Hebrew and the Christian Scriptures.[127] He maintained that Marx, who must have been trained in the Hebrew Scriptures by his Jewish parents, both of whom were descended from rabbis, could not forget the words of the prophet Amos, "Let judgment roll down as waters and righteousness as a mighty stream."[128] He asserted that since Marx's parents adopted Christianity when he was a child, Marx could not forget the message of the gospels about Jesus' concern for the welfare of the poor, for the "least of these."[129] He also praised Marx for developing a theory that aimed at the creation of a classless society. *The Communist Manifesto* clearly revealed this goal: "In place of the old bourgeois society, with its classes and class antagonisms, we shall have an association in which the free development of each is the condition for the free development of all."[130] King saw that not only did the theory dispense with the distinction of class but it also rejected any distinction based on race, color or caste. The color of a man's skin theoretically could not disqualify him from membership in the Communist Party. In sharp contrast to this humanitarian message in Marx's doctrine, the Christian Church was a major force in perpetuating segregation in American society.[131]

While acknowledging that the capitalism attacked by Marx was not identifiable with American capitalism, King nevertheless believed that Marx's critique of capitalism was applicable to our system to the extent that it exposed the gulf between superfluous wealth and abject poverty. Necessities are taken from the many in order to allow luxuries to the few, and this system has allowed some to remain apathetic to the suffering of humanity. King synthesized insights from Marx and Buber when he contended, "The profit motive, when it is the sole basis of an economic system, encourages a cutthroat competition and selfish ambition that inspire men to be more I-centered than thou-centered."[132] Instead of making a life, individuals become more concerned about making a living. Our salary and material possessions become the criteria of our success and not "the quality of our service and relationship to humanity."[133]

Although King expressed his genuine admiration for Marx's passionate concern for the underprivileged, still he felt it necessary to level several serious criticisms against Communist theory and practice. He repudiated the Communist doctrines on man and history. He was convinced that reality cannot be reduced to matter and motion, and that history cannot be reduced to the interplay of economic forces.[134] Marx highlighted this materialism as the feature of his system that most clearly separated it from Hegel's idealism:

> To Hegel . . . the real world is only the external, phenomenal form of "the Idea." With me, on the contrary, the ideal is nothing else than the material world reflected by the human mind and translated into forms of thought.[135]

King criticized Marx for rejecting Hegel's idealism and spiritualism.[136] He regarded Marx's reductions as distortions since they ignored the Spirit Who as Infinite Love and Power is the Ground of all reality, and Who works through history for the salvation of His children. He considered Communism to be unacceptable also because it declares this God to be a figment of the imagination, religion to be the result of fear and ignorance, and the Church to be an invention of rulers to control the masses. He maintained that Communism suffers under the illusion that man without divine help can create a new society. This atheistic humanism is inadequate since man, as a result of his sin and finiteness, needs a Saviour especially in the task of self-improvement. He believed too that Marx, by his explanation of the historical process solely in terms of collisions between economic classes, neglected the vast array of moral, psychological, political, and religious factors also responsible for the formation of institutions and ideologies.[137]

King felt compelled to reject Communism also because of its denial of the existence of eternal and unchangeable moral principles. Instead of affirming the existence of absolute right and wrong, Communists endorse any method that can promote the goal of a classless society, even if that method involves lying, violence, torture, and murder. King appealed to the words of Lenin to reinforce this charge. "We must be ready to employ trickery, deceit, lawbreaking, withholding and concealing truth."[138] While King could praise the noble nature of the goal of a classless society, he could only condemn the use of immoral means to this goal. "Christianity at its best refuses to live by a philosophy of ends justifying means."[139] In contrast to Communism, Christianity affirms that unchangeable moral principles do exist and are rooted in the divine will. These principles should govern not only the choice of our goals but also the choice of the means to our goals:

> In a real sense, the means represent the ideal in the making and the end in process. So in the long run destructive means cannot bring about constructive ends because the end is preexistent in the means.[140]

In his dissertation King quoted Henry Nelson Wieman's conviction about this truth:

> To say that the process is mere means and therefore of less value than the possibility which is the end is to set up a wholly vicious dichotomy between means and ends. The highest possibilities of value can never be attained except by way of [the] process which leads to them.[141]

As already seen, Gandhi emphasized the necessity of moral means. "Means are after all everything. As the means, so the end. There is no wall of separation between means and end. . . ."[142]

Furthermore, King denounced the political totalitarianism of Communism. He recognized that Communist theory declares that the state is but an "interim reality" which will be replaced by a classless society.

However, he stressed that for the sake of the goal of a classless society, the Communist state suppresses freedoms of the press, vote, and assembly.[143] *The Communist Manifesto* proclaimed the necessity of "despotic inroads on the rights of property and on the conditions of bourgeois production."[144] In this system man becomes little more than a depersonalized cog in the wheel of the state. Communism divests the individual of his dignity as a person since his dignity springs from his freedom.[145] Communism would smother the individual in order to save him. King found Communism guilty of the same evil as segregation since, by depriving man of freedom, it relegates him to the status of a thing. In Kantian terms King protested, "Man is not made for the state; the state is made for man. . . . Man must never be treated as a means to the end of the state, but always as an end within himself."[146] He contended that the Kingdom of God can be found neither in the thesis of traditional capitalism since it failed to see that life is also social nor in the antithesis of Marxism since it failed and continues to fail to see that life is also personal. Yet, since each of these systems does contain a partial truth, the Kingdom of God may be found in a synthesis of these truths in the form of a socially conscious democracy, which recognizes both the rights of the community and the rights and dignity of the individual.[147]

Because of its materialism, ethical relativism, and totalitarianism, King regarded Communism as fundamentally incompatible with Christianity. "A true Christian cannot be a true Communist, for the two philosophies are antithetical and all the dialectics of the logicians cannot reconcile them."[148] Although King maintained that these two philosophies are fundamentally opposed in the ways in which they view the world, he claimed that Communism can reawaken the Church to its social mission. He warned that, after condemning the philosophy of Communism, the best way the Church can combat Communism, its "most formidable rival," is to use its influence to open the doors of opportunity and to seek to eliminate economic insecurity, injustice, racial discrimination, and poverty—all of which provide a fertile soil for Communism. He claimed that any religion that claims to be concerned with the souls of men and is not concerned with the economic and social conditions that cripple men is the kind the Marxist describes as "an opiate of the people."[149] He agreed with the judgment of William Temple, former Archbishop of Canterbury, that Communism is a Christian heresy since it theoretically seeks social justice, and King admonished the Church to assume the lead in social reform if it is to overcome the threat of this heresy:[150]

We must not engage in a negative anti-Communism, but rather in a positive thrust for democracy, realizing that our greatest defense against Communism is to take offensive action in behalf of justice and righteousness.[151]

The Beloved Community: The Ultimate Norm and Goal

King maintained that the social mission of the Christian Church requires that it have as its primary goal the development of the beloved community. The stated ultimate aim of SCLC was to seek reconciliation and the formation of a community based on love.[152] King's conception of the beloved community represented a synthesis of insights from several sources including the Hebrew prophets, the New Testament, the founding fathers, Kant, Hegel, Marx, Rauschenbusch, the existentialists, Nygren, Gandhi, Niebuhr, Ramsey, Thurman, and the Personalists, especially DeWolf, Brightman, Muelder, and Davis. While several thinkers contributed to King's conception of the beloved community, Personalism emerged as the dominant influence in his thoughts about this community which was the goal of all his endeavors.

King explained that members of the beloved community would allow the spirit of *agape* to direct all their individual and social relationships; hence they would manifest a persistent willingness to sacrifice for the good of the community and for their own spiritual and temporal good. In their private lives and as members of a caring community, they would regard each person as an image of God and an heir to a legacy of dignity and worth with rights that are not derived from the state but from God. Inspired by a vision of "total interrelatedness" and of the solidarity of the human family, they would be aware that what directly affects one person affects all persons indirectly. By their laws, actions, and attitudes they would never reduce persons to mere means but always treat them as ends-in-themselves with the right of rational self-determination. They would judge persons not on the basis of the color of their skin but on the content of their character. King maintained that such an ideal community not only would exclude all forms of discrimination in education, employment, housing, and public accommodations but also would consistently exemplify full integration, that is, "genuine intergroup and interpersonal living."[153] Every member of such a community would welcome the participation of every other member in every phase of social life, not because of the pressure of laws but because of a commitment to brotherhood. Their industries would be more concerned with persons than with profits, would respect the rights of consumers, and would so improve job opportunities, working conditions, human relations, and the sharing of profits that all workers would be free of a destructive feeling of alienation from their work, their co-workers, and themselves. Their governments would concentrate on developing moral power, would arrange to share political power with their citizens, and would recognize that their resources, when possible, should be compassionately used as instruments of service for all their citizens and for the rest of humanity. Their governments would also work to preserve international harmony and would establish domestic justice by ensuring equality under law for all citizens, and by providing the necessary educational, social, and economic opportunities and assistance so that all persons could preserve their dignity and channel their creativity. Their schools would provide quality education for all. Their churches would open their doors to all races, actively promote ecumenical endeavors, be involved in community programs to enhance the spiritual and temporal well-being of all, and when necessary, be willing to speak as the conscience of the nation.

At times King alluded to the ideal of the beloved community as if it could be achieved. Thus in 1965, he stated, "It is the keystone of my faith in the future that we will someday achieve a thoroughly integrated society."[154] Nonetheless, despite statements of this kind, there were certain elements in his thought which indicated that he could not have expected that the perfect beloved community in its fullness could ever become an historical reality.

First, King emphasized in his writings that man is a sinner. He acknowledged his indebtedness to Reinhold Niebuhr's "realism" for helping him recognize the illusions of a superficial optimism concerning human nature and the dangers of a false idealism, and to be more aware of "the glaring reality of collective evil."[155] In *Strength To Love* he asserted, "Man collectivized in the group, the tribe, the race, and the nation often sinks to levels of barbarity unthinkable even among lower animals."[156] He indicated that Niebuhr emphasized that thinkers such as Kierkegaard, Nietzsche, and Freud in their explorations of the dark depths of the human heart confirmed the biblical doctrine of the sinfulness of man.[157] King maintained that Niebuhr's theology "is a persistent reminder of the reality of sin on every level of man's existence," and affirmed:

Evil is with us as a stark, grim, and colossal reality. The Bible affirms the reality of evil in glaring terms. It symbolically pic-

tures it in the work of a serpent which comes to inject a discord
into the beautiful, harmonious symphony of life in a garden. . . .
The whole history of life is the history of a struggle between good
and evil.[158]

King stressed that all the great religions have recognized that in the
midst of the upward thrust of goodness there is the downward pull of
evil. They have discerned a tension at the very core of the universe.
Thus Hinduism regards this tension as a conflict between reality and
illusion; Zoroastrianism, as a conflict between the god of light and the
god of darkness; and Judaism and Christianity, as a conflict between
God and Satan.[159] As we have seen in his essay, "How Modern Christians Should Think of Man," King described as "perilous" the tendency of some liberal theologians to regard sin as a mere "lag of
nature" that can be progressively eliminated as man climbs the evolutionary ladder.[160] He defined man as "a being in need of continuous
repentance."[161] Niebuhr had contended, "Even in our highest moral
achievements we continue to be in contradiction to God and therefore
require his mercy."[162] Given King's conviction about human sinfulness, he could not believe that humanity could create the perfect beloved community.

Personalism intensified King's awareness of the reality of sin. In *A
Theology of the Living Church* DeWolf developed the notion of "the
prevalence of sin."[163] He indicated that the New Testament often refers
to the universality of sin, and that Jesus stated, "No one is good but
God alone."[164] But he also explained that when the Scriptures teach
that all men are sinners, this does not imply that every human deed is a
sin or that sin prevails in every life. He alluded to St. Paul's praise of
those Gentiles who did not have the law but who lived in conformity
with the law, and to Jesus' Parable of the Last Judgment in which he
referred to the "righteous people" and described them in concrete
terms as caring for the needy. Having made these qualifications, De-
Wolf still maintained:

> Yet whatever good deeds any person has done, who can claim to
> have fulfilled the command to "be perfect as your heavenly
> Father is perfect"? While acknowledging that men do good as
> well as evil, the Scripture clearly teaches that "all have sinned and
> fall short of the glory of God."[165]

DeWolf added that all human beings who live to maturity are probably
involved in material sin, that is, action not in conformity with God's

will, whether or not they are aware of this lack of conformity.[166] He questioned whether even those who have renounced all evils could say that they are free of all of them, and that they are doing everything possible to prevent and relieve the suffering and guilt that result from evils. He also questioned whether persons could be certain that they are not engaged in active participation or acquiescent involvement in sin. He claimed that since the human capacity for self-deception is so great, it is at least highly probable that if we are convinced that we are free from active participation or acquiescent involvement in sin, we are mistaken in this conviction. Furthermore, DeWolf questioned whether any one of us can claim to know the will of God for ourself at every moment:

> Imperfect in knowledge as we are, we may make a choice with the best of intentions to do God's will and yet miss the mark, perhaps with most destructive consequences, affecting even those persons whom we love most dearly.[167]

In the light of these considerations alone it would be difficult to contend that King's commitment to Personalism could allow him to believe that humanity could fully concretize the ideal of the beloved community.

Second, although King spoke of "an amazing potential for goodness" in human nature, he accepted the notion developed by Tillich, the existentialists, and others that man's freedom is limited, and that man is a finite child of nature.[168] When King admitted that the laws of nature and the elements of "natural necessity" they involve interfere with the higher life of man, he recognized that these laws interfere with the human commitment to *agape,* and therefore with the perfect actualization of the beloved community.

Third, King acknowledged that the existentialists contributed to our understanding of man's estrangement from his own essential nature and to our perception of the anxiety that permeates individual and social existence. He believed that man's cooperation with divine grace could empower man to deal constructively with this anxiety and self-estrangement, but never completely to eliminate these basic conditions that increase the limitations on man's freedom and restrict his capacity to love and hence his ability to achieve the perfect actualization of the beloved community.

Fourth, King identified with Hegel's conviction that it belongs to the nature of the human spirit to develop dialectically as it struggles against objective evils, so that he could not also consistently affirm that humanity could arrive at a beloved community in any final form that, in effect, would eliminate the necessity for continuous struggle.

Fifth, King accepted the Personalist view of human nature, that emphasized the need for continual progress. According to Brightman, this view of human nature is "an affirmation of the possibility of infinite progress," and "a denial that any limit can be set, as long as man is conscious, which would render progress impossible."[169] "Wherever there are men and God in a universe there are always inexhaustible possibilities of progress."[170]

Sixth, King also accepted the Personalist law that all persons ought to will the best possible values in every situation. As Brightman explained, "The ideal of the best possible is relatively modest in comparison with the ideal of absolute and complete perfection. . . ."[171]

Seventh, while King stressed that court orders and Federal enforcement agencies were of inestimable value in achieving desegregation and while he did refer to the day when all citizens in every court would receive equal protection of the laws, he also warned that desegregation would be only a partial step toward the goal of "genuine intergroup and interpersonal living."[172] He asserted that desegregation would bring people together physically but not necessarily spiritually. "A vigorous enforcement of civil rights laws . . . cannot bring an end to fears, prejudice, pride, and irrationality, which are the barriers to a truly integrated society."[173] He cautioned that laws cannot reach inner attitudes and change the heart.[174] Although he believed that religion and education could help to transform attitudes, there is no evidence that he felt that their efforts could create a perfect beloved community.

If King did not expect that humanity could achieve the perfect actualization of the ideal of the beloved community, then what purpose did this ideal serve in his Movement? As early as the Montgomery Boycott he stressed that while nonviolent resistance had become the technique of the Movement, love stood as its regulating ideal.[175] Although he agreed with Niebuhr on the reality of collective evil, he was able to avoid Niebuhr's pessimism about challenging this evil:

Although man's moral pilgrimage may never reach a destination point on earth, his never-ceasing strivings may bring him ever closer to the city of righteousness. And though the Kingdom of God may remain *not yet* as a universal reality in history, in the present it may exist in such isolated forms as in judgment, in personal devotion, and in some group life.[176]

Though mindful of human limitations, King could still affirm with the Personalists the power of divine grace, the human capacity for *agape*, and the moral obligation to will the best possible values in every situation. DeWolf has indicated that without believing that the beloved community will be perfectly fulfilled in history, we can preserve this beloved community as a very realistic and active goal, and use it for normative measuring of different policies that are proposed to determine whether or not these policies move in the direction of this ideal.[177] In *Crime and Justice in America: A Paradox of Conscience*, which he dedicated to "the revered memory of my student and cherished friend Martin Luther King, Jr., who stirred many Americans to seek justice with new urgency," DeWolf stressed that even Reinhold Niebuhr allowed for a crucial role for love in the creation of social justice:

> Even Reinhold Niebuhr with all his "realistic" warnings about the "impossible possibility" of love in the social order, assumes it as the Christian ideal. He says too that "the law of love is involved in all approximations of justice, not only as the source of the norms of justice, but as an ultimate perspective by which their limitations are discovered."[178]

King could identify with Brightman's affirmation:

> This world is such that in all its history it will never be perfect; yet it is such that the other world, the world of the perfect ideal, will always be at work in it. As surely as there is a world against which we protest, so surely the ideal in the name of which we protest is more potent than the world's evils.[179]

Gandhi argued that the fact that the individual cannot reach the perfect state while still in the body allows for the constant striving after the ideal that is the basis of all spiritual progress.[180] The ideal must remain the goal:

> Man will ever remain imperfect, and it will always be his part to try to be perfect; so that perfection in love or non-possession will remain an unattainable ideal as long as we are alive but towards which we must ceaselessly strive.[181]

In proposing nonviolence as the ideal he acknowledged:

> We may never be strong enough to be entirely non-violent in thought, word, and deed. But we must keep non-violence as our goal and make steady progress towards it.[182]

In Rauschenbusch King could have found a similar emphasis. In *Christianity and the Social Crisis,* without promoting any utopian delusion, he appealed for faith in the possibility of a new social order:

> We know well that there is no perfection for man in this life; there is only growth toward perfection. . . . We make it a duty to seek what is unattainable. We have the same paradox in the perfectibility of society. We shall never have a perfect social life, yet we must seek it with faith.[183]

By emphasizing humanity's moral obligation to struggle against injustice and by affirming its capacity to move closer to the ideal of the beloved community, King not only rejected the excessive optimism of liberal theology, which taught that religion and education without social pressure could make the actualization of the ideal inevitable, but he also transcended Niebuhr's pessimism. King was convinced that we can adequately understand human nature not by adopting the thesis of liberalism or the antithesis of neo-orthodoxy but by relying on a synthesis that includes the truths of both.[184] His realistic view of humanity ignored neither the human capacity for good nor its capacity for evil. Thus he concluded, "Even though all progress is precarious, within limits real social progress may be made."[185]

While recognizing the human potential for both good and evil, King maintained that humanity is moving toward the beloved community. In 1959, he spoke of the period after the 1954 Supreme Court decision on school desegregation as one of "constructive integration . . . in which men seek to rise to the level of genuine intergroup and interpersonal living."[186] In his Nobel Lecture in 1964 he asserted:

> What we are seeing now is a Freedom Explosion, the realization of "An idea whose time has come". . . . The deep rumbling of discontent that we hear today is the thunder of disinherited masses, rising from the dungeons of oppression to the bright hills of freedom.[187]

In his Nobel Acceptance Speech he expressed his belief that nonviolent redemptive goodwill would proclaim the rule of the land, and reaffirmed the prophetic vision of an era in which "the lion and the lamb shall lie down together and every man shall sit under his own vine and fig tree and none shall be afraid."[188]

Even though King often expressed his confidence about the direction of history, there are references in his writings and speeches to the possibility that the nation and the world may choose the road of injustice and even self-destruction. He concluded a 1965 interview by warning, "If the problem [of injustice to blacks] is not solved, America will be on the road to its self-destruction."[189] In his last published interview he warned:

> The question that now faces us is whether we can turn the Negro's disillusionment and bitterness into hope and faith in the essential goodness of the American system. If we don't, our society will crumble.[190]

He claimed that even as ancient Rome when it began to disintegrate turned to strengthening its military establishment instead of correcting the corruption within its society, so too America had turned to militarism and would probably suffer a similar end if blacks did not provide a new soul-force for all Americans.[191] In a speech on the night before his assassination he again warned:

> And also in the human rights revolution, if something isn't done, and in a hurry, to bring the colored peoples of the world out of their long years of poverty, their long years of hurt and neglect, the whole world is doomed.[192]

Despite this type of reference, the more frequent and dominant emphasis in his writings and speeches was on his faith that humanity would proceed toward a community based on love and justice. This was evident in the conclusion to the same speech. "And I've seen the promised land. I may not get there with you. But I want you to know tonight, that we, as a people, will get to the promised land."[193] It was also evident in his last book, *The Trumpet of Conscience*, which stated, "We are marching . . . in legions of thousands. . . . Today, the question is not whether we shall be free but by what course we will win."[194]

King's faith and hope that humanity would put an end to the external forms of segregation and discrimination and would continue to progress toward the beloved community, the Kingdom of God, was rooted in his Personalist conviction that God is in control of history and wills that humanity progress toward justice and freedom:

> Let us realize that as we struggle for justice and freedom, we have cosmic companionship. . . . The God that we worship . . . is an other-loving God Who forever works through history for the establishment of His kingdom.[195]

God is more fundamental than sin or evil. Good Friday must give way to Easter:

> The cross is the eternal expression of the length to which God will go in order to restore broken community. The resurrection is a symbol of God's triumph over all the forces that seek to block community. The Holy Spirit is the continuing community creating reality that moves through history.[196]
>
> All reality hinges on moral foundations . . . and the whole cosmic universe has spiritual control.[197]
>
> There is something in this universe which justifies Carlyle in saying, "No lie can live forever." There is something in this universe which justifies William Cullen Bryant in saying, "Truth crushed to earth will rise again." There is something in this universe which justifies James Russell Lowell in saying, "Truth forever on the scaffold, wrong forever on the throne. Yet, that scaffold sways the future, and behind the dim unknown stands God—within the shadow keeping watch above His own."[198]

In 1963, King appealed to the fact that within twenty-five years vast numbers of Asians and Africans had been freed from oppression and colonialism as evidence that the development of man under God is in the direction of freedom.[199]

King spoke often of his dream of a land where everyone would respect the dignity of human personality. In 1967, in *The Trumpet of Conscience* he reaffirmed his faith in this dream that he had so eloquently described at the March on Washington. He asserted that despite widespread poverty, riots, and the Vietnam War, he still had a dream that men would come to see that they are made to live together as brothers.[200] In his efforts to bring about even the incomplete realization of this dream, King believed that he was not only executing God's will but also helping to realize the American dream of the freedom, equality, dignity, and worth of every human being.[201] He designed his protests for civil rights to lead the nation to live its professed values. In his Nobel Lecture he explained that the nonviolent demonstrators had taken the nation back to "those great wells of democracy which were dug deep by the founding fathers in the formulation of the Constitution and the Declaration of Independence."[202] Speaking for those in the Movement he proclaimed:

> We feel that we are the conscience of America—we are its troubled soul—we will continue to insist that right be done because both God's Will and the heritage of our nation speak through our echoing demands.[203]

King contended that because of the unresolved race question, our Government from the day of its birth had been "weakened in its integrity, confused and confounded in its direction."[204] American officials were hypocritical when they advocated free elections in Europe while elections were not held in great sections of America. America must struggle for democracy at home. King declared that black Americans thought it ironic that they were governed, taxed, and given orders, but had no representation in a nation that would defend the right to vote abroad.[205] He concluded that America had a "schizophrenic personality on the question of race" since it had proclaimed a dream marked by "an amazing universalism" that stated that all men are endowed by their Creator with certain inalienable rights, that among these are life, liberty, and the pursuit of happiness, and yet it had practiced the very antithesis of these principles in the form of slavery and segregation. He judged the issue of civil and human rights as "the most weighty social problem of this century" and as "an eternal moral issue which may well determine the destiny of our nation in the ideological struggle with Communism."[206] However, he contended that the primary reason the nation should abandon racial discrimination was not the need to respond to the Communist challenge or to appeal to Asian and African peoples but because discrimination was morally wrong and prevented us from realizing the sublime principles of our Judeo-Christian tradition.[207]

To highlight his message that the nation should live in conformity with its professed principles and should reject racism by its actions King quoted the 1944 judgment of Gunnar Myrdal, the Swedish economist, in *An American Dilemma*:

. . . the Negro problem is not only America's greatest failure but also America's incomparably great opportunity for the future. If America should follow its own deepest convictions, its well-being at home would be increased directly. At the same time America's prestige and power abroad would rise immensely. The century-old dream of American patriots, that America should give to the entire world its own freedoms and its own faith, would come true. America can demonstrate that justice, equality and cooperation are possible between white and colored people. . . . *America is free to choose whether the Negro shall remain her liability or become her opportunity.*[208]

King maintained that in all of their nonviolent protests black Americans were aiming to become more American, not less.[209] In his appeals for social justice he frequently alluded to the loyalty of black Americans to the nation, and to their sacrifices in peace and war. It was through appeals such as these that he aimed to arouse the conscience of the nation:

And so our most urgent message to this nation must be summarized in these simple words: "We just want to be free." We are not seeking to dominate the nation politically or hamper its social growth; we just want to be free. . . . America, in calling for our freedom we are not unmindful of the fact that we have been loyal to you. We have loved you even in the moments of your greatest denial of our freedom. And now we are simply saying that we want to be free. We have stood with you in every major crisis. Since Crispus Attucks gave his life on Boston's Commons black men and women have been mingling their blood with other Americans in defense of this Republic. For the protection of our honored flag which still floats untarnished in the breeze, Negro men and women have died on the far-flung battlefields of the world. And so, America, we think we have a right to insist on our freedom. For your security, America, our sons . . . died in the trenches of France, in the foxholes of Germany, on the beachheads of Italy, and on the islands of Japan. And now, America, we are simply asking you to guarantee our freedom. . . .[210]

If this is done, we will be able to emerge from the bleak and desolate midnight of man's inhumanity to man into the bright and glittering daybreak of freedom and justice. This will be a great day, not only for America, but for the whole human family.[211]

Chapter 6

King's Critiques of Other Responses to Collective Evil

Since King believed that oppressed people have a moral obligation to resist any system that refuses to treat them as persons, he believed it necessary to expose and denounce any type of response by the oppressed that would ignore this duty to resist or would resort to immoral forms of resistance. Therefore, he rejected Booker T. Washington's method of the passive acceptance of segregation since he thought that it involved a lack of self-determination, robbed the black man of his dignity, and allowed the oppressor to feel justified. Nor could he accept W. E. B. DuBois's method of resistance because it depended mainly upon the efforts of a "Talented Tenth" instead of relying on the masses. Neither could he approve of Marcus Garvey's call for a "return to Africa" since it provided no solution for blacks who had their roots in America. King contended that the Black Power Movement suffered from serious defects such as the emphasis on separatism and the approval by some of its members of aggressive violence. He maintained that the Black Muslims also were deficient in their appeals for separatism, retaliatory violence, and hatred of whites. Moreover, he denounced the individual reactions of self-pity, bitterness, apathy, silence, and fatalism as inadequate and immoral responses to oppression. The basis for his critiques of these responses was his conviction that nonviolent resistance in conjunction with education, political action, and litigation is the only moral and effective way of overcoming oppression.

Booker T. Washington's "Passive Acceptance"

In rejecting passive acceptance as the path to social justice, King found it necessary to criticize the philosophy of Booker T. Washington. Born a slave on a Virginia plantation, Washington became founder and president of Tuskegee Normal and Industrial Institute in Alabama. Through his achievements with the institute and his speeches and writings calling for Negro self-improvement and for interracial cooperation, he won national and international acclaim, and even the friendship of Presidents Cleveland, Coolidge, Roosevelt, and Taft. Washington outlined his philosophy in his Atlanta Exposition Address of 1895. He warned Negroes, "It is at the bottom of life we must begin, and not at the top."[1] He advised them that they would prosper to the extent that they learned to dignify and glorify common labor, and to apply their intelligence and skill to the common occupations of life. He claimed that it was the Negro's lack of knowledge and experience that caused him to seek first a seat in Congress or in the state legislature rather than a real estate or an industrial skill, and which led him to prefer the activity of a political convention to starting a dairy farm or a truck garden.

In this address, as part of his appeal for harmony between the races, Washington issued a challenge to those Negroes who thought that they could better their condition in a foreign land and to those who were reluctant to cultivate friendly relations with their Southern white neighbors, " 'Cast down your bucket where you are.'—Cast it down in making friends in every manly way of the people of all races by whom we are surrounded."[2] He directed the same challenge to those whites who chose to bypass Negroes and to look to immigrants for the future prosperity of the South. He reminded them of the fidelity, love, and contributions of eight million Negroes to the progress of the South. If those whites did "cast down their bucket" with his people, he promised them that in the future, as in the past, they and their families would be "surrounded by the most patient, faithful, law-abiding, and unresentful people that the world has seen."[3] It is significant that he added an assurance that revealed the limited nature of his goals as well as his passive acceptance of social segregation. "In all things that are purely social we [Negroes and whites] can be as separate as the fingers, yet one as the hand in all things essential to mutual progress."[4]

Washington repudiated any agitation on questions of social equality as the "extremest folly," and indicated that progress by Negroes in the enjoyment of privileges that would come to them had to be the result of "severe and constant struggle" rather than "artificial forcing."[5] Evidently, he wanted the Negro to struggle with self and not against the legal and economic injustices within the system of segregation. While granting that all the privileges of the law should belong to Negroes, he stressed that it was much more important that they be prepared for the exercise of these privileges. He concluded the speech by praying for the abolition of sectional differences, racial animosities, and suspicions, for the determination to administer absolute justice, and for the willingness of all classes to obey the mandates of law. It is not surprising that President Cleveland understood this speech not as a protest to whites for social justice but rather as an appeal to Negroes to work for self-development within existing opportunities already offered by the system. In a letter to Washington he stated:

> Your words cannot fail to delight and encourage all who wish well for your race; and if our coloured fellow-citizens do not from your utterances gather new hope and form new determinations to gain every valuable advantage offered them by their citizenship, it will be strange indeed.[6]

In his discussion of the Atlanta Address in his autobiography *Up From Slavery*, published in 1901, Washington explained that some Negroes had criticized him for being too liberal in his remarks toward Southern whites and for not speaking out strongly enough for the rights of his race, but he claimed that later he had become successful in winning over these critics to his belief and practice.[7] However, despite this claim, some Negroes did continue to feel resentment at his program which they thought surrendered their civil and political rights, even though it provided them with greater opportunities for economic development. William E. B. DuBois led the opposition to this program, and in *The Souls of Black Folk* denounced it for becoming a "Gospel of Work and Money" to such an extent that it apparently almost completely overshadowed the higher aims of life.[8] He labeled the Atlanta Address the "Atlanta Compromise" since it asked Negroes for the present to give up political power, insistence on civil rights, and the higher education of their youth, and to devote their energies to industrial education, the accumulation of wealth, and the conciliation of the South. He declared that Washington's program represented the traditional Negro attitude of adjustment and submission, and that it practically accepted the alleged inferiority of the Negro. "Manly self-respect is worth more than lands and houses, and . . . a people who voluntarily surrender such respect, or cease striving for it, are not worth civilizing."[9]

DuBois examined the "accomplishments" of Washington's program after fifteen years and concluded that it had served only to promote the Negro's disfranchisement, the creation of a distinct legal status of civic inferiority for the Negro, and the steady withdrawal of aid from institutions for the higher education of the Negro.[10] In this work DuBois also exposed the "triple paradox" that beset Washington. *First*, Washington was making a noble effort to change Negro artisans into businessmen and property owners but modern competitive methods made it impossible for businessmen and property-owners to defend their rights and exist if they did not have the right to vote.[11] *Second*, he emphasized thrift and self-respect, but proposed a silent submission to civic inferiority, which could only emasculate the Negro.[12] *Third*, he defended the value of common school and industrial training, and depreciated institutions of higher learning, but the former, including Tuskegee Institute, could not function if the teachers were not trained in Negro colleges or trained by their graduates.[13] DuBois appealed to the patriotism and loyalty of Negroes to oppose their own industrial slavery and civic death by all civilized methods "even though such opposition involves disagreement with Mr. Booker T. Washington."[14] In calling upon Negroes to state their legitimate demands and to oppose this honored leader, he stressed their responsibility not only to themselves but to the entire nation, "this common Fatherland." "We have no right to sit silently by while the inevitable seeds are sown for a harvest of disaster to our children, black and white."[15]

King praised DuBois for counteracting to some degree the attitude of resignation in Washington's philosophy.[16] While King maintained that Washington was sincere in his belief that the South eventually would respond voluntarily to the needs of Negroes if they did not force it to do what at the time it did not want to do, and while he conceded that Washington was not guilty of compromising his principles for the sake of keeping peace, he could not share his optimism that the Negro's possession of intelligence, high character, and property would lead the South to the full recognition of his political rights.[17] He lamented the fact that Washington's method underestimated the structures of evil and allowed for too little freedom in the present and too little promise in the future. He felt that the method of patient persuasion was so patient that it deteriorated into mere passive acceptance, and he thus summarized Washington's message, "Be content, he said in effect, with doing well what the times permit you to do at all."[18] King contended that passive acceptance of an unjust system is evil since it constitutes cooperation with that system. "Noncoöperation with evil is as much a moral obligation as is coöperation with good."[19] While he acknowledged that acquiescence is often the easier way, he warned that it is not the moral way but rather can be the way of the coward. He was convinced that the Negro cannot win the respect of his oppressor by acquiescing; he thereby merely increases the oppressor's arrogance and contempt since the oppressor interprets acquiescence as proof of the Negro's inferiority. "His [Washington's] philosophy of pressureless persuasion only served as a springboard for racist Southerners to dive into deeper and more ruthless oppression of the Negro."[20]

DuBois's Reliance on the Talented Tenth

In *Why We Can't Wait* King indicated that DuBois at the turn of the century had urged the Talented Tenth of the black race to rise and pull behind it the rest of the race. King expressed his dissatisfaction with this approach since he felt that it provided "no role for the whole people."[21] He rejected it as "a tactic for an aristocratic elite who would themselves be benefited while leaving behind the 'untalented' 90 percent."[22] His criticism was not without some basis. DuBois did explicitly refer to the need to provide special educational opportunities for the Talented Tenth. In a speech in 1903 entitled "The Training of Negroes for Social Power," he proclaimed:

> The history of civilization seems to prove that no group or nation which seeks advancement and true development can despise or neglect the power of well-trained minds; and this power of intellectual leadership must be given to the talented tenth among American Negroes before this race can seriously be asked to assume the responsibility of dispelling its own ignorance.[23]

In *The Souls of Black Folk* as he pointed with pride to the significant increase in the number of blacks who had graduated from Northern and Southern colleges, he asserted:

> Here, then, is the plain thirst for training; by refusing to give this Talented Tenth the key to knowledge, can any sane man imagine that they will lightly lay aside their yearning and contentedly become hewers of wood and drawers of water?[24]

Although DuBois did emphasize the mission of the Talented Tenth, it would be inaccurate to conclude that he did not also have a concern for the educational development of other black students. His editorials in *The Crisis*, the journal of the NAACP, frequently revealed this concern. Thus in a 1912 editorial, while he argued that black parents in educating their children should be careful "to conserve and select ability, giving to their best minds higher college training," he also maintained:

They should endeavor to give all their children the largest possible amount of *general training and intelligence* before teaching them the technique of a particular trade, remembering that the object of all true education is not to make men carpenters, but to make carpenters men.[25]

He advised parents to give their children "the broadest and highest education possible," and to "train them to the limit of their ability. . . ."[26] In a 1918 editorial he declared, ". . . The object of a school system is to carry the child as far as possible in its knowledge of the accumulated wisdom of the world. . . ."[27] He argued that Hampton Institute with its limited programs ought to be the finishing school for nine-tenths of its students, but he might well have estimated that at the time because of limited opportunities only about 10 percent of black students were qualified to receive higher education.[28] His emphasis on the widest educational opportunity for all would indicate that he was not opposed in principle to a greater number of blacks in higher education if they were qualified. Moreover, his concern for the Talented Tenth must be seen in part as a reaction to Southern efforts to halt the drive of blacks for higher education, and also as a corrective for Booker T. Washington's emphasis on industrial training for black students. DuBois proclaimed the need to challenge Washington to the extent that the latter opposed the higher training and ambition of brighter minds.[29] "We have a right to inquire . . . if after all the industrial school is the final and sufficient answer in the training of the Negro race. . . ."[30] DuBois's purpose was to ensure that *at least* the most deserving would receive a higher education and to encourage others to assimilate as much education as their abilities and condition would allow. Then too, his emphasis on the Talented Tenth may be understood as another manifestation of his concern for quality education since it allowed him to discourage the proliferation of inferior colleges for blacks. He was careful to urge black parents to strive to send their children to the best colleges.[31]

Despite his disagreement with DuBois's doctrine of the Talented Tenth, in a speech in February 1968 King spoke of his admiration for DuBois, and alluded to the fact that DuBois, though he had degrees from Harvard University and the University of Berlin, gave up the substantial privileges of a highly educated Negro in the North in order that he could live among Negroes in the South "to share their daily abuse and humiliation."[32] In this speech King selected *Black Reconstruction in America* for special praise from DuBois's eighteen books, since it refuted the almost universal interpretation that because Negroes had political power during Reconstruction, civilization in the South virtually collapsed.[33] DuBois marshalled evidence to demonstrate that during Reconstruction the economy was recovering, and free public education came into being not only for Negroes but also for poor whites. King affirmed that DuBois proved that, far from being the tragic era that white historians depicted, Reconstruction was the only period in which democracy existed in the South.[34] While discerning that Negroes were robbed of so many things decisive to their existence that the theft of their history appeared to them to be only an insignificant part of their losses, DuBois also realized that "to lose one's history is to lose one's self-understanding and with it the roots for pride."[35] He claimed that DuBois by his scholarship had rescued a heritage whose loss would have impoverished American Negroes. He asserted that DuBois was first and always a black man who took pride in being black and who dedicated his life to demolishing the myth of the inferiority of the Negro, but he added that DuBois with all his pride and spirit did not make a mystique out of blackness:

> He was proud of his people, not because their color endowed them with some vague greatness but because their concrete achievements in struggle had advanced humanity and he saw and loved progressive humanity in all its hues, black, white, yellow, red, and brown.[36]

Garvey's "Back to Africa" Movement

Marcus Garvey aimed to capture the imagination and loyalty of the black masses when he established the Universal Negro Improvement Association in Jamaica in 1914 and in Harlem in 1917.[37] In 1919, he could claim a membership of one million in the United States, the Caribbean, Latin America, and Africa. In the preamble to the constitution of the association, he defined the organization as "a social, friendly, humanitarian, charitable, educational, institutional, constructive and expansive society," and as "founded by persons, desiring to the utmost to work for the general uplift of the Negro peoples of the world."[38] He stated that one of the principal objectives of the association was the establishment of a nation in Africa where blacks, whether they were born in Africa or in the Western world, would be given the opportunity to develop by themselves, "without creating the hatred and animosity that now exist in countries of the white race through Negroes rivaling them for the highest and best positions in government, politics, society, and industry."[39] He maintained that the 400 million blacks throughout the world should have a country and government of their own that would compel the respect of all nations and races. They could free themselves from universal oppression if they could wrest Africa from the grasp of European tyranny and build a united black Africa. He affirmed that there was no other salvation for blacks but a redeemed, free, and independent Africa, which would provide protection for blacks everywhere. To achieve this emancipation of their race, New World blacks had to unite with blacks in Africa under the slogan "Africa for the Africans." Garvey repudiated the objection that fighting for the "redemption" of Africa would constitute disloyalty to the United States:

> Fighting for the establishment of Palestine does not make the American Jew disloyal; fighting for the independence of Ireland does not make the Irish-American a bad citizen. Why should fighting for the freedom of Africa make the Afro-American disloyal or a bad citizen?[40]

Garvey attempted to develop in American blacks a sense of collective pride and individual worth by emphasizing their history, tradition, and culture as a people. He reminded them that three thousand years ago on the banks of the Nile black men excelled in government, and were founders and teachers of art, science, and literature.[41] "Be as proud of your race today as our fathers were in the days of yore. We have a beautiful history, and we shall create another in the future that will astonish the world."[42] Garvey's message of a proud and independent Africa so inspired Kwame Nkrumah, first president of Ghana, that he wrote in his autobiography: "Of all the literature I studied, the book that did more than any other to fire my enthusiasm was *Philosophy and Opinions of Marcus Garvey.*"[43] W. E. B. DuBois had to concede that Garvey's influence "penetrated every corner of Africa."[44]

In *Why We Can't Wait* King acknowledged that Garvey's Movement "attained mass dimensions and released a powerful emotional response because it touched a truth which had long been dormant in the mind of the Negro. There was reason to be proud of their heritage as well as of their bitterly won achievements in America."[45] He granted that Garvey's emphasis on race pride had the virtue of rejecting concepts that fostered a sense of inferiority. King affirmed:

> We must teach every Negro child that rejection of heritage means loss of cultural roots, and people who have no past have no future.[46]
>
> With a spirit straining toward true self-esteem, the Negro must boldly throw off the manacles of self-abnegation and say to himself and the world: "I am somebody. I am a person. I am a man with dignity and honor. I have a rich and noble history, however painful and exploited that history has been. I am black *and* comely."[47]
>
> Our heritage is Africa. We should never seek to break the ties, nor should the Africans.[48]

Though King did not indicate them, there were several other themes in Garvey's philosophy that also were present in his own thought, namely, leadership involves pain, blood, and even martyrdom for the cause; every fighter for freedom must be willing to die for the realization of his dream; persecution should only increase one's determination to fight for the cause—opposition can contribute to success; much racial discrimination is due to the failure of the majority of Christians to understand and hence to practice the message of Christ; it is an insult to God Who has created everyone to be free, equal, and autonomous to assume the fatalistic attitude that God has accorded each of us a position and a condition, and that we should not attempt to change them; and the black race may well be the race that will teach humanity the way to life, liberty, and true happiness.[49]

In *Where Do We Go From Here: Chaos or Community?* King maintained that Garvey's Movement represented "a dashing of hope, a conviction of the inability of the Negro to win. . . ."[50] King thought that it was similar to the Black Power Movement in this respect. "Today's despair is a poor chisel to carve out tomorrow's justice."[51] Evidently, he was here evaluating Garvey's call for a return to Africa from his own perspective that the only authentic victory for the Negro must be within the context of an integration that recognizes the dignity of every black person. In *Why We Can't Wait* he claimed that Garvey's plan was doomed because a return to Africa in the twentieth century by a people who had established roots in America for three and a half centuries did not have the ring of progress.[52]

Garvey's call for a return to Africa was not the only way his philosophy differed from that of King. There were several other specific differences related to the call for separatism that King did not mention. *First*, King in his nonviolent crusades to bring about an integrated community remained consistent with his pronouncements about the necessity of universal love, the dignity of the self as the image of God, and the brotherhood of man. Although Garvey also wrote of the Negro's desire to love all mankind, of the duty to recognize man as the reflection of the very being of God, and of the necessity to practice the brotherhood of man with the spirit of Christ's universal love, at times in his writings he seemed to repudiate these ideals when he contended that a struggle between the white race and the black race was inevitable if the blacks did not return to Africa.[53] He seemed to foster the spirit of retaliation when he favored the possibility that "one day Africa will colonize Europe, even as Europe has been endeavoring to colonize the world for hundreds of years."[54] Even though in the preamble to the constitution of the Universal Negro Improvement Association he wrote that the members pledged themselves to do all in their power to respect the rights of all mankind, believing always in the brotherhood of man and the fatherhood of God, and that the reign of peace and plenty would be heralded into the world with "love, faith, and charity towards all," later he wrote, "Man is becoming so vile that today we cannot afford to convert him with moral, ethical, [and] physical truths alone, but with that which is more effective—implements of destruction."[55]

Apparently, Garvey could never harmonize his understanding of the spirit of universal love within Christianity with his thesis that within a few centuries the white race, pressured by its overpopulation and dwindling food supply, would attempt to move from subjugation and exploitation of the black race to its extermination as it did with the American Indian, and that this prospect should compel the black race to strengthen itself so that it would be the race to survive the conflict.[56] He stated that one of the purposes of the Universal Negro Improvement Association was to build an Africa so powerful as to make it impossible for the black race to be exterminated. His concern about a threat of racial extermination in effect caused him to reduce the unity of humanity to a unity among blacks and to restrict brotherhood to black brotherhood. King's vision of the ideal of the integrated beloved community allowed him to transcend such a limited and pessimistic understanding of the direction of history.

Second, while King believed that American blacks could achieve constitutional rights by the power of nonviolent direct action, Garvey was convinced that black agitation for full equality with whites in this civilization created by whites was doomed to failure. Garvey warned:

> Teach the Negro to do for himself, help him the best way possible in that direction; but to encourage him into the belief that he is going to possess himself of the things that others have fought and died for, is to build up in his mind false hopes never to be realized.[57]

King could not accept Garvey's premise that Western civilization, and the United States in particular, did not belong also to blacks. On many occasions King felt the need to detail for his audience how the labors and sacrifices of blacks in peace and war had amply demonstrated that they deserved an equal place in this society.

Third, although both King and Garvey made explicit appeals to the conscience of white America for justice, their appeals were quite different. King sought equal rights for blacks as citizens, but Garvey appealed to the conscience of whites only to allow blacks to create a new civilization in Africa. At times, Garvey seemed quite confident that the conscience of white America would recognize the legitimacy of his appeal.

> I believe that true justice is to be found in the conscience of the people, and when one is deprived of it by the machinations and designs of the corrupt, there can be no better tribunal of appeal than that of public opinion, which gives voice to conscience, and that is why I now appeal to the conscience of the American people for justice.[58]

While acknowledging that materialism had to a great extent destroyed the innocence and purity of the national conscience, he maintained that beyond the politics and the "soulless industrialism" there was a deep feeling of sympathy for the unfortunate that touched the soul of white America. "Surely the soul of liberal, philanthropic, liberty-loving, white America is not dead."[59] It seems that Garvey felt no need to reconcile this belief with his expectation that white America would attempt to exterminate blacks.

Fourth, while King wrote of the difficulties that confronted interracial marriage in the United States, still his convictions about the fundamental equality of human beings and about the morality of integration led him to approve of such a marriage.[60] Without King's vision of the basic unity of humanity, Garvey denounced such a marriage since it destroyed the purity of the black race. Garvey maintained that blacks only forfeited their identities through miscegenation and social intercourse with whites. "The unfortunate condition of slavery, as imposed upon the Negro, and which caused the mongrelization of the race, should not be legalized and continued now to the harm and detriment of both races."[61] He predicted that the continued social intermingling of the races would lead to more violence for the Negro:

So long as white men believe that black men want to associate with, and marry white women, then we will ever have prejudice, and not only prejudice, but riots, lynchings, burnings, and God to tell what next will follow![62]

The white man of America will not, to any organized extent, assimilate the Negro, because in so doing, he feels that he will be committing racial suicide.[63]

Fifth, King and Garvey differed in their attitudes toward black self-help. Since King believed that government, industry, and society in general should and eventually under pressure would substantially extend special assistance to blacks in compensation for centuries of deprivation, he devoted most of his efforts to securing the ballot for blacks so as to compel the white power structure to make political, economic, and social concessions. Consequently, he *did not frequently* stress the need for black self-help. For example, when he emphasized the need for blacks to secure an education, it was usually as part of his efforts to qualify them to register to vote. In contrast with King's view, Garvey felt that the ballot could not help blacks when they were jim-crowed, segregated, burned, and lynched, even though he did encourage them to achieve as much political freedom as possible.[64] Instead of relying heavily on the ballot, Garvey *repeatedly* underscored the necessity for the black race to achieve self-reliance through education and economic development. "Education is the medium by which a people are prepared for the creation of their own particular civilization, and the advancement and glory of their own race."[65] "A race that is solely dependent upon another for its economic existence sooner or later dies. . . ."[66] Garvey expressed his indebtedness to Booker T. Washington for demonstrating to him the value of black initiative in industrial development. He established colleges in Jamaica modelled after Washington's Tuskegee Institute. In 1919, Garvey initiated an impressive economic program when he established the Negro Factories Corporation and the Black Star Line. The corporation developed numerous successful businesses, but the shipping line failed because of the inexperience and incompetence of its directors.

Sixth, while King's Personalism regarded the body as an integral part of the self that, together with the soul, is subject to God's Providence, Garvey proclaimed, "God is not and Jesus is not interested in the bodies of men. . . . All that God is interested in is the spiritual. . . ."[67] Garvey here introduced a dichotomy between the spiritual and the physical that King could not accept. Moreover, King had witnessed too many instances in which environmental restrictions so debilitated the body that the soul was crippled in its spiritual development.

Seventh, King and Garvey differed in their attitudes toward the NAACP. Garvey not only disagreed with the strategies and the tactics of the NAACP in its struggles for social equality but also was quite hostile toward its president, DuBois. He criticized DuBois for using his ability to fight for a place for Negroes among whites in society, industry, and politics instead of creating something that would be a credit to the black race, and warned that this kind of leadership would lead to the destruction of the Negro in America.[68] In his concern to denounce what he regarded as the hypocrisy of the whites in the NAACP, Garvey wrote:

> Between the Ku Klux Klan and the Moorfield Storey National Association for the Advancement of "Colored" People group, give me the Klan for their honesty of purpose towards the Negro. They are better friends to my race, for telling us what they are, and what they mean, thereby giving us a chance to stir for ourselves, than all the hypocrites put together with their false gods and religions, notwithstanding.[69]

While rejecting the value of black membership in white unions, Garvey created much controversy by his willingness to cooperate with the Klan to achieve his goal of "Africa for the Africans." Such cooperation was scarcely consistent with Garvey's own declaration:

> The new Negro shall not be deceived. The new Negro refuses to take advice from anyone who has not felt with him and suffered with him. . . . It takes the suffering Negro to interpret the spirit of his comrade.[70]

DuBois, in turn, did not hesitate to attack Garvey for his separatism and methods. In contrast to Garvey's attitude, King from his early ministry maintained membership in the NAACP, frequently addressed their meetings, and cooperated with them in several projects such as the 1963 March on Washington. Despite later criticisms by the leadership of the NAACP for his public opposition to the Vietnam War, King refused to develop hostility toward the organization and continued to affirm that the method of litigation for civil rights complemented his own method of nonviolent direct action.

The Black Power Movement

"Black Power" was first used as a slogan in the civil rights movement by Stokely Carmichael during the Freedom March through Mississippi in June 1966. Outraged by the shooting of James Meredith, who had begun the march, Carmichael agreed to join with King and Floyd McKissick, national director of the Congress of Racial Equality (CORE), to continue the march. At a mass meeting in Greenwood, Carmichael delivered a speech to the marchers that denounced Mississippi "justice," and when he had sufficiently aroused the audience, he proclaimed, "What we need is black power."[71] Willie Ricks of SNCC then mounted the platform and shouted to the crowd, "What do you want?" They responded, "Black Power." Again and again, Ricks repeated the question until the response "Black Power" reached fever pitch. The audience could not resist the appeal of the slogan. They had too long felt the pressure of white power. Moreover, they knew that the speakers who offered them the slogan were members of SNCC, the organization that had worked so courageously in their community during the turbulent summer of 1964. They knew Carmichael's history. In the struggle for their freedom he had been arrested twenty-seven times. When he had been director of the Freedom School in Greenwood in 1964, white terrorists firebombed the school and savagely beat nonviolent local black activists.

King thought that the term "Black Power," which had been used long before by Richard Wright and others, should not be adopted as a slogan for the march or the Movement. He witnessed how the slogan caused division in the ranks of the marchers as some speakers called for the chant of "Black Power" while others called for "Freedom Now." To resolve the problem, he met with Carmichael and McKissick to convince them to abandon the slogan. He advised them that the leader of a group has to be concerned about the problem of semantics. He explained that a term may have both a denotative meaning, that would be its explicit and recognized sense, and a connotative meaning, its suggestive sense.[72] While granting that the *concept* of legitimate Black Power might be denotatively sound, he argued that the *slogan* "Black Power" conveyed the wrong connotations. He reminded them of how the press had already associated this slogan with violence and of how rash statements by a few of the marchers had tended to substantiate this interpretation by the press. Carmichael responded by declaring that the question of violence versus nonviolence was irrelevant. He indicated that the real issue was the need for blacks to consolidate their political and economic resources for the acquisition of power. He stated, "Power is the only thing respected in this world, and we must get it at any cost," and contended that almost every other ethnic group in America had acted on this conviction.[73] King reminded Carmichael that the Jews, the Irish, and the Italians had not publicly chanted slogans referring to power, but rather had worked hard to achieve power through "group unity, determination, and creative endeavor."[74] King maintained that blacks should do exactly the same, using every constructive means to obtain economic and political power and to build racial pride. While agreeing that a movement needs slogans, he argued that the slogan "Black Power" would only confuse allies, isolate the black community, and allow many whites who otherwise would be ashamed of their prejudice to rationalize their hostility to blacks. He felt that the slogan "Black Power" conveyed the impression that the Movement aimed at black domination. He proposed instead the slogan "Black Consciousness" or "Black Equality." Carmichael rejected these, claiming that "Black Power" was far more persuasive. When King saw that he could not convince them of the necessity of substituting a new slogan, he proposed that for the rest of the march they would not chant either "Black Power" or "Freedom Now." Carmichael and McKissick agreed to accept this compromise so that they would minimize the appearance of conflict within the Movement.[75] However, Carmichael later chose to reject the spirit of this compromise when he engaged in abuse of white participants in the march.

King maintained that Black Power is essentially an emotional concept that can mean different things to different persons, and can vary in meaning even for the same person on different occasions.[76] In his evaluation of the concept that attempted to go "beyond personal styles, verbal flourishes and the hysteria of the mass media," King explained that it was necessary to understand that "Black Power" was a cry of disappointment and that the causes of the disappointment were many. White power had left blacks empty-handed. Mississippi, where the slogan was born, symbolized the most blatant abuse of white power, with its unpunished lynchings, bombings of Negro churches, and murders of civil rights workers. King indicated that many of the young who proclaimed Black Power had been participants in the Nonviolent Movement and proponents of black-white cooperation. But as they labored and suffered courageously to expose the disease of racism, they came to feel that "a real solution is hopelessly distant because of the inconsistencies, resistance and faintheartedness of those in power."[77] He attempted to understand how some of them in their anger could repudiate nonviolence even though he did not justify their position:

> If Stokely Carmichael now says that nonviolence is irrelevant, it is because he, as a dedicated veteran of many battles, has seen with his own eyes the most brutal white violence against Negroes and white civil rights workers, and he has seen it go unpunished.[78]

King stated that members of SNCC, including Carmichael, had the impression that the life of a black in white America had no meaning. He recalled how this impression was reinforced during the Selma Movement when both Jimmy Lee Jackson, a Negro, and the Reverend James Reeb, a white Unitarian minister, had been killed by white racists, but President Johnson in his "We Shall Overcome" speech, felt it appropriate to mention only Reeb.[79]

King had no difficulty in adding to the list of disappointments that caused the frustrated to advocate Black Power. The refusal of the Federal Government to implement the civil rights laws helped lead the Black Power advocates to develop a contempt for the legislative process. As he indicated in 1967, although the 1965 Voting Rights Act required the appointment of hundreds of registrars and thousands of Federal marshals to protect the voters, fewer than sixty registrars were appointed, and not one Federal law officer with the power to arrest was sent into the South. As a result, the economic coercion, terrorism, and murder continued unchecked.[80] He asserted that the disappointment of the Black Power advocates could only increase as they considered the educational, economic, and social conditions that oppressed blacks in Northern ghettos. These Black Power advocates could experience only further disappointment as they witnessed a Goverment that was more concerned about winning the Vietnam War than about winning the war against poverty and that praised blacks whenever they remained nonviolent while it asked them to commit violence in Vietnam; a Christian Church that appeared to be more white than Christian; white moderates who believed that they had the right to set a timetable for the freedom of blacks; black ministers more concerned about material rewards than about the quality of their service to the black community; and a black middle class that had forgotten its black brothers.[81]

King explained that Black Power in its positive sense was a call to black people to acquire the political and economic strength to achieve their legitimate goals. He felt that the acquisition of legitimate power was crucial to the solutions of the problems of the ghetto. "The problem of transforming the ghetto is, therefore, a problem of power—a confrontation between the forces of power demanding change and the forces of power dedicated to preserving the status quo."[82] He was careful to add that power should be creative and positive, and should implement the demands of justice and love. Blacks must not imitate those white Americans who had sought their goals through power without love and conscience. He agreed with the Black Power advocates on the necessity of developing political power in the black community. The many voter registration campaigns conducted by SCLC testified to his awareness of this need. He agreed also with the Black Power advocates on the necessity of blacks' pooling their resources to achieve economic security. While he called for a massive Federal program to help the poor, he contended that blacks could help shape the policies of American businesses and thus improve their own conditions by the ways in which they used the buying power in their collective annual income of $30 billion.[83]

Given King's own dedication to the principle of the dignity of the person, it was not difficult for him to find positive value in Black Power as "a psychological call to manhood."[84] He recognized that the demand of the Black Power Movement that the black man should assert his manhood was a reaction to the psychological indoctrination begun in slavery and continued in segregation. He found a penetrating analysis of this indoctrination in *The Peculiar Institution* by the historian Kenneth Stampp.[85] To understand the indoctrination that the master used to develop a good slave, Stampp had consulted manuals on the training of slaves. He discovered certain recurring rules in these manuals. *First*, the master had to maintain strict discipline so as to achieve the unconditional submission of the slave to his absolute authority. *Second*, for the purpose of maintaining this control, the

master was to inculcate in the slave "a consciousness of personal inferiority."[86] Therefore he was to convince the slave that bondage was his
natural status, that his African background had tainted him, and that
his color was "a badge of degradation."[87] *Third,* the master had to
instill in the slave an awe of his enormous power. Though King did not
indicate it, Stampp here referred to Frederick Douglass's contention
that few slaves could free themselves altogether from the notion that
their masters were "invested with a sort of sacredness."[88] *Fourth,* the
master had to attempt to persuade the slave to be concerned about
his master's interests and to accept his standards of good conduct.
Fifth, the master had to implant in the slave a sense of helplessness
and to develop in him a habit of perfect dependence.[89] King viewed
the Black Power defiance of white authority as one that contained
a legitimate concern of blacks to break away from the "unconditional submission" lingering from slavery, and to affirm one's own
selfhood.

King saw the desire of the Black Power Movement to glory in blackness and in the African heritage as a further reaction to the system of
slavery. Moreover, he acknowledged that although he felt that he
could not justify how some Black Power advocates encouraged contempt for white authority and called for uncivil disobedience, he did
understand how these responses could arise as alternatives to the system of slavery with its fear, awe, and obedience to the master. When
proponents of Black Power went to the extreme of rejecting all forms
of white help and the accepted "standards of good conduct," they
were reacting against the slave pattern of total dependence on the master. Carmichael frequently attacked the systematic way in which
whites continued their "colonization" of blacks in America by im-
posing their definitions on them. "They define what education is, they
define what work is, they define how we move, what we do, and
how we look—the oppressor defines even the standards of beauty
for the victims of colonialism."[90] Carmichael endorsed the contention of the French philosopher Albert Camus in *The Rebel* that
it is only when a slave stops accepting definitions imposed on him by
his master that he begins to move and create a life.[91] While not en-
dorsing the absolute independence and isolation in this reaction,
King felt that it did have merit in that it emphasized the need for
the black to develop a new awareness of his own value as a person:

One must not overlook the positive value [in Black Power] in
calling the Negro to a new sense of manhood, to a deep feeling of

racial pride and to an audacious appreciation of his heritage. The Negro must be grasped by a new realization of his dignity and worth. He must stand up amid a system that still oppresses him and develop an unassailable and majestic sense of his own value. He must no longer be ashamed of being black.[92]

Even though King found positive values in the Black Power Movement, he believed that it had defects that were so serious that it could not become the basic strategy for the civil rights movement. At the foundation of the Black Power Movement he found a nihilistic philosophy that stood in sharp contrast to Gandhi's doctrine that hope and love must permeate an effective revolution. Some Black Power advocates rejected the possibility that blacks could find fulfillment within the American system. King tried to understand the depth of the frustration of blacks trapped in despair. He related that the only time he was booed by an audience was by young members of the Black Power Movement at a Chicago mass meeting, and that upon reflection he recognized that the youths were responding to the fact that promises of social justice had not been fulfilled. Nonetheless, he affirmed that, despite the lamentable rate of progress, blacks should not descend to a despair and a nihilism that seeks disruption for the sake of disruption. He stressed that hope is what keeps the fire of a revolution burning. God is in control of history, directs it toward righteousness, and demands our cooperation.[93]

King contended that the implicit and often explicit belief of the Black Power Movement in separatism was totally unrealistic. He argued that if blacks chose to develop their political strength through separatism and by concentration on those few cities and counties where they constituted a majority, such a strategy would leave most blacks outside the mainstream of American political life. The Black Power Movement seemed to fail to realize that it was far more preferable for blacks to establish coalitions with white moderates to seek the election of fifteen or twenty representatives in Congress from Southern districts than for blacks on their own to secure the election of two or three black representatives from predominately black districts. King denounced any policy as morally unjustifiable and politically unsound that would elect candidates because they were black and reject all white candidates because they were white. He argued further that blacks could not achieve significant economic power through separatism. Though the proper use of black buying power could effect some improvements, only Federal programs involving billions of dollars could bring about the necessary basic reforms in jobs, housing, and education; blacks through their own efforts could not secure these programs. Only an alliance of liberal, labor, and civil rights forces could move the Government to create the necessary programs. Certain ethnic groups, such as the Jews, the Irish, and the Italians, did emphasize group unity, as the Black Power advocates maintained, but these groups also perceived the value of alliances with other groups such as political machines and trade unions. In recommending alliances, King stressed the need for vigilance against possible betrayal as well as the need to avoid an excess of skepticism that would constitute a denial of the contributions of some whites to the civil rights struggle and would cripple any alliance:

> While Negro initiative, courage and imagination precipitated the Birmingham and Selma confrontations and revealed the harrowing injustice of segregated life, the organized strength of Negroes alone would have been insufficient to move Congress and the administration without the weight of the aroused conscience of white America.[94]

King denied that by entering alliances blacks were relying on white leadership or ideology. Rather, the black man was "taking his place as an equal partner in a common endeavor."[95] King's Personalist belief in the interconnectedness of all humanity reinforced his conviction on the value of black-white alliances:

> There is no separate black path to power and fulfillment that does not intersect white paths, and there is no separate white path to power and fulfillment, short of social disaster, that does not share that power with black aspirations for freedom and human dignity. We are bound together in a single garment of destiny.[96]

In their desire for separatism many Negroes regarded themselves only as Africans. Others rejected their African heritage and defined goodness and beauty in terms of the standards of white society. King rejected the narrowness of each of these approaches and chose again to appeal to the Hegelian synthesis as "the best answer to many of life's dilemmas." "The American Negro is neither totally African nor totally Western. He is Afro-American, a true hybrid, a combination of two cultures."[97] By this description he was attempting to respond to

Carmichael's charge that "integration" meant that black people had to give up their identity and deny their heritage.[98]

King felt that the Black Power Movement was deficient also because some of its members called for aggressive violence. In Atlanta and Chicago he had many dialogues with proponents of Black Power who argued for the validity of violence and riots. He not only denounced aggressive violence as morally wrong and practically absurd for the American Negro but he also opposed the unconscious and often conscious call for retaliatory violence in the Black Power Movement. He did not deny the right to defend one's home and person, but he rejected the role of retaliatory violence in a civil rights demonstration:

> It is dangerous to organize a movement around self-defense. The line of demarcation between defensive violence and aggressive violence is very thin. The minute a program of violence is enunciated, even for self-defense, the atmosphere is filled with talk of violence, and the words falling on unsophisticated ears may be interpreted as an invitation to aggression.[99]

King uncovered a paradox in the Black Power Movement. While its members continued to insist on not imitating the "values" of white society, by advocating violence they were imitating the worst and the most brutal "value" of American life.

Carmichael's writings and speeches revealed his position to be more antithetical to King's philosophy of nonviolence than King indicated. While King conceded that Carmichael thought that the question of violence versus nonviolence was irrelevant, he also maintained that Carmichael had declared himself to be an opponent of aggressive violence.[100] King was implying that the only violence Carmichael proposed was defensive violence. Although it is true that Carmichael often advocated defensive violence, it is also true that he did not consistently reject aggressive violence. Thus in an October 1966 speech to a predominately white liberal audience at the University of California at Berkeley he issued the challenge, "You show me a black man who advocates aggressive violence who would be able to live in this country," but he concluded the speech by warning white America, "Move on over, or we're going to move on over you."[101] In the same speech he asserted, "If South America were to rebel today, and black people were to shoot the hell out of all the white people there, as they should, Standard Oil would crumble tomorrow."[102] While in a January 1967 speech at Morgan State College in Baltimore he reminded the black students of their obligation to help those in the ghetto, and of the fact that if they failed in this obligation, they would be responsible when rebellions increased that summer, in the same speech he referred to a grocer who for years had overcharged customers in the ghetto, and declared, "His store should have been bombed five years ago."[103] At the Congress on the Dialectics of Liberation in London in June 1967 he attacked the "system of international white supremacy coupled with international capitalism," and threatened, "We're out to smash that system. People who see themselves as part of that system are going to be smashed with it—or we're going to be smashed."[104] He explained that the Black Power Movement was the catalyst for bringing together young bloods who had the hatred that Che Guevera extolled. He then quoted Guevera's description of this hatred:

. . . hatred as an element of the struggle, relentless hatred of the enemy that impels us over and beyond the natural limitations of man, and transforms us into effective, violent, selected and cold killing machines.[105]

The only concession Carmichael made to nonviolence was to recommend that blacks should adopt nonviolence as a guiding philosophy in their relationships with each other. "We must develop an undying love for our people. . . ."[106] This was in line with his plan to define and encourage a new consciousness among black people. In *Black Power: The Politics of Liberation of America* he and Charles Hamilton described this consciousness as "a sense of peoplehood; pride, rather than shame, in blackness, and an attitude of brotherly, communal responsibility among all black people for one another."[107] In another speech Carmichael contended that this communal responsibility was for blacks alone. "In order to fight a war of liberation, you need an ideology of nationalism. We do not have this country. The nationalism can be nothing but black nationalism."[108] "The concept 'community' is simply one of 'our people.'"[109] This "community" included 900 million black people, but no whites. He contended that the black community could secure survival only by organizing its people and "orienting them toward an African ideology that speaks to our blackness—nothing else."[110] Carmichael combined this message of love, nonviolence, and communal responsibility among blacks with a declaration of war on the white man, "the enemy." "The major enemy is the honky and his institutions of racism—*that* is the major enemy. And whenever anybody prepares for revolutionary warfare, you concentrate on the major enemy."[111]

The Black Muslim Gospel of Separatism

In recent years the largest group in the black community that proclaimed the necessity for a permanent separation of the races was Elijah Muhammad's Black Muslim Movement, the Nation of Islam. The Black Muslims under his leadership believed that integration could yield only further tragedy and frustration for blacks. King explained that this Movement was composed of people who had lost faith in America, rejected Christianity, and concluded that the white man is an incorrigible devil.[112] He repudiated the philosophy of this black nationalism as an expression of bitterness and hatred and warned that it came close to advocating violence.

Under Elijah Muhammad the Black Muslims developed a mythology that declared that Black is Absolute Perfection and that all black men are divine and represent Allah or at least participate in Him. White men, devoid of color, are incomplete and imperfect. Only the black man is truly wise and creative.[113] Elijah Muhammad commanded his followers to separate themselves as far as possible from whites, "the children of the devil," and contended, "God did not intend for the two races to mix."[114] The Black Muslim philosophy called for an end to all personal relationships between the races, and warned that the Black Nation would only be weakened physically and morally by a further admixture of white blood.[115] Only through separation could the "Negro" dispense with the image of himself that had been created by the white man. Instead of seeing himself as the white man saw him, he could move on to attain authentic self-identity through self-knowledge. Muhammad wished to establish a Black Republic in the United States and indicated that a few states should provide the necessary land and assistance for this republic. He claimed that this would be compensation to blacks for hundreds of years of exploitation.

Eric Lincoln revealed the essence of the strategy of the Black Muslims under Elijah Muhammad by indicating that they defined their movement in terms of a contrast with Negroes, Jews, orthodox Moslems in America, and the hated whites. By denouncing the weakness and the depravity that they thought that they had found in these other groups, they attempted to assert their own strength and purity.[116] George Kelsey charged that the Black Muslims were guilty of a "counter-racism." He cited as typical of the Black Muslim image of the white man a statement by Elijah Muhammad that identified the white race as "the human beast—the serpent, the dragon, the devil, and Satan," and described whites as "the great universal deceivers of nonwhite people, the greatest murderers . . . whoever lived or ever will live on our planet earth."[117] Muhammad warned that though some whites seem to show friendship to black people, they are deceivers and are intent on continuing their six thousand years of deception and oppression of black nations.[118] In *Message to the Black Man* he stated that the basic aim of Christianity was to allow the white race to deceive other races and to prey upon them.[119]

The doctrine of the Black Muslims was diametrically opposed to King's belief in the basic unity of humanity, and to his conviction that since everyone is made in the image of God, all distinctions based on color are diabolical. He would agree with Kelsey that the Black Muslims failed to recognize that any race that regards itself as a superior race, whether black or white, defeats itself by its own self-glorification.[120] He could endorse Kelsey's further criticisms that the Black Muslims, like white racists, were guilty of refusing to enter into dialogue, of stereotype thinking, and of thereby using ignorance of facts about the out-race as an "escape apparatus."[121] King's repeated emphasis on the interrelated structure of humanity could reinforce Kelsey's criticism that despite the Black Muslims' desire for separation, they still had to live with an economic, political, and cultural dependence on the larger community. Moreover, King's own experiences with nonviolence supported Kelsey's further criticism:

> Muslim dedication to the idea that all white men are devils, beasts, and oppressors obscures all perception of justice, humanitarianism, and affection expressed in the lives of whites toward non-whites.[122]

Aside from his philosophical and theological commitment to love as a practical ideal, King knew from his crusades that the willingness of many whites to suffer for the cause demonstrated that they were genuine humanitarians and integrationists. Although King described the white man as the Negro's adversary, he was careful to add that there were millions of whites who had transcended prevailing prejudices, and were willing to share power and accept structural changes in society:

> To deny their existence as some ultranationalists do is to deny an evident truth. . . . To develop a sense of black consciousness and peoplehood does not require that we scorn the white race as a whole. It is not the race per se that we fight but the policies and ideology that leaders of that race have formulated to perpetuate oppression.[123]

While Black Muslims under Elijah Muhammad did not teach that their members should initiate violence, they did advocate retaliation if whites injured them. They regarded the law of retaliation as a divine law, as having an intrinsic moral value, and as especially appropriate when used against the white man, the natural enemy. Malcolm X, a member of the Black Muslims, affirmed that the law of retaliation is the only thing that will affect the white man since he himself applies it, and it can only enhance respect for the black man throughout the world. King had to reject the Muslims' law of retaliation. He claimed that Jesus taught in effect that this "eye-for-an-eye philosophy" would leave everyone blind, and he could point to the history of human tragedies because men ignored Jesus' gospel of love:[124]

> The ultimate weakness of violence is that it is a descending spiral, begetting the very thing it seeks to destroy. . . . Returning violence for violence multiplies violence, adding deeper darkness to a night already devoid of stars.[125]

Malcolm X rejected nonviolence in his "Message to the Grass Roots:"

> Revolution is bloody, revolution is hostile, revolution knows no compromise, revolution overturns and destroys everything that gets in its way. And you, sitting around here like a knot on the wall saying, "I am going to love these folks no matter how much they hate me." No, you need a revolution.[126]

As early as 1958 King had anticipated this objection when he indicated that the phrase "passive resistance" often gives the false impression that nonviolent resistance is a sort of "do-nothing method" in which the resister quietly and passively accepts evil.[127] He explained that

Gandhi's notion of love did not involve a passive nonresistance to evil but rather a strongly active nonviolent resistance to evil. "Gandhi resisted evil with as much vigor and power as the violent resister, but he resisted with love instead of hate."[128]

In a 1963 interview the black social psychologist Kenneth Clark confronted King with Malcolm X's criticism that his Movement and philosophy played into the hands of the white oppressors, and that the latter were happy to hear King call for love for the oppressor since this disarmed the Negro and conformed to the stereotype of the Negro as "a meek, turning-the-other-cheek sort of creature."[129] King replied that he did not regard the love motivating his protests as "emotional bosh" but as a strong force that organized itself into powerful direct action. He emphasized that there was a great deal of difference between nonresistance to evil, which results in a stagnant passivity and a deadly complacency, and nonviolent resistance, which involves strong and determined resistance. "I think some of the criticisms of nonviolence or some of the critics fail to realize that we are talking about something very strong and they confuse non-resistance with nonviolent resistance."[130]

In 1963, Malcolm X pointed with justifiable pride to the widespread success of the Black Muslims in achieving the rehabilitation of blacks in prison. He explained that many black prisoners had realized that the system was not designed for their rehabilitation and had turned to the religion of Islam:

> Then when he [the black prisoner] hears the religious teaching of the Honorable Elijah Muhammad, that restores to him his racial pride, his racial identity, and restores to him also the desire to be a man, to be a human being; he reforms himself.[131]

Malcolm X could claim that this religious teaching was able to do what psychologists, sociologists, penologists, and criminologists had failed to do. Without ignoring his substantial differences with the Black Muslims, King did not fail to praise their achievements in rehabilitation:

> While I strongly disagree with their separatist black supremacy philosophy, I have nothing but admiration for what our Muslim brothers have done to rehabilitate ex-convicts, dope addicts and men and women who, through despair and self-hatred, have sunk to moral degeneracy. This must be attempted on a much

larger scale, and without the negative overtones that accompany Black Muslimism.[132]

When Wallace Muhammad succeeded his father Elijah Muhammad as spiritual leader of the Black Muslims, he rejected the philosophy of separatism. Whereas his father had warned that integration meant self-destruction for blacks, Wallace Muhammad invited whites to join the movement. This development seemed to reflect the transformation that Malcolm X had experienced. In his autobiography, written after his separation from the Black Muslims and shortly before his death, Malcolm X explained how in his travels abroad he was able to share brotherly love with many whites who were Muslims and "who never gave a single thought to the race, or to the complexion, of another Muslim":[133]

In the past, yes, I have made sweeping indictments of *all* white people. I never will be guilty of that again—as I know now that some white people *are* truly sincere, that some truly are capable of being brotherly toward a black man. The true Islam has shown me that a blanket indictment of all white people is as wrong as when whites make blanket indictments against blacks.[134]

Other Immoral Responses to Collective Evil

King indicated that some individuals respond to frustration in the face of oppression by indulging in self-pity or by descending into bitterness and resentment. He warned that self-pity can lead to a "self-defeating black paranoia," and that bitterness and resentment can destroy the personality.[135] Bitterness causes some to lash out against God, those around them, and themselves. Their lives lack respect, love, and trust. Bitterness does not have the capacity to make the distinction between some and all. When some members of the dominant group, especially those who have power, are guilty of racist attitudes and practices, bitterness accuses the whole group.[136] Some of those victimized by bitterness resort to antisocial behavior, overt delinquency, and gang warfare to express their defiance. King emphasized the role of segregation in producing their hostility. "The 'behavior deviants' within the Negro community stem from the economic deprivation, emotional frustration, and social isolation which are the inevitable concomitants of segregation."[137] Bitterness causes others to seek the path of racial isolation to express their hostility.

Another reaction to collective evil, not unrelated to passive acceptance, is to withdraw in apathy from the struggle. King noted that the
black community in Montgomery prior to the boycott was marked by
indifference and complacency, and that in 1954 in Montgomery
County only about two thousand out of thirty thousand blacks of
voting age were registered.[138] True, Alabama law had created obstacles, but blacks did betray a lack of interest. He indicated the sources
of this apathy.[139] Many blacks were apathetic concerning their basic
rights because they had a sense of inferiority and a real lack of self-
respect. Some other blacks were apathetic because they felt that
freedom would be handed to them on a silver platter. They failed to
realize that freedom could be achieved only through suffering and
sacrifice, and simply waited for the coming of what they regarded as
the inevitable:

> Even a superficial look at history reveals that no social advance
> rolls in on the wheels of inevitability; it comes through the tireless
> efforts and persistent work of dedicated individuals. Without
> this hard work time itself becomes an ally of the primitive forces
> of irrational emotionalism and social stagnation.[140]

King thought that the apathy of others was rooted in their pessimistic
conclusion that they could do nothing to better the racial situation.

In *Strength To Love* King indicated how some react to a world in
which their hopes are not fulfilled:

> Detachment is the word which best describes them. Too uncon-
> cerned to love and too passionless to hate, too detached to be
> selfish and too lifeless to be unselfish, too indifferent to expe-
> rience joy and too cold to experience sorrow, they are neither
> dead nor alive; they merely exist.[141]

He would agree with the contention of the psychotherapist Rollo May
that apathy, not hate, is the opposite of love.[142] While maintaining that
in the past the apathy of blacks in the face of collective evil was a moral
failure, King warned that the time had come when such apathy was "a
form of moral and political suicide."[143] He made this judgment even
though he also acknowledged that blacks developed a disinterest in
politics as a defense against further exploitation.[144]

To arouse some in the black community from apathy, King appealed
to the example of American Jews, who in large numbers, despite op-

pression, sacrificed to achieve educational competence, combined it with social action, and became enormously effective in political life.[145] He stressed that many of the Jews who remained poor and uneducated still were politically active. He also appealed to the example of extraordinary blacks who rose above their circumstances to make significant contributions. He referred to the achievements of Booker T. Washington, Roland Hayes, Marian Anderson, George Washington Carver, Leontyne Price, Ralph Bunche, James Weldon Johnson, Paul Lawrence Dunbar, Countee Cullen, Claude McKay, Langston Hughes, Harry Belafonte, Sammy Davis, Mahalia Jackson, Ray Charles, Duke Ellington, Sidney Poitier, W. E. B. DuBois, Richard Wright, Ralph Ellison, James Baldwin, Joe Louis, Jack Johnson, Muhammad Ali, Jackie Robinson, Roy Campanella, Don Newcombe, Willie Mays, Henry Aaron, Frank Robinson, James Brown, Bill Russell, Wilt Chamberlain, Jesse Owens, Buddy Young, Althea Gibson, and Arthur Ashe. "These are only a few of the examples which remind us that, in spite of our lack of full freedom, we can make a contribution here and now."[146] It is at least debatable whether this appeal would dispel the apathy in the vast majority who knew that they did not possess the exceptional talents of these individuals.

King endorsed the view of E. Franklin Frazier in *Black Bourgeoisie* that many blacks were engaged in a middle-class struggle for status and prestige, were more concerned about "conspicuous consumption" than about the cause of justice, and probably were not prepared for the sacrifices and ordeals required by nonviolent protest.[147] King lamented the fact that many middle-class blacks, because they had achieved academic and economic security, chose to ignore their origins and their debt to the uneducated who had helped make their success possible. They became insensitive to the agonies and struggles of the underprivileged, and their selfish detachment alienated many of their black brothers. He emphasized that the black professional should not ask himself what will happen to his position or safety if he participates in the Movement to end segregation but rather should ask himself what will happen to the cause of justice and the masses of black people who have never had economic security if he does not participate courageously in the Movement. King was quite certain that the future of the black middle class would be connected with the future of the black masses:

> The relatively privileged Negro will never be what he ought to be until the underprivileged Negro is what he ought to be. The salva-

tion of the Negro middle class is ultimately dependent upon the salvation of the Negro masses.[149]

It was disheartening to discover how little money middle-class blacks were willing to invest in the struggle for *their own* freedom and dignity. "It will be tragic indeed if future historians are able to record that the Negro spent more on transitory pleasure than he spent on the eternal values of freedom and justice."[150]

King contended that it was when young blacks abandoned their middle-class values that they made a historic social contribution. When these youths decided to assign a secondary role to their careers and wealth and made a commitment to work with the poor in the rural South, by their example they challenged white youths to emulate them.[151] He claimed that the work of these young blacks and whites served as the inspiration for the organization of the Peace Corps on an international scale.

King also condemned the reaction of the millions who remained silent in the presence of the collective evil of segregation. He realized that much of their silence was due to fear of social, political, and economic reprisals, but he warned, "Our generation will have to repent not only for the acts and words of the children of darkness but also for the fears and apathy of the children of light."[152] In responding to the clergy who criticized the Birmingham Movement he said, "We will have to repent in this generation not merely for the hateful words and actions of the bad people but for the appalling silence of the good people."[153] He noted with considerable anguish that no white official in Birmingham attended the funeral of the four black girls who were killed by a bomb while they were at Sunday school. "The ultimate tragedy of Birmingham was not the brutality of the bad people, but the silence of the good people."[154] He repeated Einstein's warning, "The world is in greater peril from those who tolerate evil than from those who actively commit it."[155] In 1965, he reminded the members of the Association of the Bar of the City of New York of the message of Rabbi Joachim Prinz at the 1963 March on Washington. Rabbi Prinz spoke of what he had learned from his experience as the Rabbi of the Jewish Community in Berlin under the Hitler regime:

The most important thing that I learned in my life and under tragic circumstances is that bigotry and hatred are not the most urgent problems. The most urgent, the most disgraceful, the most shameful and the most tragic problem is silence.[156]

A further reaction to oppression is to adopt a fatalistic attitude which believes that what does happen must happen and that man can do nothing about the course of external circumstances but must resign his will to the foreordained necessary flow of events which constitute his fate. King rejected this reaction as immoral since by promoting a passivity that waits upon preordained forces to regulate all events, it implicitly denies the reality of freedom. In accepting the Nobel Peace Prize he asserted, "I refuse to accept the idea that man is mere flotsam and jetsam in the river of life, unable to influence the unfolding events which surround him."[157] He regarded the denial of freedom as a denial of human personality. "Freedom is that vital, intrinsic value which determines one's selfhood."[158] One of the reasons he judged segregation as morally wrong was that it made decisions for blacks and hence robbed them of their freedom, i.e., of their humanity. In his doctoral dissertation he alluded to Tillich's doctrine that freedom belongs to the essence of man. "Man is man because he has freedom."[159] Tillich's affirmation of human creativity was a further rejection of fatalism. Man is "existentially creative" because he has the power to transform himself and the world.

King's commitment to Personalism as his own philosophy grounded his conviction about the reality of human freedom. DeWolf in *A Theology of the Living Church* presented the following arguments to support the belief in free will.[160] *First,* many texts in the New Testament seem to presuppose man's capacity for free choice. "Jesus' many admonitions, instructions, warnings, and persuasive appeals seem made to free wills rather than to human puppets predetermined in their courses."[161] The Epistle of St. James also calls for righteous action and defines sin as a responsible act of a person who knows the right thing and does not do it.[162] St. Paul presupposes man is free when he warns, "Therefore, let anyone who thinks that he stands, take heed lest he fall."[163] Even in the Epistle to the Romans, which is often cited in favor of a strict predestinarianism, St. Paul implies the need for a responsible use of freedom when he underscores the necessity of standing fast in faith and of practicing kindness.[164] While recognizing that there are a very few passages in the Scriptures that seem to cast doubt on the freedom of the will, DeWolf argued:

> Since the pleas for righteousness, calls to repentance, numerous promises and warnings, conditional on human choice, are in the central stream of the entire Biblical message and are constantly recurrent from beginning to end, they must be given precedent consideration.[165]

Second, our immediate intuition of our consciousness testifies to some self-determination.

> At the moment when a man is making a deliberate conscious choice between alternative courses of action he feels free and his anxious thought about the choice he has to make presupposes his freedom so that the choice itself, *as he makes it*, is an *assertion* of his freedom. Such empirical evidence is not to be taken lightly.[166]

DeWolf considered that it is possible that we may be self-deluded in thinking that we are free, but he contended that the burden of proof is on those who make this claim. He cited the conviction of Max Planck, the physicist, that the freedom of the ego and its independence of the causal determinism of the world is a truth that comes from the immediate dictate of the human consciousness.[167] He also presented the argument for freedom by Sir Arthur Eddington, the astronomer, that if he could be deluded over such a matter of immediate knowledge as the very nature of his being, it would be difficult to see where any trustworthy beginning of knowledge could be found.[168]

Third, moral life with its obligations presupposes the freedom of the will. "Whenever I say that I ought to perform act A or when a neighbor condemns me for not performing act A, it is presupposed that I am or was free to choose act A."[169] Only a free being can be subject to obligation or be held morally responsible for its acts.

Fourth, the whole intellectual life presupposes the freedom of the will.[170] If the will were not free but subject to causal necessity, then there could be no genuine weighing of reasons for the purpose of discovering truth. If all reasoning were but the result of rigorously predetermined, causally driven mechanisms, then it would not be possible for any mind ever to discover that any proposition is either true or false. However, since the mind is ordinarily capable of such discovery, it must be free to weigh alternatives.

Fifth, the experience of the Christian community makes a substantial contribution to the evidence for belief in the freedom of the will. In contrast with the cyclical views of history prevalent in ancient times and in the Orient, Christians have found a profound meaning in life. Their acts, words, and thoughts in the presence of Jesus have continually assumed new significance:

> As Jesus said, "My Father is working still and I am working," so his disciples are aware of a divine calling to fulfill the responsibil-

ities of their special tasks and stations as in God's sight, and every day lived in that spirit is full of novelty and fresh adventure.[171]

DeWolf added the consideration that if God denied man freedom by predetermining that he must sin and refuse redemption and by compelling man to bear all the burden of guilt and suffering as if he were a free agent responsible for his acts, then God could not be considered either as good or just. The Christian belief in God's goodness and justice presupposes that God allows man to respond freely to His offer of salvation.

DeWolf regarded man's freedom as a special manifestation of the divine creativity. Man's capacity for self-determination and novelty constitutes one basis for affirming that he is made in the divine image. Strictly speaking, only God can create, but man, as a "steward," does possess a power from God to direct to some degree the development of his life and to participate in the continuation of creation in each moment of growth. "We thus stand at the yet unfinished edge of His creation where we are given a significant part in determining what is to be."[172]

Chapter 7

King's Rejection of Violent Resistance

The Immorality and Impracticality of Violence

When King engaged in dialogue with some of the proponents of
Black Power who passionately held that violence was the only means
to achieve their liberation, they appealed to the thought of Frantz
Fanon, a black psychiatrist from Martinique who went to Algeria to
assist the National Liberation Front in its struggle against the French.[1]
In *The Wretched of the Earth* Fanon argued that it is psychologically
healthy and tactically sound for the oppressed to resort to violence:

> At the level of individuals, violence is a cleansing force. It frees
> the native from his inferiority complex and from his despair and
> inaction; it makes him fearless and restores his self-respect.[2]

Fanon contended that the native who decides to participate in the
process of decolonization, which involves "a complete calling in question of the colonial situation" so that "the last shall be first, and the
first last," is always ready for violence.[3] "From birth it is clear to him
[the native] that this narrow world, strewn with prohibitions, can only
be called in question by absolute violence."[4] King thought it contradictory for Fanon to issue the challenge, "For Europe, for ourselves, and
for humanity, comrades, we must turn over a new leaf, we must work
out new concepts, and try to set afoot a new man," and at the same
time to be willing to imitate the old concepts of violence.[5]

King consistently condemned violence as both immoral and impractical. It is immoral because it thrives on hatred rather than love. It
wants to humiliate the opponent rather than to win his understanding.
It seeks to injure rather than to redeem the other. Violence is opposed

to creativity and wholeness, aims to destroy community, and renders brotherhood impossible. Hatred and violence intensify the fears of the white majority and lessen their shame in their prejudice against blacks. Violence is immoral also because it deepens the brutality of the perpetrator of violence. He too is a victim. King in effect reaffirmed the insight of Socrates that one who injures another injures himself spiritually since he disrupts the harmony within his own soul, whereas the soul of his victim may remain intact. "Like an unchecked cancer, hate corrodes the personality and eats away its vital unity."[6] King identified with Booker T. Washington's warning, "Let no man pull you so low as to make you hate him."[7] King contended that when another makes you hate him, he leads you to work against community and to defy creation. Through his hate the hater becomes depersonalized because the design of creation demands that personality can be fulfilled only in community:

> Hate is rooted in fear, and the only cure for fear-hate is love.[8]
> Hatred and bitterness can never cure the disease of fear; only love can do that. Hatred paralyzes life; love releases it. Hatred confuses life; love harmonizes it. Hatred darkens life; love illumines it.[9]

King explained that after he had seen hate on the faces of so many sheriffs, members of White Citizens Councils, and Klansmen in the South, he had to conclude that hate is too great a burden to bear.[10] He claimed that he who hates stands in immediate candidacy for non-being.[11]

Furthermore, violence is immoral because it increases the existence of evil. During the Montgomery Boycott, at the weekly meetings of the MIA, King emphasized this in his rejection of violence in the struggle. "To meet hate with retaliatory hate would do nothing but intensify the existence of evil in the universe. Hate begets hate; violence begets violence; toughness begets a greater toughness."[12] Violence may seek to eliminate an evil, but it only intensifies evil. Violence cannot eradicate another violence. Only love can break the chain reaction of violence. If we seek power not for itself, but only to improve society, violence is not the moral answer. Violence solves no social problem but rather creates new and more complicated ones. While it often brings temporary victory, it never brings permanent peace.[13] King conceded that some historical victories such as the American Revolution had been won by violence, but he stressed that the Negro Revolution was seeking integration, not independence.[14] The official slogan of the MIA was "Justice Without Violence."[15]

King was painfully aware that moral reasons might not deter some Negroes from violence, and so he presented reasons to demonstrate that violence is impractical. *First*, the limited history of Negro insurrection in this country reveals the futility of violent rebellion. "The courageous efforts of our own insurrectionist brothers, such as Denmark Vesey and Nat Turner, should be eternal reminders to us that violent rebellion is doomed from the start."[16] The well-armed white majority could easily suppress a violent rebellion, and the fanatical right wing of this majority would take delight in exterminating thousands of black men, women, and children.[17] In 1968, King predicted that if the rioting continued, it would provoke a right-wing takeover and a Fascist development in the cities.

Second, the futility of violence is evident in the consequences of the riots:

At best the riots have produced a little additional anti-poverty money being allotted by frightened government officials, and a few water-sprinklers to cool the children of the ghettos. It is something like improving the food in a prison while the people remain securely incarcerated behind bars. Nowhere have the riots won any concrete improvement such as have the organized protest demonstrations.[18]

Then too, those who live in the ghetto suffer most directly from any riot. Most of those who lie dead in the streets after a riot are black. King considered rioting not as revolutionary but as reactionary since it invites defeat:[19]

A riot is at bottom the language of the unheard. It is the desperate, suicidal cry of one who is so fed up with the powerlessness of his cave existence that he asserts that he would rather be dead than ignored.[20]

Third, violence negates some of the very goals the rioters seek to achieve. They desire to participate in the very things that they attempt to destroy, namely, the economy, the housing market, and the educational system. To burn down a factory is scarcely an effective way to secure a job at that factory.[21] Destruction cannot be constructive. The destroyers are left only with the debris.

Fourth, King repeated one of his moral arguments against violence and dealt with it pragmatically. A violent approach would be crippled from the outset since it cannot appeal to the conscience of the opponents. The future of blacks depends to a great degree on their capacity to awaken the conscience of white America:

> It is perfectly clear that a violent revolution on the part of American blacks would find no sympathy and support from the white population and very little from the majority of the Negroes themselves.[22]

Confronted with violence, the white majority would only grow in fear and prejudice, and render any reconciliation impossible. "Darkness cannot drive out darkness; only light can do that. Hate cannot drive out hate; only love can do that."[23] King observed that few if any violent revolutions would have been successful if the nonresisting majority had not extended their sympathy and support to the violent minority. He cited Castro's revolution and maintained that if the majority of the Cuban people had not supported Castro, he would never have overthrown the Batista regime.[24]

Some white groups claimed that blacks, by participating in the riots, revealed that they had no capacity for constructive change, surrendered their rights, and justified any form of repressive measures. King rejected this argument and added that the riots were not the root causes of white resistance. Rather, riots were the consequences of white resistance to the legitimate demands of blacks. He acknowledged, "It is incontestable and deplorable that Negroes have committed crimes. . . ." However, he added the necessary qualification, ". . . but they are derivative crimes."[25] He was not excusing these crimes, but he did want to determine their ultimate causes. "The best way to solve any problem is to remove its cause."[26] He contended that crimes by blacks were born of greater crimes in the white society. Those who determined policy in the white society generated the demoralizing conditions that filled blacks with frustration and rage, and led them to riot and to crime. While blacks were expected to observe the law, whites could ignore building codes in the ghettos and violate laws on equal employment, welfare, education, and provisions for civic services. King thought it both ironical and tragic that some in the white society protested that if there were no riots, great reforms would occur while their governments continued to create the conditions that bred the riots. He urged these whites to direct demands for reform to their municipal, state, and national governments. Merely to demonstrate their resentment against black rioters as if they were the only villains was to allow those with greater responsibility to evade blame and to permit the situation to worsen. Instead of being horrified at the conditions of Negro life, Congress was horrified at the product of these conditions—the Negroes themselves:

> It [Congress] could, by a single massive act of concern expressed in a multibillion-dollar program to modernize and humanize Negro communities, do more to obviate violence than could be done by all the armies at its command.[27]

In detailing the causes of the riots, King attacked the evil of the white backlash. He regarded this as a primary cause because it explained the ferocity of the emotional content of the riots as well as their spontaneity. He explained that, as a result of the protest demonstrations, a growing sensitivity to the justice of the demands by blacks had developed in the white community, and certain concessions were made in several areas. However, when blacks indicated that they wanted to move toward full equality, a firm resistance emerged in the white community, which revealed that it did not feel that blacks deserved this equality.[28] The force and range of this resistance became evident to blacks in a variety of ways, including the systematic withdrawal of support by some former white allies. Apparently, some white liberals and moderates were more committed to order than to equality. As early as 1958, King called for a genuine liberalism that not only would hold that the goal of integration is morally and legally right but also would involve a positive and active commitment to the ideal of integration even in one's own community.[29] Even though white moderates for the most part would consider themselves as friends of the civil rights movement, he did not hesitate to state that the white moderate was "the Negro's great stumbling-block in his stride toward freedom."[30] The white moderate with his concern for tranquillity rather than justice did not see the necessity of tension for progress. Since he professed to agree with blacks on their goals, he paternalistically believed that he could determine for them the methods and timetable for achieving these goals, and thus he remained an obstacle to effective direct action. The moderate felt that the blacks had made significant strides toward equality, and that they should not be so greedy as to seek more so soon. Therefore, the moderate was quite content with tokenism in his schools, unions, churches, and politics. "These moderates had come some distance in step with the thundering drums, but at the point of mass application they wanted the bugle to sound a retreat."[31]

Another cause of the riots, according to King, was the practice of discrimination that haunted black persons on a daily basis. Discrimination was borne with resignation by the older generation, but it incited intense hostility in a more aware young generation. "Discrimination cuts off too large a part of their life, to be endured in silence and apathy."[32] He was not wielding the threat of violence, but was disclosing a fact that he had frequently experienced. Discrimination was especially cruel to those whom the power structure had allowed to enjoy some of its blessings and then in subtle but certain ways impeded their further development. One devastating consequence of discrimination for black youths was massive unemployment, which could have been expected to induce rage and rebellion in the midst of historic prosperity. In 1967, King charged that unemployment for black youths was as high as 30 to 40 percent in many cities.[33] He observed that when mass unemployment occurs in the white community, it is called a depression, but when it exists only in the black community, it is called a social problem. He claimed that the unemployment of blacks and their underemployment or lack of meaningful work constituted probably 90 percent of the basic motivation for the riots.[34]

King contended that a further cause of the riots was the Vietnam War, a moral outrage.[35] Blacks were asked to fight for democracy in Vietnam when in fact the Saigon government was far from being a democracy. Even if blacks were recognized as heroes in the war, they still had to return home to the same lack of recognition in the form of second-class citizenship. He viewed the war also as the enemy of the poor since it consumed funds and energies that could have been used for their rehabilitation. In 1967, he asserted that whenever he spoke to the people in the ghettos, the one time they rose to their feet was when he spoke out on Vietnam.[36]

He maintained that urban life itself with its many degenerating conditions was another cause of the riots.[37] Black persons were expected to live in cities suffering from financial crisis, polluted air and water, obsolete and inadequate public facilities, and slums so squalid that they were unparalleled in any other industrial nation. The situation in the slums was further aggravated by the extensive migration from the South in recent years. King blamed the Federal Government for not developing plans to assist blacks to deal with the reduction of agricultural employment in the South. "Though other minorities had encountered obstacles, none was so brutally scorned or so consistently denied opportunity and hope as was the Negro."[38]

The National Advisory Commission on Civil Disorders in its 1968 Report in effect substantially agreed with most of King's analysis of the causes of the riots and with some of his other judgments. The commission stated that white racism was "essentially responsible" for the explosive mixture that had been accumulating in cities since the end of World War II. The commission identified the basic components of this mixture.[39] *First*, great numbers of blacks were continually excluded from the benefits of economic progress through pervasive discrimination in employment and education and through enforced confinement in segregated housing and schools. *Second*, the migration of blacks from the rural South, rapid population growth, and the continuing movement of middle-class whites to the suburbs created massive concentrations of impoverished blacks in major cities, producing a growing crisis of deteriorating facilities and services and unmet human needs. *Third*, in the ghettos segregation and poverty converged on blacks to destroy opportunity and hope and to enforce failure. Life in the ghettos too often meant unemployment, families without men, and schools that did not educate children, but only processed them and caused the young to turn to crime, drug addiction, dependency on welfare, and to bitterness and resentment against society in general and white society in particular. While blacks in the ghettos experienced these conditions, television and the other mass media added to their bitterness by endlessly flaunting before their eyes the affluence of most whites and of many blacks outside the ghettos.

The commission maintained that these conditions alone could not have caused the disorders. It cited other and more immediate factors that recently had begun to catalyze the explosive mixture.[40] *First*, while the great judicial and legislative victories of the civil rights movement had aroused the expectations of blacks, the failure to fulfill these expectations led to frustration, hostility, and cynicism. The struggle for equal rights in the South had sensitized Northern Negroes to the inequities in ghetto life. *Second*, a climate had developed that tended toward the approval and encouragement of violence as a form of protest. Several forces had contributed to this climate, such as white terrorism directed against nonviolent protest, open defiance of the law and of Federal authority by state and local officials in their attempts to block desegregation, and the use of violence by some protest groups that abandoned nonviolence and went beyond the constitutionally protected rights of petition and free assembly in their efforts to alter laws and policies. The commission observed that this climate was reinforced by a general erosion of respect for authority in American society and by a reduced effectiveness of social standards and of community restraints on violence and crime. *Third,* with a sense of powerlessness in the face of political and economic exploitation by the white power structure some blacks developed the conviction that there was no effective alternative to violence as a means of expression and redress and as a way of "moving the system." *Fourth,* white racists had appealed to violence, and their appeals were echoed by black racists across the country and reported by the media. Local militants and organizations resorted to the same inflammatory rhetoric, thus creating a mood of acceptance and expectation of violence. *Fifth,* many blacks regarded the police as symbolic of white power, white racism, and white repression, and many police did express white racist attitudes. Moreover, there was a widespread perception among blacks of the existence of police brutality and corruption, and of a double standard of justice and protection—one for blacks and another for whites.[41]

In the light of all these conditions that were the fuel of riots, King agreed with the judgment of Kenneth Clark that it was a surprise only that the outbreaks did not occur earlier.[42] In September 1965, Dr. Clark wrote an article for *The New York Times Magazine* entitled "The Wonder Is There Have Been So Few Riots."[43] Clark marveled at the fact that Negroes generally were law-abiding in a world where the law itself seemed to be their enemy. He quoted Senator Robert Kennedy, who said after the Watts riot, "There is no point in telling Negroes to observe the law. . . . It has almost always been used against [them]."[44] In Clark's analysis of the causes of riots he observed that appeals from governmental and civil rights leaders to the rioters for moderation and reason did not take into consideration the fact that individuals who had been systematically excluded from the privileges of middle-class life could not be expected to regard themselves as middle-class or to behave in terms of middle-class values.[45] How could prisoners of the ghetto be expected to respect property if instead of possessing it, they were possessed, exploited, and degraded by it as they suffered the daily damages of overcharges and usury? In the Northern ghettos, in particular, the rage and frustration of the Negro grew as he was told about progress in civil rights through Supreme Court decisions, civil rights legislation, and firm Presidential commitment, but his suffering continued as he experienced discrimination in employment and housing, and his children were subjugated in *de facto* segregated and inferior schools. It was these conditions that contributed to the outbreaks of rage that reached the point of being suicidal, "reflecting the ultimate in self-negation, self-rejection and hopelessness."[46]

The actions of some white liberals contributed to the rage of the Negro since often they owned his decaying home and administered the "criminally inefficient" public education of his children while their liberal labor unions either excluded him or accepted him only in token numbers or accepted him en masse but prevented him from assuming leadership or policy-making roles.[47] The Negro was pained by the interpretation of his "white friends" that his protest was a sign of his insatiability, irrationality, and ingratitude. This interpretation saw his equal rights not as something due to him as a human being and an American citizen but rather as a reward for good behavior. He had found it more difficult psychologically to bear this interpretation from those who professed to be his friends than to be a victim of the bigotry of acknowledged segregationists.

Clark rejected the racist use of a "double standard of social morality" in the evaluation of the riots. While emphasizing that the riots could not be understood by attempts to excuse them, he deplored the fact that while the lawlessness of Negroes was seen as a reflection on all Negroes and was countered by the full force of police and other governmental authority, the lawlessness of whites was considered the primitive reactions of a small group of unstable individuals and was often ignored by the police.[48]

Clark contended that if racism was to be eliminated, whites had to give more than financial contributions and intellectual support. They had to give their compassion, reveal a willingness to accept hostility, and increase their resolve to make race and color irrelevant for participation in American society. He called for the inclusion of Negroes within the economy at all levels of employment, for the improvement of their living conditions, and for the reorganization, improvement, and integration of public schools, which were also necessary in order to reeducate white children and prepare them to live in the present and future world of racial diversity. If realistic programs were to be implemented to achieve these minimum goals to change the lives of human beings confined within the ghetto, "the ghetto will be destroyed rationally, by plan, and not by random self-destructive forces. Only then will American society not remain at the mercy of primitive, frightening, irrational attempts by prisoners in the ghetto to destroy their own prison."[49]

In his 1967 analysis of the riots King discovered at least two facts that indicated hope for the future of nonviolence. First, the violence by blacks to a startling degree was directed against property rather than against persons.[50] While the property damage exceeded a billion dollars, the injury inflicted by blacks on whites was "inconsequential" by comparison. The death toll during the riots largely consisted of rioters killed by the military. Blacks did not use the riots to vent their rage by physical injury to whites. King claimed that we cannot dismiss the significance of this fact by asserting that most black rioters were prompted by a fear of retribution since the military forces dealt with the acts of petty larceny as if they were murder. Most rioters were willing to risk their lives to attack property because it was symbolic of the power structure they wished to oppose. He reinforced this interpretation by referring to the fact that after the riots police received hundreds of calls from blacks wanting to return merchandise they had stolen. These persons were not interested in the possession of this property, but they were expressing their anger at the imbalance of power evident in the inequitable distribution of property. He contended that even arson, though more dangerous than looting, was an attack on property as a symbol.

A second fact about the riots that, according to King, offered promise for the future of nonviolence was that 99 percent of blacks in the ghettos did not commit violence during the riots.[51] Then too, no report on the riots indicated that more than one or two dozen people were engaged in sniping. He concluded:

> From the facts, an unmistakable pattern emerges: a handful of Negroes used gunfire substantially to intimidate, not to kill; and all of the other participants had a different target—property.[52]

While rejecting violence, he still praised even those radicals among the young who asserted the political and psychological need for violence to the extent that they with the other radicals understood "the need for action—direct self-transforming and structure-transforming action."[53]

The Necessity of Exposing the Violence of Racism

Many of King's critics have implied that he was guilty of a self-contradiction by practicing a type of nonviolent protest that generated violence. *Time* in a 1964 article on him as "Man of the Year" asserted, "King preaches endlessly about nonviolence, but his protest movements often lead to violence."[54] *U.S. News & World Report* in its analysis of how he won the Nobel Peace Prize indicated that many Americans thought it "extraordinary that this prize should go to a man whose fame is based upon his battle for civil rights for Negroes—and whose activities often led to violence."[55] Hanes Walton, Jr., in *The Political Philosophy of Martin Luther King, Jr.,* maintained that in one respect King's nonviolence was similar to violence in that it could result in the destruction of property and life.[56] Frank Meyer, in a 1965 article in *National Review*, "The Violence of Nonviolence," accused King of employing a nonviolence that had a "violent essence" since it involved "the provocation of violence," "the use of force against civil society," and a "violent assault upon representative, constitutional government."[57] Unlike Walton, who conceded that King's intentions and means differed from the advocates of violence, Meyer charged King's Nonviolent Movement with "hypocrisy on a grand scale" since the Movement aimed to provoke the supporters of the civil order so that they would initiate the first act of violence, and proceeded by "relying upon the terror inspired by mobs to destroy the processes of constitutional government."[58]

In an attempt to substantiate his criticisms, Meyer appealed to an article by King in *Saturday Review* entitled "Behind the Selma March," which explained that the goal of the demonstrations in Selma, as elsewhere, was to dramatize injustice and to bring about justice by nonviolent methods, and that these demonstrations could achieve this goal of justice when four things occurred:[59]

1. Nonviolent demonstrators go into the streets to exercise their constitutional rights.
2. Racists resist by unleashing violence against them.
3. Americans of conscience in the name of decency demand federal intervention and legislation.
4. The Administration, under mass pressure, initiates measures of immediate intervention and remedial legislation.[60]

In commenting on the second march from Selma, King asserted, "I felt that we had to march at least to the point where the troopers brutalized the people on Sunday even if it would mean a recurrence of violence, arrest, or even death."[61]

By this explanation did King concede to his critics that his nonviolent demonstrations precipitated violence? Clearly, he did not intend that his demonstrators should commit any violent act that would arouse and justify violent reactions by their opponents. His demonstrators were trained in workshops in nonviolence so that their disciplined resistance would not initiate violence but only endure it. Guided by the spirit of *agape*, they were not to let their protest lose its dignity and degenerate to the crippling level of violence. During the Montgomery Boycott he frequently appealed to his followers to continue their nonviolence. At the weekly prayer meetings he stressed the immorality and impracticality of violence. When his home was bombed, he pleaded with enraged blacks not to resort to retaliatory violence.[62] After he received many threats to his life, he told his followers at a mass meeting, "If one day you find me sprawled out dead, I do not want you to retaliate with a single act of violence."[63] His "Integrated Bus Suggestions" in many ways revealed the spirit of nonviolence.[64] At the beginning of the sit-ins when he addressed a civil rights student conference at Shaw University, he recommended the study and adoption of the philosophy of nonviolence that would aim for reconciliation. "Our ultimate end must be the creation of the beloved community."[65] When he was asked in 1960 whether he thought that the picketing and sit-ins might lead to violence, he replied:

> I don't believe that the Negro people will precipitate the violence, that they will inflict violence upon the white community, because we have stressed over and over again the need for nonviolence.[66]

During the Albany Movement when some blacks who were not adequately trained in nonviolence battled with police, King declared a "Day of Penitence" and cancelled further demonstrations until the community adopted nonviolence. During the Birmingham Movement he was careful to prepare the demonstrators with extensive training in nonviolence. During the 1966 Mississippi Freedom March it was he who attempted to persuade activists from CORE and SNCC to adopt nonviolence.[67] He explained that in all the marches he organized, it was routine for his march leaders to collect hundreds of knives from the marchers in case of momentary weakness. During the Chicago Movement he could report that day after day he had walked through the lines of march and had never seen anyone, even members of black gangs, retaliate with violence, even though they were injured by white spectators.[68]

Though the evidence reveals that King was highly successful in convincing his demonstrators not to commit violence, he was not able to eliminate it completely from his demonstrattions. While 90 percent of the blacks in Birmingham agreed to accept nonviolence for the duration of the movement and thus were committed to "tactical nonviolence," and thirty thousand of them were trained in nonviolence workshops and accepted the "ten commandments of nonviolence," still he had to witness some retaliatory violence by a few blacks who were not members of the movement but were spectators at some of the demonstrations.[69] In the march from Selma to Montgomery he had to listen to reports of those who followed along the fringe of the march and began to talk of arming themselves. In Memphis he had to endure the eruption of violence because some black youths, not disciplined in nonviolence, joined the march. Since he was attempting to arouse the conscience of the nation by the nonviolence of the demonstrators, these acts of violence by those outside the Movement were a source of special frustration for him. The public would read of the violence and not know who was responsible. In a speech on the night before his assassination he protested the way the press in its accounts of the Memphis march emphasized the window breaking, but seldom mentioned the injustice to the sanitation workers that was the reason for the march.[70] Moreover, if he had little control over the blacks who were not adherents of nonviolence and still joined his demonstrations, he had less control over the blacks elsewhere for whom the Movement served as a catalyst for releasing pent-up resentments. He called for protest and love, but they heard only the call for protest. Despite his appeals, his Nonviolent Movement could not avert the violent protests. Yet, he knew that if he did not continue to protest, he would be guilty of cooperating with the evil system of segregation.

However, in another way King did design his nonviolent demonstrations to precipitate violence since he intended them to unmask the violence that permeates society. He argued that hostilities rooted in racism are present in individuals and institutions, and direct action is necessary to expose them. He claimed that the strength of American democracy consists in its relentless and insistent struggle to expose and overcome social evils.[71] In a January 1965 interview he explained the need to precipitate a crisis for social transformation:

Our nonviolent direct-action program has as its objective not the creation of tensions, but the *surfacing* of tensions already present. We set out to precipitate a crisis situation that must open the door to negotiation. I am not afraid of the words "crisis" and "tension." I deeply oppose violence, but constructive crisis and tension are necessary for growth. Innate in all life and all growth is tension. Only in death is there an absence of tension. To cure injustices, you must expose them before the light of human conscience and the bar of public opinion, regardless of whatever tensions that exposure generates. Injustices to the Negro must be brought out into the open where they cannot be evaded. [72]

To expose the evil of injustice, he was willing to precipitate even a crisis that would result in violence to the demonstrators. During the Birmingham Movement he dispatched demonstrators to the streets, even though he knew that they would be met with further violence by the police because he also knew that such violence would in part reveal the latent violence of racism to the American public and would arouse their conscience to pressure the Federal Government to pass legislation that would begin to eradicate this evil. [73] While leading a march in Chicago, he was hit by a rock. As his aides went to assist him, he said, "I have to do this—to expose myself—to bring this hate into the open." [74] When he was confronted with the charge that his demonstrations precipitated violence in this sense, he responded by comparing this charge to a condemnation of Socrates because his commitment to truth and his philosophical inquiries precipitated the act of the misdirected Athenians who sentenced him to death, and to a condemnation of Jesus because his unique consciousness of God and his consistent devotion to God's will precipitated his crucifixion. [75]

It might be objected that King, by using the violence of his opponents as a means of focusing public attention on social evils, in effect repudiated his own principle that the means must always be as pure as the end. However, this objection ignores his explanation of his method. When his protests caused violence to erupt, they were not creating evil but were causing the existing violence in individuals to surface so that it might be cured. In *Why We Can't Wait* he explained:

> Just as a doctor will occasionally re-open a wound because a dangerous infection hovers beneath a half-healed surface, the revolution for human rights is opening up unhealthy areas in American life and permitting a new and wholesome healing to take place. [76]

He argued that even as it would be strange to condemn a doctor who discovers cancer in a patient, so too it would be strange to condemn nonviolent direct actions for revealing the dangerous cancer of hatred and racism in this society. "We did not cause the cancer; we merely exposed it. Only through this kind of exposure will the cancer ever be cured."[77] He thought that it would be immoral to allow these evils to continue unchecked. His explanation of his intention to expose latent violence by his demonstrations was reminiscent of Gandhi's explanation of his protests. Gandhi replied to the charge that his civil disobedience might lead to violence by stating that such a result was likely, but he added that such disobedience would not be the cause of violence:

> Violence is there already corroding the whole body politic. Civil disobedience will be but a purifying process and may bring to the surface what is burrowing under and into the whole body.[78]

King highlighted the significance of the fact that the nonviolent demonstrations helped bring about several achievements, including the passage of the 1964 Civil Rights Act and of the 1965 Voting Rights Act with a minimum loss of life, and he was able to claim, "Fewer people have been killed in ten years of nonviolent demonstrations across the South than were killed in one night of rioting in Watts."[79] He explained that a minimum of whites were casualties in the demonstrations because the demonstrators were trained not to engage in retaliatory violence, and that a minimum of blacks were casualties because their white oppressors were aware that the world was watching their actions and because for the first time these whites were being confronted by blacks who did not display fear.[80]

In his explanation of the second march from Selma in 1965 King revealed his intent to keep violence by the opposition to a minimum:

> We determined to seek the middle course. We would march until we faced the troopers. We would not disengage until they made clear that they were going to use force. We would disengage then, having made our point, revealing the continued presence of violence, and showing clearly who are the oppressed and who [are] the oppressors, hoping finally that the national administration in Washington would feel and respond to the shocked reactions with action.[81]

King's desire to reduce the violence that might result from his demonstrations was apparent also in his approval of the use of Federal marshals to protect the demonstrators. During the Freedom Rides he welcomed the presence of U.S. marshals and the federalized Alabama

National Guard when they dispersed a mob that threatened the lives of the demonstrators.[82] In a 1962 editorial in *The Nation* he commented upon the use of U.S. marshals and troops of the National Guard and the U.S. Army in securing the admission of James Meredith to the University of Mississippi:

> Whereas I abhor the use of arms and the thought of war, I do believe in the intelligent use of police power. . . . Mississippi's breakdown of law and order demanded the utilization of a police action to quell the disorder and enforce the law of the land. Armed force that intelligently exercises police power, making civil arrests in which full due process is observed, is not functioning as an army in military engagement, so I feel the presence of troops in Oxford, Mississippi, is a police force seeking to preserve law and order rather than an army engaging in destructive warfare.[83]

After the march from Selma to Montgomery he could claim, "We were reminded that the only reason that this march was possible was due to the presence of thousands of federalized troops, marshals, and a Federal Court order."[84] During the Mississippi Freedom March he appealed to President Johnson for Federal marshals to protect the marchers. In the Chicago Movement he welcomed all the police protection for his marchers that he could receive. He expressed his gratitude to Governor Otto Kerner of Illinois for ordering the National Guard to remain on alert to provide protection for a proposed march to Cicero, a Chicago suburb.

When critics focus on the violence that resulted from King's demonstrations, they generally say nothing of the violence he was attempting to eliminate from society. This may be due in part to their limited conception of violence that would restrict violence to physical violence and perhaps to civil disobedience. King had a comprehensive conception of violence that included a keen awareness of "systemic violence." He was opposed not only to physical violence by his demonstrators but to that sometimes subtle and yet devastating violence that assaults the disinherited on a daily basis. He denounced the brutal discrimination that can occur when a Negro tries to buy a house, and the "brutal violence against the Negro's soul when he finds himself denied a job that he knows he is qualified for."[85] He also condemned the violence of having to live in a community where one must pay higher prices for goods or higher rent for equivalent housing than are charged in the white areas of the city. During the Chicago Movement when he chose to live with his family in a slum in Lawndale, he witnessed numerous instances of this violence. To reduce this type of daily violence, he was willing to have himself and his followers endure physical suffering in a demonstration:

> It is better to shed a little blood from a blow on the head or a rock thrown by an angry mob than to have children by the thousands finishing high school who can only read at a sixth-grade level.[86]

Julian Bond, who has been active in the civil rights struggle since the 1960 sit-ins, in *A Time To Speak, A Time To Act* in 1972 compiled a list of instances that attempted to reveal some of the depth and prevalence of systemic violence in America.[87] His examples can serve to help correct a narrow conception of what constitutes violence—a conception that identifies violence only with physical aggression. He explained that violence occurs when black children go to school for twelve years and receive the equivalent of six years of education, when almost thirty million people remain hungry in the richest nation in the world, when a country spends $900 per second to stifle the Vietnamese but only $77 a year per poor person to feed the hungry at home, when a country places more value on property than on persons, when Congress gives priority to cotton, tobacco, rice, and cattle over people, when six thousand farmers receive as much as $25,000 each year not to farm, when Congress is quick to pass a loan guarantee of hundreds of millions of dollars to rescue an inefficient aerospace company while a congressional committee remains inactive on a welfare reform bill, when $78 billion is spent each year to kill and only $12 billion to heal, when black men represent a disproportionate share of the casualties in Vietnam, or when the President of the United States ignores the demands of millions for peace.

On the night of King's assassination Robert Kennedy spoke of this violence that permeates so many lives:

> For there is another kind of violence, slower but just as deadly, destructive as the shot or the bomb in the night. This is the violence of institutions; indifference and inaction and slow decay. This is the violence that afflicts the poor, that poisons relations between men because their skin has different colors. This is

a slow destruction of a child by hunger, and schools without books, and homes without heat in the winter. This is the breaking of a man's spirit by denying him the chance to stand as a father.[88]

In the light of this more realistic and comprehensive conception of violence, it can be argued that King's nonviolent demonstrations were exchanging the possibility of minimal violence, most of which was inflicted on the demonstrators, who were willing to endure it, for the removal of a significant amount of the massive violence that plagued millions of people on a daily basis.

Related to the charge that King's demonstrations precipitated violence was the charge, made by Hanes Walton, Jr. and others, that King and other leaders of nonviolent groups employed the implicit threat of violence, and that such a threat was crucial to their successes.[89] Walton maintained that King and these leaders persistently warned their opponents that if they did not receive what they demanded, they would not be able to restrain their followers. He indicated that King did not hesitate to warn his opponents that the Black Muslims were quite prepared to exploit the frustrations of blacks in the large industrial areas of the North. Frank Meyer contended that King's demonstrators were in fact a "mob . . . devoted to overawing constitutional processes, which represent a balance of the rights of the majority and of many minorities, by the threat of creating terror and civil chaos," and that "the political morality of Dr. King and his nonviolent movement would destroy the very possibility of representative government."[90] "It is a program for government by force and the threat of terror."[91] Lionel Lokos in *The Life and Legacy of Martin Luther King*, which contains an account of the Montgomery Boycott, also charged King's Movement with relying on threats of violence. When King was arrested on the charge of traveling 30 miles an hour in a 25-mile-an-hour zone, and a large crowd gathered outside the jail, the jailer out of fear immediately released King. In recounting this incident Lokos concluded, "This was the first time—but hardly the last—that the threat of violence would come to the rescue of nonviolence."[92]

Does a warning that violence might erupt if certain demands are not met constitute a threat of violence? King repeatedly issued such warnings. In a February 1964 interview he stated that it was imperative to get the civil rights bill through Congress, and cautioned, "If it doesn't get through, the nation will face a great deal of social disruption."[93] In November 1965, he warned that it could not be taken for granted that blacks in the North would adhere to nonviolence under any conditions:

> When there is rock-like intransigence or sophisticated manipulation that mocks the empty-handed petitioner, rage replaces reason. . . . The cohesive, potentially explosive Negro community in the North has a short fuse and a long train of abuses.[94]

In 1966, he wrote:

> There are more Negroes in Chicago than in the whole state of Mississippi, and if we don't get nonviolent groups, the alternative is Watts. And, without another alternative, Watts will look like a Sunday School teaparty compared to what will happen.[95]

How are these warnings to be understood? In a 1959 address to the MIA King reminded his audience that Governor John Patterson of Alabama had predicted violence if the schools in the state were integrated, and King added, "Of course, the continuous prediction of violence is a conscious or unconscious invitation to it."[96] In the light of this contention may it then be said that King's own warnings were in fact invitations to violence? Such an interpretation would be erroneous since it would have to ignore his repeated emphasis on the discipline of nonviolence and his detailed rejection of the immorality and impracticality of riots:

> The riots, North and South, involved mobs—not the disciplined, nonviolent, direct-action demonstrators with whom I identify. We do not condone lawlessness, looting, and violence committed by the racist or the reckless of *any* color.[97]

King's critics have here ignored the fact that he also warned that riots would create the danger of a right-wing takeover of the Fascist type. While reactionaries may interpret predictions of violence as invitations to violence, such predictions can be intended as warnings that arise from a genuine desire to avert violence. King felt that he had a moral obligation to warn of the possibility of violent alternatives if the nation did not move toward social justice:

> Those who argue that it is hazardous to give warnings, lest the expression of apprehension lead to violence, are in error. Vio-

lence has already been practiced too often, and always because remedies were postponed. It is now the task of responsible people to indicate where and why spontaneous combustion is accumulating.[98]

He warned that if the repressed emotions were not released nonviolently they would be expressed violently. ". . . This is not a threat, but a fact of history."[99] He repeated President Kennedy's warning:

We are confronted primarily with a moral issue. It is as old as the Scriptures and is as clear as the American Constitution. The heart of the question is whether all Americans are to be afforded equal rights and equal opportunities. . . . Those who do nothing are inviting shame as well as violence. . . .[100]

The Immoral War in Vietnam

Several years before King decided to declare his opposition to the Vietnam War, he had attempted to determine the validity of pacifism. At Crozer Theological Seminary he studied Gandhi's pacifism with George Davis, a pacifist, and Reinhold Niebuhr's "realism" with Kenneth Smith. Initially, he was impressed with Niebuhr's critique of pacifism, but when he began to compare this critique with Gandhi's thought, he realized that Niebuhr had distorted pacifism by interpreting it as passive nonresistance to evil and as expressing a naive trust in the power of love, whereas true pacifism, as exemplified by Gandhi, involves a courageous confrontation of evil by the power of love.[101] Even after considering this limitation in Niebuhr's thought, he conceded that Niebuhr had led him to realize the human potential for evil and to recognize that many pacifists had an excessive optimism concerning human nature and unconsciously tended toward self-righteousness:

It was my revolt against these attitudes under the influence of Niebuhr that accounts for the fact that in spite of my strong leaning toward pacifism, I never joined a pacifist organization. After reading Niebuhr, I tried to arrive at a realistic pacifism. In other words, I came to see the pacifist position not as sinless but as the lesser evil in the circumstances.[102]

King indicated that while a student at Boston University, he came to see that Niebuhr's view of human nature was too pessimistic and failed to appreciate the redeeming power of divine grace.[103] L. Harold DeWolf, Edgar Brightman, Allen Chalmers, Peter Bertocci, and Walter Muelder provided King with the philosophy of Personalism, which *for him* had the effect of developing tendencies toward pacifism. Both Chalmers and Muelder had a deep sympathy for pacifism.[104] Howard Thurman, dean of the chapel at Boston University at that time, was a pacifist. In 1963, in *Strength To Love* King stated that he had recently realized the necessity for nonviolence in international relations.[105] Previously he had thought that war could serve as a negative good to prevent the growth of an evil force and would be preferable to surrender to a totalitarian system, but he had come to believe that the potential destructiveness of modern weapons completely ruled out the possibility that war could ever again achieve a negative good. In 1964, in his Nobel Lecture he reaffirmed this belief, and added:

> But wisdom born of experience should tell us that war is obsolete. . . . A so-called limited war will leave little more than a calamitous legacy of human suffering, political turmoil, and spiritual disillusionment.[106]

He maintained that it is necessary to love peace and to sacrifice for it. "We must concentrate not merely on the negative expulsion of war, but [on] the positive affirmation of peace."[107]

Since 1965 King had been publicly expressing his moral concern about the Vietnam War. At a civil rights rally in Petersburg, Virginia, he warned that unless the Johnson Administration found a way to negotiate peace in Vietnam, he might mass his followers in teach-ins and peace rallies.[108] That August, when a SCLC convention passed a resolution giving King the power to turn the "full attention" of the organization to Vietnam and world affairs if he thought that the international situation made this necessary, he urged the U.S. Government to rebuild some destroyed Vietnamese villages as "a solid indication to the people of Vietnam that our interest is in the development of Vietnam, and not in its destruction."[109] In September 1965, he conferred with Arthur Goldberg, U.S. Ambassador to the United Nations, to press for a negotiated settlement to the war. Senator Thomas Dodd of Connecticut, who considered King "a man of unquestioned competence in the field of civil rights," criticized his effort as "an ill-advised adventure in the sphere of foreign policy."[110] Later that year Dr. Benjamin Spock told King that he could become the most important symbol for peace in the country, and urged him to make a world tour for peace and upon his return to unify the forces for peace in the nation.[111] In January 1966, King spoke out in defense of Julian Bond, who had been deprived of his elective seat by the Georgia legislature because of his endorsement of SNCC's anti-Vietnam platform.[112] At a SCLC convention early in 1966 King called for American withdrawal from Vietnam, and in May he agreed to serve as one of the co-chairmen of Clergy and Laymen Concerned about Vietnam with Dr. John Bennett, Rabbi Abraham Heschel, the Reverend John McKenzie and Philip Scharper.

During 1966 King agonized over whether he should increase his opposition to the war and even lead peace marches. He knew that if he did escalate his opposition, he would run the risk of producing further division not only within the civil rights movement but even within the SCLC national organization. He had already been criticized by black leaders for his pronouncements against the war. He knew also that his heightened opposition to the war would infuriate President Johnson, who in many ways had identified with the civil rights struggle. Then too, he was warned by some of his financial advisers that his further opposition to the war would so discourage supporters of SCLC that it would mean the ruin of the organization. His previous statements on the war had already substantially reduced donations to SCLC.

King had become keenly aware, however, that it would have been morally inconsistent for him to preach against violence at home and by silence to condone it abroad. Also, there were evident signs that if he did not vigorously protest the war, the Nonviolent Movement could not hope to secure the allegiance of black youths in the ghetto who were already sympathetic to the antiwar message of Stokely Carmichael. He was aware that white liberals were increasingly moving from the civil rights movement to the peace movement. Moreover, Bayard Rustin, whose wisdom in the strategy and tactics of nonviolence contributed so much to the crusades, agreed that King had a moral obligation to oppose the war, but advised him not to attempt to combine the civil rights and the peace movements. Coretta Scott King, an active member of Women Strike for Peace, urged him to take a strong stand against the war. Since her student days she had been a pacifist, and in June 1965 had been a speaker at a rally of the National Committee for a Sane Nuclear Policy (SANE). L. Harold DeWolf, who remained an adviser to King and had long been an active member of SANE, encouraged him to intensify his opposition to the war. James Bevel, a member of King's staff, consistently urged him to become more critical of the war, and asked for a leave of absence from SCLC to recruit black youths for the antiwar movement.

On March 25, 1967, in an antiwar march in Chicago, King proclaimed, "We must combine the fervor of the civil rights movement with the peace movement."[113] Five days later the directors of SCLC unanimously condemned the war as "morally and politically unjust," and pledged to do everything in their power to end it.[114] On April 4, at The Riverside Church in New York City, King delivered a speech, "Beyond Vietnam," later entitled "Vietnam and the Struggle for Human Rights," that condemned the involvement of the United States in the war.[115] Evidently, he chose not to employ his usual dialectical approach that attempted to discover some truths on both sides of a conflict. He explained that he was addressing his "beloved nation," not Hanoi, the National Liberation Front, China, or Russia. Although he admitted that there was a need for a collective solution to this tragic war, and indicated that he would not attempt to present North Vietnam or the National Liberation Front as "paragons of virtue" or overlook the role they could play in the resolution of the conflict, he directed his criticisms only against the U.S. Government:

> Here is the true meaning and value of compassion and non-violence when it helps us to see the enemy's point of view, to hear his questions, to know his assessment of ourselves.[116]

Acknowledging that the calling to speak against the policy of one's nation is often "a vocation of agony," King affirmed, "My conscience leaves me no other choice."[117] He declared that the U.S. Government in the name of peace and freedom was "the greatest purveyor of violence in the world today."[118] With its firepower it was responsible for twenty times the number of casualties caused by the Viet Cong, and it tested its weapons on the peasants of Vietnam "just as the Germans tested out new medicine and new tortures in the concentration camps of Europe."[119] He stated that since the U.S. Government assumed the initiative in this war, it should assume the initiative in stopping it. He proposed five actions that it should carry out immediately to begin the long process of extricating itself from the conflict:

1. End all bombing in North and South Vietnam.
2. Declare a unilateral cease-fire in the hope that such action will create the atmosphere for negotiation.
3. Take immediate steps to prevent other battlegrounds in

Southeast Asia by curtailing our military build-up in Thailand and our interference in Laos.

4. Realistically accept the fact that the National Liberation Front has substantial support in South Vietnam and must thereby play a role in any meaningful negotiations and in any future Vietnam government.

5. Set a date that we will remove all foreign troops from Vietnam in accordance with the 1954 Geneva Agreement.[120]

He stated that ministers should challenge young men with the alternative of conscientious objection, and he encouraged ministers of draft age to give up their ministerial exemptions and seek status as conscientious objectors.[121] In an interview two days before this speech he had warned that if the nation continued the escalation of the war, it might be necessary to engage in civil disobedience to arouse further the conscience of the nation.[122]

Critics arose from many directions to challenge this assault. Many of them had supported King in the civil rights struggle. Roy Wilkins, Whitney Young, Jr., Senator Edward Brooke of Massachusetts, Ralph Bunche, and Jackie Robinson publicly expressed their disagreement with him on the war. The NAACP, which had assisted him for years in many ways, unanimously passed a resolution that said in part:

> To attempt to merge the civil rights movement with the peace movement, or to assume that one is dependent upon the other, is, in our judgment, a serious tactical mistake. It will serve the cause neither of civil rights nor of peace.[123]

The directors of Freedom House, which had honored King in the past, called his position "demagogic and irresponsible in its attack on our government."[124]

The Washington Post, which had often supported King, maintained:

> Dr. King has done a grave injury to the great struggle to remove ancient abuses from our public life. He has diminished his usefulness to his cause, to his country, and to his people.[125]

The New York Times in an editorial "Dr. King's Error" rejected as erroneous King's argument that stated the "war should be stopped not only because it is a futile war waged for the wrong ends but also because it is a barrier to social progress in this country and therefore prevents Negroes from achieving their just place in American life."[126] The editorial claimed that this was "a fusing of two public problems that are distinct and separate," that it was "a disservice to both," and that "linking these hard, complex problems will lead not to solutions but to deeper confusion."[127]

Life in its editorial "Dr. King's Disservice to His Cause" claimed that, by linking the civil rights movement with total opposition to the U.S. position on the war, he came "close to betraying the cause for which he has worked so long."[128] The editorial accused him of going off on a tangent when, instead of providing a share of the leadership for the civil rights movement, he suggested that American Negroes boycott the war. It objected that, by his characterization of the war as "colonialist," he introduced matters that had nothing to do with the legitimate battle for equal rights in America. While conceding that "Dr. King, a Nobel Prize winner justly honored for his philosophy of nonviolence, could be expected to have strong personal reservations about our involvement in Vietnam," it contended that he went beyond his personal right to dissent when he connected progress in civil rights in the United States with a proposal that amounted to abject surrender in Vietnam and recommended that youths become conscientious objectors.[129] After criticizing his attack on the United States for the violence in Vietnam and rejecting his comparison of the American tactics with those of the Nazis, the editorial concluded:

> Dr. King has claimed that the budgetary demands of the war in Vietnam are the key hindrance to progress in civil rights. Not so. If the drive for equal rights falters now, in the difficult time when life must be given to laws already on the books, Dr. King and his tactics must share the blame.[130]

In an article in *The Reader's Digest* entitled "Martin Luther King's Tragic Decision" Carl Rowan, a black journalist, who had been of assistance to King during the Montgomery Boycott, affirmed that King's deep involvement in a conflict between the United States and the Communists would likely cause more murmurings that he was influenced by enemies of the United States.[131] Rowan argued that such murmurings might produce powerfully hostile reactions that would imperil chances for the passage of a bill that would protect civil rights workers in the South and make housing discrimination illegal. He granted that it might not make any difference to King that he had become a *persona non grata* to President Johnson and that he had lost his influence with his friends in Congress, but Rowan contended that it could make a difference to millions of Negroes who could not break out of the vicious circle of poverty if the President did not provide the leadership and if Congress did not create the necessary programs and laws. Rowan charged that, by recommending that Negroes not respond to the draft or fight in Vietnam, King was adopting a course of action that many Americans of all races considered utterly irresponsible. He contended that King had created the impression that the Negro was disloyal. With evident sadness he concluded:

> It is a tragic irony that there should be any doubt about the Negro's loyalty to his country—especially doubt created by Martin Luther King, who has helped as much as any one man to make America truly the Negro's country too.[132]

Any meaningful evaluation of King's position on the Vietnam War must include an examination of the *moral* reasons he offered for his dissent. Instead of confronting these reasons, his critics chose to level charges against him, such as disloyalty to his country and betrayal of the civil rights movement. Analysis of his speeches and writings reveals that he presented at least ten *moral* reasons for his opposition to the war, all of which he mentioned in his April 4 speech, however briefly. Personalist themes such as the sacredness of human personality, the fundamental unity of humanity, the right to moral self-determination, and the necessity for logical and moral consistency permeate these reasons.

First, King had to oppose the war because of the violence to human life:

> This business of burning human beings with napalm, of filling our nation's homes with orphans and widows, of injecting poisonous drugs of hate into the veins of peoples normally humane, of sending men home from dark and bloody battlefields physically handicapped and psychologically deranged cannot be reconciled with wisdom, justice, and love.[133]

He contended that a war in which Vietnamese children were incinerated and in which American soldiers died in increasing numbers was a war that mutilated the conscience.[134] He maintained that these casualties were sufficient to cause all people to rise up with righteous in-

dignation to protest the very nature of this war. His Personalistic conviction about the sacred value of every person served to intensify his
horror at the inhumanity of the war. "And it is out of this moral commitment to [the] dignity and the worth of human personality that I feel
that it is necessary to stand up against the war in Vietnam."[135]

Second, he indicated that he was concerned that the constant escalation of the war could lead to a war with China and to a world war that
might mean the annihilation of the human race. He granted that war
might have been a negative good in the past since it stopped the growth
of tragically evil and sick forces like Hitler. Despite its horror, war
might have been preferable to surrender to a Nazi, Fascist, or Communist totalitarian system. However, he was convinced that, because
of the destructive power of nuclear weapons, war was no longer
morally legitimate. "It is no longer a choice between violence and nonviolence. It is either non-violence or non-existence. . . ."[136] He repeated President Kennedy's warning, "Mankind must put an end to
war or war will put an end to mankind."[137] He reminded his critics who
wanted him to restrict his protests to civil rights that it would be absurd for him to work for integration and not be concerned with the
survival of the world in which the integration was to take place.[138]

Third, he maintained that it would have been morally inconsistent
for him to raise his voice against violence by the oppressed in American ghettos and at the same time condone the violence of his Government in Vietnam. He explained that when for three summers he had
walked among the rejected, angry, and desperate young men in the
Northern ghettos, and had attempted to speak to them of nonviolence
for social change and to tell them that Molotov cocktails and rifles
would not solve their social problems, they responded by asking him if
the nation was not using massive doses of violence in Vietnam to solve
its problems.[139] He acknowledged that this experience in the ghettos
increased his awareness of his obligation to challenge violence on an
international scale:

> Their questions hit home, and I knew that I could never again
> raise my voice against the violence of the oppressed in the ghettos
> without having first spoken clearly to the greatest purveyor of
> violence in the world today—my own government.[140]
>
>   If destruction of property [in riots] is deplorable, what is the
> word for the use of napalm on people?[141]

King questioned how an Administration guilty of this violence in
Asia could denounce the violence of blacks in the ghettos. "Only those

who are fighting for peace have the moral authority to lecture on non-violence."[142] He also became more conscious of the inconsistency in some Americans who applauded the nonviolence of Negroes at home and still supported the violence of Negroes abroad. They commended Negroes for their disciplined nonviolence in the Montgomery Boycott, the sit-ins, the Freedom Rides, and in the Albany, Birmingham, and Selma Movements, and yet they commissioned Negroes to do violence in Vietnam. King denounced as immoral the strange inconsistency of a nation and a press that were so noble in their praise of him when he appealed for nonviolence toward "Bull" Connor and Sheriff Jim Clark, and that cursed and damned him when he called for nonviolence toward brown children in Vietnam.[143]

Fourth, he felt compelled to oppose the war because, "like some demoniacal destructive suction tube," it absorbed the skills and funds desperately needed to implement the economic and social domestic programs for the poor.[144] He explained that the Poverty Program a few years before had seemed to offer hope to the poor, both black and white, but when the war became a national obsession, then poverty and other social problems were generally ignored. He thought it tragic and immoral that the Government was willing to spend $322,000 for each enemy soldier killed, but in the war on poverty only $53 a year for each person classified as poor, and that much of the $53 went for the salaries of people who were not poor.[145] While the Government spent some 70 billions each year for military purposes, it spent not even 2 billion for the security of 20 million blacks in anti-poverty programs.[146] The war had destroyed the promises of the Great Society. "The bombs in Vietnam explode at home; they destroy the hopes and possibilities for a decent America."[147]

King granted that the Government had resources for both the war and for domestic programs, but he maintained that it would never voluntarily pursue both at the same time for two reasons. The Administration and the majority of Congress, as distinguished from the majority of the people, were single-mindedly devoted to the war. While they were emotionally committed to the war, they were emotionally hostile to the needs of the poor. Moreover, in conformity with the logic of war, they reasoned that beyond using the wealth of the nation for immediate combat, they needed to maintain a substantial reserve so that the military power of the nation would not be diminished by draining off resources for social programs.[148] King warned that a nation is moving toward spiritual death when year after year it spends more on military defense than on social programs.[149] At times, he offered the disastrous effect of the war on domestic programs for the poor as the first reason for his dissent.[150] On May 16, 1966, at an antiwar rally in Washington, D.C., the Reverend William Sloane Coffin, Jr., chaplain of Yale University, read a statement by King that contained the protest, "The pursuit of widened war has narrowed domestic welfare programs, making the poor, white and Negro, bear the heaviest burdens at the front and at home."[151]

Fifth, King recognized that the war was a special evil for young black Americans. He lamented the fact that blacks who had been crippled by American society were sent eight thousand miles to guarantee liberties in Southeast Asia that had been denied them in southwest Georgia and East Harlem. He thought it a cruel irony that Americans could watch on television blacks and whites killing and dying together for a nation that in many places refused to educate them together in the same school and to allow them to live together on the same block.[152] Then too, he indicated that at the beginning of 1967, considering their proportion in the population, there were twice as many blacks as whites in combat in Vietnam and twice as many blacks had died in action.[153] He contended that he could not be silent in the face of such a cruel manipulation of the poor.

Sixth, he explained that he spoke against the war also because he loved America and passionately desired that it stand as the moral example of the world.[154] He emphasized that he spoke not in anger but out of anxiety, sorrow, and disappointment with America, and added that there is no great disappointment where there is no great love.[155] In reply to his critics who wanted to exclude him from the peace movement, he frequently appealed to the fact that since 1957 the motto of SCLC had been "To Save the Soul of America."[156] He had come to understand that this redemption had to involve the eradication not only of racism and materialism but of militarism as well. He maintained that the soul of America could never be saved as long as it destroyed the deepest hopes of men. "If America's soul becomes totally poisoned, part of the autopsy must read Vietnam."[157] He contended that no one who had any concern for the integrity and life of America could ignore the moral outrage of a war that was leading to a national disaster. Creative dissenters were needed to challenge the clamor of war hysteria and to perpetuate the best in our tradition. He expressed his agreement with Dante that the hottest places in hell are reserved for those who in a time of moral crisis preserve their neutrality.[158] Polls indicated that fifteen million Americans explicitly opposed the war, but he summoned all people of conscience to call upon the nation to return to brotherhood and peaceful pursuits and to demonstrate to the world its moral power:

> We must demonstrate, teach and preach until the very foundations of our nation are shaken. We must work unceasingly to lift this nation that we love to a higher destiny, to a new plateau of compassion, to a more noble expression of humane-ness.[159]

To convey the notion that true patriotism at times demands criticism of the policies and methods of the nation, he stressed that Emerson, Thoreau, and even Lincoln in his first term as a Congressman all criticized the Government for its war with Mexico.[160] He quoted from a statement of the executive committee of Clergy and Laymen Concerned about Vietnam, "A time comes when silence is betrayal."[161] He was quick to perceive the unique moral significance of this interdenominational organization:

> And we must rejoice as well, for surely this is the first time in our nation's history that a significant number of its religious leaders have chosen to move beyond the prophesying of smooth patriotism to the high grounds of a firm dissent based upon the mandates of conscience and the reading of history.[162]

In a speech on February 6, 1968, he asserted that in a recent poll taken at Harvard University 24 percent of the students said that they would rather go to jail or leave the country before they would serve in Vietnam and 96 percent of the students polled said that they opposed the United States policy in Vietnam. He affirmed that ministers, rabbis, and priests were ordained to stand with these young students in their moments of conscience.[163]

Seventh, he explained that he had to oppose the war also because he understood that his Nobel Peace Prize was not only an honor to him and to those who had engaged in the civil rights struggle but also was a commission for him to go beyond national allegiances and to work harder than ever before for peace and the brotherhood of man.[164] When Gunnar Jahn presented him with the prize in 1964, he seemed to be encouraging him to speak out on Vietnam:

> Though Martin Luther King has not personally committed himself to the international conflict, his own struggle is a clarion call to all who work for peace. He is the first person in the western

world to have shown us that a struggle can be waged without violence. He is the first to make the message of brotherly love a reality in the course of his struggle, and he has proclaimed a message to all men, to all nations and races.[165]

In his Nobel Lecture King recommended that the philosophy of nonviolence immediately become a subject for study and for serious experimentation in every field of human conflict, including relations among nations. He proclaimed that loyalties must become ecumenical rather than sectional. "We must now give an overriding loyalty to mankind as a whole in order to preserve the best in our individual societies."[166] Charles Fager, who had been on the staff of SCLC, in an article entitled "Dilemma for Dr. King" in *The Christian Century* in 1966 stated that when King accepted the Nobel Peace Prize, "He baptized all races into his congregation and confirmed the world as the battleground for his gospel of nonviolence and reconciliation."[167]

Eighth, he believed that he had to oppose the war because the very nature of his commitment to the ministry of Jesus Christ demanded his efforts for peace. He explained that the relationship of the ministry to the making of peace was so evident to him that he sometimes had to wonder at those who asked him why he was hurting the cause of his people by speaking against the war. He indicated that he was greatly saddened by this question since it revealed a lack of knowledge of him and of his commitment and calling.[168] Did they not realize that the good news was meant for all men? Did they forget that his ministry was in obedience to the one who loved his enemies so fully that he died for them? "What then can I say to the Vietcong or to Castro or to Mao as a faithful minister of this one? Can I threaten them with death or must I not share with them my life?"[169] Shortly after King's speech on April 4, Reinhold Niebuhr defended his right to speak against the war:

But after all he is one of the great religious leaders of our time and he has a right to speak on any issue which concerns mankind. . . . Let us simply say that Dr. King has the right and a duty, as both a religious and civil rights leader, to express his concern in these days about such a major human problem as the Vietnam War.[170]

Ninth, King felt that he had to oppose the war also because he shared with all men the calling to be a son of God and to strive to make the brotherhood of man a reality. ". . . the Vietnamese are our brothers, the Russians are our brothers, the Chinese are our brothers; and one day we've got to sit down together at the table of brotherhood."[171] This call summoned men to transcend the self-defined goals and positions of their nation, and to speak for the weak, the voiceless, the victims of the nation and for those it calls enemy, ". . . for no document from human hands can make these humans any less our brothers."[172] "I speak as a child of God and brother to the suffering poor of Vietnam."[173] He warned that there could be no meaningful solution to the conflict until there was some attempt to know these victims and to hear their broken cries.

Tenth, he opposed the war because it violated the right of self-determination of the Vietnamese. His Personalism allowed him to recognize this right to be not only political but moral. He claimed that the United States had clearly violated the charter of the United Nations by not submitting to the Security Council its charge of aggression against North Vietnam and by entering the civil war. Chapter I of the charter provided that:

> All members shall refrain in their international relations from the threat or use of force against the territorial integrity or political independence of any state or in any other manner inconsistent with the purposes of the United Nations.

Chapter VII provided that:

> The Security Council shall determine the existence of any threat to peace, breach of the peace, or act of aggression, and shall make recommendations or shall decide what measures shall be taken . . . to maintain or restore international peace and security.[174]

King argued that while the United States claimed to be fighting for the liberation of the Vietnamese and for peace, democracy, and land reform, the Vietnamese people must have regarded as "strange liberators" the Americans who destroyed their families, corrupted their women, caused their children to run "in packs on the streets like animals," poisoned their water, ruined their crops, herded them off their lands into fortified hamlets that were concentration camps where minimal social needs were rarely met, and helped crush the nation's only non-Communist revolutionary political force—the unified Buddhist Church.[175] He maintained that these same "liberators" for more than twenty years had suppressed the Vietnamese drive for self-determination. When the Vietnamese proclaimed their independence in 1945 after the French and Japanese occupations, and quoted the American Declaration of Independence in their document of freedom, the U.S. Government with its "deadly western arrogance" decided that the Vietnamese were not ready for independence, refused to recognize them, and for nine years supported the French in their abortive attempt to recolonize Vietnam. After the defeat of the French, the U.S. Government conspired to prevent elections that surely would have brought Ho Chi Minh to power, and it supported Premier Ngo Dinh Diem, "one of the most vicious modern dictators," who protected the extortionist landlords and who refused even to discuss reunification with the North.[176]

When Diem was overthrown, the U.S. Government increased its military support to South Vietnamese governments that were corrupt and inefficient, and did not have popular support. Prompted by a feeling that it had some divine messianic mission to police the whole world, the United States, which began its own history with a revolution, chose, without the consent of its own people, to devote its energies to counterrevolution not only in Vietnam but also in many other countries such as Venezuela, Guatemala, Colombia, and Peru:

> The greatest irony and tragedy of all is that our nation, which initiated so much of the revolutionary spirit of the modern world, is now cast in the mold of being an arch anti-revolutionary. We are engaged in a war that seeks to turn the clock of history back and perpetuate white colonialism.[177]

He affirmed that the only hope for the United States lay in its ability to recapture the revolutionary spirit and to abandon its morbid fear of Communism, and with unconditional love for all men to remove those conditions of poverty, insecurity, and injustice that fostered the growth of Communism.[178] If it did not change its policies, it would suffer the fate reserved for those nations who possess "power without compassion, might without morality, and strength without sight."[179]

In his speech "The Casualties of the War in Vietnam" King contended that the nightmarish physical casualties of the war were not the only catastrophes:

> The casualties of principles and values are equally disastrous and injurious. Indeed, they are ultimately more harmful because they

are self-perpetuating. If the casualties of principle are not healed, the physical casualties will continue to mount.[180]

His list of casualties alone expressed the comprehensive nature of his protest. The casualties were the charter of the United Nations, the principle of self-determination, the Great Society, the humility of our nation, the principle of dissent, and the prospect of the survival of humanity. In "The Domestic Impact of the War in Vietnam" he in effect mentioned another casualty, already indicated, when he referred to the young Americans who fought in the war and could not understand the purpose of their sacrifice. "It is harrowing under any circumstances to kill, but it is psychologically devastating to be forced to kill when one doubts that it is right."[181]

King felt that he had to respond to the NAACP resolution that charged him with a "serious tactical mistake" in advocating a merger of the civil rights movement with the peace movement. He explained that he had recently spoken out more frequently about the war and the way it drew attention from progress in civil rights because Negroes in many circles had urged him to voice their concern and frustration.[182] He rejected as a myth the view that he was calling for a fusion of the civil rights movement with the peace movement and related that SCLC and he had just recently declared in a formal public resolution that they had no intention of diminishing their civil rights activities in any respect and had outlined extensive programs for these activities in the South and Chicago. Expressing his sorrow that the Board of Directors of the NAACP would help to perpetuate a myth about his views, he challenged the NAACP and other critics of his position to take a definite stand on the rightness or wrongness of the war instead of creating a nonexistent issue. He warned against pretending that the war did not have a detrimental effect on the destiny of the civil rights movement. He affirmed that as a clergyman he should be concerned about the moral roots of our war policy and about justice for all people, and that as a civil rights leader he had manifested this concern for universal justice. Guided by his Personalist conviction that all persons and all things in the universe constitute an interacting system, he asserted:

I have always insisted on justice for all the world over, because justice is indivisible, and injustice anywhere is a threat to justice everywhere. I will not stand idly by when I see an unjust war taking place and fail to take a stand against it.[183]

He was here proclaiming a conviction that he had related to students at Howard University several years before. On that occasion he contended that the moral principles that guide the conduct of individuals in the social field must also guide their conduct in the political and international fields. We cannot devise different sets of moral values for different departments of life since life refuses to be compartmentalized. "There cannot be two consciences, one in civil and another in political life."[184] He then quoted Gandhi:

The whole gamut of man's activities today constitutes an indivisible whole. You cannot divide life, social, economic, political, and purely religious, into watertight compartments. . . . Some friends have told me that truth and nonviolence have no place in politics and worldly affairs. I do not agree.[185]

Notes

Abbreviations of Titles of Works by Martin Luther King, Jr.

CCG   "A Comparison of the Conceptions of God in the Thinking of Paul Tillich and Henry Nelson Wieman." Ph.D. Dissertation in Systematic Theology, Boston University, 1955.

MM   *The Measure of a Man* (Boston: Pilgrim Press, 1968). First published in 1959 by the Christian Education Press, Philadelphia.

STL   *Strength To Love* (New York: Harper & Row, Publishers, 1963).

STF   *Stride Toward Freedom: The Montgomery Story* (New York: Harper & Row, Publishers, 1958).

TC   *The Trumpet of Conscience* (New York: Harper & Row, Publishers, 1967).

WDWGFH   *Where Do We Go From Here: Chaos or Community?* (New York: Harper & Row, Publishers, 1967).

WWCW   *Why We Can't Wait* (New York: Harper & Row, Publishers, 1963).

Chapter 1: The Redemptive Power of *Agape*

1. Catherine Johnston et al., eds., *The Wisdom of Martin Luther King in His Own Words*, (New York: Lancer Books, 1968), pp. 189–90.

2. STF, pp. 95–96.

3. Friedrich Nietzsche, *The Antichrist* in *The Portable Nietzsche*, ed. Walter Kaufmann (New York: The Viking Press, 1954), pp. 570–73. For a defense of pity as the essence of spiritual love see Miguel de Unamuno, *Tragic Sense of Life*, trans. J. E. Crawford Flitch (New York: Dover Publications, 1954), pp. 135–55.

4. Nietzsche, *The Genealogy of Morals* in *The Birth of Tragedy* and *The Genealogy of Morals*, trans. Francis Golffing (New York: Doubleday & Co., 1956), passim.

5. Nietzsche, *The Will To Power*, trans. Walter Kaufmann and R. J. Hollindale (New York: Vintage Books, 1968), p. 129.

6. Ibid., p. 126.

7. STF, pp. 96–97.

8. Ibid., p. 97. Donald Smith noted that in King's first address in the boycott he made sixteen references to God, Jesus, and Christianity. "Martin Luther King, Jr.: Rhetorician of Revolt" (Ph.D. diss., University of Wisconsin, 1964), p. 288.

9. Quoted in Johnston et al., eds. *The Wisdom of Martin Luther King in His Own Words*, p. 61.

10. STF, p. 96.

11. Gandhi, *From Yeravda Mandir* (Ahmedabad: Navajivan Publishing House, 1932) in *Gandhi: Selected Writings*, ed. Ronald Duncan, Colophon Edition (New York: Harper & Row, Publishers, 1972), p. 41.

12. Gandhi, *Harijan,* Mar. 27, 1949, p. 26, quoted in Joan Bondurant, *Conquest of Violence: The Gandhian Philosophy of Conflict* (Berkeley: University of California Press, 1971), p. 19.

13. Gandhi, *An Autobiography or the Story of My Experiments with Truth* (Ahmedabad: Navajivan Publishing House, 1948), p. 6, quoted in *All Men Are Brothers: Life and Thoughts of Mahatma Gandhi As Told in His Own Words*, ed. Krishna Kripalani (New York: World Without War Publications, 1972), p. 60.

14. Ibid., pp. 65–66.

15. Gandhi, *Non-violent Resistance (Satyagraha)*, ed. Bharatan Kumarappa (New York: Schocken Books, 1961), p. 6.

16. Gandhi, Apr. 3, 1924, quoted in Bondurant, *Conquest of Violence*, p. 20.

17. Gandhi, *An Autobiography*, p. 337, quoted in *All Men Are Brothers*, ed. Krishna Kripalani, pp. 23–24.

18. Gandhi, *Non-violent Resistance*, pp. 41–42.

19. Gandhi, *Young India*, Oct. 1, 1931, quoted in *All Men Are Brothers*, p. 78.

20. Gandhi, *Non-violent Resistance*, p. 6.

21. Gandhi, *From Yeravda Mandir*, 1935, quoted in *All Men Are Brothers*, p. 74.

22. Gandhi, speech, 1931, quoted in *All Men Are Brothers*, p. 64.

23. *The Collected Works of Mahatma Gandhi* (Ahmedabad: Navajivan Press, 1971), 47:217.

24. Gandhi, n.d., quoted in *All Men Are Brothers*, p. 84.

25. Gandhi, *Young India*, Aug. 6, 1928, quoted in *All Men Are Brothers*, p. 37.

26. Gandhi, *Non-violent Resistance*, p. 134.

27. Ibid., pp. 161–62.

28. Ibid., p. 112.

29. King, "My Trip to the Land of Gandhi," *Ebony* 14, no. 9, Jul. 1959, p. 86.

30. King, "Integrated Bus Suggestions," no. 8, King Collection, Special

Collections Division, Mugar Memorial Library, Boston University, file drawer I, folder no. 11. All subsequent references to the King Collection will be to this collection.

31. King, "Our Struggle: The Story of Montgomery" in *Black Protest in the Twentieth Century*, 2nd ed., eds. August Meier et al. (New York: Bobbs-Merrill Co., 1971), p. 300.

32. Quoted in STF, p. 103.

33. King, "The Montgomery Story," Address to the NAACP Convention, Jun. 27, 1956 in "Alabama's Bus Boycott—What's It All About?" *U.S. News & World Report*, Aug. 3, 1956, p. 89.

34. King, Address to the National Bar Association, Milwaukee, Aug. 20, 1959, King Collection, I, no. 11, p. 9.

35. STL, p. 138.

36. Paul Tillich, *Love, Power, and Justice* (New York: Oxford University Press, Galaxy Book, 1960), pp. 11, 49–50. First published in 1954.

37. WDWGFH, p. 37.

38. Ibid.

39. CCG, p. 147.

40. STF, p. 104. See also TC, pp. 72–73.

41. Ibid., p. 104.

42. CCG, p. 149. See Paul Tillich, *Systematic Theology*, 2 vol. (Chicago: The University of Chicago Press, 1951), 1:280.

43. King, "Nonviolence and Racial Justice," *The Christian Century* 74 (Feb. 6, 1957):166.

44. King, "A Christmas Sermon on Peace " in TC, p. 74.

45. King Collection, XVI, no. 3.

46. Anders Nygren, *Agape and Eros*, trans. Philip Watson (New York: Harper & Row, Publishers, 1969). Part I was first published in England in 1932; Part II, vol. 1 in 1938; Part II, vol. 2 in 1939; and it was revised, in part retranslated, and published in one volume in 1953 by the Westminster Press.

47. King, "Contemporary Continental Theology," King Collection, XIV, no. 3, p. 12.

48. Reinhold Niebuhr in *An Interpretation of Christian Ethics* (New York: Harper & Brothers, 1935, p. 211) referred to Nygren's contrast between *eros* and *agape* and accepted his interpretation of the gospel as excluding all self-interest. King's research papers indicate that he had read this work. Niebuhr found a rigorism in the gospel ethic since it made no concessions to even the inevitable and natural self-regarding impulses. He interpreted Jesus as condemning all concern for physical existence and for love of possessions as forms of self-assertion (pp. 41–42). While Niebuhr thought that *agape* had some application in individual lives, he felt that it could not be achieved in social relationships since they demanded the more realistic goal of justice.

49. Nygren, *Agape and Eros*, pp. 160–81.

50. Ibid., p. 174. *Symposium* 210.

51. Ibid., *Symposium* 211d.

52. Ibid., pp. 175–76.

53. Against Nygren it could be argued that Plato did conceive of a love which was not merely acquisitive when in the dialogue *Timaeus* he had Timaeus say, "Let me tell you then why the creator made this world of generation. He was good, and the good can never have any jealousy of anything. And being free from jealousy, he desired that all things should be as like himself as they could be." *Timaeus*, 29e in *The Collected Dialogues of Plato*, ed. Edith Hamilton and Huntington Cairns (New York: Pantheon Books, 1961), p. 1162.

54. Nygren, *Agape and Eros*, p. 176.

55. Ibid., pp. 179–81.

56. Ibid., pp. 179–80.

57. Ibid., pp. 215–16.

58. Ibid., p. 218.

59. Ibid., pp. 75–76.

60. Ibid., p. 77.

61. Ibid., pp. 77–78.

62. Ibid., p. 222.

63. Ibid., p. 80. Nygren interpreted Plato to mean that *eros* and the salvation it produces are due solely to human effort (p. 210), but this interpretation ignored Plato's explanation in the "Allegory of the Cave" in the *Republic* that the prisoner who symbolizes the plight of humanity must be freed from the chains of illusion and be dragged from the cave of half-truths (*Republic* 515c). Nygren's interpretation also ignored Plato's reference in the *Meno* to the necessity for a "divine dispensation" for individuals to practice virtue (Meno 99e). These references reveal Plato's recognition of the moral insufficiency of humanity in its natural state and may be seen as adumbrations of the Christian doctrine of grace.

64. Ibid., pp. 85–91.

65. Ibid., p. 90.

66. Ibid., p. 91.

67. Ibid., p. 96.

68. Ibid., p. 97.

69. Ibid., p. 102.

70. Ibid., p. 215.

71. Ibid., p. 217.

72. Ibid., p. 130. Rom. 8:39.

73. Ibid., p. 131.

74. STF, p. 104.

75. Ibid., pp. 104–5.

76. Ibid., p. 105.

77. Ibid.

78. While a student at Boston University, King attended three courses for transfer credits at Harvard University, viz., "History of Modern Philosophy," "Philosophy of Plato," and "Philosophy of Whitehead."

79. Nygren, *Agape and Eros*, p. 119.

80. STL, p. 33.

81. Mrs. George Davis sent a copy of this Dec. 1, 1953, letter to the author on Sept. 1, 1974.

82. George Davis, "The Origins and Principles of Evangelical Christianity," *The Crozer Quarterly* 23, no. 3 (July 1946): 238–39.

83. Ibid., p. 239.

84. Ibid., p. 226.

85. Davis, "God and History," *The Crozer Quarterly* 20, no. 1 (Jan. 1943): 32.

86. Ibid., p. 25.

87. Davis, "Some Theological Continuities in the Crisis Theology," *The Crozer Quarterly* 27, no. 3 (July 1950): 219.

88. Davis, "God and History," p. 31.

89. Davis, "Liberalism and a Theology of Depth," *The Crozer Quarterly* 28, no. 3 (July 1951): 204–5.

90. Ibid., p. 204.

91. King, Dec. 1, 1953, letter to George Davis.

92. STF, p. 100.

93. Coretta Scott King, *My Life with Martin Luther King, Jr.* (New York: Holt, Rinehart and Winston, Inc., 1969), p. 88.

94. L. Harold DeWolf, *A Theology of the Living Church*, rev. ed. (New York: Harper & Row, Publishers, 1960), p. 201. First published in 1953. No reference will be made here to sections in the revised edition that were not in the original edition which King used.

95. Ibid.

96. Ibid., pp. 201–2.

97. Ibid., p. 202.

98. Ibid.

99. Ibid., Gen. 1:27, 31.

100. Ibid., Ps. 82:6.

101. Ibid., 1 Cor. 11:7.

102. DeWolf, *A Theology of the Living Church*, p. 203, Letter of St. James 3:9.

103. DeWolf, *A Theology of the Living Church*, p. 203.

104. Ibid., pp. 205–07.

105. DeWolf must have intended to mean "feel" and "desire" in a specifically human mode that is quite distinct from the experience of animals, which is devoid of spiritual objects and self-reflection.

106. Ibid., p. 206.

107. Ibid., p. 207.

108. Ibid.

109. Ibid.

110. King, "Man in a Revolutionary World," July 6, 1965, Palmer House, Chicago, *Minutes of the Fifth General Synod of the United Church of Christ,*

pp. 237–38. Archives of the Martin Luther King, Jr. Center for Nonviolent Social Change.

111. Ibid.

112. STL, p. 123.

113. In *Strength To Love* King presented the message of Rabbi Joshua Liebman in *Peace of Mind* that we must love ourselves properly before we can adequately love others (p. 69). Liebman proposed that the commandment "Thou shalt love thy neighbor as thyself" must best be interpreted to mean "Thou shalt love thyself properly and *then* thou wilt love thy neighbor" (p. 43). He questioned how can the neighbor be loved as oneself if the self is not loved. In anticipation of the objection that he was merely approving an intensified selfishness, he explained that the love for oneself, which he regarded as the foundation of a "brotherly society and personal peace of mind," does not involve "coddling oneself, indulging in vanity, conceit and self-glorification," but rather a proper self-regard which involves reverence for oneself (*Peace of Mind* [New York: Simon & Schuster, 1946], p. 45). King also indicated that Erich Fromm had highlighted the interdependence of the right kind of self-love and the right kind of love of others (STL, p. 111). In *The Art of Loving* Fromm rejected the common belief that it is virtuous to love others but sinful and selfish to love oneself, and that to the extent that one loves oneself one does not love others. Fromm traced this belief back to Freud, who in identifying self-love as narcissism frowned on self-love as mere selfishness, and to Calvin, who regarded self-love as a "pest" (p. 57). In defending authentic self-love, Fromm argued, "If it is a virtue to love my neighbor as a human being, it must be a virtue—and not a vice—to love myself, since I am a human being too" (p. 58). He contended that the biblical command to love thy neighbor as *thyself* implies that a person must respect his own integrity and uniqueness, and love and understand himself if he is to be capable of a productive love of others. "If he (an individual) can love only *others,* he cannot love at all" (p. 60; *The Art of Loving,* Colophon Edition [New York: Harper & Row, Publishers, 1962]). Howard Thurman, who was dean of the Chapel at Boston University when King was a student there, in *Deep Is the Hunger* maintained, "All love grows basically out of a qualitative self-regard and is in essence the exercise of that which is spiritual" (New York: Harper & Brothers, 1951, p. 109). Edgar Brightman in "The Essence of Christianity" affirmed, "Christians agree almost unanimously with their Master's evaluation of the individual human personality. Jesus taught that, as every sheep is precious to the good shepherd, so every soul is precious to God. . . . Christianity is a religion of self-evaluation. 'Thou shalt love thy neighbor as thyself' is a fundamental Christian essential, if following Jesus means anything at all. 'As thyself' means that the root virtue is respect for personality in one's own self. . . . Jesus treats self-respect as a basis for respect for all persons" (*The Crozer Quarterly* 18 [1941]: 119–20, Brightman Papers, Boston University School of Theology Faculty Archives).

114. DeWolf, *A Theology of the Living Church*, p. 299.

115. DeWolf, "A Theology of Maximum Involvement," *The Drew Gateway* 28, no. 2 (Winter 1958):86, DeWolf Papers, Boston University School of Theology Faculty Archives.

116. This law in one of DeWolf's class syllabi was quoted in Walter G. Muelder, *Moral Law in Christian Social Ethics* (Richmond, Va.: John Knox Press, 1966), p. 53.

117. Brightman, "The Essence of Christianity," pp. 119-20.

118. Brightman, "The Best Possible World," *The Journal of Bible and Religion* (Feb. 1943):11, Brightman Papers, Boston University School of Theology Faculty Archives.

119. Peter A. Bertocci and Richard M. Millard, *Personality and the Good: Psychological and Ethical Perspectives* (New York: David McKay, 1962), p. 593.

120. Muelder, *Moral Law in Christian Social Ethics*, p. 170.

121. DeWolf, *A Theology of the Living Church*, p. 303.

122. Ibid., p. 305.

123. Class notes of L. Harold DeWolf, quoted in Muelder, *Moral Law in Christian Social Ethics*, p. 53.

124. DeWolf, "A Theology of Maximum Involvement," p. 87.

125. DeWolf, *A Theology of the Living Church*, p. 302.

126. Ibid.

127. Ibid., p. 300. See DeWolf, *Responsible Freedom*, for further objections to Nygren's requirement that the Christian ought to love and serve another without any thought of any good that might accrue to him (New York: Harper & Row, Publishers, 1971, pp. 104-6). See also Paul Johnson's detailed critique of Nygren's concept of *agape* in *Christian Love* (New York: Abingdon-Cokesbury Press, 1951), pp. 23-48.

128. Brightman, "The Best Possible World," p. 14.

129. Brightman, *Moral Laws* (New York: Abingdon Press, 1933), p. 223.

130. Bertocci and Millard, *Personality and the Good*, p. 591.

131. Ibid., p. 403.

132. Muelder, *Moral Law in Christian Social Ethics*, p. 106.

133. Ibid.

134. Ibid., p. 169.

135. Ibid., p. 104. Joseph Washington, Jr., claimed that King's protest had its roots outside the teachings of American Protestantism. *Black Religion: The Negro and Christianity in the United States* (Boston: Beacon Press, 1964), p. 240. This claim overlooked King's special debt to Davis, DeWolf and other Boston Personalists.

136. Paul Ramsey, *Basic Christian Ethics* (New York: Charles Scribner's Sons, 1950), pp. 1-45, 92-132, 153-90, 234-48, 326-66. Kenneth Smith and Ira Zepp, Jr. indicated some of King's dependence on Ramsey in *Search for the Beloved Community: The Thinking of Martin Luther King, Jr.* (Valley Forge: Judson Press, 1974), pp. 62-65. Smith and Zepp's work was based mainly on Zepp's Ph.D. dissertation, "The Intellectual Sources of the Ethical

Thought of Martin Luther King, Jr. As Traced in His Writings with Special Reference to the Beloved Community" (St. Mary's University and Seminary, Baltimore, 1971).

137. STF, pp. 104–5. August Meier claimed that the real credit for developing and projecting the techniques and the philosophy of the nonviolent direct action in the civil rights arena should be given to CORE, founded in 1942. "The Conservative Militant," *Martin Luther King, Jr.—A Profile*, ed. C. Eric Lincoln (New York: Hill & Wang, 1970), p. 144. This chapter by Meier first appeared as an article, "On the Role of Martin Luther King," *New Politics* 4 (Winter 1965):52–59. In another work Meier, with Elliott Rudwick and Francis Broderick as the other editors, claimed, "Although King traced his intellectual antecedents to a number of philosophers and religious thinkers, his outlook was closely akin to, and largely derived from that of the founders of CORE" (*Black Protest in the Twentieth Century*, p. 291). Both of these claims ignored the fact that *agape*, central to King's nonviolence, was not emphasized in CORE's nonviolent resistance.

138. Ramsey, *Basic Christian Ethics*, p. 92.

139. Ibid., pp. 94–95, quoted in Smith and Zepp, *Search for the Beloved Community*, p. 64.

140. STF, p. 105. See also STL, p. 36. Smith and Zepp quoted only the second part of this text (p. 64). Herbert Richardson did not consider King's distinction between *agape* and *philia* nor his identification of Christian love as *agape* when he referred to King's "vision of Christian love as friendship" and when he contended that "according to King self-sacrificing love grows naturally out of the love of friendship. . . ." "Martin Luther King, Unsung Theologian," in *New Theology*, no. 6, eds. Martin Marty and Dean Peerman (New York: The Macmillan Co., 1969), p. 183. See STL, p. 37, and TC, p. 73. William Miller also did not consider King's distinction between *agape* and *philia* when he supported Richardson's interpretation. *Martin Luther King, Jr.: His Life, Martyrdom and Meaning for the World* (New York: Weybright and Talley, 1968), p. 298. Richardson also portrayed King as opposed to ideological conflict whereas King regarded nonviolent conflict and tension as essential to life (Richardson, p. 180; WDWGFH, pp. 90–91).

141. Ramsey, pp. 96, 98–99. Peter Bertocci defended the values of self-love and self-realization within community as motives for Christian love in his critique of Ramsey's call for an altruism that has no hope of requital. "Ramsey's *Basic Christian Ethics*: A Critique," *The Crozer Quarterly* 29, no. 1 (Jan. 1952): 24–38. Like Ramsey, Gandhi's notion of the nature of love also had emphasized that true love seeks no return. "Love becomes a sordid bargain when it asks for return or compensation; it degrades. Spontaneous service of love purifies and elevates" (Quoted in *A Day Book of Thoughts from Mahatma Gandhi*, ed. K. T. Narasimha Char [London: Macmillan & Co., 1951], p. 58). Gandhi also stated, "A love based on the goodness of those who love is a mercenary affair; whereas true love is self-effacing and demands no consideration" (Quoted in *The Wit and Wisdom of Gandhi*, ed.

Homer Jack [Boston: The Beacon Press, 1951], p. 69; also quoted in Donald Bishop, "Gandhi and the Concept of Love," *Gandhi Marg* 11 [1967]: 323).

142. STF, p. 105. Ramsey, pp. 92–95. See Smith and Zepp, *Search for the Beloved Community*, p. 64.

143. Ramsey, p. 94. He also stated, "Nor should the correctness of such a universal definition of neighbor be demonstrated by reference to some divine spark in every man providing an element of worth . . ." (p. 94). In one passage King seemed to agree with Ramsey. "At this level [of *agape*], we love men not because we like them, nor because their ways appeal to us, nor even because they possess some type of divine spark; we love every man because God loves him" (STL, p. 37).

144. STF, p. 105.

145. Ramsey, p. 238, quoted in Smith and Zepp, *Search for the Beloved Community*, p. 64.

146. Ibid., p. 241.

147. Ibid., pp. 241–42. Ramsey's conception of Christian love included a rejection of nonviolent resistance. "Non-violent or passive resistance and violent resistance are *equally* far removed from non-resistance. Non-resistance is incommensurable with *any form* of resistance" (*Basic Christian Ethics*, p. 69).

148. Howard Thurman, *Jesus and the Disinherited* (Nashville: Abingdon Press, 1949). Lerone Bennett, Jr. referred to the fact that King read this work during the boycott in *What Manner of Man*, 2nd rev. ed. (Chicago: Johnson Publishing Co., 1976), pp. 74–75.

149. Ibid., p. 89.

150. Ibid., pp. 93–94.

151. Ibid., pp. 94–95.

152. Ibid., pp. 104–5.

153. Ibid., p. 108.

154. King, "Three Dimensions of a Complete Life," in STL, pp. 69, 71–73.

155. Ibid., p. 76.

156. Ibid.

157. Ibid., p. 71.

158. Tillich, *Love, Power, and Justice*, p. 78.

159. STL, p. 76. See also King, "The Most Durable Power," *The Christian Century* 74 (Jun. 1957): 709.

160. Ibid., pp. 17–24.

161. Ibid., p. 17.

162. King, "I've Been to the Mountain Top," p. 5. Address, April 3, 1968, Memphis, Archives of the Martin Luther King, Jr. Center for Nonviolent Social Change.

163. King, "On Being a Good Neighbor," in STL, p. 20.

164. WDWGFH, p. 101.

165. STL, p. 28.

166. Ibid., p. 26.

167. STF, p. 157.

168. Ibid., p. 137–38.

169. Ibid., p. 88.

170. Quoted in Johnston et al., eds., *The Wisdom of Martin Luther King in His Own Words*, p. 115.

171. Interview with Rev. Ralph Abernathy by the author on Jan. 10, 1973, in Atlanta.

172. King, Nobel Lecture, Dec. 11, 1964, Oslo University, Norway, in *Dear Dr. King* (New York: Buckingham Enterprises, 1968), p. 73.

173. Ibid., pp. 72–73.

174. WWCW, p. 135.

175. Ibid., p. 61.

176. King, "Facing the Challenge of a New Age," *Phylon* 18, no. 1 (1957): 28.

177. King, address at the Convocation on "Equal Justice under Law" of the NAACP Legal Defense Fund, May 28, 1964, New York City, King Collection, XIII, no. 27, p. 8.

178. WDWGFH, p. 86.

179. STL, p. 23.

180. King, "I Have a Dream" address at the March on Washington for Civil Rights on Aug. 28, 1963 at the Lincoln Memorial, *Negro History Bulletin* 31 (May 1968): 16.

181. Coretta Scott King's "Scrapbook on Montgomery Bus Boycott," p. 8, The Martin Luther King, Jr. Center for Nonviolent Social Change.

182. King, "The Rising Tide of Racial Consciousness," address at the Golden Anniversary Conference of the National Urban League, Sept. 6, 1960, New York City, King Collection, XIII, no. 27, p. 3.

183. "Revolt without Violence—The Negroes' New Strategy," *U.S. News & World Report*, Mar. 21, 1960, p. 78.

184. King, "Youth and Social Action," in TC, p. 50.

185. King, "A Testament of Hope," *Playboy Magazine*, reprint, Jan. 1969, p. 4.

186. WDWGFH, p. 54.

187. Ibid., p. 50.

188. Ibid., Introduction to the Bantam edition, 1968, no page given.

189. King, Commencement Address on Jun. 6, 1961 at Lincoln University, *Negro History Bulletin* 31 (May 1968): 11.

190. King, Nobel Lecture, p. 67.

191. Ibid., p. 69.

192. King, "A Christmas Sermon on Peace," in TC, p. 68.

193. King, "Honoring Dr. DuBois," address on Feb. 23, 1968 at Carnegie Hall, New York City, *Freedomways*, second quarter, (1968): 110–11. Hanes Walton, Jr. in *The Political Philosophy of Martin Luther King, Jr.* (Westport, Conn.: Greenwood Publishing Corporation, 1971, pp. 78–89) made the fol-

lowing claims that questioned the necessity, practicality and even the possibility of *agape* in social protest: (1) King gave no criteria for judging the practice of *agape*; (2) *agape* is not necessary for effective nonviolent direct action; (3) King used *agape* also as a negative force to prevent and control destructive conflict; (4) no action can be motivated entirely by *agape*; (5) man by his own reason or nature cannot produce *agape* in his life but can be only a recipient and transmitter of God's grace; (6) *agape* cannot survive and be effective in a world of excessive self-assertion; (7) it is questionable that the ordinary person is capable of *agape*; (8) groups cannot be expected to practice *agape*; (9) you cannot hate the deeds of a person and love the person; (10) *agape* as a disinterested love should not seek for a return in terms of freedom, equality, and personal dignity; (11) *agape* seeks the impossible when it seeks perfection; (12) reliance on just a few outstanding individuals such as Jesus and Gandhi constitutes a despair for humanity; (13) *agape* need not be added to nonviolent tactics; (14) King did not provide for alternative attitudes to *agape*; (15) a controlled use of violence can be used to achieve highly legitimate ends; (16) it may be impossible to remove all traces of violence from one's actions; (17) nonviolence resorts to coercion; (18) ordinary individuals cannot be expected voluntarily to suffer in the face of persecution; (19) *agape* may arouse only rage and hatred in the opponent; (20) the continual sublimation of violent impulses that nonviolence demands may be psychologically unhealthy; (21) power, and not love and morality, creates change; and (22) a nonviolent attitude that relies on an appeal to conscience may lead to a feeling of self-righteousness. (The above numbers have been added.) In this critique Walton neglected some of the main principles of King's central strategy of nonviolence as well as the history of the Nonviolent Movement. The following responses could be made to Walton's claims: (1) King developed several criteria for judging the practice of *agape*, as indicated in this chapter; (2) *agape* is necessary for the success of nonviolence in terms of the transformation of the demonstrator and the preservation of discipline within the demonstrations; (3) *agape* in preventing and controlling destructive conflict was, in Hegelian terms, negating a negation and was thus a positive force in the Movement; (4) man by using *agape* as a regulating ideal can seek to realize and share in values; (5) through cooperation with God's grace man can practice *agape* and become a "co-worker with God;" (6) *agape* can sacrifice and, when successful, can also enjoy the results achieved; (7) the history of the Movement demonstrates that ordinary persons are capable of *agape*; (8) *agape* through individuals can transform collectivities; (9) *agape* can grasp that much of the evil that people commit is due to their moral blindness; (10) it can risk all for the beloved community and still achieve and enjoy the values of freedom, equality, and personal dignity; (11) *agape* may not be perfectly actualized but it can and must serve as a norm for attitudes and actions; (12) the nonviolent crusades showed that Providence can use also ordinary individuals to further the cause of *agape*; (13) nonviolent techniques without *agape* have not had the same effect on the demonstrator or his opponent; (14) King allowed for those who practiced nonviolence only as a technique and not as a way of life, and in his crusades assigned other tasks to those incapable even of this technique; (15) violent means, however controlled, contaminate the pursuit of even a noble end; (16) the Nonviolent Movement proved that large numbers of individuals could remove every trace of violence from their actions; (17) ethical appeals must be supported by some form of constructive coercive power in the sense of the application of political and economic pressure; (18) the Movement provided ample evidence of the capacity of the ordinary person for voluntary unearned suffering; (19) the rage of the opponent scarcely adds to his efficiency, and may well succumb to public pressure or to the example of the demonstrators; (20) nonviolent direct action is a healthy and creative method to channel discontent whereas hate destroys the personality; (21) power is necessary to implement the demands of love and justice; and (22) King warned his followers that a person may be self-centered in his self-denial and self-righteous in his self-sacrifice. For a detailed evaluation of Walton's claims see my article, "Martin Luther King's Conception of *Agape,*" *Gandhi Marg*—Journal of the Gandhi Peace Foundation, New Delhi, India, Second Series, 2, no. 10 (Jan. 1981): 556–71.

Chapter 2: The Dimensions of Divine Providence

1. King, "The Death of Evil Upon the Seashore," sermon, May 17, 1956, Cathedral of St. John the Divine, New York City, p. 4, Archives of the Martin Luther King, Jr. Center for Nonviolent Social Change. See also STL, p. 141.

2. King, address to the Montgomery Improvement Association, Mar. 22, 1956, Holt Street Baptist Church, King Collection, I, no. 20, p. 1. See also STF, p. 138.

3. STF, p. 171.

4. Ibid., p. 106. See also King, Address to the MIA, Mar. 22, 1956, p. 1.

5. King, "Nonviolence and Racial Justice," pp. 166–67. See also King, "The Current Crisis in Race Relations," *New South* (Mar. 1958): 11.

6. Ibid., p. 167.

7. King, "A Testament of Hope," p. 1.

8. STF, p. 100.

9. DeWolf, *A Theology of the Living Church*, p. 46.

10. Ibid., p. 48.

11. Ibid.

12. Ibid., p. 49.

13. Plato, *Timaeus* 28, 29, in *The Collected Dialogues of Plato*, ed. Edith Hamilton and Huntington Cairns, pp. 1161–62.

14. DeWolf, *A Theology of the Living Church*, p. 49.

15. Ibid., pp. 49–50.

16. Ibid., p. 50.

17. STL, p. 74. In his dissertation King challenged Wieman's naturalism by asking what is the being that stands behind the system of events to account for its systematic character (p. 267).

18. Ibid., pp. 75, 103.

19. DeWolf, *A Theology of the Living Church*, p. 50.

20. Ibid., p. 51.

21. Ibid.

22. Ibid., p. 52.

23. Ibid.

24. Ibid., p. 53. Sir James Jeans, *Physics and Philosophy* (Cambridge: Cambridge University Press, 1935), p. 216.

25. STL, p. 55.

26. DeWolf, *A Theology of the Living Church*, pp. 53–54.

27. Ibid., p. 54.

28. Ibid., p. 55.

29. Ibid.

30. Ibid., p. 56. Rom. 1:19–20.

31. DeWolf, *A Theology of the Living Church*, p. 56.

32. Ibid., p. 57.

33. Ibid.

34. Ibid.

35. Ibid., p. 58.

36. Ibid., p. 59. James Hannigan contended that King had not examined his religious beliefs, and that he had held that the rational grounds of faith are experiential and practical, and not logical and theoretical. "Martin Luther King, Jr. and the Ethics of Militant Nonviolence" (Ph.D. diss. in religion, Duke University, 1973), pp. 57, 67. It is not surprising that Hannigan drew these conclusions since he made no reference to DeWolf's developments of the evidences for God's existence. What is surprising is that Hannigan did not explore King's dependence on DeWolf's doctrine, especially when he did refer to King's acknowledgement of his debt to Personalism for providing him with a philosophical grounding for the idea of a personal God (p. 44).

37. Ibid., p. 97.

38. St. Thomas Aquinas, *Summa Theologica*, I, Q. 2, a. 3.

39. DeWolf, *A Theology of the Living Church*, p. 99.

40. STF, p. 92.

41. DeWolf, *A Theology of the Living Church*, p. 100.

42. Ibid. In his dissertation King referred to Tillich's rejection of the description of God as "actus purus" since it excluded the dynamic side of His life (p. 138). See Tillich, *Systematic Theology*, 1:246. In his dissertation King found in Wieman's thought a similarity to Whitehead in his preference for dynamic terminology as he stressed the activity of God as against "a static *ens necessarium*, absolute Being" (p. 291).

43. Ibid., p. 101. John 5:17, Rom. 1:20.

44. Aristotle, *Physics* 8 and *Metaphysics* 12 in *The Basic Works of Aris-*

totle, ed. Richard McKeon (New York: Random House, 1941), pp. 354–77, 872–88.

45. Ibid., p. 885.

46. King, address at the Prayer Pilgrimage for Freedom, May 17, 1957, Washington, D.C., King Collection, VI, no. 4, p. 4.

47. STL, p. 6.

48. Ibid., p. 7.

49. DeWolf, "A Theology of Maximum Involvement," p. 88. In "A Personalistic View of Human Nature" Brightman asserted, "Suffering and tragedy, cross and pain, are (on this Personalistic view) not merely the lot of human nature, but also of the eternal divine nature" (*Religion in Life* [Spring 1945]: 11). Ralph Tyler Flewelling in his exposition of the reasons for Brightman's position on the finitude of God referred to the Divinity Who "suffers in the suffering of His creatures in the process of completing his own creative experience, perfected through suffering" ("Brightman: Ex Umbras in Lucem," *The Personalist* 34 [August 1953]: 346).

50. DeWolf, *A Theology of the Living Church*, p. 102.

51. Ibid., p. 103.

52. Ibid., pp. 104–9.

53. In "A Personalistic Philosophy of History" Brightman affirmed, "History, then, with its wars and bombs and bacterial warfare, is the price that God pays in order to have men who are free." He also maintained that despite sufferings, errors, and sins the purpose of history is rational since it gives evidence of a controlling purpose that creates possibilities for cooperative love, no matter how dark and hateful the situation may be (*The Journal of Bible and Religion* 18, no. 1 [Jan. 1950]: 10). Ernest Lyght did not allow for the qualifications DeWolf placed on the power of God when he contended that DeWolf held that God's power is infinite (*The Religious and Philosophical Foundations in the Thought of Martin Luther King, Jr.* [New York: Vantage Press, 1972], p. 41; this was a Th.M. thesis at Princeton Theological Seminary).

54. DeWolf, *A Theology of the Living Church*, p. 109.

55. Ibid.

56. Ibid., p. 111.

57. Ibid., p. 112. Rev. 15:4.

58. DeWolf, *A Theology of the Living Church*, p. 112.

59. Ibid., pp. 112–13. Ps. 119:142, Isa. 2:3–4.

60. STL, p. 95.

61. Ibid., p. 131.

62. STF, p. 117.

63. STL, p. 128.

64. DeWolf, *A Theology of the Living Church*, p. 115.

65. Ibid., p. 121. Matt. 6:26–30.

66. DeWolf, *A Theology of the Living Church,* p. 123.

67. CCG, p. 281.

68. STL, pp. 86, 115.

69. Ibid., p. 141.

70. STF, p. 134.

71. Ibid., pp. 134–35.

72. DeWolf, *A Theology of the Living Church*, pp. 130–43.

73. Ibid., p. 131. Ps. 35, 37.

74. Ibid., p. 132.

75. Ibid.

76. Ibid.

77. Ibid., p. 133.

78. Ibid., pp. 133–35.

79. Ibid., pp. 138–39.

80. King, "Paul's Letter to American Christians" in STL, p. 132.

81. DeWolf, *A Theology of the Living Church*, p. 139.

82. Ibid.

83. Ibid., p. 140.

84. Ibid., p. 141.

85. Ibid., p. 142.

86. DeWolf in *The Religious Revolt Against Reason* charged that, by attempting to account for evil in the world by referring to such a nonrational Given in the nature of God, Brightman used a rational method to arrive at an "explanation" in terms of the ultimately nonrational. DeWolf denied that the nonrational because of its unintelligibility could be the basis of a valid explanation of evil in the world (New York: Greenwood Press, 1968), pp. 94, 96. This work was first published by Harper & Brothers in 1949.

87. DeWolf, *A Theology of the Living Church*, p. 142.

88. In "The Essence of Christianity" Brightman also stressed the spiritual value of suffering. "It is safe to say that no one at any stage of Christian development has ever read the story of Good Friday and Easter without seeing in it the drama of faith in the spiritual value of sacrifice. Out of voluntary submission to undeserved suffering come resurrection and redemption" (p. 119).

89. STF, p. 179.

90. King, "Suffering and Faith," *The Christian Century* 77 (April 27, 1960): 510.

91. STL, p. 82.

92. Ibid., p. 85.

93. Ibid., p. 101.

94. Ibid.

95. King, address to the MIA, Dec. 3, 1959, Bethel Baptist Church, Montgomery, King Collection, I, no. 14, p. 17. See also STL, p. 141.

96. CCG, pp. 298–99.

97. STL, p. 64.

98. CCG, p. 298.

99. STL, p. 64.

100. CCG, p. 298.

101. STL, pp. 33, 94. In his dissertation King compared Brightman's finite God to Wieman's (p. 229). In one passage King did tend to speak as a finitist when he referred to the presence of physical evil in human life. "Although God permits evil in order to preserve the freedom of man, he does not cause evil. That which is willed is intended, and the thought that God intends for a child to be born blind or for a man to suffer the ravages of insanity is sheer heresy that pictures God as a devil rather than a loving Father" (STL, p. 82).

102. DeWolf, *A Theology of the Living Church*, p. 143.

103. TC, p. 69.

104. CCG, p. 271.

105. Ibid., p. 303.

106. Ibid., p. 158.

107. Ibid.

108. Ibid.

109. Ibid., pp. 158-59.

110. STL, pp. 141-42. In "A Meeting of Extremes: Operationalism and Personalism," Brightman affirmed the personal nature of God. "True it is that God could not be supposed to experience specifically human limitations, such as sin or a physiological organism, for example. He is not ignorant or petty. He is superhuman. All this is granted. But the personalist is puzzled when an operationalist seems to assert that mindlessness is (or is essential to being) greater than mind, that blank unconsciousness is somehow greater than any possible personal consciousness, or that God is value (hence experience) but not personal experience. Such value judgments and such metaphysical assertions seem to the personalist to be warranted neither by experience nor by reason. As empiricist, the personalist is too cautious to dare to make assertions about something that so far transcends all possible experience as to lack basic traits of actual experience" (*The Journal of Religion* 31, no. 4 [Oct. 1951]: 239).

111. CCG, p. 159. See Tillich, *Systematic Theology*, 1:251, 282.

112. Ibid., p. 160.

113. Ibid., p. 312.

114. Ibid., pp. 159-63.

115. Ibid., p. 163.

116. Ibid., p. 219. Henry Nelson Wieman, *The Wrestle of Religion with Truth* (New York: Macmillan Co., 1927), p. 182.

117. Ibid., p. 220.

118. Ibid., pp. 194, 240. See Henry Nelson Wieman and Walter Marshall Horton, *The Growth of Religion* (Chicago: Willett Clark & Co., 1938), p. 363. King included in his dissertation some of Wieman's other definitions of God (pp. 166, 167, 207, 230, 231, 240, 263).

119. Ibid., p. 240.

120. Ibid., p. 242.

121. Ibid.

122. Ibid., pp. 234-35. Henry Nelson Wieman, *The Source of Human Good* (Carbondale, Ill.: Southern Illinois University Press, 1946), pp. 265-66.

123. Ibid., pp. 234. Henry Wieman, "God Is More Than We Can Think," *Christendom* 1 (1936): 432.

124. Ibid., pp. 262, 268.

125. Ibid., pp. 268-69.

126. Ibid., p. 269.

127. Ibid., p. 275.

128. When King was asked to explain the Montgomery Boycott, he replied, "So every rational explanation breaks down at some point. There is something about the protest that is suprarational; it cannot be explained without a divine dimension. Some may call it a principle of concretion, with Alfred N. Whitehead; or a process of integration, with Henry N. Wieman; or Being-in-Itself, with Paul Tillich; or a personal God" (STF, p. 69). Louis Lomax cited this passage to "show why he [King] should never be called an intellectual" (*The Negro Revolt* [New York: Signet Books, 1962], p. 100). Lomax would not have made this criticism if he had traced the source of King's statement and had read his dissertation. Lomax also claimed that King would be "the first to testify to the narrowness of his training" (p. 100). Lomax's account revealed little knowledge of the scope of King's training, which in addition to his studies in theology and scripture included a major in sociology at Morehouse College and extensive training in philosophy at Morehouse, Crozer Theological Seminary, the University of Pennsylvania, Boston University, and Harvard University. John Rathbun seemed to be unaware of King's detailed rejections of Tillich's and Wieman's conceptions of God when he claimed, "King does not particularly care which philosophical or theological terms are used to describe God. He finds himself equally sympathetic with Whitehead's principle of concretion, Wieman's theory of integration, or Tillich's idea of Being-in-Itself" ("Martin Luther King: The Theology of Social Action," *American Quarterly* 20, no. 1 [Spring 1968]: 42-43). Rathbun wrote another version of this article with the same title which was included in *Martin Luther King—Profile of Greatness—A Student Symposium*, ed. Lucy Bolds (Atlanta: Interdenominational Theological Center for the Religious Heritage of the Black World, April 1973), Unit III: 1-15.

129. Davis, "God and History," p. 19. John 5:17.

130. Davis, "God and History," p. 19. Davis returned to this idea in "Liberalism and a Theology of Depth," p. 204. King indicated in his letter to Davis on Dec. 1, 1953, that this article had been quite influential on his own thinking.

131. Ibid.

132. Davis, "Liberalism and a Theology of Depth," p. 211.

133. Davis, "God and History," p. 20. See Smith and Zepp's references to these "shifts" in *Search for the Beloved Community,* pp. 27-28.

134. Ibid., p. 21.

135. Ibid., pp. 22–23.
136. Ibid.
137. Ibid., p. 24.
138. Ibid., p. 25.
139. Ibid.
140. Ibid., p. 27.
141. King, "The Death of Evil Upon the Seashore," p. 4.
142. In "In Praise of Liberalism" Davis wrote, "In the long run it is well with the righteous and ill with the evil" (*Theology Today* 4, no. 4 [Jan. 1948]: 491).
143. Davis, "God and History," p. 26.
144. STL, p. 63.
145. King, "I've Been to the Mountain Top," p. 1.
146. Davis, "God and History," p. 27.
147. Ibid., p. 29.
148. STL, p. 63.
149. Ibid., p. 103.
150. King, "The Death of Evil Upon the Seashore," p. 2.
151. STL, pp. 95, 105.
152. WDWGFH, p. 180.
153. Davis, "God and History," pp. 29, 33.
154. Ibid., p. 34.
155. STL, p. 73.
156. TC, p. 50.
157. Ibid., pp. 49–50.
158. STL, p. 53.
159. Ibid., p. 23.
160. Davis, "God and History," p. 35. In his dissertation King presented Wieman's doctrine that God's judgment is the "mutual destructiveness" that comes to individuals and groups as a result of their opposition to the transformation required by the new life of interdependence. "The closer drawn the cords of love, the more destructive of one another do men become when they resist the transformation brought forth by these closer connections" (p. 247). See Wieman, "What is Most Important in Christianity," *Religion in the Making* 1 (1940): 156.
161. Ibid., p. 30.
162. Davis, "Some Theological Continuities in the Crisis Theology," p. 219.
163. Davis, "Liberalism and a Theology of Depth," p. 205.
164. TC, p. 68. See also STF, p. 224.
165. Davis, "Some Theological Continuities in the Crisis Theology," pp. 208–219, and passim.
166. STL, p. 123.
167. Ibid.
168. Ibid., p. 122.

169. King, "Facing the Challenge of a New Age," p. 31. Vincent Harding focused on a statement in *Where Do We Go From Here: Chaos or Community?* that indicated King's faith that the struggle for justice would enable blacks to achieve humanity's full stature. "Our most fruitful course is to stand firm, move forward nonviolently, accept disappointments and cling to hope. Our determined refusal not to be stopped will eventually open the door to fulfillment. By recognizing the necessity of suffering in a righteous cause, we may achieve our humanity's full stature. To guard ourselves from bitterness, we need the vision to see in this generation's ordeals the opportunity to transfigure both ourselves and American society" (pp. 46–47). Since the statement did not explicitly refer to God, Harding concluded that the object of King's faith was vague, and that "King's God often seems no less dead than anyone else's—at least if one judges life by appearance in the printed pages" ("The Crisis of Powerless Morality," *Martin Luther King, Jr.: A Profile*, ed. C. Eric Lincoln, p. 183). In making this criticism, Harding was unaware of or chose to ignore King's numerous references to God and His Providence in his other works, including *The Trumpet of Conscience*, his last work. Many of these references have been included in this chapter. Even *Where Do We Go From Here: Chaos or Community?*, mentioned by Harding, developed the notions that man's rights are God-given, that our religious heritage is the Judeo-Christian tradition, and that man is made in the image of God, and concluded with a quote from the First Epistle of St. John affirming that only through love of each other can we know and love God (pp. 82, 97, 99, 180, 190, 191; 1 John 7–8, 12).

Chapter 3: The Sacredness of Human Personality

1. WDWGFH, p. 97.

2. TC, p. 11.

3. Immanuel Kant, *Foundations of the Metaphysics of Morals*, trans. Lewis Beck (New York: The Library of Liberal Arts Press, 1959), p. 52.

4. Ibid., p. 58.

5. Kant, *Critique of Practical Reason*, trans. Lewis Beck (New York: The Library of Liberal Arts Press, 1956), p. 90.

6. WWCW, p. 84.

7. STL, p. 18.

8. Ibid., p. 95. See also STF, p. 93.

9. STL, p. 19.

10. Kant, "On the Common Saying 'This May Be True in Theory But It Does Not Apply in Practice,' " *Kant's Political Writings*, ed. Hans Reiss, trans. H. B. Nisbet (Cambridge: The University Press, 1970), p. 74.

11. In *The Metaphysics of Morals* (1797) Kant again emphasized this principle of freedom in his proclamation of "The Universal Principle of Right," "Every action which by itself or by its maxim enables the freedom of each individual's will to co-exist with the freedom of everyone else in accord-

ance with a universal law is *right*" (*Kant's Political Writings*, ed. Reiss, p. 133). In the Appendix to the *Critique of Pure Reason* (1781) he indicated the need for a constitution that would permit the greatest possible human freedom in accordance with laws which would ensure that the freedom of each could co-exist with the freedom of all the others (Reiss, p. 191).

12. Kant, "On the Common Saying 'This May Be True in Theory But It Does Not Apply in Practice' " (Reiss, p. 74).

13. Ibid., p. 75.

14. Ibid., p. 74.

15. Ibid., p. 77.

16. Ibid., p. 78.

17. Kant, *The Metaphysics of Morals* (Reiss, p. 139).

18. One difficulty with Kant's assumption that the "active citizens" through their representatives would demonstrate a concern for the interests of the "passive citizens" is that it was inconsistent with a persistent theme in his political writings, i.e., man's perpetual inability to transcend his own egoism. Thus, in the same essay in which he implied a confidence in the altruism and justice of the voters, he observed, "Perhaps no recognized and respected duty has ever been carried out by anyone without some selfishness or interference from other motives; perhaps no one will ever succeed in doing so, however hard he tries" (Reiss, p. 69). In another essay, "Idea for a Universal History with a Cosmopolitan Purpose" (1784), he claimed that as a rule men are concerned about pursuing their own selfish ends. "Nothing straight can be constructed from such warped wood as that which man is made of" (Reiss, p. 46). He also claimed, "We find that, despite the apparent wisdom of individual actions here and there, everything as a whole is made up of folly and childish vanity, and often of childish malice and destructiveness" (Reiss, p. 42). Kant viewed man's social incompatibility, enviously competitive vanity, and insatiable desires for possession and power as the necessary conditions for the development of his natural capacities.

19. King, address at the Prayer Pilgrimage for Freedom, May 17, 1957, Washington, D.C.

20. In the *Critique of Practical Reason* (1788) Kant argued that we have to postulate the reality of *freedom* if our obedience to the categorical imperative of the moral law is to be intelligible. Moral law would be meaningless without the *freedom* to respond to this law. Moreover, he designated the concept of *freedom* as the keystone of the whole architecture of the system of pure reason and even of speculative reason and contended that the concepts of immortality and of God gain their stability and objective reality through this concept of freedom (trans. Beck, p. 3).

21. Nor could King suspect that Kant condemned all civil disobedience. Thus in *The Metaphysics of Morals* Kant proclaimed, "A law, which is so sacred (i.e. inviolable) that it is practically a crime even to cast doubt upon it and thus to suspend its effectiveness for even an instant, cannot be thought of as coming from human beings, but from some infallible supreme legislator"

(Reiss, p. 143). He granted citizens in his proposed "rational state" the right to criticize the measures of the ruler only if the ruler consents (Reiss, p. 84). For a detailed examination of Kant's proposed "rational state" see my articles in *The New Scholasticism*, "Kant's Limitations on Individual Freedom" (Winter 1973): 88-99, and "Kant's Concessions to Particular Interests" (Autumn 1975): 492-502.

22. STF, p. 18.

23. Ibid.

24. Ibid., p. 19.

25. Ibid., p. 20.

26. *Playboy Interviews* (Chicago: Playboy Press, 1967), p. 349.

27. Interview with Dr. Brailsford Brazeal, former dean of Morehouse College, by the author on July 26, 1973 in Atlanta.

28. Ibid.

29. "Man of the Year," *Time*, Jan. 3, 1964, p. 14.

30. David Lewis, *King: A Critical Biography* (New York: Praeger Publishers, 1971), pp. 4-5. The civil rights activities of King's father and grandfather certainly rendered debatable the judgment of *Newsweek* that there was nothing in his origins that marked him for his role ("King Is the Man, Oh Lord," Apr. 15, 1968, p. 36).

31. Brightman defined Personalism as "a system of philosophy that regards the universe as an interacting system of persons (or selves). According to it, everything that exists is either a person, or some experience, process, or aspect of a person or persons in relation to each other. Reality is social or interpersonal. A person is taken to be a complex unity of consciousness that is able to develop rational thought and ideal values" ("A Personalistic Philosophy of History," p. 3).

32. King wrote a research paper for DeWolf entitled "The Personalism of J. M. E. McTaggart Under Criticism" in which he referred to Brightman's emphasis on freedom in *Moral Laws* (p. 74). King contended that in rejecting freedom McTaggart was rejecting the most important characteristic of personality (King Collection, XVI, no. 3, p. 13).

33. Brightman, *Moral Laws*, p. 45.

34. Ibid.

35. Ibid., p. 46.

36. Ibid.

37. Ibid.

38. Ibid., p. 112.

39. Ibid., p. 98.

40. Brightman, "Some Definitions for Personalists," *The Personalist*, 27:366.

41. Brightman, *Moral Laws*, p. 101.

42. TC, p. 24.

43. Brightman, *Moral Laws*, p. 106.

44. Ibid., p. 110.

45. WWCW, p. 85.

46. Brightman, *Moral Laws*, p. 122. He here argued that while the Aristotelian and Epicurean types of ethical theory have stressed more the values to be chosen than the intention, the Christian and Kantian ethics have emphasized the intention, spirit, or will more than the values. Brightman contended that an ethical theory to be complete must give ample emphasis to both factors.

47. Ibid., p. 125.

48. Brightman, "Some Definitions for Personalists," p. 370.

49. King, "Love, Law, and Civil Disobedience," *New South* 16, no. 11 (Dec. 1961): 7.

50. Ibid., p. 8.

51. Brightman, *Moral Laws*, p. 142.

52. In "The Conservative Militant" August Meier claimed that in a movement that took pride in its militancy and in its rejection of compromise with the white power structure and with racial discrimination, King maintained close relationships with and seemed to be influenced by Democratic Presidents and their emissaries, appeared to be amenable to compromises that some regarded as half a loaf or less, and frequently seemed to be willing to postpone or to avoid a direct confrontation in the streets (p. 145).

53. King, "Love, Law, and Civil Disobedience," p. 3.

54. CCG, p. 85. See also Tillich, *Systematic Theology*, 1:191.

55. King, Nobel Lecture, p. 66.

56. King, Address on the Fourth Anniversary of the MIA, Dec. 3, 1959, p. 5.

57. Brightman, *Moral Laws*, p. 156.

58. Ibid., p. 171.

59. Ibid., p. 181.

60. *Playboy Interviews*, pp. 350–51. Rev. Wyatt Tee Walker, King's associate, asserted that the Albany campaign was a historic highpoint in the nonviolent social revolution partly because it launched an unprecedented assault upon the entire system of segregation ("Albany, Failure or First Step," *New South* [June 1963]: 3–4. What King regarded as a mistake Walker regarded as an achievement.

61. Brightman, *Moral Laws*, p. 183.

62. Ibid., p. 185.

63. Ibid., p. 184.

64. STL, p. 10.

65. Brightman, *Moral Laws*, p. 194.

66. Ibid., p. 200.

67. Ibid., p. 201.

68. Ibid., p. 202.

69. Ibid., p. 204.

70. Ibid., p. 223.

71. King, Nobel Lecture, p. 73.

72. Brightman, *Moral Laws*, p. 227.

73. Ibid., p. 242.

74. Ibid., pp. 242–43. Brightman indicated that he meant "Personalistic Laws" to refer to the Laws of Individualism, Altruism, and the Ideal of Personality.

75. King, "How Modern Christians Should Think of Man," King Collection, XVI, no. 3.

76. Ibid., p. 1.

77. Ibid.

78. Ibid., p. 2.

79. Ibid.

80. Ibid., p. 3.

81. Ibid. Reinhold Niebuhr examined the notion of man as "the image of God" in the doctrines of St. Paul, St. Augustine, St. Gregory of Nyssa, St. Thomas Aquinas, and the leaders of the Reformation in *The Nature and Destiny of Man: A Christian Interpretation* (New York: Charles Scribner's Sons, 1941), 1: 150–66. King cited this work as one of the sources for his paper.

82. Ibid. Brightman maintained that the acts of the will combine necessity and possibility. "The necessity is implied in the givenness of the situation, the psychological mechanisms involved, and the necessary consequences of the act" (*Moral Laws*, p. 76). Paul Tillich developed the notion of "finite freedom" in *The Courage To Be* (New Haven: Yale University Press, 1965), pp. 52, 124, 152. This work was first published in 1952.

83. Ibid.

84. Ibid., p. 4.

85. Ibid.

86. Ibid.

87. Ibid., p. 5.

88. Ibid.

89. Reinhold Niebuhr examined the nature of pride in *The Nature and Destiny of Man: A Christian Interpretation*, 1: 186–207.

90. King, "How Modern Christians Should Think of Man," p. 5.

91. Ibid.

92. Ibid., p. 6. W. N. Clarke, *An Outline of Christian Theology* (New York: Scribner's, 1898), p. 403.

93. King, "What Is Man?" in MM, p. 17. Another version of this sermon was published in STL., pp. 87–92.

94. Ibid., p. 18.

95. Ibid., p. 19. Ps. 8:6.

96. MM, p. 17.

97. Ibid., p. 29.

98. Plato, *Phaedrus* 253d. Niebuhr discussed this myth in *The Nature and Destiny of Man: A Christian Interpretation*, 1: 31–32.

99. MM, p. 30. Rom. 7:15. See also St. Augustine, *Confessions*, VIII, vii, 17.

100. King, "Pilgrimage to Nonviolence," *The Christian Century* 77 (Apr. 13, 1960): 439. See also STL, pp. 136-37.

101. King, "What the Mystics Say about God," King Collection, XIV, no. 73.

102. Sören Kierkegaard, *Purity of Heart Is To Will One Thing*, trans. Douglas Steere (New York: Harper & Brothers Publishers, Torchbook Edition, 1956), p. 184. King encountered different interpretations of Kierkegaard. DeWolf criticized him for his irrationalism (*The Religious Revolt Against Reason,* passim). Brightman criticized him for his extreme individualism (*Moral Laws*, p. 205), while Reinhold Niebuhr claimed "Kierkegaard has interpreted the true meaning of human selfhood more accurately than any modern, and possibly than any previous Christian theologian" (*The Nature and Destiny of Man*, 1: 170-71).

103. Ibid., p. 185.

104. Ibid., p. 191. Kierkegaard acknowledged that in a positive way Socrates inspired him to defend the value of the individual. " 'The masses,' that is really the aim of my polemic; and I learnt that from Socrates." " 'The individual'; that category has only been used once before and then by Socrates, in a dialectical and decisive way, to disintegrate paganism. In Christianity it will be used once again—in order to make men (the 'Christians') into Christians" (*The Journals of Kierkegaard*, trans. Alexander Dru [New York: Harper & Brothers, Torchbook Edition, 1959], pp. 118, 135).

105. STL, pp. 8, 14. In describing part of King's legacy, Coretta Scott King reaffirmed his conviction that the hope of a secure world depends on disciplined nonconformists who are dedicated to justice, peace, and brotherhood. She noted, as did King, that Emerson wrote in his essay "Self-Reliance," "Whoso would be a man must be a nonconformist" ("The Legacy of Martin Luther King, Jr.: The Church in Action," *Theology Today* 27, no. 2 [July 1970]: 136). See also STL, p. 12.

106. King, "What the Mystics Say about God," p. 4.

107. King, "Love, Law, and Civil Disobedience," p. 11.

108. Kierkegaard, *Concluding Unscientific Postscript,* trans. David Swenson (Princeton: Princeton University Press, 1941), p. 188.

109. George Davis referred to Kierkegaard's doctrine of Christ as the "Absolute Paradox" and to the need for faith in the midst of suffering in "Liberalism and a Theology of Depth," p. 208.

110. Kierkegaard, *Training in Christianity*, trans. Walter Lowrie (New York: Oxford University Press, 1941), p. 67.

111. Kierkegaard, *Purity of Heart Is To Will One Thing*, p. 148.

112. DeWolf in *The Religious Revolt Against Reason* presented a description, analysis, and critical evaluation of the irrational trend in recent theology, as developed especially by Karl Barth and Emil Brunner, who, despite their differences, contended that human reason cannot furnish evidence

for the existence of God. He also examined in detail Kierkegaard's "charges against reason," which served as the foundation for this trend, and after exploring the possible strength and relevance of these charges, he responded to each of them (pp. 106-37).

113. DeWolf, "A Theology of Maximum Involvement," p. 83.

114. King, "Why I Oppose the War in Vietnam," sermon, Apr. 16, 1967, Ebenezer Baptist Church, Atlanta, Motown Record, 1970.

115. Brightman, "How Much Truth Is There in Nietzsche?, *The Christian Century* (June 16, 1948): 593.

116. Ibid., p. 594.

117. Ibid.

118. Ibid., p. 595.

119. Paul Tillich, *The Courage To Be*, pp. 142, 148-49.

120. CCG, pp. 4, 87, 88, 328. In STL (p. 111) King alluded to Tillich's notion that courage is self-affirmation and referred to the same doctrines of Epictetus and Fromm that Tillich appealed to in *The Courage To Be* (pp. 13, 22). Rev. Hosea Williams in an interview with the author stated that King in his last meetings with his staff made many references to Tillich (Jan. 11, 1973, Atlanta).

121. Martin Heidegger, *Being and Time*, trans. John Macquarrie and Edward Robinson (New York: Harper & Row, Publishers, 1962), pp. 279-311. King would have seen a reference to Heidegger's doctrine of "the anticipation of death" in Tillich's *The Courage To Be*, p. 142.

122. Ibid., p. 294. Tillich in *The Courage To Be* contended that the first assertion that must be made about anxiety is that it is a state in which man is aware of his possible nonbeing (p. 35). He also dealt with two other forms of anxiety which belong to existence as such, viz., the anxiety of meaninglessness and the anxiety of condemnation (pp. 41-63).

123. Heidegger, *Being and Time*, p. 311.

124. Ibid., p. 297.

125. Ibid., p. 298.

126. Ibid., pp. 308, 309. Tillich in *The Courage To Be* presented Heidegger's notion of "resolve" which requires the individual to will to liberate himself from average and ordinary behavior that contains no independent ethical decision (pp. 148-49).

127. In his dissertation King presented some of Tillich's reflections on death, and these closely resembled those of Heidegger. "Experienced on the human level, finitude is nonbeing as the threat to being, ultimately the threat of death. Yet, in order to experience his finitude, man must look at himself as a potential infinity. In grasping his life as a whole as moving toward death, he transcends temporal immediacy" (p. 85).

128. After stating "The threat of nonbeing to man's ontic self-affirmation is absolute in the threat of death," Tillich attempted to relate creatively to this threat by seeking "a courage to be, a courage to affirm oneself in spite of the threat against man's ontic self-affirmation" (*The Courage To Be*, p. 45).

129. *Playboy Interviews*, p. 361.

130. Quoted in Johnston et al., eds., *The Wisdom of Martin Luther King in His Own Words*, p. 144.

131. *Playboy Interviews*, p. 362.

132. King, address at Howard University, n.d., King Collection, XIII, no. 28, p. 12.

133. "Andrew Young: New South," Part I, *Assignment America*, Educational Broadcasting System, Apr. 1, 1975, transcript, p. 6.

134. Stephen Gayle, "Man in the News: Martin Luther King, Sr.—Carrying On," *New York Post*, July 6, 1974, p. 22.

135. King, "Notes on *De Trinitate, the Instructor*, Irenaeus, Justin, and Ignatius," King Collection, XIV, no. 45, p. 3. In fact, the text states that Ignatius wants the Christians to entice the beasts so that they might become his tomb. In this epistle Ignatius also wrote, "I am the wheat of God, and am ground by the teeth of the wild beasts, that I may be found the pure bread of God" (*Epistle of Ignatius to the Romans* [chap. 4] in *The Ante-Nicean Fathers: Translations of the Writings of the Fathers down to A.D. 325*, ed. Rev. Alexander Roberts and James Donaldson [New York: Charles Scribner's Sons, 1925], 1:75).

136. King, address to the First Annual Institute on Nonviolence and Social Change, Dec. 3, 1956, King Collection, I, no. 11, p. 18.

137. Quoted in Johnston et al., eds., *The Wisdom of Martin Luther King in His Own Words,* pp. 76–77.

138. Metromedia Television interview with Merv Griffin, June 21, 1968.

139. STL, p. 111. See *Discourses of Epictetus* in *The Stoic and Epicurean Philosophers*, ed. Whitney Oates (New York: The Modern Library, 1940), p. 282.

140. *The Manual of Epictetus* in *The Stoic and Epicurean Philosophers*, ed. W. Oates, p. 469.

141. *Discourses of Epictetus*, ed. W. Oates, p. 289.

142. Ibid., p. 404. See *Apology* 41d.

143. STL, pp. 86, 106.

144. Ibid., pp. 114–15. See also pp. 75, 105.

145. Ibid., p. 85. Epictetus developed other themes which are present in King's philosophy of nonviolence. Epictetus asserted that the will can remain invincible even in the face of bodily suffering and has a divine mission to continue its struggle for peace and freedom (*Discourses*, pp. 320–21). "Difficulties are what show men's character. Therefore, when a difficult crisis meets you, remember that you are the raw youth with whom God the trainer is wrestling" (ibid., p. 264). He also affirmed that in the course of his struggles man must realize that there is a bond among all men not only because they possess reason but also because they are the children of God and hence are brothers (ibid., pp. 298–99). Moreover, he called for compassion for those who seek to injure others since they "know not what is good and what is evil" (ibid., p. 256). Furthermore, integral to Epictetus's thought was his belief in

the Divine Presence in man. "And if our minds are so bound up with God and in such close touch with Him as being part and portion of His very being, does not God perceive their every movement as closely akin to Him?" (ibid., p. 250). It was this Stoic doctrine of the immanence of God in the soul which helped to foster St. Augustine's belief that God is closer to us than we are to ourselves. Although there are these similarities between the ethic of Epictetus and that of King, there is at least one significant difference between them. King could not subscribe to Epictetus's cultivated indifference to the body and external involvements. King would have to reject his contention, "It is not poverty that we must cast out, but our judgment about poverty, and so we shall be at peace" (ibid., p. 371). King would agree with other Stoic thinkers such as Marcus Aurelius who recognized that it is man's duty as a rational being to work for the objective improvement of others while preserving the emotional detachment necessary for the successful completion of this work.

146. Karl Jaspers, *Philosophie* (Berlin: Springer, 1932), 1:3.

147. Ibid., 2, p. 180. See also Kurt Reinhardt, *The Existentialist Revolt*, rev. ed. (New York: Frederick Ungar, 1960), p. 181.

148. DeWolf, *A Theology of the Living Church*, pp. 156, 160.

149. Brightman, "A Personalistic View of Human Nature," p. 7.

150. Tillich, *The Courage To Be*, p. 52.

151. CCG, pp. 80–81.

152. Ibid., p. 80. See also Tillich, *Systematic Theology*, 1:195.

153. STL, p. 81.

154. Ibid., p. 90.

155. Jaspers, *Philosophie*, 2:469. Influenced by Jaspers's doctrine of "limit situations," Tillich referred to despair as an ultimate or "boundary-line situation" (*The Courage To Be*, p. 54).

156. Jaspers, *Philosophie*, 3:126. See Reinhardt, p. 195.

157. STL, p. 137.

158. Jaspers, *Philosophie*, 3:105. See Reinhardt, p. 197.

159. Tillich reiterated this doctrine of Jaspers when he affirmed, "A profound ambiguity between good and evil permeates everything he [man] does, because it permeates his personal being as such. Nonbeing is mixed with being in his moral self-affirmation as it is in his spiritual and ontic self-affirmation" (*The Courage To Be*, p. 52).

160. Jaspers, *Philosophie*, 3:220. See Reinhardt, p. 197. See also David Roberts, *Existentialism and Religious Belief* (New York: Oxford University Press, Galaxy Book, 1959), pp. 255–57.

161. Tillich, *The Courage To Be*, p. 150.

162. Jean-Paul Sartre, *Existentialism*, trans. Bernard Frechtman (New York: Philosophical Library, 1947), p. 18.

163. Tillich, *The Courage To Be*, pp. 149–50.

164. Sartre, *L'être et le néant* (Paris: Gallimard, 1943), p. 708.

165. Sartre, *Existentialism*, pp. 18 f.

166. King, address at the First Annual Institute on Nonviolence and Social Change of the MIA, p. 19.

167. STL, p. 137.

168. Tillich, *The Courage To Be*, p. 143.

169. STL, p. 124.

170. Ibid.

171. Ibid.

172. Gabriel Marcel, *The Mystery of Being*, 2 vols. (Chicago: Henry Regnery Company, Gateway Edition, 1960), 2:86.

173. Ibid., p. 87.

174. STL, p. 125.

175. Ibid.

176. George Kelsey, *Racism and the Christian Understanding of Man* (New York: Charles Scribner's Sons, 1965), p. 9, quoted in WDWGFH, p. 69.

177. H. Richard Niebuhr, *Radical Monotheism and Western Culture* (New York: Harper & Row, Publishers, 1960), p. 16, quoted in Kelsey, *Racism and the Christian Understanding of Man*, p. 26.

178. Kelsey, *Racism and the Christian Understanding of Man*, p. 53.

179. Ibid., p. 27.

180. Ibid.

181. WDWGFH, p. 70.

182. Quoted in Kelsey, p. 27, and in H. Richard Niebuhr, p. 119.

183. Kelsey, p. 29.

184. Ruth Benedict, *Race, Science and Politics*, rev. ed. (New York: Viking Press, 1947), p. 98, quoted in Kelsey, p. 29.

185. Kelsey, p. 32.

186. WDWGFH, p. 70.

187. Ibid.

188. Kelsey, p. 43. Kelsey referred to Gordon Allport's treatment of stereotypes in *The Nature of Prejudice* (New York: Doubleday & Company, Anchor Book, 1958), pp. 184–200.

189. Ibid., p. 47. Kelsey acknowledged his dependence on Kyle Haselden's treatment of "stereotyping" in *The Racial Problem in Christian Perspective* (New York: Harper & Row, Publishers, 1959), p. 143.

190. Ibid., pp. 36, 48, 54.

191. WDWGFH, p. 70.

Chapter 4: The Moral Obligation To Resist Collective Evil

1. STF, p. 91. King used the title, *Essay on Civil Disobedience*.

2. Henry Thoreau, "On the Duty of Civil Disobedience," *Social and Political Philosophy*, ed. John Somerville and Ronald Santoni (New York: Doubleday & Company, 1963), p. 287.

3. Ibid., p. 289.

4. Ibid., p. 291.

5. Ibid., p. 294.

6. Ibid., p. 283.

7. Ibid., p. 291.

8. Ibid., pp. 290-91.

9. *Civil Disobedience, Walden and Other Writings of Henry David Thoreau* (New York: The Modern Library, 1937), p. 669. Hannah Arendt maintained that Thoreau did not believe that an individual has any obligation to improve the world, and she quoted from his essay on civil disobedience. "I came into this world not chiefly to make this a good place to live in, but to live in it, be it good or bad" (p. 290; *Crises of the Republic* [New York: Harcourt Brace Jovanovich, Inc., 1969], p. 60). While Thoreau did not regard the reform of society as his chief obligation, it is a distortion of his doctrine to maintain that he felt that he or any individual has no obligation to reform an unjust system and to claim, as Arendt did, that he did not think that non-cooperation could lead to reform. As already indicated, he was convinced that the withdrawal of support by individuals from the system of slavery would lead to its abolition.

10. STF, p. 51. In 1962, Martin Buber recalled how when he first read Thoreau's essay he had the strong feeling that it concerned him directly, and only later did he realize that it was the concrete and personal elements in the essay that had impressed him. "He [Thoreau] addressed his reader within the very sphere of this situation (a specific historical-biographic situation) common to both of them in such a way that the reader not only discovered why Thoreau acted as he did at that time but also that the reader—assuming him of course to be honest and dispassionate—would have to act in just such a way whenever the proper occasion arose, provided he was seriously engaged in fulfilling his existence as a human person. . . . By speaking as concretely as he does about his own historical situation, Thoreau expresses exactly that which is valid for all human history" (quoted in *Massachusetts Review* 4, no. 1 [Autumn 1962]: 55).

11. Thoreau, "On the Duty of Civil Disobedience," pp. 285, 289-291.

12. WWCW, pp. 84-85.

13. Francis Dedmond, "Thoreau and the Ethical Concept of Government," *The Personalist* 26 (1945), p. 43. *Walden* expressed Thoreau's faith in the unquestionable ability of man to elevate his life by conscious endeavor.

14. Ibid., p. 45.

15. Thoreau, "On the Duty of Civil Disobedience," p. 282. Satish Kalekar contended that Thoreau was not a philosophical anarchist, but he did not consider Thoreau's doctrine that when men are prepared for it, they will have a government which "governs not at all" ("Thoreau and Mahatma Gandhi," *Gandhi Marg* 8 [Jan. 1964]: 60).

16. Thoreau, "A Plea for Captain John Brown," *Thoreau: People, Principles, and Politics*, ed. Milton Meltzer (New York: Hill and Wang, 1963), p. 187, quoted in Richard Regan, S.J., *Private Conscience and Public Law: The American Experience* (New York: Fordham University Press, 1972), p. 228.

17. Ibid., pp. 228–29. Dedmond's claim that Thoreau relied on passive resistance and did not counsel the use of force ignored Thoreau's defense of Brown's raid ("Thoreau and the Ethical Concept of Government," p. 42). Lawrence Reddick stressed that Gandhi and King derived from Thoreau only the element of noncooperation with evil and not the principle of nonviolence (*Crusader without Violence* [New York: Harper & Brothers, 1959], p. 17).

18. King, "A Legacy of Creative Protest," *Massachusetts Review* 4 (Autumn 1962): 43.

19. Ibid.

20. WWCW, p. 87.

21. "Memo to Martin Luther King," editorial, *National Review* 19 (Dec. 12, 1967): 1368.

22. *Crito* 50b, *The Collected Dialogues of Plato*, ed. Edith Hamilton and Huntington Cairns, p. 35.

23. Ibid., 52, p. 37.

24. *Apology* 29d, *The Collected Dialogues of Plato*, p. 15. S. M. Tewari noted that Gandhi admired Socrates' moral courage in being willing to take the hemlock rather than agree to abandon his pursuit of truth and his nonviolent resistance to the superstitious beliefs of his people ("Four Questions on Gandhi's Philosophy," *Gandhi Marg* 13, no. 3 [July 1969]: 220. A. D.). Woozley argued that there is no real contradiction between the *Apology* and the *Crito* since it is not the doctrine of the *Crito* that a man must always, and no matter what, obey the laws of the state ("Socrates on Disobeying the Law," *The Philosophy of Socrates*, ed. Gregory Vlastos [New York: Doubleday & Company, Anchor Book, 1971], pp. 300–08).

25. King, "Letter from Birmingham Jail," WWCW, p. 84. See Augustine, *De libero arbitrio*, I, 5, *Patrologia Latina*, 32: 1227. Aquinas referred to this doctrine of Augustine in the *Summa Theologica*, Ia, IIae, Q. 95, a. 2.

26. John 19:11, cited by Augustine, *Contra Faustum*, 22: 20, quoted in Herbert Deane, *The Political and Social Ideas of St. Augustine* (New York: Columbia University Press, 1963), p. 143.

27. Rom. 13:1, 2, 5, quoted in Deane, p. 143.

28. John Figgis, *The Political Aspects of St. Augustine's City of God* (Gloucester, Mass.: Peter Smith, 1963), p. 9. See Augustine, Sermo CCCII, 21, *Patrologia Latina*, 38: 1392–93. See also Deane, p. 144.

29. Deane, p. 147.

30. Augustine, *Confessions*, book 3, chap. 8, *The Basic Writings of St. Augustine*, 2 vols., ed. Whitney Oates (New York: Random House, 1948), 1:37.

31. Augustine, Sermo 62, 8, *Patrologia Latina*, 38: 421. See Deane, pp. 148–49.

32. DeWolf, *A Theology of the Living Church*, p. 112.

33. Augustine, *De Vera Religione*, LV, 3, *Patrologia Latina*, 34: 171, quoted in Deane, p. 152. "Et aliud est servitus animae, aliud servitus corporis." Hegel declared as sophistic any doctrine which separates body and

soul and claims that the soul is a thing-in-itself and hence is unaffected when wrong treatment is accorded to the body and it is subjected to the power of another (*The Philosophy of Right*, trans. T. M. Knox [New York: Oxford University Press, 1967], p. 43).

34. Augustine, *De Civitate Dei*, 19: 15, quoted in Deane, p. 114.

35. Augustine, *De Sermone Domini*, 1, 19, *Patrologia Latina*, 34: 1260, quoted in Deane, p. 115.

36. WWCW, p. 85.

37. Aquinas, *Summa Theologica*, Ia, IIae, Q. 93, a. 1, *Introduction to St. Thomas Aquinas*, ed. Anton Pegis (New York: The Modern Library, 1948), p. 629.

38. Ibid., Ia, IIae, Q. 91, a. 2, p. 618.

39. Ibid., Ia, IIae, Q. 95, a. 2, p. 649.

40. Aquinas, *Quodlibetum*, 3, 27, quoted in Frederick Copleston, *Aquinas* (Baltimore: Penguin Books, 1957), p. 220.

41. Aquinas, *De Regimine Principum*, 1, 15. See Copleston, *Aquinas*, p. 230.

42. Aquinas, *Summa Theologica*, Ia, IIae, Q. 96, a. 4, quoted in Copleston, p. 232. Will Herberg seemed to be unaware of this doctrine of Aquinas when he judged King's doctrine of civil disobedience as "not Christian at all but seriously deviant and heretical" since it did not have a foundation in the Christian tradition ("A Religious Right to Violate the Law?" *National Review* 16, no. 28 [July 14, 1964]: 579).

43. WWCW, p. 85.

44. Aquinas, *Summa Theologica*, Ia, IIae, Q. 96, a. 4, quoted in Copleston, p. 232.

45. WWCW, p. 86.

46. King, "Facing the Challenge of a New Age," p. 25.

47. *Hegel's Lectures on the History of Philosophy*, 3 vols., trans. E. S. Haldane (New York: The Humanities Press, 1955), 1:279.

48. Brightman, "Hegel's Influence in the Contemporary Social Situation," *The Crozer Quarterly* 12, no. 1 (Jan. 1935):52.

49. King, "Notes on Hegel," King Collection, XIV, no. 40. Lerone Bennett, Jr., in his biography of King seemed not to know that Brightman became ill during the first month of King's seminar on Hegel and that it was Professor Peter Bertocci who guided King through Hegel's *Phenomenology of Mind* and *Philosophy of Right* (*What Manner of Man*, 4th rev. ed. [Chicago: Johnson Publishing Co., 1976], p. 48).

50. "Heraclitus," *The Presocratics*, ed. Philip Wheelwright (New York: The Odyssey Press, 1966), p. 70, no. 20.

51. Ibid., p. 71, no. 26–27.

52. Ibid., p. 77, no. 98.

53. Ibid., p. 75, no. 81.

54. Ralph Flewelling, "Studies in American Personalism," *The Personalist* 31 (July 1950): 229.

55. DeWolf, "A Personalistic Re-examination of the Mind-Body Problem," *The Personalist* 34 (Winter 1953): 21.

56. King Collection, XIV, no. 67.

57. Brightman, "A Personalistic View of Human Nature," p. 9.

58. Ibid., p. 8.

59. Ibid., p. 7.

60. Ibid., p. 8. In "A Personalistic Philosophy of History" Brightman reemphasized this doctrine of Heraclitus. "As Heraclitus said, 'You cannot find the boundaries of the soul no matter how far down you go.' The creative resources of freedom are illimitable. Personality is inexhaustible history" (p. 6).

61. Interview of King by Tom Johnson of *The Montgomery Advertiser*, published on Jan. 19, 1956. See Lerone Bennett, Jr., *What Manner of Man*, p. 72.

62. STF, p. 101.

63. Ibid., p. 100. King found in Hegel an additional confirmation of the value of community and the futility of any attempt by any individual or group to dominate another. Professor Peter Bertocci recalled how King in the seminar on Hegel "almost took over the class" in his enthusiasm for Hegel's insight that the master is dependent on the slave for his consciousness of himself as master (interview by the author at Boston University on June 13, 1973). Hegel had perceived that just when the master achieves lordship, he achieves a dependent consciousness and finds his truth to be "the unessential consciousness" (*The Phenomenology of Mind*, rev. ed., trans. J. Baillie [New York: The Macmillan Company, 1955], pp. 236–37). Joseph Barndt emphasized that James Baldwin reaffirmed the message of President Lincoln that when the black man is emancipated, the white man will discover that he is the one who has been set free. Barndt maintained that when a man controls another by force, he himself is the most controlled, and when he denies the humanity of another by enslaving him, his actions deny even more his own humanity (*Why Black Power?* [New York: Friendship Press, 1968], p. 55).

64. Hegel, *The Philosophy of History*, trans. J. Sibree (New York: Dover Publications, 1956), p. 77.

65. STF, p. 101.

66. Hegel, *The Phenomenology of Mind*, p. 81. See also STF, p. 197.

67. WDWGFH, pp. 12–13. When Malcolm X criticized King for a readiness for making compromises and charged him with a "sellout," he did not understand that King's tactics were designed not merely for partial gains but as stages in a drive toward total equality. See Kenneth Clark's interview with Malcolm X in *The Negro Protest*, ed. Kenneth Clark (Boston: Beacon Press, 1963), p. 27.

68. STL, p. 1.

69. STF, p. 213.

70. STL, p. 1. King's notes on his seminar on Hegel contain Brightman's comment that Hegel's early theological writings viewed love as the central religious idea (King Collection, XIV, no. 40).

71. Ibid., pp. 2, 5.

72. Ibid., p. 136.

73. CCG, p. 279.

74. Ibid., pp. 297–98.

75. King, address at Mississippi Christian Leadership Conference, Sept. 23, 1959, King Collection, XI, no. 8, p. 14.

76. King, "Our Struggle," *Black Protest in the Twentieth Century*, pp. 296–97.

77. King's appeal to these examples renders unacceptable C. Eric Lincoln's judgment, "There was nothing in Hegel or Thoreau or Gandhi which could have prepared Martin Luther King to confront the evil and the racial hatred endemic in a people who neither knew nor cared about Hegel or Thoreau or Gandhi" (*Martin Luther King, Jr.: A Profile*, p. xi). Lincoln's claim that in Montgomery King was confronting history and not ideology did not allow for the central role of ideology in the direction of history.

78. Hegel, *The Philosophy of History*, p. 33.

79. Ibid., p. 30.

80. STF, p. 44.

81. Quoted in Bennett, *What Manner of Man*, p. 106.

82. King, Nobel Lecture, p. 63. See also King, "Dreams of Brighter Tomorrows," *Ebony*, 20, no. 5, Mar. 1965, p. 35. In 1965, King contended, "Consciously or unconsciously, the American Negro has been caught up by the black *Zeitgeist*" (*Playboy Interviews,* p. 370).

83. It would seem, however, that Kierkegaard was not accurate in some of his criticisms of Hegel. Kierkegaard's criticism that Hegel's system was pantheistic ignored Hegel's emphasis on the eternal Trinity, distinct from and prior to creation, which is its manifestation (Hegel, *Lectures on the Philosophy of Religion*, 3 vols., trans. E. B. Spiers and J. B. Sanderson [New York: Humanities Press, 1895], 3: 38–39). His further criticism that Hegel emphasized the importance only of the movements of the World-Spirit or Absolute in the development of "objective truth " and deprived the individual of his self-identity, self-determination, and dignity neglected Hegel's emphasis on the value of the individual's achievement of "subjective freedom" by consciously interiorizing and contributing to the rational elements in the objective political, artistic, religious, and philosophical orders (Hegel, *The Philosophy of History*, p. 104). The criticisms that the Hegelian system pretended to have achieved total truth even in the historical order and that the system made the existing state the court of last resort in ethical matters disregarded Hegel's specific proposals for political freedoms that did not exist in the Prussian state of his day (*Hegel's Philosophy of Right*, trans. T. M. Knox [New York: Oxford University Press, 1967], pp. 141–42, 201, 289). The criticism that Hegel destroyed the meaning of Christianity failed to appreciate the role of belief in the unique person of Christ as the source of the insight in the Hegelian system that the divine and the human have already been implicitly reconciled in the Incarnation (Hegel, *Lectures on the Philosophy of Religion*, 3:72, 75).

84. Brightman, *The Problem of God* (New York: Abingdon Press, 1930), p. 135, quoted in Donald Smith, "An Exegesis of Martin Luther King, Jr.'s Social Philosophy," *Phylon* 31 (Spring 1970): 97.

85. Brightman, "Hegel's Influence in the Contemporary Social Situation," pp. 51, 53.

86. STF, pp. 100–101.

87. CCG, p. 311.

88. STL, p. 137. King's criticisms of Hegel would not invalidate Tom Johnson's report, already cited, that Hegel was King's favorite philosopher, but these criticisms would dispel any notion that King endorsed the Hegelian system.

89. *Laws of Manu*, 6: 47–48, quoted in William Stuart Nelson, "The Tradition of Nonviolence and Its Underlying Forces," *Gandhi: His Relevance for Our Times*, rev. ed., ed. G. Ramachandran and T. K. Mahadevan (Berkeley: World Without War Council, 1971), p. 4.

90. Nelson, p. 4.

91. *Bhagavad-Gita* (*The Blessed Lord's Song*), chap. 1: 35, 46, *The Wisdom of China and India*, ed. Lin Yutang (New York: Random House, The Modern Library, 1942), pp. 59–60. P. Nagaraja Rao indicated that Gandhi and Sankara have been the exceptions among the many students of the *Gita* who have regarded it as supporting and enjoining the use of violence against an evildoer, and he referred to its several appeals for violence ("Gandhi and the Hindu Concept of *Ahimsa*," *Gandhi Marg* 11, no. 1 [Jan. 1967]: 65–66). Gene Sharp asserted that the *Bhagavad-Gita* dwelt upon the justification for fighting and that Gandhi reinterpreted it symbolically ("Gandhi's Political Significance Today," *Gandhi: His Relevance for Our Times*, p. 143). Gandhi explained that "under the guise of physical warfare, it [the *Gita*] described the duel that perpetually went on in the hearts of mankind and that physical warfare was brought in merely to make the description of the internal duel more alluring" (Gandhi, *The Gita according to Gandhi* [Ahmedabad, 1951], p. 127, quoted in George Hendrick, "The Influence of Thoreau's 'Civil Disobedience' on Gandhi's Satyagraha," *The New England Quarterly* 29, no. 4 [Dec. 1956]: 468). Hendrick sent a copy of this article to King in 1957.

92. Gandhi, *All Religions Are True*, ed. Anand Hingorani (Bombay: Pearl Publications Private Limited, 1962), p. 196, quoted in S. M. Tewari, "Four Questions on Gandhi's Philosophy: An Attempt at Their Answers," p. 217.

93. K. J. Mahale presented Albert Schweitzer's acknowledgement of this contribution by Buddha to the development of the doctrine of nonviolence in "Gandhian *Ahimsa* in French Opinion," *Gandhi Marg* 13, no. 1 (Jan. 1969): 74.

94. *Vinaya*, 1, 342–49; *Cula-Hatthi-Padopama Sutta* (*Sacred Books of Buddhism*) 5: 128, 129, quoted in William Nelson, "The Tradition of Nonviolence and Its Underlying Forces," p. 5.

95. Quoted in Jawaharlal Nehru, *The Discovery of India* (New York: The John Day Company, 1946), p. 119, also quoted in Nelson, p. 5.

96. Quoted in Tewari, "Four Questions on Gandhi's Philosophy: An Attempt at Their Answers," p. 220.

97. Gandhi, *An Autobiography or The Story of My Experiments with Truth*, p. 49, quoted in Tewari, p. 220.

98. Tewari, p. 220.

99. Ibid., p. 224. See also Mahale, "Gandhian *Ahimsa* in French Opinion," p. 75.

100. Quoted in Tewari, p. 224.

101. Ibid., p. 223.

102. Gandhi, *In Search of the Supreme*, 2:302-03, quoted in Tewari, p. 221.

103. Ibid.

104. Leo Tolstoy, "The Law of Force and the Law of Love," *The Fortnightly Review* (London: Chapman & Hall, Ltd., 1909), p. 474, quoted in Gene Sharp, "A Study of the Meanings of Nonviolence," *Gandhi: His Relevance for Our Times*, p. 32.

105. Tolstoy, *The Kingdom of God Is Within You* (London: William Heinemann, 1894), p. 160. See Sharp, "A Study of the Meanings of Nonviolence," p. 32.

106. Quoted in Ernest Simmons, *Leo Tolstoy* (Boston: Little, Brown and Company, 1945), p. 467, and quoted also in Nelson, p. 12.

107. Hendrick repeated Gandhi's denial that he had derived the idea of civil disobedience from Thoreau ("The Influence of Thoreau's 'Civil Disobedience' on Gandhi's Satyagraha," p. 471). Satish Kalekar discussed this letter in "Thoreau and Mahatma Gandhi," p. 57.

108. Gandhi, *Indian Opinion*, Oct. 26, 1907, *The Collected Works of Mahatma Gandhi* (Ahmedabad: Navajivan Press, 1962), 7: 304.

109. Donald Smith observed that it is intriguing how the lines of Eastern and Western thought were intertwined in the formation of King's social philosophy since King and Gandhi were strongly affected by the example of Thoreau while Thoreau and his mentor, Ralph Waldo Emerson, in their development toward transcendentalism often discussed the *Bhagavad-Gita* and the sacred *Upanishads* ("An Exegesis of Martin Luther King, Jr.'s Social Philosophy," p. 92).

110. *The Gandhi Reader*, ed. Homer Jack (New York: Grove Press, 1961), p. 219, quoted in Thomas Merton, "The Meaning of Satyagraha," *Gandhi Marg* 10 (1966): 115.

111. *The Essential Gandhi*, ed. Louis Fischer (New York: Random House, 1962), p. 166.

112. Gene Sharp, "Gandhi's Political Significance Today," p. 144.

113. Chester Bowles recounted how Gandhi during his first train ride in South Africa was ordered to leave a compartment reserved for whites; when he refused, he was forced to leave the train. It was soon after this incident that he began the organized struggle against discrimination ("What Negroes Can Learn from Gandhi," *Saturday Evening Post*, Mar. 1, 1958, pp. 20-21). King retained a copy of this article. As already indicated, he too attached a special

significance to the first time that he had experienced discrimination on a train (STF, p. 20).

114. See Bondurant, *Conquest of Violence* (pp. 36-104) for a detailed discussion of Gandhi's methods. See also Ram Rattan, "The Anatomy of Gandhi's Satyagraha," *Gandhi Marg* 17, no. 1 (Jan. 1973): 84-105. Gene Sharp has made an inestimable contribution to the study of the history of nonviolence with his work, *The Politics of Nonviolent Action* (Boston: Porter Sargent Publishers, 1973). In Part 2 of this work he explained 198 methods of nonviolent resistance and provided historical examples of these methods.

115. Louis Waldman, who served as chairman of the Committee on Civil Rights of the Association of the Bar of the City of New York, has offered the most detailed critique of King's civil disobedience. On April 21, 1965, King defended his civil disobedience in an address before the association, "The Civil Rights Struggle in the United States Today." The address contained arguments he had developed in his "Letter from Birmingham Jail" (*The Record of the Association of the Bar of the City of New York*—Supplement—20, no. 5, May 1965, pp. 3-19.) Waldman developed the following criticisms of King's position in an address before the association, "Civil Rights—Yes: Civil Disobedience—No" *(New York State Bar Journal* 37 [Aug. 1965]: 331-37. Reprinted in *Civil Disobedience: Theory and Practice*, ed. Hugo Bedau [New York: Pegasus, 1969], pp. 106-15): (1) The 1954 *Brown* v. *Board of Education* decision, "the foundation for the progress made in the last 10 years," had been achieved not by civil disobedience, sit-ins, lie-ins, or marches but by reason and an appeal to traditional constitutional principles. (2) King's doctrine that he and his followers could refuse to obey laws that they thought were unjust was not only illegal and for that reason alone should be rejected, but also immoral, destructive of the principles of democratic government, and a danger to the very civil rights he sought to promote. (3) King's definition of an unjust law as "one in which people are required to obey a code that they had no part in making because they were denied the right to vote," and as "one in which the minority is compelled to observe a code that is not binding on the majority" would logically imply that every person under 21 or the millions of non-citizens who are denied the right to vote have no obligation to obey the law. (4) King and his followers by their open violation of laws were less virtuous than those who violated laws secretly because an open violator by his actions invites others to join in such a violation and is shameless in his defiance of his neighbor's judgment and his fellow man's disapproval, whereas the secret violator understands the antisocial nature of his action and seeks to avoid the disapproval of his neighbors. (5) If King's doctrine that citizens on the basis of conscience have a right to disobey unjust laws were carried out by twenty million American Negroes, it would produce chaos and deny individual liberty to every other American. What would happen to our freedom and civil rights if the members of the Labor Movement or other economic or religious groups followed King's doctrine? (6) By his statement that everything that Hitler did in Germany was

legal King made an invidious comparison between Hitler's Germany and the United States. Then too, Hitler, prior to becoming Chancellor, also practiced civil disobedience. (7) King declared the need for civil disobedience in the North since he thought that it was guilty of broad injustice in the areas of unemployment, housing, and education. However, honest men may in good conscience differ on the justice or injustice of the laws relating to these problems. (8) In response to a question after his address King implied that if you state your goal you are justified in proceeding with marches and demonstrations, but this position is constitutionally indefensible. (9) King's demonstrations provoked violence, and he trifled with the plain meaning of words when he described such provocations as nonviolent. (The numbers have been added.) King chose not to respond to these criticisms but he could have made the following responses: (1) In 1963, in *Why We Can't Wait*, I indicated that although the 1954 decision had called for the desegregation of the schools "with all deliberate speed," it had been "heeded with all deliberate delay," and that at the beginning of 1963 only 9 percent of Southern Negro students were attending integrated schools (p. 5); without minimizing the importance of legislation, nonviolent direct action including civil disobedience has been necessary. (2) I would grant that illegality belongs to the essence of civil disobedience, but I would emphasize that many of the local laws we opposed with civil disobedience were illegal in the sense that they conflicted with the law of the land. Moreover, I would regard Waldman's conception of man's obligations as too limited. The individual must answer ultimately to his own conscience, and when the laws of men conflict with his conscience, he has a moral obligation to disobey those laws. Confronted with legal obligations, the individual must preserve his moral autonomy, and not be guilty of an uncritical identification of legality as morality. He must not surrender his dignity as a moral agent. Furthermore, I have indicated that the civil disobedience in the Birmingham Movement did not prove to be a danger to civil rights but helped to secure them by generating the 1964 Civil Rights Act. (3) In protesting unjust local laws that denied the franchise, I was referring not to children, nor to non-citizens, who could become citizens of the society and vote, but to adults who were citizens and were denied this fundamental right of a citizen simply because of their color. (4) I have affirmed that the nonviolent resister acts in conformity with his conscience, is appropriately conscious of the justice of his cause, and hence cannot be regarded as shameless. Then too, during the Birmingham Movement the majority of the nation could perceive that the civil disobedients were not antisocial but were concerned with nonviolently promoting the common good and were willing to accept imprisonment for their open disobedience to demonstrate their respect for law. Besides, how could the secret violators of the law who used violence be considered as "virtuous"? I have condemned the end result of their defiance of the law as anarchy. (5) As a result of our civil disobedience the nation did not turn to civil disobedience on a massive scale. If our civil disobedience had assumed such proportions that it threatened national order,

I would have been compelled by my repudiation of anarchy to limit our use of this tactic. Also, an act of civil disobedience may confirm more citizens in their legal rectitude than it induces to violate laws. (6) My references to Hitler's actions as legal when he was the Chancellor were intended to challenge those in this country who would emphasize legality at the expense of morality. I affirmed that if I had lived in Hitler's Germany I would have aided my Jewish brothers and would have openly disobeyed the law that declared such aid illegal. Waldman's further reference to Hitler's civil disobedience ignored the fact that our civil disobedience aimed to apply democratic principles to the republic and not to destroy them. (7) I have granted that many of our opponents have acted in good conscience and have believed that they have been quite moral in their opposition as they executed what they regarded as God's will, but I have also stressed that pressure must be applied to bring about the *objective* moral good of justice. (8) Civil disobedience becomes necessary when an ordinance that requires a permit for a parade is used unjustly to maintain segregation and disfranchisement by denying citizens the First-Amendment privilege of peaceful assembly and protest. (9) Our demonstrations were designed to cause the violence of racism to come to the surface so that it might be healed. For a detailed evaluation of Waldman's criticisms see my article "Martin Luther King's Civil Disobedience—A Rejoinder," *Gandhi Marg,* Second Series, 3, no. 12 (Mar. 1982): 709–21.

A further refutation of the type of perception that permeated Waldman's criticisms may be found in "Religious Obedience and Civil Disobedience," a policy statement of the National Council of the Churches of Christ in the U.S.A. on June 7, 1968. The General Board of the Council called upon Christians and other men of good will to recognize the form of civil disobedience practiced by King, Thoreau, Tolstoy, and Gandhi as a valid instrument for those who seek justice and as consistent with both the Christian tradition and the American political and legal heritage (*Policy Statement* in *Political Obligation and Civil Disobedience: Readings*, ed. Michael Smith and Kenneth Deutsch [New York: Thomas Y. Crowell Company, 1972], pp. 66–72).

116. See the following articles by King that contain many of his petitions: "Equality Now: The President Has the Power," *The Nation* 192 (Feb. 4, 1961): 91–95; "The Time for Freedom Has Come," *The New York Times Magazine* (Sept. 10, 1961): 25; "Fumbling on the New Frontier," *The Nation* 194 (Mar. 3, 1962): 190–93; "The Case Against Tokenism," *The New York Times Magazine* (Aug. 5, 1962): 11, 49, 52–53; "Bold Design for a New South," *The Nation* 196 (Mar. 30, 1963): 259–62; "In a Word: Now," *The New York Times Magazine* (Sept. 29, 1963): 91–92; "Hammer on Civil Rights," *The Nation* 198 (Mar. 9, 1964): 230–34; "Civil Right No. 1—The Right to Vote," *The New York Times Magazine* (Mar. 14, 1965): 26, 27, 94–95; "Let Justice Roll Down," *The Nation* 200 (Mar. 15, 1965): 269–74; "The Last Steep Ascent," *The Nation* 202 (Mar. 14, 1966): 288 ff. For King's detailed petition to President Kennedy see *A Martin Luther King Treasury* (New York: Educational Heritage, Inc., 1964), Book 3, pp. 289 ff.

117. STF, p. 33.

118. Ibid. See King, address to the First Annual Institute on Nonviolence and Social Change, Dec. 3, 1956, p. 16.

119. "Boycotts Will Be Used," interview with King, *U.S. News & World Report*, Feb. 24, 1964, p. 60.

120. King, address to the National Bar Association, Milwaukee, Aug. 20, 1959, p. 8.

121. STF, p. 33. See King, Commencement address at Lincoln University, Jun. 6, 1961, p. 14.

122. King, address to the National Bar Association, Milwaukee, Aug. 20, 1959, p. 8.

123. WWCW, p. 23.

124. King, address at Freedom Fund Report Dinner, NAACP 53rd Annual Convention, July 5, 1962, Atlanta, p. 10.

125. King, address at the Convocation on Equal Justice Under Law of the NAACP Legal Defense Fund, New York City, May 28, 1964, pp. 3–4.

126. Louis Lomax referred to Roy Wilkins's denial that the NAACP was primarily a legalistic organization, and to the fact that Wilkins had pointed with pride to the participation of "NAACP youth demonstrators" in the sit-ins (*The Negro Revolt*, p. 163).

127. King, "Advice for Living," *Ebony* 13, no. 7, May 1958, p. 112.

128. WWCW, p. 23.

129. King, address to the Convocation on Equal Justice Under Law of the NAACP Legal Defense Fund, New York City, May 28, 1964, p. 1. See also King, address at Freedom Fund Report Dinner, Atlanta, July 5, 1962, p. 2.

130. STF, p. 81.

131. Ibid., pp. 160, 186.

132. King, address to the Convocation on Equal Justice Under Law of the NAACP Legal Defense Fund, New York City, May 28, 1964, p. 2. See also *The Negro Protest*, ed. Kenneth Clark, pp. 43–44. Rev. Wyatt Tee Walker stated that King received one dollar for raising more than $400,000 for SCLC in one year. See Robert Penn Warren, *Who Speaks for the Negro?* (New York: Random House, 1965), p. 231.

133. STF, pp. 49–51.

134. Ibid., p. 51.

135. Ibid., p. 102.

136. King, "Love, Law, and Civil Disobedience," p. 6.

137. King, address at Conference of Religious Leaders under the sponsorship of the President's Committee on Government Contracts, May 11, 1959, Washington, D.C., King Collection, XVI, no. 6, p. 3.

138. Quoted in Ernest Dunbar, "A Visit with Dr. King," *Look*, Feb. 12, 1963, p. 96.

139. STL, p. 40.

140. STF, pp. 171–72.

141. Quoted in S. M. Tewari, "The Concept of Nonviolence in the Philosophy of Mahatma Gandhi," *Gandhi Marg* 13, no. 4 (Oct. 1969): 90.

142. King, address at the First Annual Institute on Nonviolence and Social Change, Dec. 3, 1956, p. 3.

143. Coretta Scott King, Foreword, TC, p. xii.

144. STL, pp. 28–31.

145. Ibid., p. 29.

146. Ibid.

147. Ibid.

148. Ibid., p. 30.

149. Ibid., p. 29.

150. King, "Who Speaks for the South?" *Liberation* 3, no. 1 (Mar. 1958): 13.

151. STF, p. 139. In his dissertation King presented Wieman's doctrine that "most sin is unconscious and unintended" (p. 224).

152. King, Statement to Judge Eugene Loe, Sept. 5, 1958, Montgomery.

153. King, "Love, Law, and Civil Disobedience," p. 6.

154. King, "Philosophy of Plato" notebook, King Collection, XIV, no. 57, n.p. Raghavan Iyer explained that Gandhi, by asserting that evil is good or truth misplaced, implied that a mistaken belief or a failure to see things as they really are is the basis of every evil action (*The Moral and Political Thought of Mahatma Gandhi* [New York: Oxford University Press, Galaxy Book, 1978], p. 159).

155. However, King seemed to allow for the traditional Christian view of the source of moral evil when he wrote, "Slavery in America was perpetuated not merely by human badness but also by human blindness" (STL, p. 29).

156. STF, p. 102. See also King, "The Current Crisis in Race Relations," p. 9.

157. King, "An Experiment in Love," *Jubilee* 6, no. 5 (Sept. 1958): 14. In this article King did add that Gandhi made this statement conscious of the fact that there is always an alternative to violence.

158. Gandhi, *Young India*, Aug. 11, 1920. Gandhi also affirmed, "He who cannot protect himself or his nearest and dearest or their honor by non-violently facing death, may and ought to do so by violently dealing with the oppressor" (*Gandhi, Nonviolence in Peace and War* [Ahmedabad: Navajivan Publishing House, 1948], 1:77, quoted in Manick Samuel, "A Comparative Study of the Methods of Nonviolence As Used by Martin Luther King, Jr. and Mahatma Gandhi" [M.A. diss., Interdenominational Theological Center, Atlanta, 1970], p. 35). Samuel emphasized that it was natural for the Eastern mind to fight to protect one's honor.

159. Quoted in S. M. Tewari, "The Concept of Nonviolence in the Philosophy of Mahatma Gandhi," p. 106.

160. *Playboy Interviews*, p. 366.

161. "Montgomery Sparked a Revolution," *The Southern Courier*, Dec. 11, 1965, p. 1.

162. See Keith Rae, "The Theology and Ethics of Dr. Martin Luther King, Jr. with Special Reference to the Thought of Paul Tillich and Reinhold

Niebuhr" (Th.M. thesis, Boston University School of Theology, 1971), p. 48.

163. STL, p. 84.

164. Bondurant, *Conquest of Violence,* p. 19.

165. Quoted in William Nelson, "Satyagraha: Gandhian Principles of Non-violent Non-cooperation," *The Journal of Religious Thought* (Autumn-Winter, 1957–58): 16. Nelson sent King a copy of this article.

166. King, "Our Struggle," p. 299.

167. STF, p. 102. Maurice Friedman was mistaken in stating that King would confirm an enemy even in opposing him, i.e., "confirm his right to stand where he stands" ("Martin Luther King: An American Gandhi and a Modern Job," *Gandhi Marg* 12 [1968]: 231).

168. Bondurant, *Conquest of Violence*, pp. 180–81.

169. Ibid., p. 67.

170. Ibid., p. 91.

171. Quoted in *The Essential Gandhi*, ed. Louis Fischer, p. 230.

172. Ibid., p. 145.

173. Ibid., p. 91.

174. Gandhi, *An Autobiography or The Story of My Experiments with Truth*, p. 365.

175. Nelson, "Satyagraha: Gandhian Principles of Non-violent Non-cooperation," p. 23.

176. Bowles, "What Negroes Can Learn from Gandhi," p. 87.

177. WWCW, p. 151. In 1964 King proposed that the Republican party include in its platform an endorsement and support for a plan for a Bill of Rights for the Disadvantaged. See his statement before the Platform Committee of the Republican National Convention, July 7, 1964, San Francisco, King Collection, XV, no. 11, p. 10. In 1963, he called for the "systematic liquidation of ghetto life" ("In a Word *Now*," p. 92).

178. WDWGFH, pp. 162–63.

179. WWCW, p. 11.

180. WDWGFH, p. 87. President Carter in a press conference on July 28, 1977 stated that the Government and private business should try to compensate for past discrimination.

181. King, "Advice for Living," *Ebony* 13, no. 5, Mar. 1958, p. 92.

182. STF, pp. 222–23.

183. King, address to the MIA, Dec. 3, 1959, pp. 2–3.

184. King, "My Trip to the Land of Gandhi," p. 90.

185. STL, p. 71.

186. "Constitution and By-Laws of the Montgomery Improvement Association," art. 1, sects. 2–3, King Collection, VII.

187. James Baldwin, "The Dangerous Road Before Martin Luther King," *Harper's Magazine*, Feb. 1961, p. 36. Gandhi had stated, "We can't blame the whites for all our troubles. . . . We can begin to clean up our homes, to teach illiterate Indian adults to read, and to provide free schools for the children of the poor" (quoted in Bowles, "What Negroes Can Learn from Gandhi," p. 87).

188. King, "Nonviolence: The Only Road to Freedom," *Ebony* 21, Oct. 1966, p. 34.

189. WDWGFH, pp. 143–46.

190. Ibid., p. 38.

191. Ibid., p. 125.

192. King, "A Proper Sense of Priorities," address to the Clergy and Laity Concerned about Vietnam, Feb. 6, 1968, Washington, D.C. *Martin Luther King Speaks*, Southern Christian Leadership Conference Collection.

193. King, "Showdown for Non-violence," *Look* 32, no. 8, Apr. 16, 1968, p. 24.

194. José Yglesias, "Dr. King's March on Washington, Part 2," *The New York Times Magazine*, Mar. 31, 1968, in *Black Protest in the Sixties*, ed. August Meier and Elliott Rudwick (Chicago: Quadrangle Books, 1970), pp. 268, 272. See also William Schulz, "Martin Luther King's March on Washington," *The Reader's Digest* 92, Apr. 1968, p. 68.

195. Quoted in Yglesias, p. 272.

196. Quoted in Yglesias, pp. 270–71.

197. William Miller, "Gandhi and King—Pioneers of Modern Nonviolence," *Gandhi Marg* 13, no. 1 (Jan. 1969), p. 24. After his public fasting as a political act in 1918 Gandhi told Mahadev Desai that the fast had been "the most valuable lesson of my life," and his "best deed so far" (quoted in Erik Erikson, *Gandhi's Truth* [New York: W. W. Norton & Co., Inc., 1969], pp. 50–51).

198. William Cenkner, "Gandhi and Creative Conflict," *Thought* 45, no. 178 (Autumn 1970): 427.

199. *Playboy Interviews*, p. 382. June Yungblut reported that a few days before his assassination King told her that he had decided to accept Father Thomas Merton's invitation to make a retreat at Gethsemani Monastery before the completion of his plans for the Poor People's Campaign ("Martin Luther King: The Man and the Vision," *Gandhi Marg* 12 [1968]: 277).

200. Kenneth Smith and Ira Zepp, Jr., *Search for the Beloved Community*, pp. 48, 59.

201. Richard Gregg, *The Power of Nonviolence*, 2nd rev. ed. (New York: Schocken Books, 1971), p. 44.

202. Ibid.

203. Ibid.

204. Ibid., p. 45.

205. Ibid., p. 46.

206. Ibid., p. 47.

207. Ibid., p. 48.

208. Ibid., p. 49.

209. Ibid., p. 50.

210. Ibid., p. 51.

211. Ibid.

212. *The Negro Protest*, ed. Kenneth Clark, p. 39.

213. King, Commencement address at Lincoln University, June 6, 1961, p. 14.

214. STF, pp. 98-99. See also King, "Nonviolence and Racial Justice," p. 166.

215. King, address at the First Annual Institute on Nonviolence and Social Change, Dec. 3, 1956, pp. 18-19.

216. *The Negro Protest*, p. 42.

217. King, address at the First Annual Institute on Nonviolence and Social Change, p. 19. In commenting on how demonstrators in Birmingham had remained nonviolent as they were confronted with police dogs and fire hoses, King affirmed that it was then that the power of nonviolence became manifest since in magnified strokes it made evident who was the evildoer and who was the undeserving and oppressed victim ("A New Sense of Direction," *Worldview* 15, no. 4 [Apr. 1972]: 5).

218. STF, p. 99.

219. STL, pp. 135-36.

220. Ibid.

221. STF, p. 99.

222. King, "Reinhold Niebuhr's Ethical Dualism," May 9, 1952, King Collection, XIV, no. 58, p. 1.

223. Ibid. Quoted by King from Reinhold Niebuhr, *The Contribution of Religion to Social Work* (New York: Columbia University Press, 1932), p. 77.

224. Ibid., p. 2. See Niebuhr, *The Contribution of Religion to Social Work*, p. 80.

225. Ibid. See Niebuhr, *The Contribution of Religion to Social Work*, p. 82.

226. Ibid., pp. 2-3. Quoted by King from Niebuhr, *Moral Man and Immoral Society* (New York: Charles Scribner's Sons, 1932), pp. xi-xii.

227. Niebuhr, *Moral Man and Immoral Society*, p. xi.

228. King, "Reinhold Niebuhr's Ethical Dualism," p. 5. Quoted from *Moral Man and Immoral Society*, p. 257.

229. Ibid., p. 4. See Niebuhr, *An Interpretation of Christian Ethics*, pp. 149-50.

230. Ibid., p. 5. See *An Interpretation of Christian Ethics*, p. 145.

231. Ibid. See *An Interpretation of Christian Ethics*, pp. 147-48.

232. Ibid., p. 6. Quoted by King from *Moral Man and Immoral Society*, p. 48.

233. Ibid., pp. 6-7. Quoted from *An Interpretation of Christian Ethics*, p. 131.

234. Ibid., p. 7. Quoted from *An Interpretation of Christian Ethics*, p. 144.

235. Ibid., pp. 7-8. Quoted from *An Interpretation of Christian Ethics*, p. 176.

236. Ibid., p. 9.

310 NOTES TO PP. 156-162

237. Ibid., p. 10. Quoted from Niebuhr, *The Children of Light and the Children of Darkness* (New York: Charles Scribner's Sons, 1944), pp. 46–47.

238. Ibid., p. 10.

239. Ibid., p. 11. Quoted from Niebuhr, *Reflections on the End of an Era* (New York: Charles Scribner's Sons, 1934), p. 154.

240. Ibid., p. 12.

241. Ibid. Quoted from *An Interpretation of Christian Ethics*, p. 189.

242. Ibid.

243. Ibid., p. 14.

244. Ibid.

245. Walter Muelder, "Reinhold Niebuhr's Conception of Man," *The Personalist* 36 (1945): 282–93.

246. Ibid., p. 292.

247. *Moral Man and Immoral Society*, p. 252.

248. Ibid., p. 253.

249. Ibid., p. 254.

250. WDWGFH, p. 143. Albert Cleage, Jr.'s contention that King and SCLC had little theology to justify their attempt to change the world neglected the impact on King of the doctrines of the Boston Personalists, Niebuhr, and the theology of the social gospel (*Black Christian Nationalism: New Directions for the Black Church* [New York: William Morrow & Co., Inc., 1972], p. 183).

251. CCG, p. 220. See Henry Nelson Wieman and Walter Horton, *The Growth of Religion*, p. 358.

252. STL, p. 58.

253. Ibid., p. 60.

254. WWCW, p. 82.

255. King, address at the Pilgrimage for Democracy, Dec. 15, 1963, Atlanta, King Collection, I, no. 11, p. 5.

256. WDWGFH, p. 128.

257. King address to the National Bar Association, Milwaukee, Aug. 20, 1959, pp. 2–4.

258. Ibid., p. 3.

259. Ibid.

260. Ibid., pp. 3–5.

261. Ibid., pp. 4, 6. See also STF, pp. 192–93.

262. King, "The Civil Rights Struggle in the United States Today," pp. 22–23.

263. King, address to the National Press Club, July 19, 1962, Washington, D.C., p. 11.

264. WDWGFH, p. 78.

265. STL, p. 62. *Douglass' Monthly*, Jan. 1, 1863, p. 1.

266. WDWGFH, p. 79.

267. Quoted in ibid., p. 79.

268. King, "A New Sense of Direction," p. 7.

269. WDWGFH, p. 80.

270. King, "The Un-Christian Christian," *Ebony* 20, no. 10, Aug. 1965, p. 80.

271. Quoted in Bennett, *What Manner of Man*, p. 11.

Chapter 5: The Social Mission of the Christian Church

1. Walter Rauschenbusch, *Christianity and the Social Crisis*, ed. Robert D. Cross (New York: Harper & Row, Publishers, Torchbook Edition, 1964). First published in 1907 by The Macmillan Company.

2. The present name of the seminary is Colgate Rochester Divinity School-Bexley Hall-Crozer Theological Seminary.

3. STF, p. 91. King emphasized his debt to Rauschenbusch also in STL, pp. 137–38.

4. Quoted in Harry Emerson Fosdick, Introduction, *A Rauschenbusch Reader: The Kingdom of God and the Social Gospel*, ed. Benson Landis (New York: Harper & Brothers, 1957), pp. xv–xvi.

5. Rauschenbusch, *Christianity and the Social Crisis*, p. 2.

6. Ibid., p. 5; Hosea 6:6.

7. Ibid., p. 5; Isaiah 1:15–17.

8. Ibid., p. 6; Micah 6:7–8.

9. Ibid., p. 6; Amos 5:25; Jeremiah 7:22–23.

10. Ibid., p. 29. In *A Theology for the Social Gospel* Rauschenbusch maintained, "If the prophets ever talked about the 'plan of redemption,' they meant the social redemption of the nation" (New York: Macmillan Publishing Co., Inc., 1917), p. 24.

11. Ibid., p. 11.

12. Ibid., p. 12.

13. WWCW, p. 78. See also King, "The Negro Is Your Brother," *Atlantic Monthly* 212, Aug. 1963, p. 78.

14. King, annual address on the Fourth Anniversary of the MIA, Dec. 3, 1959, p. 11; King, address at Mississippi Christian Leadership Conference, Sept. 23, 1959, pp. 17–18.

15. TC, p. 77; Amos 5:24. See also "I Have a Dream."

16. Cf. Mic. 6:8.

17. Cf. Isa. 2:4.

18. Cf. Isa. 11:6 and Mic. 4:4.

19. Cf. Isa. 40:4–5. See also "I Have a Dream."

20. Amos 5:24; STF, p. 210; "The Current Crisis in Race Relations," p. 12; "The Future of Integration," Nov. 11, 1959, The State University of Iowa, King Collection, XIV, pp. 11–12; "I Have a Dream," p. 2; WWCW, p.

92; address at Pilgrimage for Democracy, Dec. 15, 1963, Atlanta, p. 5; "Let Justice Roll Down," p. 274; "I've Been to the Mountain Top," p. 3.

21. King, Commencement address at Lincoln University, June 6, 1961, p. 15.

22. "Let Justice Roll Down," p. 274. See also "I've Been to the Mountain Top," p. 3.

23. STF, p. 210.

24. DeWolf, *A Theology of the Living Church*, p. 77.

25. Rauschenbusch, *Christianity and the Social Crisis*, p. 53.

26. Ibid., p. 54. Mark 1:15.

27. Rauschenbusch, *Christianity and the Social Crisis*, p. 67. In *A Theology for the Social Gospel* Rauschenbusch warned, "A religious experience is not Christian unless it binds us closer to men and commits us more deeply to the Kingdom of God" (p. 105).

28. Rauschenbusch, *Christianity and the Social Crisis,* p. 67.

29. Ibid.

30. Ibid., p. 68. In *A Theology for the Social Gospel* Rauschenbusch indicated that "the Reign of God" came to mean for Jesus "the organized fellowship of humanity acting under the impulse of love" (p. 155).

31. Ibid., pp. 70–77.

32. Ibid., p. 82; Luke 4:17–19.

33. Rauschenbusch, *Christianity and the Social Crisis*, p. 82; Matt. 11:2–5.

34. Rauschenbusch, *Christianity and the Social Crisis*, p. 84.

35. Ibid., pp. 85–92.

36. Ibid., p. 87.

37. STF, p. 40.

38. Rauschenbusch, *Christianity and the Social Crisis*, p. 287.

39. Ibid., p. 355.

40. Ibid., p. 363. John C. Bennett referred to the fact that the representatives of the social gospel did not understand and had little to say about the organized and pervasive oppression and humiliation of American blacks as a confirmation of Marx's and Niebuhr's contention that the comfortable, no matter how just their intentions, do not deal seriously with the burden of injustice until the oppressed become articulate and begin to gain power ("Realism and Hope after Niebuhr," *Worldview* 15, no. 5 [May 1972]: 4).

41. STF, p. 91. See also STL, p. 138.

42. Ibid.

43. Ibid.

44. MM, pp. 21–22.

45. STL, p. 52.

46. King, "Advice for Living," *Ebony* 13, no. 11, Sept. 1958, p. 68.

47. STL, p. 89.

48. King, "I've Been to the Mountain Top," p. 3.

49. King, address at Conference of Religious Leaders under the sponsor-

ship of the President's Committee on Government Contracts, May 11, 1959, Washington, D.C., p. 3.

50. STF, p. 36. E. Franklin Frazier in alluding to the predominately other-worldly outlook in the Negro's religion emphasized that in many of the spirituals death was viewed as a means of escape from the woes and weariness of this world (*The Negro Church in America* [New York: Schocken Books, 1966], pp. 14–15).

51. Ibid., p. 35. See also WWCW, pp. 24–25.

52. Ibid., pp. 116–17.

53. Quoted in "The Prophetic Ministry?," *Newsweek* 60, Aug. 20, 1962, p. 80.

54. WWCW, p. 65.

55. Ibid.

56. WDWGFH, p. 124.

57. King, "I've Been to the Mountain Top," p. 3.

58. Rauschenbusch, *A Theology for the Social Gospel*, p. 142.

59. Ibid.

60. Ibid.

61. Ibid., p. 143.

62. Ibid.

63. Ibid.

64. Ibid.

65. STF, p. 91.

66. Rauschenbusch, *A Theology for the Social Gospel*, pp. 58, 87. Lois Wasserman claimed that King's critique of what he had regarded as Rauschenbusch's "superficial optimism" revealed that he had not read Rauschenbusch's later works. She noted that World War I had caused a change in Rauschenbusch's optimistic view of man and produced in his consciousness a sense of individual and social perversity ("Martin Luther King, Jr.: The Molding of Nonviolence as a Philosophy and Strategy—1955–1963" [Ph.D. diss. in history, Boston University, 1972], p. 11). In making this claim, Wasserman did not know that Kenneth Smith, King's professor and friend at Crozer, maintained that in his conversations with King as a student it had been evident that Rauschenbusch was King's favorite author in the field of ethics and that King had read and pondered all of his major works ("Martin Luther King, Jr.: Reflections of a Former Teacher" *Bulletin of Crozer Theological Seminary* 57, no. 2, Apr. 1965, p. 3).

67. Rauschenbusch, *Christianity and the Social Crisis*, p. 421.

68. DeWolf, *A Theology of the Living Church*, pp. 324–26.

69. Ibid., pp. 325–26; Mark 10:43–44.

70. DeWolf, *A Theology of the Living Church*, p. 326.

71. Ibid.

72. Ibid., p. 317.

73. Ibid.

74. DeWolf, *Responsible Freedom*, p. 208.

75. Ibid.; John 14:17; 16:33.

76. DeWolf, *Responsible Freedom*, p. 209.

77. Ibid., p. 207.

78. Quoted in CCG, p. 36. See Tillich, *Systematic Theology*, 1:23.

79. King, address at Howard University, n.d., p. 6.

80. Ibid.

81. Quoted in S. M. Tewari, "Four Questions on Gandhi's Philosophy: An Attempt at Their Answers," p. 209.

82. King, "Man in a Revolutionary World," p. 257, Martin Luther King, Jr. Center for Nonviolent Social Change. See also King, "The Church and the Race Crisis," *The Christian Century* 75 (Oct. 8, 1958): 1140-41.

83. WDWGFH, p. 99.

84. King, "Man in a Revolutionary World," p. 238. See also King, "Advice for Living," *Ebony* 12, no. 12, Oct. 1957, p. 53.

85. Ibid., p. 240.

86. Ibid.

87. STF, pp. 206-7.

88. King, "Man in a Revolutionary World," p. 240.

89. King, address at Conference of Religious Leaders under the sponsorship of the President's Committee on Government Contracts, May 11, 1959, Washington, D.C., pp. 2, 4.

90. Ibid., pp. 6-7.

91. STF, pp. 25-26.

92. WWCW, pp. 90-91.

93. King, "Man in a Revolutionary World," p. 241. In "The Burning Truth in the South" King stressed that the black religious tradition enabled his philosophy of nonviolence to become a living reality (*The Progressive* 24 [May 1960], pp. 8 ff).

94. E. Franklin Frazier ignored certain basic similarities between Gandhism and Christianity when he made the claim, "Gandhism as a philosophy and a way of life is completely alien to the Negro and has nothing in common with the social heritage of the Negro" (*The Negro Church in America*, p. 75).

95. STF, p. 89.

96. King's interview with Tom Johnson, published in *The Montgomery Advertiser*, Jan. 19, 1956, quoted in Bennett, *What Manner of Man*, p. 72.

97. King, "The Power of Nonviolence," *The Intercollegian,* May 1958, p. 9.

98. Gunnar Jahn's Presentation Speech, *Dear Dr. King*, p. 53.

99. James Smylie highlighted the irony that in the Negro quest for identity in America the theme of exodus and deliverance from bondage derives from the Hebrew experience of slavery in Africa ("On Jesus, Pharaohs, and the Chosen People: Martin Luther King as Biblical Interpreter and Humanist," *Interpretation* 24 [Jan. 1970]: 75).

100. Rathbun, "Martin Luther King: The Theology of Social Action," p. 42. WDWGFH, p. 124.

101. King, "Out of the Long Night of Segregation," *The Presbyterian Outlook*, Feb. 10, 1958, p. 6.

102. For some of the ways in which the Negro Church served as the social and political center of Negro life, see Alex Willingham, "The Religious Basis for Action in the Political Philosophy of Martin Luther King, Jr." (M.A. thesis in political science, University of Iowa, 1965), pp. 52–56.

103. Bayard Rustin, "Montgomery Diary," *Liberation* 1, no. 2 (April 1956): 8.

104. WWCW, p. 96.

105. Ibid., p. 95. See STF, pp. 207. See also King, "The Un-Christian Christian," p. 77, and King, "Advice for Living," *Ebony* 13, no. 4, Feb. 1958, p. 84.

106. STF, p. 208. See also King, "The Current Crisis in Race Relations," p. 11.

107. Quoted in Benjamin Mays, *Seeking To Be a Christian in Race Relations* (New York: Friendship Press, 1957), p. 51.

108. STF, p. 208.

109. Quoted in John Williams, *The King God Didn't Save* (New York: Coward McCann, 1970), p. 129.

110. Quoted in Williams, p. 127. Msgr. Joseph Gremillion's *The Gospel of Peace and Justice* contains documents of Catholic social teaching since Pope John XXIII with commentary by the founding director of the Pontifical Commission on Justice and Peace (Maryknoll, N. Y.: Orbis Books, 1976).

111. STF, p. 208.

112. Benjamin Mays, "The Churches Will Follow," *The Christian Century* 81 (Apr. 22, 1964): 513. In his autobiography Mays revealed that he believed that throughout his lifetime the local white church had been society's most conservative and hypocritical institution in the area of race relations. "When the church maintains a segregated house and simultaneously preaches the fatherhood of God and the brotherhood of man, then surely 'hypocrisy' is the mildest term one can apply. 'Whitened sepulchre' comes to mind" (*Born to Rebel* [New York: Charles Scribner's Sons, 1971], p. 241).

113. WWCW, p. 94.

114. King, address to the National Press Club, July 19, 1962, Washington, D.C., p. 5.

115. See the copy of this statement in the file of the Episcopal Society for Cultural and Racial Unity in The Martin Luther King, Jr. Center for Nonviolent Social Change. Rev. Jerry Falwell felt it necessary to criticize King for using his ministry to achieve social change. Years later, Falwell reversed his position. As a guest on "Firing Line" he stated, "I feel that what King was doing is exactly what we are doing" ("Are We Menaced by the Moral Majority?," Feb. 15, 1981).

116. While criticizing most white clergymen for their refusal to participate in the struggle for civil rights, King did praise some of the white clergymen and churches that had joined the struggle. He indicated that Robert Graetz, a

white minister of the Lutheran Church, who had served on the executive committee of the MIA, had been a constant reminder during the Montgomery Boycott that many white people were applying Christian love in their daily lives (STF, p. 74). King acknowledged that some white churches outside Montgomery had given financial support to the boycott. During the Albany Movement seventy-five white ministers and rabbis came to the community to lend their support to his efforts. In his "Letter from Birmingham Jail," while expressing his disappointment with the white church, King did mention that he was mindful that each of the clergy who had signed the statement criticizing his demonstrations in Birmingham had taken some significant stands on the race issue, and he singled out for commendation Rev. Earl Stallings for welcoming blacks to his worship service at the First Baptist Church on a nonsegregated basis. He also praised the Catholic leaders of Alabama for having integrated Spring Hill College several years before (WWCW, p. 93). After the publication of this letter, Rev. Eugene Carson Blake, national head of the United Presbyterian Church, participated in a protest march with two dozen other clergymen and was arrested. In his account of the Birmingham Movement King was pleased to report that nationally renowned religious leaders such as Rev. Blake had joined the demonstrations and had taken their place in jail cells, and that Catholic priests and rabbis were in the front lines of these demonstrations (WWCW, p. 129). He stressed that the March on Washington had been officially endorsed by the National Council of Churches of Christ in the U.S.A., the American Baptist Convention, the Brethren Church, the United Presbyterian Church in the U.S.A., and by thousands of congregations and ministers of the Lutheran and Methodist churches (WWCW, p. 135). He reported that in the archdiocese of New York letters had been read in all the parishes containing Cardinal Francis Spellman's call for accelerated activity on racial justice with an additional appeal from the auxiliary bishop, Most Rev. John Maguire. He referred to the fact that Cardinal Richard Cushing of Boston had named eleven priests to represent him at the march. He also indicated that the American Jewish Congress and virtually every other major Jewish organization, religious and secular, had endorsed the march and had been heavily represented at the gathering, and that Dr. Joachim Prinz, president of the American Jewish Congress, had been one of the chairmen of the march (ibid.). King contended that in 1963 he witnessed an unprecedented coalition of conscience. "Church groups came out in 1963 in a way they never had come out in the past in terms of active participation by white clergymen and many of the lay leaders in white churches" ("Boycotts Will Be Used," p. 60). A *Newsweek* poll in 1963 reported that 58 percent of the blacks questioned thought that Catholic priests were helpful in their cause (cited in Williams, *The King God Didn't Save*, p. 128). King acknowledged that religious bodies had done extensive lobbying for the passage of the Civil Rights Bill in 1964 ("The Un-Christian Christian," p. 79). Andrew Young claimed that the Church is the key to any social change in America. In an interview with James McGraw he stated, "The passage of the 1964 Civil Rights Bill taught me this. When you finally needed to cut off the Southern filibuster, it was Eugene Carson Blake, the Methodist Bishops Lord and Mathews, Bob Spike and the NCC's Commission on Religion and Race, Anna Hedgeman and that bunch that mobilized the churches in the Middle West to put pressure on Senator Hickenlooper of Iowa. He called in other senators and about five to seven votes in that block swung. And that gave the two-thirds majority to cut off the debate and get the Civil Rights Bill passed" ("An Interview with Andrew J. Young," *Christianity and Crisis*, Jan. 22, 1968, p. 330). During the Selma Movement more than a hundred white ministers picketed and were arrested, and hundreds more participated in the march to Montgomery. The participation of clergymen of many denominations in this march caused Mary McGrory to describe it as "America's first dramatic display of ecumenical power" ("Spring Campaign for the Poor," *America*, Feb. 24, 1968, p. 247). James McClendon, Jr. in a review of books on King claimed, "When Methodist and Orthodox bishops. nuns and priests, ministers, rabbis and laymen of every sort linked arms with Martin King to march in Selma or Montgomery, the ecumenical dimension of faith came to life in America as never before" ("M. L. King: Politician or American Church Father?," *Journal of Ecumenical Studies* 8, no. 1, Winter 1971, p. 115). In commenting on the Meredith Mississippi March, King praised Bishop Paul Moore of the Episcopal Church for declaring his intention to join the march despite opposition by some of the young black activists who had objected to participation by whites (WDWGFH, p. 95). During the Chicago Movement Archbishop John Cody marched with King through a hostile white neighborhood.

117. STF, p. 209.

118. Ibid.

119. Rev. John Morris, address before the Michigan chapter of the Episcopal Society for Cultural and Racial Unity, May 29, 1962, at St. Paul's Episcopal Cathedral, Detroit. A release containing excerpts from this address is in the ESCRU file at The Martin Luther King, Jr. Center for Nonviolent Social Change.

120. Ibid.

121. Ibid. At that time Dr. Joseph Jackson, president of the National Baptist Convention, also was a critic of King, vigorously opposed his civil disobedience, supported "law and order," and rejected all proposals to help King during the Albany Movement (Williams, *The King God Didn't Save*, p. 54).

122. STF, pp. 96–97, 101. James Cone affirmed that King's life and message demonstrated that the "soul" of the black community cannot be separated from liberation which is always grounded in Jesus Christ (*A Black Theology of Liberation* [New York: J. B. Lippincott Company, 1970], p. 78).

123. STL, p. 99.

124. STF, p. 92.

125. Ibid., p. 93, 95.

126. STL, p. 96.

127. Ibid.

128. Ibid.; Amos 5:24. Erich Fromm described Marx's aim of socialism with its concern for the emancipation of man as essentially prophetic Messianism in the language of the nineteenth century (*Marx's Concept of Man* [New York: Frederick Ungar Publishing Co., 1966], p. 5).

129. Ibid.

130. Karl Marx and Friedrich Engels, *The Manifesto of the Communist Party* in *Marx and Engels: Basic Writings on Politics and Philosophy*, ed. Lewis Feuer (New York: Doubleday & Company, Anchor Book, 1959), p. 29. Wilson Record noted that Marx had been critical of President Lincoln for his hesitation in issuing the Emancipation Proclamation ("The Development of the Communist Position on the Negro Question in the United States," *Phylon* 19, no. 3 [Fall 1958]: 312).

131. STL, p. 98.

132. WDWGFH, p. 186.

133. STL, p. 98.

134. STF, pp. 92, 94. See also STL, p. 94. Alan Stang did not take into account King's explicit rejection of materialism when he charged that although King did not say it he knew that in the context of his program to think in terms of thesis, antithesis, and a new synthesis was nothing else but dialectical materialism. Stang seemed to be unaware that his own logic would have compelled him to regard Hegel, whose philosophy rested on the recognition of the reality of spirit, as a dialectical materialist (*It's Very Simple: The True Story of Civil Rights* [Boston: Western Islands Publishers, 1965], p. 149).

135. Karl Marx, *Capital: A Critique of Political Economy* in *Marx and Engels: Basic Writings on Politics and Philosophy*, p. 145.

136. King, "Let Us Be Dissatisfied," *Gandhi Marg* 12 (1968): 226.

137. STF, p. 94.

138. Quoted in STL, p. 94.

139. Ibid., p. 95. C. J. Curtis, in effect if not in intention, distorted King's doctrine on this point when he wrote, "Such a theology of social change, as King proposed, insisted that the end justifies the means. The end is reconciliation, forgiveness, and authentic human communion. This end justifies the means of sit-ins, demonstrations, boycotts, and the refusal to cooperate with social structures which serve unjust ends" (*Contemporary Protestant Thought* [New York: The Bruce Publishing Co., 1970], p. 205).

140. King, address to the National Press Club, July 19, 1962, Washington, D.C., p. 8.

141. Quoted in CCG, p. 208.

142. Quoted in William Nelson, "Satyagraha: Gandhian Principles of Non-Violent Non-Cooperation," p. 19.

143. STL, p. 95.

144. Marx and Engels, *The Manifesto of the Communist Party*, p. 28.

145. Adam Schaff presented an elaborate defense of Marx's concern for

the individual and his happiness in *Marxism and the Human Individual* (New York: McGraw-Hill, 1970).

146. STF, p. 93.

147. King, "Let Us Be Dissatisfied," p. 226. See also STF, p. 95, and WDWGFH, p. 187.

148. STL, p. 93.

149. Ibid., pp. 93, 97, 100.

150. Ibid., p. 96.

151. Ibid., p. 100.

152. WWCW, p. 37. See also the last section of "This Is SCLC," brochure, The Martin Luther King, Jr. Center for Nonviolent Social Change.

In *The Problem of Christianity* Josiah Royce stated, "The principle of principles in all Christian morals remains this: 'Since you cannot find the universal and beloved community, create it' " (New York: Archon Books, 1967, p. 359). (This work was published by the Macmillan Company in 1913.) In sharp contrast to the later view of Nygren, Royce in his development of the "Idea of the Universal Community" rejected the notion that Christian love demands self-abnegation, and he affirmed that man has an essentially infinite value (pp. 79–80). Royce's works were part of the recommended reading in DeWolf's courses. Paul Johnson in *Christian Love* maintained that Christian love "reaches out to the enemy to reconcile him, to the stranger to make him a friend, and to the neighbor to unite in creating a beloved community" (p. 46).

153. STL, p. 23. See also King, "The Ethical Demands of Integration," *Religion and Labor* (May 1963): 3 ff.

154. *Playboy Interviews*, p. 381.

155. STF, p. 99.

156. STL, p. 91.

157. King, "Reinhold Niebuhr," Research Paper, King Collection, XIV, no. 58, p. 4.

158. King, "The Death of Evil upon the Seashore," p. 1.

159. STL, p. 59. The editors of *Commonweal* seemed not to know of this emphasis in King's thought when in an editorial, "Dr. King's Legacy," they repeated the argument that nonviolence cannot work since it seems to presuppose an angelic conception of man's dignity rarely encountered in reality (Apr. 19, 1968, p. 125).

160. King, "How Modern Christians Should Think of Man," p. 5.

161. Ibid.

162. Niebuhr, *The Christian Century* (Dec. 18, 1940), n.p., quoted in Marvin Green, "A Theory of Evil in the Tension Ethics of Reinhold Niebuhr," *The Personalist* 26, no. 4 (Autumn 1945): 371.

163. DeWolf, *A Theology of the Living Church*, pp. 187–89.

164. Ibid., p. 187; Mark 10:18.

165. DeWolf, *A Theology of the Living Church*, p. 188; Matt. 5:48; Rom. 3:23.

166. DeWolf, *A Theology of the Living Church*, pp. 182, 188.

167. Ibid., p. 188.

168. King, "Love, Law, and Civil Disobedience," p. 6.

169. Brightman, "A Personalistic View of Human Nature," p. 9.

170. Brightman, "A Personalistic Philosophy of History," p. 5.

171. Brightman, "The Best Possible World," p. 8.

172. STL, p. 23.

173. Ibid.

174. King, address to the National Bar Association, Aug. 20, 1959, Milwaukee, p. 8.

175. STF, p. 85.

176. STL, p. 64. Smith and Zepp used this same text as evidence for their intrepretation that King believed that the beloved community would be actualized within history. *Search for the Beloved Community*, p. 140. The text seems *at least* to indicate that the beloved community might not be realized within history. Then too, Smith and Zepp's interpretation contradicted their previous correct statement that Niebuhr's Christian "realism" qualified King's initial optimism about the possibility of actualizing the beloved community within history (p. 119). In an article, "Martin Luther King's Vision of the Beloved Community," Smith and Zepp presented the same interpretation (*The Christian Century* [Apr. 3, 1974]: 361–63). Zepp should not have abandoned his earlier interpretation, which was based mainly on King's dependence on Niebuhr. At the conclusion of his dissertation Zepp had stated that perhaps King's dream, as King understood it, remained a dream which should be the object of our strivings but which would never be totally realized in history (p. 318).

177. Interview with L. Harold DeWolf by the author on July 18, 1974 in Washington, D.C.

178. DeWolf, *Crime and Justice in America: A Paradox of Conscience* (New York: Harper & Row Publishers, 1975), p. 144. See Niebuhr, *An Interpretation of Christian Ethics*, p. 140.

179. Brightman, "A Personalistic View of Human Nature," p. 12.

180. B. Sharma, "The Ideal and the Actual in Gandhi's Philosophy," *Gandhi: His Relevance for Our Times*, p. 312.

181. Nirmal Bose, ed., *Selections from Gandhi* (Ahmedabad: Navajivan Publishing House, 1948), p. 8, quoted in Donald Bishop, "Gandhi and the Concept of Love," p. 324.

182. Gandhi, *Non-violence in Peace and War*, 1:58, quoted in Manick Samuel, "A Comparative Study of the Methods of Non-violence as Used by Martin Luther King, Jr. and Mahatma Gandhi," p. 26.

183. Rauschenbusch, *Christianity and the Social Crisis*, p. 420, quoted in Smith and Zepp, *Search for the Beloved Community*, p. 45.

184. STL, p. 136.

185. Ibid., p. 64.

186. King, "The Future of Integration," p. 2.

187. King, Nobel Lecture, *Dear Dr. King*, p. 62.

188. King, Nobel Acceptance Speech, *Dear Dr. King*, p. 58.

189. *Playboy Interviews*, p. 383.

190. King, "A Testament of Hope," p. 7.

191. Ibid., p. 6.

192. King, "I've Been to the Mountain Top," p. 2.

193. Ibid., p. 6.

194. TC, p. 4.

195. King, address at Prayer Pilgrimage for Freedom, May 17, 1957, Washington, D.C., p. 4.

196. STF, pp. 105-6.

197. King, "The Death of Evil upon the Seashore," p. 4.

198. King, address at the Prayer Pilgrimage for Freedom, May 17, 1957, p. 4.

199. STL, pp. 58-63.

200. TC, pp. 76-77.

201. Smith and Zepp stated that according to DeWolf King regarded himself as a medium for the communication of a dream from God to his people (*Search for the Beloved Community*, p. 126).

202. King, Nobel Lecture, p. 66.

203. King, address to the National Press Club, July 19, 1962, Washington, D.C., p. 13.

204. King, address at the 30th Anniversary of District 65, Oct. 23, 1963, New York City, King Collection, X, no. 9, p. 2.

205. King, "Who Speaks for the South?," p. 13.

206. King, "A View of the Dawn," address accepting 1957 Social Justice Award of the Religion and Labor Foundation, *Interracial Review* 30, no. 5 (May 1957): 84.

207. King, "The Rising Tide of Racial Consciousness," p. 6.

208. WDWGFH, pp. 84-85.

209. Ralph McGill, former publisher of the *Atlanta Constitution*, in "The South Will Change" asserted that the historically unique feature of the Negro struggle was that the Negro was trying to become more American, not less (*We Dissent*, ed. Hoke Norris [New York: St. Martin's Press, 1962], p. 62).

210. King, address at the Bethel Baptist Church, Dec. 3, 1959, Montgomery, pp. 9-10.

211. King, address to the National Bar Association, Aug. 20, 1959, Milwaukee, p. 12.

Chapter 6: King's Critiques of Other Responses to Collective Evil

1. Booker T. Washington, *Up From Slavery* (New York: Doubleday & Company, 1963), p. 159.

2. Ibid., p. 158.

3. Ibid., pp. 159–60.

4. Ibid., p. 160.

5. Ibid., p. 161.

6. Ibid., pp. 163–64.

7. Ibid., p. 165.

8. William E. B. DuBois, *The Souls of Black Folk* (New York: Fawcett Publications, 1961), p. 48.

9. Ibid.

10. Ibid., pp. 48–49.

11. Ibid., p. 49.

12. Ibid.

13. Ibid.

14. Ibid., p. 51.

15. Ibid.

16. WWCW, p. 22.

17. WDWGFH, p. 129.

18. WWCW, p. 22.

19. STF, p. 212.

20. WDWGFH, p. 129. Although Washington during most of his public life did not speak out forcefully against most forms of racial segregation, in an article shortly before his death he strongly denounced the attempt to maintain residential segregation ("My View of Segregation Laws," *The New Republic* 5 [Dec. 4, 1915]: 113–14). Daniel Walden alluded to the claim that Washington's own correspondence revealed extensive efforts against segregation and disfranchisement. Without identifying with this claim, Walden did indicate that there was some evidence for it in the Francis J. Garrison Papers in the Schomburg Library in New York City, especially letters to T. T. Fortune, Nov. 10, 1899, and to Garrison, Feb. 27 and Mar. 11, 1900 ("The Contemporary Opposition to the Political and Educational Ideals of Booker T. Washington," *The Journal of Negro History* [Apr. 1960]: 112).

21. WWCW, p. 22.

22. Ibid.

23. W. E. B. DuBois, "The Training of Negroes for Social Power," *W. E. B. DuBois Speaks*, ed. Philip Foner (New York: Pathfinder Press, 1970), 1:133.

24. DuBois, *The Souls of Black Folk*, p. 85.

25. *W. E. B. DuBois: The Crisis Writings*, ed. Daniel Walden (New York: Fawcett Publications, Inc., 1972; June 1912), pp. 136–37.

26. Ibid., p. 139.

27. Ibid. (Feb. 1918), p. 151.

28. Ibid. (Nov. 1917), p. 143.

29. DuBois, *The Souls of Black Folk*, pp. 53–54.

30. Ibid., pp. 77–78.

31. *W. E. B. DuBois: The Crisis Writings* (July 1914), p. 142.

32. King, "Honoring Dr. DuBois," p. 105. Lenneal Henderson, Jr.,

maintained that the ingredients which led Washington and DuBois to their respective race ideologies lay largely in their different backgrounds ("W. E. B. DuBois: Black Scholar and Prophet," *The Black Scholar* [Jan.–Feb. 1970]: 53–54).

33. Ibid., p. 107. In this speech King also praised two more of DuBois's works, viz., *The Suppression of the African Slave-Trade to the United States of America*, 1638–1870 (New York: The Social Science Press, 1954), and *The Philadelphia Negro: A Social Study* (New York: Benjamin Blom, 1967, first published in 1899). The former became Volume One of the Harvard Classics. The latter revealed to King the painstaking quality of DuBois's scientific method since he conducted five thousand interviews for this work.

34. Ibid.

35. Ibid., p. 108.

36. Ibid., p. 109.

37. In 1910, Garvey sought to promote the interests of the working class in Jamaica through his first political organization, the National Club.

38. Amy Jacques-Garvey, ed., *Philosophy and Opinions of Marcus Garvey*, 2 vols. (New York: Atheneum Publishers, 1971), 1:102.

39. Ibid., 2:37.

40. Ibid., 2:35–36. Garvey opened the first International Convention of the Universal Negro Improvement Association in New York City on August 1, 1920, by reading the message that he had sent to Eamon DeValera, president of the Irish Republic. The message in part read, "Please accept sympathy of the Negroes of the world for your cause. We believe Ireland should be free even as Africa shall be free for the Negroes of the world. Keep up the fight for a free Ireland" (quoted in Elton C. Fax, *Garvey: The Story of a Pioneer Black Nationalist* [New York: Dodd Mead and Company, 1972], p. 3).

41. Amy Jacques-Garvey, ed., *Philosophy and Opinions of Marcus Garvey*, 2:19.

42. Ibid., 1:7.

43. Quoted by Hollis Lynch in the Preface to *Philosophy and Opinions of Marcus Garvey*, n.p.

44. Ibid., Preface. See W. E. B. DuBois, *Dust of Dawn* (New York: Harcourt Brace and Co., 1940), p. 277.

45. WWCW, pp. 22–23.

46. King, "Advice for Living," *Ebony* 13, no. 3, Jan. 1958, p. 34.

47. WDWGFH, pp. 43–44.

48. *Playboy Interviews*, p. 370.

49. *Philosophy and Opinions of Marcus Garvey*, 1:14, 27, 32, 65, 78, 89, 91, 93, 94.

50. WDWGFH, p. 47.

51. Ibid., p. 48.

52. WWCW, p. 23.

53. *Philosophy and Opinions of Marcus Garvey*, 1:12, 72, 91; 2:32.

54. Ibid., 2:19.

55. Ibid., 1:9, 102.

56. Ibid., 1:12, 54, 66; 2:34.

57. Ibid., 2:43.

58. Ibid., 1:98.

59. Ibid., 2:1.

60. King, "Advice for Living," *Ebony* 13, no. 5, Mar. 1958, p. 92 and 13, no. 4, Feb. 1958, p. 84.

61. *Philosophy and Opinions of Marcus Garvey*, 2:38.

62. Ibid., 2:3.

63. Ibid., 1:26.

64. Ibid., 1:53.

65. Ibid., 1:6.

66. Ibid., 1:48.

67. Ibid., 2:32.

68. Ibid., 2:43.

69. Ibid., 2:71. William Foster described Garvey's development as a transition from an early radicalism to a conservatism that amounted to a surrender of the Negro people into the hands of their worst enemies on a national and international scale. He accused Garvey of abandoning his demands for Negro rights and of concentrating totally on his utopian plan for a mass return to Africa (*The Negro People in American History* [New York: International Publishers, 1954], pp. 447–49).

70. *Philosophy and Opinions of Marcus Garvey*, 1:75.

71. WDWGFH, p. 29.

72. Ibid., p. 30.

73. Ibid.

74. Ibid.

75. Ibid., p. 32.

76. Ibid.

77. Ibid., p. 33.

78. Ibid., pp. 33–34.

79. Ibid., p. 34.

80. Ibid., pp. 34–35.

81. Ibid., pp. 35–36.

82. Ibid., pp. 36–37.

83. Ibid., p. 38.

84. Ibid.

85. Ibid., p. 39. See Kenneth Stampp, *The Peculiar Institution: Slavery in the Ante-Bellum South* (New York: Alfred A. Knopf, 1972), pp. 141–48 (first published in 1956).

86. Ibid. See Stampp, p. 145.

87. Ibid. See Stampp, p. 145.

88. Stampp, *The Peculiar Institution*, p. 146.

89. WDWGFH, p. 39. See Stampp, p. 147.

90. Stokely Carmichael, "A New World To Build," speech at A & T University, Greensboro, N. C., Dec. 9, 1968, *Stokely Speaks: Black Power Back to Pan-Africanism*, ed. Ethel Minor (New York: Vintage Books, 1971), p. 147.

91. Stokely Carmichael, speech before the Congress on the Dialectics of Liberation in London on July 18, 1967, *Stokely Speaks*, p. 80. See Albert Camus, *The Rebel* (New York: Vintage Books, 1956), pp. 23–25.

92. WDWGFH, p. 41.

93. Ibid., p. 46.

94. Ibid., p. 51. When Albert Cleage, Jr., wrote that while King was organizing mass demonstrations, whites were showing that when blacks appeared to threaten white institutions, all whites would come together, Cleage did not consider the participation of whites in the second and third marches from Selma in 1965 as well as the passage of the Civil Rights Bill in 1964 and the Voting Rights Bill in 1965 by a predominately white Congress (*Black Christian Nationalism: New Directions for the Black Church*, Introd., p. xxxiii).

95. Ibid., p. 52.

96. Ibid.

97. Ibid., p. 53.

98. Stokely Carmichael and Charles Hamilton, *Black Power: The Politics of Liberation in America* (New York: Vintage Books, 1967), p. 55.

99. WDWGFH, p. 56. See King, "Nonviolence: The Only Road to Freedom," p. 29.

100. Ibid., p. 30.

101. *Stokely Speaks*, pp. 59–60.

102. Ibid., p. 56.

103. Ibid., pp. 72–74.

104. Ibid., p. 78.

105. Ibid., p. 88. While James Cone acknowledged that King may not have endorsed the concept of Black Power, he claimed that the advocates of Black Power attempted to make King's dream a reality (*Black Theology and Black Power* [New York: The Seabury Press, 1969], p. 109). This claim overlooked King's insistence on nonviolent means as an integral part of his dream of freedom and equality.

106. Ibid., p. 114.

107. Stokely Carmichael and Charles Hamilton, *Black Power*, Preface, p. viii.

108. Stokely Carmichael, speech at Oakland Auditorium, Feb. 17, 1968, *Stokely Speaks*, p. 125.

109. *Stokely Speaks*, p. 115.

110. Ibid., p. 124.

111. Ibid., p. 115.

112. WWCW, p. 90.

113. C. Eric Lincoln, *The Black Muslims in America* (Boston: Beacon Press, 1961), p. 73. See also George Kelsey, *Racism and the Christian Understanding of Man,* pp. 68–69.

114. Quoted in Kelsey, p. 121.

115. Ibid., p. 166. See Lincoln, p. 89.

116. Ibid., p. 38. See Lincoln, p. 135.

117. Elijah Muhammad, "Mr. Muhammad Speaks," *The Pittsburgh Courier,* Dec. 13, 1958, p. 14, quoted in Kelsey, p. 39.

118. Kelsey, pp. 42–43.

119. Quoted in Arthur Littleton and Mary Burger, eds., *Black Viewpoints* (New York: The New American Library, 1971), p. 156.

120. Kelsey, p. 152.

121. Ibid., pp. 51–52.

122. Ibid., p. 55.

123. TC, pp. 8–9.

124. STL, p. 28.

125. WDWGFH, p. 62.

126. George Breitman, ed., *Malcolm X Speaks* (New York: Pathfinder Press, 1965), p. 9. John Williams related that his conversation with Malcolm X in early 1964 revealed that the "distance" between Malcolm and King was "small indeed," but Williams contradicted this when he ironically added, "Malcolm was even willing to sing, 'We Shall Overcome,' just so long as all who were singing had .45s firmly in hand" (*The King God Didn't Save,* p. 77).

127. STF, p. 102.

128. Ibid., p. 98.

129. Kenneth Clark, ed., *The Negro Protest*, p. 41.

130. Ibid.

131. Ibid., p. 23.

132. WDWGFH, p. 125.

133. Malcolm X and Alex Haley, *The Autobiography of Malcolm X* (New York: Grove Press, 1965), p. 362.

134. Ibid.

135. WDWGFH, p. 46. See STL, p. 83.

136. Ibid., p. 26.

137. STF, p. 222–23.

138. Ibid., pp. 29–69. King also stated that the arrest of Claudette Colvin, who had refused to give up her seat to a white passenger, caused the black community shortly before the boycott to begin to shed its apathy and to develop a new spirit of courage and self-respect (STF, pp. 41–42).

139. King, "Advice for Living," *Ebony* 13, no. 10, Aug. 1958, p. 78.

140. King, address to the National Press Club, July 19, 1962, Washington, D.C., p. 12.

141. STL, p. 80.

142. Rollo May, *Love and Will* (New York: W. W. Norton & Company, 1969), p. 29.

143. STF, p. 222. See King, speech at the Crusade for Citizenship, Feb. 12, 1958, Miami, p. 3.

144. WDWGFH, p. 154.

145. Ibid., p. 155. See also King, address on the Fourth Anniversary of the MIA, Dec. 3, 1959, p. 11.

146. Ibid., p. 127. See also STL, p. 70, and King, address on the Fourth Anniversary of the MIA, p. 12.

147. STF, p. 218.

148. STL, p. 20.

149. WDWGFH, p. 132.

150. King, address at Mississippi Christian Leadership Conference, Sept. 23, 1959, p. 28.

151. TC, p. 46.

152. STF, p. 202.

153. WWCW, p. 89.

154. Ibid., p. 43.

155. King, "The Civil Rights Struggle in the United States Today," p. 12.

156. Ibid.

157. King, Nobel Acceptance Speech, *Dear Dr. King*, pp. 57–58.

158. King, address on the Fourth Anniversary of the MIA, p. 10.

159. Quoted in CCG, p. 312. See Tillich, *Systematic Theology*, 1:182.

160. DeWolf, *A Theology of the Living Church*, pp. 165–67, 171–76.

161. Ibid., p. 165.

162. Ibid., James 4:17.

163. 1 Cor. 10:12, DeWolf, p. 165.

164. DeWolf, p. 166. Rom. 11:15; 20:23.

165. Ibid.

166. Ibid., p. 172.

167. Ibid., p. 171. See Max Planck, *Where Is Science Going?* in *The New Science* (New York: Meridian Books, 1959), p. 118 (first published in 1932).

168. Ibid. See Arthur Eddington, *New Pathways in Science* (New York: The Macmillan Co., 1935), p. 90.

169. Ibid., p. 172.

170. Ibid.

171. Ibid., p. 174.

172. Ibid., p. 177.

Chapter 7: King's Rejection of Violent Resistance

1. WDWGFH, p. 55.

2. Frantz Fanon, *The Wretched of the Earth*, trans. Constance Farrington (New York: Grove Press, 1968), p. 94.

3. Ibid., p. 37.

4. Ibid.

5. Ibid., p. 316. Quoted in WDWGFH, p. 66.

6. WDWGFH, p. 64. See also STF, p. 106.

7. STF, p. 106.

8. STL, p. 112.

9. Ibid., p. 114.

10. King, "Let Us Be Dissatisfied," p. 225.

11. STL, p. 113.

12. Kenneth Clark contended that there might be an unrealistic, if not pathological, basis in King's doctrine since it requires that a victim should love his oppressor. He asserted that such a requirement imposes an additional and probably intolerable psychological burden (*Dark Ghetto: Dilemmas of Social Power* [New York: Harper & Row, Publishers, Torchbook Edition, 1965], p. 218). Clark did not explore the possibility that *agape* with a foundation in religious faith in fact may impose a more manageable burden than do the alternatives, viz., apathy, tactical nonviolent resistance, or hate and violence.

13. King, "The Current Crisis in Race Relations," p.9.

14. *Playboy Interviews*, p. 371.

15. King, "Our Struggle," p. 295.

16. WDWGFH, p. 56. Joseph Washington, Jr., rejected what he regarded as King's assumption that Black Power as violence was "doomed from the start," and made the judgment that a growing minority of whites was fully aware that the black revolution with violence, if and when it occurred, would not be anti-white but pro-American (*Black and White Power Subreption* [Boston: Beacon Press, 1969], pp. 200–01).

17. Ibid., pp. 56–57.

18. Ibid., pp. 57–58. See King, "Let Us Be Dissatisfied," p. 224.

19. TC, p. 15.

20. WDWGFH, p. 112.

21. Ibid., p. 130.

22. Ibid., p. 59.

23. Ibid., pp. 62–63.

24. Ibid., p. 59.

25. TC, p. 8.

26. STF, p. 194.

27. TC, p. 16.

28. Ibid., pp. 6, 10. See also King, "A New Sense of Direction," pp. 6–7.

29. STF, pp. 199–200.

30. WWCW, p. 87.

31. Ibid., p. 130.

32. TC, p. 10.

33. Ibid., p. 11.

34. King, "A Testament of Hope," p. 6.

35. TC, p. 11.

36. "Which Way for the Negro?," *Newsweek*, May 15, 1967, p. 33.

37. TC, p. 12.

38. Ibid. For a quite different view of the riots see Richard M. Nixon, "What Has Happened in America?," *Reader's Digest*, Oct. 1967, pp. 49-54. He appealed to the dictim of Theodore Roosevelt, "No man is above the law and no man is below it, nor do we ask any man's permission when we require him to obey it" (p. 51). Calling for swift and sure justice for the rioters, he emphasized that the first step toward preventing riots was to have better pay, better training, and higher standards for police, and that the second step was to have a substantial increase in the number of police.

39. *Report of the National Advisory Commission on Civil Disorders*, Advance Copy (New York: Bantam Books, 1968), pp. 203-4.

40. Ibid., pp. 204-6.

41. Ibid., p. 206.

42. TC, p. 12.

43. Kenneth Clark, "The Wonder Is There Have Been So Few Riots," *The New York Times Magazine*, Sept. 5, 1965, in *Black Protest in the Sixties*, ed. August Meier and Eliott Rudwick (Chicago: Quadrangle Books, 1970), pp. 107-15.

44. Ibid., p. 109.

45. Ibid., p. 108.

46. Ibid.

47. Ibid., p. 112.

48. Ibid., p. 110.

49. Ibid., p. 115.

50. TC, p. 13.

51. WDWGFH, p. 113.

52. TC, p. 56.

53. Ibid., p. 41.

54. "Man of the Year," *Time*, Jan. 3, 1964, p. 13.

55. "How Martin Luther King Won the Nobel Peace Prize," *U.S. News & World Report*, Feb. 8, 1965, p. 76.

56. Hanes Walton, Jr., *The Political Philosophy of Martin Luther King, Jr.,* p. 85.

57. Frank Meyer, "The Violence of Nonviolence," *National Review* 17, no. 16 (Apr. 20, 1965): 327. After King's assassination this journal described him in an editorial as an apostle of peace in his own awesome fashion and contended that he had abhorred violence by blacks because he had seen that it was self-defeating ("Dr. King," Apr. 23, 1968, p. 379).

58. Ibid.

59. Ibid.

60. King, "Behind the Selma March," *Saturday Review* 48 Apr. 3, 1965, p. 16.

61. Ibid., p. 57.

62. STF, pp. 137–38.

63. Ibid., p. 133.

64. Ibid., pp. 164, 169.

65. Quoted in William Miller, *Martin Luther King, Jr.,* p. 92.

66. "Revolt Without Violence—The Negroes' New Strategy," p. 77.

67. WDWGFH, pp. 26–27.

68. TC, p. 58. John Williams in effect disregarded all of King's attempts to promote nonviolence when he chose to interpret King's description of himself as "militant" to mean not only "combative and aggressive" but also "engaged in warfare." The context of Williams's interpretation revealed that he was not referring to nonviolent warfare (*The King God Didn't Save*, p. 181). Albert Cleage, Jr., claimed that not only the people who marched but also those who looted and those who burned had been in a deep sense King's disciples (*The Black Messiah* [New York: Sheed & Ward, 1968], p. 211). Cleage refused to see that one could not be King's follower if one resorted to violence.

69. WWCW, p. 106.

70. King, "I've Been to the Mountain Top," p. 2.

71. King, "The Civil Rights Struggle in the United States Today," p. 7.

72. *Playboy Interviews*, p. 356.

73. TC, p. 5. Abraham Muste perceived that the moral revulsion Americans experienced when fire hoses and cattle prods were used on women and children in Birmingham and when four girls were murdered in a Birmingham church contributed much to the introduction of the Civil Rights Bill and its passage, and to the increase in the number of college students in support of civil rights. He maintained that the sporadic violence of blacks with which they reacted to brutality toward their women and children had not diluted this moral revulsion ("Nonviolence and Mississippi," *Gandhi: His Relevance for Our Times*, ed. G. Ramachandran and T. Mahadevan, p. 211).

74. Quoted in Lewis, *King: A Critical Biography*, pp. 338–39. August Meier was mistaken when he contended in "The Conservative Militant" that it was contrary to King's deepest wishes that his demonstrations precipitated violence from Southern whites against Negro and white demonstrators since, as we have seen, King in his explanation of the second march from Selma stated he was willing to undergo this violence (Meier, pp. 146–47).

75. WWCW, pp. 88–89.

76. Ibid., p. 168.

77. WDWGFH, p. 91.

78. Gandhi, *Young India*, Jan. 23, 1930, *Non-violent Resistance*, p. 222.

79. WDWGFH, p. 58.

80. *Playboy Interviews*, p. 358.

81. King, "Behind the Selma March," pp. 17, 57. Eldridge Cleaver contended that King by not attempting to go through the troopers on this march "denied history a great moment, never to be recaptured." Cleaver argued

that if the police had resorted again to violence, this time with nuns, priests, rabbis, preachers, and distinguished laymen, the violence and brutality of the system would have been exposed, or if the troopers had allowed them to pass, it would have indicated that the militant white South had capitulated (*Soul on Ice* [New York: McGraw-Hill Book Company, 1968], p. 74). Cleaver seemed to attach no value to King's attempts to reduce the violence from the opposition and saw no significance in the fact that the third march which King successfully conducted with the protection of the Federal Government resulted in the passage of the 1965 Voting Rights Bill. In commenting on King's refusal to attempt to march past the troopers on the second march from Selma, August Meier maintained that this refusal to occasion a possible bloodbath had helped preserve King's image in the eyes of whites as a leader of heroic moral stature, and that his willingness to be cautious and to engage in compromise had kept open the lines of communication between the activists and the majority of whites. Meier concluded that King by this type of activity had made the Nonviolent Movement respectable ("The Conservative Militant," p. 150).

82. Miller, *Martin Luther King, Jr.,* p. 108.

83. King, "Who Is Their God?," *The Nation* 195, no. 11 (Oct. 13, 1962): 210.

84. King, "After the March," n.d., p. 2, Martin Luther King, Jr. Center for Nonviolent Social Change.

85. King, "A Testament of Hope," p. 7.

86. WDWGFH, p. 56.

87. Julian Bond, *A Time To Speak: A Time To Act* (New York: Simon & Schuster, 1972), pp. 13-14.

88. Sheldon Stoff and Herbert Schwartzberg, eds., *The Human Encounter: Readings in Education* (New York: Harper & Row, Publishers, 1973), p. 137.

89. Hanes Walton, Jr., *The Political Philosophy of Martin Luther King, Jr.,* p. 85.

90. Frank Meyer, "The Violence of Nonviolence," p. 327.

91. Ibid.

92. Lionel Lokos, *The Life and Legacy of Martin Luther King* (New Rochelle, N.Y.: Arlington House, 1968), p. 99.

93. "Boycotts Will Be Used," p. 59.

94. King, "Beyond the Los Angeles Riots," *Saturday Review,* Nov. 13, 1965, p. 35.

95. Quoted from the *New South,* Winter 1966, p. 98 in Miller, *Martin Luther King, Jr.,* p. 238.

96. King, address on the Fourth Anniversary of the MIA, Dec. 3, 1959, p. 7.

97. *Playboy Interviews,* p. 365.

98. King, "Beyond the Los Angeles Riots," p. 35.

99. WWCW, p. 91.

100. Ibid., p. 21.

101. STF, p. 98. Warren Steinkraus asserted that King's satisfaction with Gandhi's nonviolent resistance had been "countered" when he studied the social thought of Reinhold Niebuhr, who argued that it was irresponsible to rely on nonviolent resistance when there was no ground for believing that it would be successful ("Martin Luther King's Personalism and Non-Violence," *Journal of the History of Ideas* 34, no. 1 [Jan.-Mar. 1973]: 99). Steinkraus neglected to add that King had explained that as he read more of Niebuhr he saw that Niebuhr had distorted the nature of true pacifism, which is not nonresistance to evil but a nonviolent resistance to evil.

102. Ibid., p. 99.

103. Ibid., p. 100.

104. Ibid. Though Chalmers and Muelder did not teach King, they did influence him. Chalmers corresponded with him after graduation, and Muelder, as we have seen, influenced him by his writings.

105. STL, p. 140.

106. King, Nobel Lecture, p. 70.

107. Ibid., p. 71.

108. "Is Vietnam To Become a 'Civil Rights' Issue?," *U.S. News & World Report*, July 19, 1965, p. 12.

109. "SCLC Looks Toward Vietnam War as Ninth Annual Convention Ends," *The Southern Courier*, Aug. 20, 1965, p. 1.

110. "King Acts for Peace," *The Christian Century* 82 (Sept. 29, 1965): 1180.

111. Coretta Scott King, *My Life with Martin Luther King, Jr.*, pp. 293–94.

112. Lewis, *King: A Critical Biography*, p. 311.

113. "Signs of Erosion," *Newsweek* 69, Apr. 10, 1967, p. 32.

114. Ibid.

115. King, "Beyond Vietnam," *Dr. Martin Luther King, Jr., Dr. John Bennett, Dr. Henry Steele Commager, Rabbi Abraham Heschel Speak on the War in Vietnam*, Reprint by Clergy and Laymen Concerned about Vietnam, 1968, pp. 10–17. (All subsequent references to "reprint" apply to this work.) A condensed version of this speech under the title "Declaration of Independence from the War in Vietnam" appeared in *Two, Three . . . Many Vietnams*, editors of *Ramparts* with Banning Garrett and Katherine Barkley (New York: Canfield Press, 1971), pp. 206–15. See also *Ramparts*, May 1967, and *Speeches by the Rev. Dr. Martin Luther King, Jr. About the War in Vietnam* (Annandale, Va.: The Turnpike Press, 1968).

116. Ibid., p. 13.

117. Ibid., p. 10. Charles Fager, who had been on the staff of SCLC, affirmed in 1966 that among national figures King was one of the few who were undeniably men of conscience, and that it seemed unlikely that he could remain silent on the war without seriously compromising his acknowledged role as a man of principle ("Dilemma for Dr. King," *The Christian Century*

83, no. 11 [Mar. 16, 1966], p. 332). King had been an editor-at-large for this journal.

118. Ibid., p. 11.

119. Ibid., p. 13.

120. Ibid., p. 14.

121. Ibid., p. 15.

122. "Dr. King To Weigh Civil Disobedience If War Intensifies," *The New York Times*, Apr. 2, 1967, p. 1.

123. NAACP Resolution, quoted in *Life* editorial, "Dr. King's Disservice to His Cause," Apr. 21, 1967, p. 4. William Hixon, Jr., in a letter to *The New York Times* on Apr. 10, 1967 argued that King stood in a solid historical tradition when as a civil rights leader he spoke out against American policy. He appealed to the protests of Moorfield Storey, first president of the NAACP, who had criticized the American acquisition of the Philippines, and while serving as president from 1910 to 1929 had condemned American interventions in the Dominican Republic, Haiti, and Nicaragua. Reprint by Clergy and Laymen Concerned about Vietnam, p. 29.

124. Quoted in Carl Rowan, "Martin Luther King's Tragic Decision," *The Reader's Digest*, Sept. 1967, p. 38.

125. Quoted in Rowan, n.d., p. 38.

126. *The New York Times*, Apr. 7, 1967, p. 36.

127. Ibid.

128. *Life*, Apr. 21, 1967, p. 4.

129. Ibid.

130. Ibid.

131. Rowan, pp. 41–42.

132. Ibid., p. 42.

133. King, "Beyond Vietnam," pp. 15–16.

134. King, "The Casualties of the War in Vietnam," *The Nation Institute*, Feb. 25, 1967, Los Angeles. Reprint by Clergy and Laymen Concerned about Vietnam, p. 5.

135. Interview with King by *The New York Times*, Apr. 2, 1967. Reprint by Clergy and Laymen Concerned about Vietnam, p. 24.

136. King, "Vietnam Is Upon Us," Feb. 6, 1968. Reprint by Clergy and Laymen Concerned about Vietnam, p. 23. In 1959, King stated that he had denounced organizers of war regardless of rank or nationality and that he had signed numerous statements condemning nuclear testing ("The Social Organization of Nonviolence," *Liberation* 4, no. 7 [1959]: 6).

137. King, "The Casualties of the War in Vietnam," p. 8.

138. "Vietnam Is Upon Us," p. 24.

139. King, "Beyond Vietnam," p. 11.

140. Ibid.

141. King, "The Domestic Impact of the War in Vietnam," Nov. 11, 1967. Reprint by Clergy and Laymen Concerned about Vietnam, p. 16. This speech

was also published in *Drum Major*, the journal of SCLC (Winter 1971): 14–17.

142. Ibid., p. 15.

143. King, "Why I Oppose the War in Vietnam," Apr. 16, 1967, Ebenezer Baptist Church, Atlanta, Motown Record, 1970.

144. TC, pp. 22–23.

145. "The Casualties of the War in Vietnam," p. 6. See also "Vietnam Is Upon Us," p. 22.

146. "The Domestic Impact of the War in Vietnam," p. 16.

147. "The Casualties of the War in Vietnam," p. 6.

148. "The Domestic Impact of the War in Vietnam," p. 16.

149. WDWGFH, p. 188.

150. "Dr. King To Weigh Civil Disobedience If War Intensifies," p. 1.

151. Miller, *Martin Luther King, Jr.*, p. 240.

152. TC, p. 23.

153. "The Casualties of the War in Vietnam," p. 7.

154. In his "Adverse Mail" file King kept a letter from Anne Barrett of London stating, "I would have preferred you to vow your love and loyalty to America and then state the injustice which exists in your country and other countries" (Nov. 14, 1961, King Collection, I, no. 47).

155. King, "Why I Oppose the War in Vietnam," Motown Record.

156. TC, pp. 24–25.

157. "Beyond Vietnam," p. 11.

158. "Why I Oppose the War in Vietnam," Motown Record.

159. "The Casualties of the War in Vietnam," p. 8.

160. "The Domestic Impact of the War in Vietnam," p. 19.

161. "Beyond Vietnam," p. 10.

162. Ibid.

163. "Vietnam Is Upon Us," p. 24.

164. TC, p. 25.

165. Gunnar Jahn, Nobel Presentation Speech, *Dear Dr. King*, p. 55.

166. King, Nobel Lecture, p. 73.

167. Fager, "Dilemma for Dr. King," p. 332.

168. TC, p. 21.

169. "Beyond Vietnam," p. 12.

170. Reinhold Niebuhr, Foreword to Reprint by Clergy and Laymen Concerned about Vietnam, p. 3.

171. TC, p. 72.

172. "Beyond Vietnam," p. 12.

173. TC, p. 31.

174. Quoted in "The Casualties of the War in Vietnam," p. 5.

175. "Beyond Vietnam," pp. 12–13.

176. Ibid., p. 12.

177. "The Casualties of the War in Vietnam," p. 6.

178. "Beyond Vietnam," p. 16.

179. TC, p. 34.

180. "The Casualties of the War in Vietnam," p. 5.

181. "The Domestic Impact of the War in Vietnam," p. 17.

182. "Dr. Martin Luther King, Jr. Comments on NAACP Resolution," Apr. 12, 1967. Reprint by Clergy and Laymen Concerned about Vietnam, p. 28.

183. Ibid. King found in Hegel a similar emphasis on "interconnection." In his seminar on Hegel, which King attended, Brightman stated, "The aim of Hegel was to discover the structure of experience. Every possible experience has meaning because of the interrelations of all experience. . . . In Hegel's view, nothing can be known if taken by itself; knowledge of anything is attained only by relating it to other principles and facts" (Minutes of Brightman's seminar on Hegel, Sept. 1952, First and Second Sessions, King Collection, XIV, no. 40). King's notes on Brightman's course, "Philosophy of Religion," contains F. H. Bradley's definition of philosophy as "the effort to comprehend the world not piecemeal but as a comprehensive whole," and H. Emil Brunner's statement that "Philosophy consists in reflection on the connection between all particular facts . . ." (King Collection, XIV, no. 46, pp. 2–3). For a recent perception of "wholistic thinking" in several fields see Alvin Toffler, *The Third Wave* (New York: Bantam Books, 1981), pp. 185, 300–303, 309, 406.

184. King, Address at Howard University, n.d., p. 6.

185. Ibid. John Maguire noted that when King's colleagues-turned-critics demanded that he confine himself to civil rights and not get involved in the cause of peace, they forgot that before he became a civil rights leader he had been a follower of Gandhi ("Martin Luther King and Vietnam," *Christianity and Crisis* 27, no. 7 [May 1, 1967]: 89).

Index